בה על
המסר שנמנקין
עלינו.

# Gluskin Family History

הספר הזה בשביל
לברך את בת שלי
רות בת דוד הלוי
היקירה

אזכרה גדולי בתורה
קדושים וטהורים
כזוהר הרקיע
אלה בבכית אבות
ואמהות
בזכרון יום הגאולה
בכבוד הב
דוד הלוי

# Gluskin Family History

Yosef Serebryanski
and
David B. Levy

2019

Dedicated to my beloved daughter Ruth
להגדלה לתורה לחופה ולמעשים טובים אמן
May you grow in torah, reach the chuppah and do acts of loving kindness, and understand that you stem from *khsidische idene* fun khsidim shtam

יְשִׂמֵךְ אֱלֹהִים כְּשָׂרָה רִבְקָה רָחֵל וְלֵאָה
יְבָרֶכְךָ אֲדֹנָי וְיִשְׁמְרֶךָ
יָאֵר אֲדֹנָי פָּנָיו אֵלֶיךָ וִיחֻנֶּךָּ
יִשָּׂא אֲדֹנָי פָּנָיו אֵלֶיךָ וְיָשֵׂם לְךָ שָׁלוֹם

David Benching his beloved daughter Ruth to whom this book as "a message in a bottle" is dedicated

# Introduction

by David B. Levy
and Yosef Yitzchok Serebryanski

The Gluskin surname dates back approximately 200 years. Before that the family name was Margolies for about 250 years and before that it was Saba.[1]

The results of dedicated research have yielded the most accurate accounting of the Gluskin family history based on information culled from a variety of sources. This is only a first step. There are several other branches of the Gluskin families that existed in approximately the past 150 years about whom we have not yet found credible information that allows us to link them into this work. It is our hope that this work may come to the attention of someone who has researched that part of the family and can contribute to enrich our knowledge of our remarkable family history.

We are blessed to have the accounting of Gita Gluskin (1922-2014) who recorded many details of her childhood that are included here in the story of Mendel Gluskin. David Levy wrote an article about Gita's husband Dr. Aryeh Vilsker.[2] Much of the information for Sonya and

Esther Gluskin comes from several articles written in Russian by family and friends.

A comprehensive account about the lives of Moshe Zev and childhood of Chaim Serebryanski was compiled and printed by Yosef Serebryanski for the first and second yahrtzeit of his father Chaim Serebryanski, which included information regarding the town of Hlusk/Glusk. The bulk of information about Reb Zalman Serebryanski was published in Beis Moshiach by his son Chaim.

As you read through the pages, you will encounter the difficulties under Soviet oppression and how the family survived in the USSR. You will also read many details about Jewish life in Czarist Russia.

David Levy's research and compillation of geneaology rounded out this work by providing a clear and concise reference on the importance of Jewish genealogy.

We would like to thank all involved for the information and assistance in preparing this book. Yosef's intention is to someday publish a separate book about his father's life and a book about his grandfather's life. David if given the time may write further on the inspiring research librarian Dr Aryeh Vilsker. Both Yosef and David's anscestors were Gluskins.

Please email any correction, additions or other comments to yosefyossi@yahoo.com.

With love and blessings,

Yosef and David

Yosef Yitzchok Serebryanski
David Levy - davidblevy@msn.com

---

1 Some trace the name Gluskin back to BT. Pesahim where a Gluskina is a fine gourmet type of challah. גלוסקא a contraction of גלוסביקא or גלופסיקא ; Rashi (ed. ורעתיה עילויה, ms m יפיפיה) a fine gluskin which he may have the intention of eating (in place of burning). Lam R. to I 16, Gluskin; a.e. Pl גלוסקאות Sabb 30b, Gen R. S. 88 beg. Lam R. To II, 12 (Ar. Ed Koh. Gluskin); a.e.-2) a superior sort of olives already pressed when appearing in the market λασται, οταφθλοες , v. Athenaeus 1, c.II, 56; cmp כלופסיו, Ab Zar. II, 7...... zethe kluska is the same as rolled olives (Ex R. S. 30 גלוסקאות v. גלוסקמא

2 2016 AJL Proceedings, Charleston, SC., copyright AJL 2016, at: http://databases.jewishlibraries.org/node/51186

# Brief Abstract

This research notes the importance of genealogical research. The study describes the methods and strategies, to uncover history of various members of the Gluskin family back about 13 generations and place this account in its historical context. As well as the revealing of an elite rabbinic history, this study brings to center stage from the margins material on matriarchal histories. The testimony is peppered with primary sources including interviews in Israel, photos, genealogical trees, letters (Iggerot), Hespadim, Hashkamot, pinkasim, maps, the historic Jewish press and current Israeli Newspapers, techinos prayers, kvitlekh, memoirs, diaries, public records, oral histories, tombstone inscriptions, original poems by family members, blog and FB posts, and demographic studies. Also many secondary sources such as Eleh Ezkarah, Minsk yizkor books, Hillel Zeitlin's portrait of Rav Gluskin, Toldot Shklov, academic articles, etc (see Hebrew Bibliography) are drawn upon. For examplc, a map of Minsk can bc found in the yizker book.

The research notes some individuals who made major impacts in the eastern European Jewish community [such as Rabbi Zev Gluskin a confidant of the Netziv and gave a hesped for the GRA), Jewish scholarship (Dr. Vilsker, Dr. Josef David Amusin, Dr, Gita Gluskin, Dr. Leah Gluskin, Dr. Sonia Gluskin), cultural history at large (Sonia's son was the international ballet dancer Sasha Minsk), Zionism and life in Israel for those fortunate to get a VISA out of the former Soviet Union in Aliya. We trace censorship and persecution under Communist Russia and how this effected family (rabbis, scholars, and members of HaShomer HaTzair) under the surveillance of the KGB. For example, Rav Menachem Gluskin with his father in law Rabbi Eliezer Rabinowitz was imprisoned twice for teaching Torah, Esther Gluskin as a Zionist sent to Siberia, Dr. Vilsker was intereogated about the Jewish elders who used his library workplace to learn "Jewish texts", and medical members of the Helfgott family were accused in the Doctor's plot, the paranoid machinations of Stalin. The work reveals the misirat nefesh of those who sacrificed as a form of Kiddush Ha-Shem, in trying times before in Tzarist Russia under the Cantonist system, and after the Communist Revolution.

The work implores us to aspire to live by the light of these noble ancestors whose holy soul sparks shine as glistening "names" in Gan Eden. We cannot know where we are going unless we know "where we have walked" in generations before. The book is an attempt to turn to the past to guide us into the future, to make us better persons, seeking wisdom from the elders, as parasha Hazinu enjoins:

זְכֹר יְמוֹת עוֹלָם, בִּינוּ שְׁנוֹת דֹּר-וָדֹר; שְׁאַל אָבִיךָ וְיַגֵּדְךָ, זְקֵנֶיךָ
וְיֹאמְרוּ לָךְ

MAPS

Maps are challenging to find because often place names have multiple transliterated spellings. Parichi appears as Paricze sometimes. Loyev appears as Lojew sometimes. Glusk appears as Hlusk sometimes.

It's a bit of a challenge to balance the needs for detail, geographic context, and time period in map requests. And it's a cliché, when working with detailed map series to locate places in proximity with each other, that each locality will be found on the edges of different but adjoining sheets. So, true to form, here are citations to multiple maps from 3 different series in the NYPL Map Divison, that show the locations of Hlusk (Glusk), Parichi, Loyev, and (in 2 out of the 3 cases) Minsk:

Topograficheskaia karta Minskoĭ gubernīi, 1846, Scale 1:210,000.

The place names on this map are in the Cyrillic alphabet. Minsk appears on Sheet VI, Glusk and Parichi on Sheet XI, and Loyev on Sheet XVI.

Specialnia Karta Europeickoi Rossii, 1890-1914, Scale 1:420,000.

Also in the Cyrillic alphabet. Minsk appears on Sheet 15 (1913), Glusk on Sheet 29 (1912), and Parichi and Loyev on Sheet 30 (1911).

This map series is not described in NYPL online catalog, but is listed under RUSSIA, EUROPEAN. SET in the Dictionary Catalog of the Map Division, vol. 8, page 761.

Generalkarte von Mitteleuropa in masse, 1:200,000, 1899-1918.

Minsk is too far north to appear on this set of maps, but Glusk appears on the sheet named Glusk (1900), Parichi appears as Paricze on the sheet named Bobrujsk (1914), and Loyev appears as Lojew on the sheet named Reczyca (1914).

This map series also is not described in NYPL's online catalog, but is listed under EUROPE, CENTRAL. SET in the Dictionary Catalog of the Map Division, vol. 3, page 815.

These maps have not been digitized for the NYPL Digital Collections, however the last set is available online at 2 other sites:
https://www.landkartenarchiv.de/oesterreich_gkm.php
http://lazarus.elte.hu/hun/digkonyv/topo/3felmeres.htm

One can also search for other maps that fit the researchers needs at oldmapsonline.org.

Of course Yizker books often have maps also. A nice map was published by URJC – Union of Religious congregations of the Republic of Belarus.

## Mission

The purpose of this book is not to speak about yichus but rather to fulfill the verse in Torah (Deuteronomy 32:7) "Ask your father and he will tell you, your elders and they will say it to you." This is the way we learn from previous generations and teach future generations. When we print things about them or words that they said, it is as if they are standing with us. This is an aspect of resurrection.

The Noam Elimelech writes that (Parshas Bo) with regard to pedigree and lineage it is prohibited to take pride. (Parshas Korach) The merit of the anscestors is an important matter that is used when a person desires to serve the Creator.

# Contents

---

1 Published in full form originally at http://databases.jewishlibraries.org/node/51186.

David at the Kotel

**Moshe Zev** (Velvel) Margolies/Margolin/Gluskin/Yaavetz

Moshe Zev also known as Wolf was born in Hlusk in 1767 to the chief Rabbi, his father Rabbi Eliezer Margolies and his mother the daughter of Yitzchok Yechiel Michel Flaya. [1](1) His mother passed away when he was a child and his father remarried Sarah whose lineage was from the Shach.

His father gave him a lot of attention with his childhood education.

*(1) Yitzchok Yechiel Michel was the son-in-law of Rabbi Dovid of Dubrowitz in Vohlin son of Mahari Heshel ab"d of Tarli (son-in-law of Rabbi Osher Enzil ab"d of Pinchov) son of Berish son of Mahari Heshel ab"d of Krakow.*

His step mother Sarah was a sister of the famous Chossid known as Binyomin Kletzker. (2) In a letter of Eliyahu Tumarkin from 5652/1892 (3) is written that Zalman Margolin of Paritz a brother of Moshe Zev was full of praise for his uncle the Gaon Reb Binyomin.

*(2) Rabinowitz, for name and family details see the book Horav p.701-740.*

*(3) Yalkut Mishpochos Alechsandorov, Odessa 1892 page 16(9).*

Moshe Zev is known as the father of the families with the surname Gluskin. The surname Gluskin/Hluskin was chosen to save a son from being conscripted into the Russian army. It is not known if Rabbi Eliezer gave his son Moshe Zev that surname so that he appeared as an only son and would thus be exempt from army service or maybe for the same reason, Moshe Zev gave that surname to one his sons. Either way in Russia it was an honor to have a child in the army but an only child was exempt from army service.[2] Czar Nicholai the first enforced conscription after 1827 for 12-year-old Jewish boys to serve with six years' military education and then 25 years in the army.[3]

Moshe Zev's oldest brother Noach kept the last name Margolies while his brother Eliyahu used the name

Margolin. Thus, it would seem that for Moshe Zev a different name was used, probably Hluskin. Moshe Zev himself had no use for a surname and thus in various books we find different surnames for him depending on who was writing. The letter h is pronounced in Russia as g.[4] Therefore, in some places the name is written Hluskin or Hluskina and in other places Gluskin or Gluskina.

One of his grandsons Yehoshua Gluskin married a daughter of Don Slonim whose sister Gute Esther was the wife of Eliyahu Tumarkin of Dubrovna. Don and his sister were children of Reb Isser Kises from Shklov, all chassidim of Rabbi Shneur Zalman the first Chabad Rebbe (1745 – 1813). Thus, we find that Moshe Zev's grandson who had the last name Hluskin was a Chabad Chossid. We do not know if Yehoshua's father, Moshe Zev's son, was a chossid or not.

Moshe Zev was a genius in Torah and that was his focus, we do not find that he was involved in opinions for or against Chassidim.[5] There was tremendous respect in the non-Chassidic world for Moshe Zev. He was very humble and did not like being called with a title.

Moshe Zev wrote:[6] When I was a child, I heard the following from my father.[7] **"Man and animal Hashem saves."** There are times when a person sins and the punishment is death. In such a case a person brings a sin offering and the animal dies in his stead. But Hashem says that a person should repent and then neither the person nor animal has to die.

He studied the Turim before he studied Talmud. When he was older he noted that had he studied the Talmud first he would have been a lamdan three times greater than he is now.[8]

When visiting Vilna, he would frequent the Vilna Gaon (1720-1797) and they would spend time discussing Torah.[9] He gave a eulogy for the Vilna Gaon, *(who passed away Monday the 3rd day of Chol Hamoed Sukkos 5558)* on Monday the 3rd of Marcheshvan 5558/1797 in Horodna.[10] He was 30 years old when the Gaon passed away. Rabbi Menachem Mendel of Shklov son of Boruch Bendet famous student of the Vilna Gaon was a maggid in Hlusk. He was a cousin to Moshe Zev since they both had the same anscestor Yehuda Yidel of Kavli.

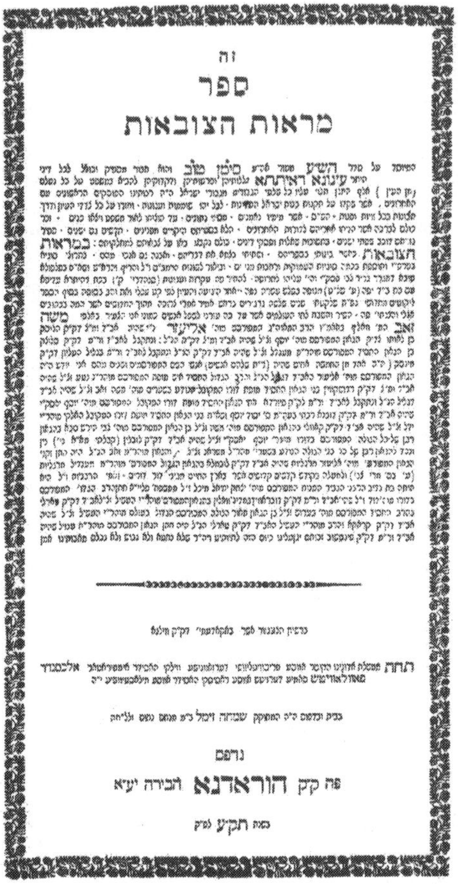

זה
ספר
מראות הצובאות

נדפס
פה קק הוראדנא הבירה יע"א

Reb Chaim Volozhin (1749 – 1821) greatly respected Moshe Zev's father Rabbi Eliezer of Hlusk as illustrated in the following story. One-time Rabbi Eliezer had to pass Volozhin with one of his sons who had been called up to the army. He did not have time to go into the city to give respect to Reb Chaim. When Reb Chaim found out that

Rabbi Eliezer would be outside the city he left the city to meet him on the road.[11]

Zev Gluskin[12] who was born in Slutsk on the ninth of Elul 5619/1859 writes in his memoirs that his father Eliezer Gluskin was born in Hlusk and that he is named after his ancestor Moshe Zev. In Kovetz Ahl Yad[13] there is an article cataloging the names of the tombstones of the city of Shklov. Shlomo Berman comments regarding a stone with the name Gluskin carved into it, that Moshe Zev is the father of the Gluskin family.

Moshe Zev and his wife had many children in Hlusk and Horodna but we know virtually nothing about them.[14] We know from Zev Gluskin that one child used the surname Hluskin/Gluskin and lived in Hlusk/Glusk and from Moshe Zev that one daughter was married.[15]

---

[1] Yitzchok Yechiel Michel was the son-in-law of Rabbi Dovid of Dubrowitz in Vohlin son of Mahari Heshel ab"d of Tarli (son-in-law of Rabbi Osher Enzil ab"d of Pinchov) son of Berish son of Mahari Heshel ab"d of Krakow.

[2] Otzar Pisgomim Mechachomim by Bershtein note 91 p.14.

[3] For details of the development of laws regarding conscription read the book "Hakantonistim" by Yosef Mendelowitz.

[4] For example, in Toldos Chabad in Russia p.126 - Rabbi Shlomo Yosef Zevin and Rabbi Yaakov Klemes mentions the last name as (Rabbi Menachem Mendel) Hluskin (av bais din in Minsk) using the letter Hey not Gimmel.

[5] There were people who did not talk about a brother or son who became a chossid and pretended they did not exist, Moshe Zev doesn't talk about any of the many children that he had while in Hlusk or Horodok but it may have nothing to do with this, just that his complete focus was in Torah study. Another Torah giant Yitzchok Eizik Halevi Epstein who became a follower of the first Chabad Rebbe learned from his grandfather in Hlusk. However, his grandfather was a misnaged and hated chassidim. (Otzar Yisroel, Epstein Family note 19) In general there was a presence of misnagdim and chassidim in Hlusk and Horodna, both places that Moshe Zev lived.

[6] Agudas Ezov Drushim p.13.

[7] Psalms 36:7.

[8] Sefer Minchas Yehuda, Warsaw 1877 in the introduction.

[9] Mokor Boruch p.416 part one, chapter 5.

[10] Agudas Ezov – Droshos p.80a.

[11] Responsa "Agudas Aizov" published in 1962 by Moshe Eliezer son of Aharon Eliyohu and Chana Margolin. Aharon Eliyohu is a descendant from Eliyohu son of Rabbi Eliezer of Hlusk. A new edition was published 5769/2009.

[12] His memoirs were published in 1946.

[13] Volume one p.167, the new edition in Jerusalem 5696/1936 is volume eleven when considered as a continuation to the volumes printed in Europe.

[14] Mokor Boruch.

[15] Introduction to his sefer Maros Hatzovos.

**Horodna/Gorodna**

Moshe Zev Wolf left Hlusk in 5558/1798 to become a Rosh Mesivta and Av Beis Din (ab''d) in Horodna for approximately 15 years.

After Pesach he gave a eulogy for Rabbi Daniel who passed away on the seventh day of Pesach 5560/1799.[1]

While in Horodna he published his first book Maros Hatzovos in 5570/1810. In the preface, he writes that most of his life was full of pain and yet he never stopped learning Torah. Now he realizes that his life has passed him by and that he has no accomplishment to show for it. He is therefore writing a book pertaining to Agunos (women who cannot remarry since they do not know if their husband is dead or alive or their husband will not give them a get) so that there will be some memory of him after he passes on. Then when people study the book, his lips will move in the grave.[2]

This book made him very famous in the Rabbinical world and he received many letters asking how to deal with agunos or if a man can return to his wife where there is concern that she was with another man, etc. In many of the cases he was able to find a way to permit the wife to continue living with her husband or that she be allowed to remarry.

On the front cover, he writes his family history son after son going back to the Maharal of Prague. In his introduction, he only mentions the name of his daughter Basya and her husband Yisroel of Sharshuv, otherwise he does not write about his wife or children. Another daughter was the wife of Nochum Tzukerman of Vitebsk.[3]

He had another daughter Zelda Riva who married Binyomin Beinish Mintz.[4]

On the cover of his first book "Maros Hatzovos" he writes that his father was the head of the Beis Din in Hlusk in past tense even though he was still alive. He then writes the name of his father Eliezer, grandfather Yosef, great grandfather Menachem Mendel, great great grandfather Moshe Zev, son of Yuda Yidel, son of Moshe son of Tzvi Hirsch Saba son of Yosef Yaski (I received from my father) a grandson of the Maharal of Prague. In the cover of his second book he only goes back as far as Yehuda Yidel.

There is much discussion among jewish historians about who Moshe was since he does not give a last name or city that he was in. There is also much discussion about how Yosef Yaski was the grandson or great grandson of the Maharal. It seems that since this comes after the words **"I received from my father"** that his intention may be that he did not receive from his father exactly how they were connected with the Maharal. Or it could be that the names he got elsewhere but the fact that they came from the Maharal he received from his father. He mentions the sefer of a relative, Morei Tzvi published in 1738 where he could have found most of the names. Thus, the main thing his father told him was that they came from the Maharal and maybe added in names that are not mentioned in Morei Tzvi.

Many of the haskomos/approbations for Maros Hatzovos are from relatives who were Rabbonim like Rabbi Binyomin Broda, Rabbi Yosef Katzenelenfogen, Rabbi Aryeh Leib Broda, Rabbi Yisroel Mirkash and his father. Rabbi Tanchum of Horodna testifies in his haskomo that Moshe Zev never stopped learning Torah and never used

Torah for his personal gain. That he was extremely humble and was not happy to be called Gaon as he never felt above others.

Moshe Zev once said, "When I was Rabbi in a small city, I was paid less than three rubles a week. I had a house full of children young and grown may Hashem bless them, and a few other family members creating a situation where my expenses were greater than my salary. Each day my wife was very concerned where to get food to feed everyone and this caused her to become bitter. Thus, even though she did not want to disturb me, she had no choice but to remind me twice a day.

We had extremely difficult times with nothing to live on. In order to borrow money, the only thing she could use as a guarantee was the money that I would be receiving from the community for the coming months. I told her not to do that since a bigger city may want me to be their Rabbi but as long as I don't pay back the money here, I would not be able to go. She responded to me that Hashem won't punish us with having to worry about having a lot of possessions since we already have the punishment of worrying by not having possessions.[5]

Moshe Zev was in continual contact with Reb Chaim of Volozhin (1741 – 1821) and in fact asked him directly what he thought of his first book. Reb Chaim's words were, **"hu sefer mechubad lemevinim"** meaning it is a precious book for those who comprehend. Reb Chaim used to ask Moshe Zev his opinion in matters of halacha, community and regarding his yeshiva. Actually[6] Leah the wife of Yosef, brother of Reb Chaim Volozhin, was the granddaughter of the sister of Moshe Zev's father Rabbi Eliezer of Hlusk. Thus, there was also a family connection.

One time, Moshe Zev was travelling through Volozhin with his brother the wealthy Reb Zalman of Paritz. When Reb Chaim heard they were in town he did not wait for them to come to him but went out to greet them.[7]

On the 18th of Sivan 5577/1816 while passing through Horodna he made a eulogy for Sholom a son-in-law of his aunt, who was buried in Hlusk.[8]

One time a tailor came to him with a case against another person. After hearing the complaint, the Rabbi ruled for the defendant. The tailor would not accept it and said that he is going to take the man to the city court. When the Rabbi heard him say that, he remarked, "A person who does not listen to a Din Torah we already know his punishment." As soon as the tailor arrived home he instantly fell dead to the floor. The Rabbi sat in mourning for him for one hour.[9]

---

[1] Agudas Ezov – Drushim p. 83b.

[2] Talmud Yevomos 96, Bechoros 31, Sanhedrin 90, etc.

[3] Shlomei Emunei Yisroel choveres three, p. 171, Odessa 5658/1898.

[4] Sefer Beis Aharon from Aharon Kevil, Pieterkov 5691. Eliezer Mintz was a son of the daughter of Moshe Zev, he passed away Tishrei 11, 5680. He had a son Dovid Shlomo Mintz. Dovid S. had three children Yehuda Aryeh Leib d. 8 Tishrei 5690, Feiga Mindel and Chaim Avigdor. (Hapardes choveres 10, year 35 p.40) Rabbi Eliezer Mintz of Warsaw was a Gerer chossid, he had a son Bunim who had a son Binyomin. Details of his accomplishments are in Hapardes.

[5] Mokor Boruch p.838, part one chapter 5.

[6] Shlomei Emunei Yisroel vol 3 p. 173.

[7] Toldos Rabbeinu Chaim of Volozhin, Vilna 1909 by Moshe Shmuel Shmukler p.32.

[8] Agudas Ezov - Drushim p.91b.

[9] Introduction to Agudas Ezov Warsaw 5764.

Tiktin[1]

He moved to Tiktin in 5574/1813 to serve as Rabbi since the city Rabbi, Mordechai Halevi had become too old and weak to serve. Three years later in 5577 when Rabbi Mordechai passed away, Moshe Zev became the Rabbi and Av Beis Din. At this period of time Tiktin was considered a more important community than Bialistok.

On erev Rosh Chodesh Nissan 5574 he eulogized Shlomo Zalman, the head Rabbi of Bialystok who passed away on the 18th of Adar 5574, he was a son in law of Moshe Zev wife's grandfather Berachia Berach. There are several letters of Torah correspondence with Shlomo Zalman that were later published in Moshe Zev's responsa.[2]

He made a eulogy on Sunday the 4th of Iyar 5574 in front of the casket of Zev Wolf son in law of his father in laws father Reb Shmuel Reb Berachs. Reb Shmuel was a son-in-law of Yosef Katz a grandson of Naftoli Katz author of Semichas Chachomim and Yosef's father-in-law was Mahari Leib also known as Reb Leib Mirkas.[3]

Eulogy for Dovid in Tiktin on Thursday the 6th of Marcheshvan 5575.[4]

During the month of Sivan 5576 he made a eulogy for Rabbi Meir of Brod and for Rabbi Nachman of Orlee son of Binyomin Biska Katz who both passed away in the year 5575.[5]

On the tenth of Teves 5580 he made a eulogy for Tzvi Hirsh known as Reb Hirsh Chossid from Simaititz who passed away in 5579 and for Tzvi Hirsh known as Reb

Hirsh Prilooker who passed away during Chanukah 5580 in Brisk.[6]

He gave a eulogy on Thursday the 28th of Sivan for Reb Chaim Volozhin who passed away the 14th of Sivan in the year 5581/1821.[7]

---

[1] Reference Sefer Tiktin published in Tel Aviv 1959 http://yizkor.nypl.org/index.php?id=2746 Sefer Tiktin in the New York library

[2] Agudas Ezov – Drushim p.85b.

[3] Agudas Ezov – Drushim p.87a.

[4] Agudas Ezov – Drushim p.88a.

[5] Agudas Ezov – Drushim p.89b.

[6] Agudas Ezov – Drushim p.84a.

[7] Agudas Ezov - Drushim p.95b.

## Bialystok

In 5584/1824 he moved to Bialystok. His move also changed the scales and put Bialystok on the map and under his guidance became a more important Jewish community than Tiktin. The investiture of Rabbi Moshe Zev of Tiktin as Bialystok's fourth Rabbi signaled the city's transformation into the regional center for Jewish affairs.[1]

The following year 5585,[2] he published his second book Agudas Ezov – Drushim Lizmanim Umoadim.[3] There were many differences between what he wrote about himself and family in the first book and the second book. He writes his brothers names and that his brother Zalman gave him money to publish this book and that they have corresponded in Torah which he will print in his next book of Agudas Ezov – responsa. He writes about his sister Rivka and her family. His present wife and two kids and his in-laws but nothing about the family that he had in Hlusk or Horodna.

His children had a few last names like Margolies, Yaavetz and Gluskin while his brother's sons used Margolies, Margolin and Saba. It seems possible that his first wife passed away close to the time that he left Horodok and that he married a second wife after or just before he arrived in Tiktin and then moved to Bialystok where he lived with his second wife Bas Sheva till he passed on in 1829. Together they had a child Shmuel Yitzchok with a surname Yaavetz.[4] She had a son from her previous marriage, Yosef Berach. Since he had a stepson[5] that means his second wife was married before. Dovid Yaavetz – Broida son of Shmuel Yitzchok writes that his father Shmuel Yitzchok was a young child when his grandfather Moshe Zev passed away.

When people spoke of him they referred to him with admiration, the Gaon Reb Velvele or simply Reb Velvele. He was also known by his book Reb Velvele Baal Maros Hatzovos, the Baal Maros Hatzovos or by the city that he was in as Reb Velvele Hatiktini or Reb Velvele Habialistoky.

In the responsa that were published after he died we find that Rabbi Akiva Eiger ab"d of Pozen addresses him as my beloved soul friend, the true Gaon prince of Israel and its beauty. In one letter Rabbi Akiva Eiger signs Akiva Ginzman and in another letter, writes about the pain he is going through due to the education system in his community, while in another letter he comments that he decided not to answer letters to people outside his city but obviously makes an exception with Moshe Zev. In two letters to two different communities[6] he writes; you can depend on the Gaon who is now in Bialystok. In the other letter he writes; I know the Gaon ab"d of Bialystok not just by his book but also through our correspondence, may there be more like him in Israel.

Efrayim Zalman Margolies of Brod, in the letters that he writes to him opens with my relative (cousin) Moshe Zev. In his book Maalas Hayuchsin, Efrayim Zalman writes his family heritage which includes some of the lineage of Moshe Zev. In his responsas, we see that Moshe Zev dealt with issues that came up in many communities. Some responses were published without any name at the beginning while some only have a city name of where it went to.

In a response dated 11th of Kislev 5590 to Binyomin, Moshe Zev writes: You ask a proper question but in my present state it is difficult to write or look deeply into the matter in order to respond at length as I have always done. I am weak and old age has come to me so that I no longer desire to look into things deeply or to write as I used to. In addition, I am consumed with matters spinning my head, spiritual as well as city and worldly matters all essential not giving me time for myself. Due to this I almost decided not to respond to your letter until I saw that you write for the sake of heaven as you revealed at the end of the letter that all you want is a brief response to which I am amicable to do in order to state the pesak halocho. From your last words is also understood that your first words are for the sake of heaven and therefore I will respond briefly in accordance with my heart.

He began to write another letter that day but did not conclude it and passed away 24 days later.

In Warsaw 5618/1858 Moshe Zev's son Menachem Dovid Yaavetz of Kanskevalli published some of his writings and called the book Chiddushei Muhoramaz. It is a commentary on Rabbi Yehonoson on the Rif and Shulchan Aruch. On the cover, he only mentions his father being Rov in Tiktin and Bialystok but does not mention Horodok. He was a son from his second wife and could be alluded to in Moshe Zev's writing, "the children of my wife, the sons that Hashem gave me and specifically my young son Shmuel Yitzchok and my stepson." The son that he mentions from his second wife had a son Dovid with the last name Yaavetz. We now find that in the last years of his life he used a surname for his children different than his father's last name. Later the name Yaavetz was also used as a surname of Shmuel Yitzchok on the front page of the reprinted derushim.

It happened one time in the area that he lived there was a person who was making trouble in the Jewish quarter by creating reports to the authorities that would hurt people.

A group of community members came to the Gaon to discuss how to be rid of the problem. The Gaon asked that they bring the person to him. When he came, the Gaon remained silent and just looked at him and that was all. The wicked man left and went to a restaurant to eat a nice piece of goose. When he started eating a bone got stuck in his throat and he choked to death. In this way, the Gaon fulfilled the saying of the sages[7] "he looked at him and he became a pile of bones."

In the introduction that the publisher writes for the publishing of Agudas Ezov in Warsaw 5664 he writes:

The head of the Rabbinical court in Sochotchov was full of praise when he saw the writings of this book and also praised the book Maros Hatzovos and its author. He said not to take any approbation from any contemporary Rabbis saying that the author of the Maros Hatzovos does not need a haskomoh from anyone in our times. Those who have read his first book will rejoice as soon as they see his name on the front of this book. Write in my name that I told you not to publish any contemporary approbation.

He also told me a story about when the Rabbi Moshe Zev was in Bialystok.

A question came before him about a man who travelled for business. The man wrote to his family that he is about to finalize a transaction but does not have the money to conclude it therefore they should send him the large sum of money that he needs. He signed his name and added the name Segal which is a common name for Levites but no-one in their family. Since the family did not know what to do they went to the Rabbi.

The Rabbi explained that he was kidnapped by thieves and they forced him to write the letter. Knowing that he cannot escape he sent a message by writing the extra name. The letters of the name Segal are an acronym for the words "Sakono Gedola Lee" meaning I am in great danger. Armed men were sent to the address and they released him from his captives.

In 5645 the responsa on even hoezer were published. In 5646 responsa agudas ezov on orach chayim and yoreh deah were published. His custom in responding was to wait a few weeks till he sent his response to fulfill the dictum of the Mishna[8] "deliberate in judgement."

When people who came to him for a court case, his custom with all Dinei Torah was to cover his face with his tallis until after a decision was made.

Rabbi Boruch Halevi Epstein (1860 – 1941)[9] writes:

My great grandfather worked with government building contracts. He had much experience under the directions of his uncle Rabbi Shimon Zimel Epstein of Warsaw. Rabbi Zimel had a business in partnership with Reb Kopel Halperin. Both these people were famous and respected throughout the lands. The following episode is something that my great grandfather personally witnessed. Due to the fame of the people the story spread as well.

After many years as business partners they found a detail of their agreement that was not clear. They could not or did not want to decide for themselves and concluded they should go to a Rabbi and decide according to Torah.

At that time, they were in Bialystock and decided to go to the head of the Beis Din there. Rabbi Moshe Zev Margolin was in his early sixties, a venerable sage already famous due to his books and an internationally respected scholar.

It was the eleventh hour of the morning and the Rabbi was sitting as usual in Tallis and Tefillin studying. His attendant was looking out through the window and saw a regal coach with fine horses stop opposite the house. The coachman jumped down and opened the door to let out two well-dressed people. As they walked to the front door, the attendant ran to the Rabbi and said with excitement, "Reb Zemil Epstein and Reb Kopel Halperin are coming."

The Rabbi responded with indifference sending the attendant to the lobby to greet the people. He took their coats and staffs and had them sit on the bench in the waiting room. They asked the attendant, "How is the Rabbi and what is he involved in at this moment?" They told the attendant that they came to have a din Torah and said that he should find out if the Rabbi can receive them.

The attendant went in to the Rabbi who gave permission for them to enter. Meanwhile the Rabbi lowered the front of his tallis over his eyes so that he would not be able to see them. When they entered he did not greet them or ask them to sit. In a dry cold voice, he said, "Zemil and Kopel, the one who is claiming should state his case first."

The two businessmen were completely taken aback by his coldness and using their name without any description. Their bodies responded with shock. Never the less they tried to overlook what had just happened and how they felt internally.

Reb Zemil said "I am the claimant."

The Rabbi said, "speak."

While they both felt like leaving, Reb Zimel swallowed his pride and stood forcefully holding the arm of my great grandfather to keep himself together. He began to present his perspective but in brief words, a lot shorter than intended, so that he could leave the house as soon as possible.

When Reb Zimel finished his words the Rabbi said, "Kopel present your words." He was standing like cast in stone from shock and therefore did not say all he intended just a synopsis.

The Rabbi then told them to wait in the outer chamber until he and the other judge with him finish discussing the case and present a ruling. They went out and sat in the other room with heads bent, in silence, lonely, depressed and feeling very bitter.

When the Rabbi came to a decision he told the attendant to call them in. When they came in, he still had his tallis over his eyes. He said, according to Torah such is the law. He gave the conclusion and explained how he came to the conclusion.

Then he said, "Zimmel do you accept the ruling?"

Zimmel responded, "I accept!"

Then the Rabbi said, "Kopel do you accept the ruling?"

Kopel responded, "I accept!"

The mood changed instantly. Rabbi Moshe Zev lifted the tallis from his head and greeted them with a smile and warm handshake. He said, "sholom aleichem Rabbi Zimel and sholom aleichem Rabbi Kopel, blessed is your coming and Hashem is with you." He gave each a seat next to him and spoke to them like a father and son. He asked about their welfare and that of their family, the business and it details, discussing it like a professional.

He told his family to serve them coffee and set the table with food and join him in welcoming the guests. They sat and spoke about all various matters of Jewish life and history and everyone had a very uplifting experience.

Before they left, they took out money to pay the Rabbi for his time. The Rabbi refused and said, I do not need your money since the community pays all my bills. If you want me to take the money just to have it in reserve, I don't need the worry about guarding it or what to do with it."

Even when I was a Rabbi in a small town and had a large family with many expenses, even then I did not take money for the cases that came to me. I accept the words of the sages[10] literally. *"A person who takes money to judge his judgment is null,"* and my heart does not accept the ways around this.

It would have been easier to listen to my wife the Rabbonis who worshipped a strange worship twice very day than to transgress an explicit Mishna from which there is no escape.

The men looked at each other, thinking what kind of strange worship his wife could have worshipped twice a day. They waited for some explanation.

The Rabbi explained. When I was Rabbi in a small city, I was paid less than three rubles a week. I had a full house of children young and grown may Hashem bless them, and a few other family members, creating a situation where my expenses were greater than my salary. Each day my wife was very concerned where to get food to feed everyone and this caused her to become bitter. Thus, even though she did not want to disturb me, she had no choice but to remind me. Once in the morning and once in the evening my wife would use the expression of the false prophets of Baal[11] and say, "Baal answer me." *(Baal means Husband and is also an idol they worshipped.)*

We had extremely difficult times with nothing to live on. In order to borrow money, the only thing she could use as a guarantee was the money that I would be receiving from the community for the coming months. While I told her not to do that since a bigger city may want me to be Rabbi but as long as I don't pay back the money here I would not be able to go. She responded to me that Hashem won't punish us with having to worry about having a lot of possessions since we already have the punishment of worrying by not having possessions.

The wealthy people still wanted to give him money. The Rabbi said, "my dear friends I do not want to change what I do and at the same time I do not want to refuse you. Therefore, let us make a compromise. Give the money to this young man with you and let him find a poor Talmud Chochom who learns constantly and in this way, we will have all done a righteous act."

They agreed and also paid the other judge who sat with the Rabbi.

Reb Kopel who had little patience and was raised in a wealthy home was still very disturbed about how they were initially received. Suddenly he said, "If this talmid chochom who you give the tzedoko to will one day be crowned an official Rabbi, will he also receive people the way you do?"

Everyone there suddenly felt shook up. And Reb Kopel as he related later suddenly felt like a fire was raging in him. Only the Rabbi showed no reaction, he was as cold as when they arrived. He responded as if he were answering a simple halachik question someone brought to him.

He thought for a moment and then said:

"Distinguished people, I see you still hold something against me in your heart for the way I acted when you arrived. You may think that I am extreme, have no manners or that I am weird and have an evil spirit in me.

You should know that it is not because of that since the way I acted was based on the teachings of the sages. In Pirkei Avos (Ethics of the Fathers chapter 1: 8) "When the litigants stand before you, they should be in your eyes as if they are wicked, but when they leave having accepted the judgment, they should be innocent in your eyes.

The reason is simple, when a judge received people and considers them righteous, he will trust them and what they say and they can use that to sway the judgment and so the truth will be compromised and so will the judgment.

With the two of you this possibility exists since you are both known as honest and upright men. Both of you do much charitable work and help many people.

Thus, when you come you need to humble yourself and not use your name to turn the law in your favor, you need to be equal to all others. In the space of your greatness you need to show your humility. When it comes to the honor of Torah and accepting what Torah says you are like all other people.[12]

Additionally, where else can I fulfill the words of Torah (Devorim 1:17) "You shall not show favoritism in judgment ... you shall not tremble before man ..." if not with you? You are well respected, famous and the sages teach "don't say that person is wealthy etc." (Proverbs 24:24) "These things are for the wise (to consider) recognizing the face during judgment is not good." This verse needs some explanation. What does King Solomon add to the verse in Devorim? Why does he write "bal tov" meaning not so good, when he should write lo tov that it is not good? Not so good means it is also not so bad. (We find such a thought in Yevomos 20a, he is not holy but also not wicked.)

The first words of the verse also are strange as it should say for judges not for wise.

Actually, the words in Devorim are extra since it is included in the previous warnings. This is what Shlomo Hamelech is coming to explain. "Lo Sakiru" is not about tilting the judgment since that is part of the previous rules and if you do you are wicked.

The intention of the verse is that when a judge sees the people and receives them at the time of judging with sholom aleichem and friendly chatter that come from seeing a person directly, this is not good. This opens channels of closeness between the judge and people being judged. Even though this is not prohibited none the less it is not good for wise people to do. Therefore, Shlomo Hamelech writes "These are things for the wise" judges who think about what they do and take everything into account. For such people, they should recognize the face during judgment.

Maybe this note will help still your feelings a little. Besides this point that I did according to the way I understand Torah, I am like all other Jews, I love and respect you with my whole soul and all the feelings of my heart and praise you and bless you for all the good you do.

Therefore, just as you accepted my decision in law, so too accept the decree of Torah in this detail with love. Don't carry anger or emotion, relax and Hashem will be with you and your families."

Everyone was moved by the words of Moshe Zev. They felt like a stone was lifted from their hearts. Most of all Reb Zemil was affected and he had to control himself from bursting into tears. When he composed himself he spoke to the Rabbi.

"Know dear great precious Rabbi, that if we search for the best times in our lives our time with you is on the first line. Don't feel bad, you are truthful and your Torah is righteous and peaceful."

Reb Zemil had been crying and cleared his eyes. Rabbi Moshe Zev walked them to the street and they kissed each other farewell.[13]

The next day Reb Zemil in honor of Rabbi Moshe Zev made a decision that one of his children will be dedicated to Torah and not be involved in business like the others.

Sometime later Moshe Zev was in Warsaw and visited Reb Zemil where he was invited for lunch. I did not hear details about their relationship since my ancestor was already living some distance from Reb Zemil.

On Wednesday, the 4th of Teves 5590/1829 he passed at the age of 62. There are two printed eulogies for Moshe Zev.[14]

---

[1] The Jews of Bialistok by Sara Benden p.6.

[2] According to the approbations, although the book was prepared for publishing in 5584 as can be seen on the cover.

[3] It was published again in 5749/1989 in Brooklyn NY.

[4] Kovetz Beis Vaad Lachachomim, Kiryas Yoel, Tishrei 2009 discusses the source of the name Yaavetz and writes that many just used it to show importance. It is based in Divrei Hayomim (1, 2:55) and the family of scribes, yoshvei Yaavetz.

[5] As he writes in his introduction in Agudas Ezov.

[6] Sefer Choot Hameshulosh 5770, previously published 5760 and originally in Drohbitch 5668 p. 219, 221.

[7] Talmud Brochos 58a.

[8] Ethics of the Fathers/Pirke Avot 1:1.

[9] Author of the Torah Temimah and Mokor Boruch on the Jerusalem Talmud writes the following story in his book Mokor Boruch pages 829 – 850 (In Hebrew 415 – 425). There are many side notes on the story in the pages which we did not translate here. On the cover of Kuntres Kinmon Bosem is mentioned his grandfather Shimon Zimel Halevi Epstein a grandson of Dovid Halevi Epstein also served as a Rabbi in Hlusk. Among the names Yehuda Yudel Halevi Epstein mentions his cousin Yitzchok Halevi Epstein ab"d Homel and that his mother is Miriam a daughter of Yaakov Grayever from Slonim.

[10] Talmud Bechoros 29a.

[11] Kings 1, 18:26.

[12] In the prayer where we say heal me like you healed Chizkiyahu the King of Judah and like the waters of Moro through Moshe Rabbeinu, the Rif and Rosh do not use the title words, the King of Judah or Rabbeinu to reflect that we are all equal.

[13] The details of what transpired with them after this are printed in Mokor Boruch.

[14] One was by Dovid ben Moshe of Navardok in his book Galye Mesechto vol. 2 p. 37d – 40d, published in Vilna 1845 and again in Jerusalem 1969. Another is from Gershon ben Moshe Chen Tov in his book Mincho Chadosho p. 43d – 44c, published in Warsaw 1873.

## Lineage of Moshe Zev

Moshe Zev's father was Eliezer ab"d of Hlusk son of Yosef ab"d of Hlusk and Slutzk son of Menachem Mendel ab"d of Hlusk, Slutzk and Minsk son of Moshe Zev ab"d of Minsk who married a Margolies and took on his wife's family name.

Moshe Zev ab"d of Minsk was the son of Yehuda Yidel ab"d Minsk and Kavli, author of Kol Yehudah son of Moshe.

Moshe was a son of Tzvi Hirsh Saba son of Yosef Yaski ab"d of Lublin. His great grandfather Yosef Yaski Saba had a son Tzvi Hirsh Saba who married Tila a daughter of the Maharal of Prague. They had a son/grandson Yosef Yaski who was the ab"d of Lublin. (see details in Sefer Ashdos Hapisgoh Choveres 2 kovetz shishi – Vilna 5660) p.101-102.

**Tzvi Hirsh son of Yosef Yoske** married **Tila** daughter of the **Maharal of Prague.**

*Where and how they are exactly connected is at present part of a varied persepctive. See Gevuros Hoari page 6.*

**Yosef Yoske from Lublin Av Beis Din of Dubno had two sons.**

1) **Shmuel** author of Lechem Rav (printed 5375/1625) to which his grandfather the Maharal of Prague and his Uncle Yitzchok Hakohain son-in-law of the Maharal gave an approbation-haskomoh. In the book is a little description of the places he lived. His wife was the daughter of Binyomin Lontshitz from Pozna.

2) **Tzvi Hirsh.**

**Tzvi Hirsh** had a son **Moshe.**

**Moshe** had a son **Yehudah Yidel** Av Beis Din of Lvov (on the outskirts of the city) and Kovli. In 5433/1673 he wrote that he is sitting in exile on the outskirts of Lvov. In 5449/1689 he signed Yehuda who is called Yidel. He also signed in his haskoma to the sefer Lev Aryeh, Moshe from Lublin son of Maharam Mahri an acronym for son of Moshe Reb Hirsh Reb Yoskes from Lublin.

**Yehudah Yidel** had two sons and one daughter.

1) **Yosef Yoske** Av Beis Din Minsk and Dubna, author of the books Yesod Yosef and Neimas Kedosho.

2) **Moshe Ze'ev** Av Beis Din Rozini, Minsk (*he was never in Fiorda,* see *Hayeshiva Horomo Befiorda vol 1 p. 387)* In the Pinkas of the community he signed that in the year 5459/1699 he gave a haskomo on the Sefer Ohr Yisroel to Rabbi Y. of Shklov. His wife was the daughter of the Gaon Eliezer son of Menachem Mendel Margoles Av Beis Din Lumblo. (The story about his burial and grave in Neimo Kedusho, is very interesting.)

3) **This daughter** was the wife of Aharon son of the Gaon Nosson Hakohain (Rappoport family) from Lvov Av Beis Din of Rezini.

**Yosef Yoske** of Dubna had one son and two daughters.

1) **Bentzion** his family history is written in the book Zichron Le Moshe by Moshe son of Nachman.

2) **Daughter** - wife of Yisroel son of Sholom Zak Av Beis Din of Birz.

3) **Daughter** - wife of Aharon son of Yaakov Halevi.

**Moshe Ze'ev** had five sons the first letters of their name make up the word "anoshim – men."

1) **Eliezer** Av Beis Din Mohilev/Mogilev. His name is signed in the Pinkas 5474/1714, 5475/1715, 5479/1719, 5480/1720, 5481/1721, 5483/1723. In a haskomo for a book he signed Eliezer son of the Gaon Moshe Ze'ev Chafetz from Mohilev.

2) **Nosson Nota** Av Beis Din Rodushkovitz.

3) **Shmuel** Av Beis Din of Rokov.

4) **Yehudah Yidel** Av beis Din Timkovitz.

5) **Menachem Mendel** Av Beis Din Hlusk and the area of Minsk. Gave a haskomo to the book Morey Tzvi of his grandson. His wife was the daughter of Simcha Bunim son of Moshe son of Nosson Shapiro author of the Megaleh Amukos.

**Eliezer** had a son **Akivah** Av Beis Din of Barisov who wrote a commentary on the Haggadah called Bizas Pesach. His wife was the daughter of Moshe son of Menachem Mendel Av Beis Din of Dubrovna, son-in-law of Yechiel the author of the Seder Hadoros. In Erchei Hakinuyim of the

Seder Hadoros is written that the family goes back to **Yehudah Hanosi**.

**Nosson Nota** had a son Yehudah Yidel Av Beis Din of Ushotz and is buried there.

**Menachem Mendel of Hlusk had three sons.**

1) **Yosef** Av Beis Din Slutzk and Hlusk. In 5532/1772 gave a haskomo to the sefer Tiferes Yisroel of his relative Yisroel Yaffa of Shklov.

2) **Simcha Bunim** Av Beis Din Puchovitz.

3) **Yehudah Yidel.** Gave a haskomoh to his son's sefer Morey Tzvi.

**Simcha Bunim had two sons.**

1) **Boruch Bendet** Moreh Tzedek of Chaslovitch.

2) **Tzvi Hirsh called Reb Tzvi Shamosh in Minsk.** He was called Simchovitch due to his father Simcha and that is the surname his descendants took on.

**YehudahYidel had a son.**

**Tzvi Hirsh** Av Beis Din of Timkovitz near Slutzsk, wrote Moreh Tzvi printed in 5498/1738.

**Yosef Av Beis Din of Slutzk and Hlusk had four sons and two daughters**

1) **Eliezer** Av Beis Din Hlusk. His first wife was the daughter of the wealthy Yitzchok Yechiel Michel

son-in-law of Dovid the Av beis Din of Dubrovitz. The second wife was Soroh a daughter of the Gaon Moshe from Kletzk whose family went back to the Shach.

2) **Yehudah Yidel** from Slutzk.

3) **Moshe** from Moholiev.

4) **Simcha.**

5) **Mera** wife of Yisroel son of Leib Mirkash (of the Ginsburg family) Av Beis Din of Minsk.

6) **Faige** wife of Eliezer Halevi Horowitz Av Beis Din of Mir son of Moshe Yehoshua Halevi Horowitz Av Beis Din in Horodna.

**Eliezer** Av Bais Din of Hlusk had four sons and four daughters.

1) **Noach** the oldest lived in Vilna.

2) **Eliyahu.**

3) **Moshe Ze'ev.** 1769-1829

4) **Zalman** the youngest. **Zalman** of Paritch was born to his second wife. There is a Zalman of Paritch mentioned in the responsa of the Tzemach Tzedek.

5) **Rivkah** married **Chaim** (son of **Tzvi Hirsh Shamosh**) of Minsk (approx. 179 km from Hlusk) and they had a son **Tzvi Hirsh** who married the

daughter of Yaakov Hillel son of Reb Michel Roveer from Warsaw.

6) **Kaila** married Menachem Mendel Rabinowitz.

7) **Chaya.**

8) **Gruna.** One of them (Chaya or Gruna) became the wife of Eliyohu ben Shmuel from Milut.

**Tzvi Hirsh Shamosh** had two sons and two daughters. **Zev Wolf** of Minsk, **Chaim** Simchovitch of Minsk, **Henna** the wife of Chaim Dovid Rotner son of Nechemiah author of Ateres Rosh and **Gittel** wife of Yitzchok Sirkin who was called Reb Itzele Gittlish son of Yehoshua Heshel Sirkin from Shklov, from the lineage of the Bach.

**Moshe Ze'ev** Av Beis Din Horodok, Tiktin and Bialystok, wrote the seforim Agudas Eizov and Maros Hatzovos printed 1810/5570) also called Volf/Wolf married **Bas-Sheva** daughter of **Naftoli** son of **Shmue**l (Av Bais Din Mohilev/Mogilev.) **Naftoli's wife** was a daughter of **Yosef** son of **Shmuel** and thus he married a first cousin.

**Shmuel** was also known as Shmuel Reb Birchas (from the Ginsburg family, **son-in-law of Yosef Katz** son of the Kohain **Naftoli Katz** author of Semichas Chachomim. Yosef Katz was the son-in-law of **Mahari Leib** known as Reb Leib Mirkas. (Yosef son of Mahari Leib Mirkas was a brother-in-law of Eliezer of Hlusk.)

**Shmuel** was a son of **Mahari Isserl** Av Beis Din Pinsk whose ancestry was from the Terumas Hadeshen, Ramoh and Maharsho.) They had two sons **Shmuel Yitzchok** and **Yosef Berach**. They had a daughter Basya who married Yisroel from Shershov.

From Moshe Ze'ev's mother's side, he was a grandson of Mahari Heshel. Until 5573 he lived in Horodna then moved to Tiktin until 5784 when he moved to Bialystok.

**Yosef** was the son of **Mendel** Av Bais Din of Slutsk. (**Yosef** took over the position as Av Bais Din in Slutsk when his father Mendel became Av Bais Din in Minsk.

**Zev Gluskin** Zichronos/memories Slutsk yizkor book

After describing the city of Slutsk its Jewish schools, shuls, Rabbis and some families he continues with his family description.

One fascinating episode is about a person called Itche der chossid. On Simchas Torah we would go to his house to see him dancing on the table. I knew nothing about chassidus and I thought the whole importance of chassidus was to dance on the table during Simchas Torah.

I remember when I first visited the dwelling of my sister in the large house that used to belong to the Iserles family. There was a cholera outbrake in the city. My mother gave me 18 rubles to give to the community charity since that was the amount designated for important families to donate.

I was born on the ninth of Elul 5619/1859, the fifth child. The first four were girls and they honored me like an only child even though two boys were born after me. After Pesach when I was four and a half, my father entered me into the "cheder" wrapped in a silk talis. In the cheder so called angels threw me sweets from the ceiling and at home it was a festive day.

For Pesach my father came from Kenigsberg where he stayed for business. He brought me a small silk talis. In Slutsk this was a new item never seen before. He brought books, siddurim, small chumoshim printed with beautiful binding and in fact every time that he returned from his trips he would bring me books in beautiful print from other countries. This brought forth my desire for books and to read them which I enjoy till today.

I grew up and was educated in comfort but without extras and waste. My mother sent me to the chadorim of the famous teachers in town who get paid well. We were six or seven children of similar age in one class. In the chadorim they started teaching komatz alef until one page of Gemoroh weekly.

There was a person called the bahelfer/assistant who brought children of all ages to the school and took them home. The mothers would give him food and sweets for their child. During school he was a guard for when the kids went outside, from dogs, wagons, a sheygetz who may want to throw stones and from anything bad.

While the parents paid the teacher, the teacher was responsible for his assistant. The students who walked without the assistant were those who learned chumash with Rashi, they obviously had to fend for themselves. This left them with fear for the rest of their life from Shegotzim and dogs. During winter when we finished studies at eight o'clock due to the fear of the dark, the students went home in groups.

In school we learned tanach, then mishnayos and began studying gemorroh with Shnayin Ochazin until we could study several pages a week then Maharsho and Maharam Shif. We studied Chaye Odom, Shulchan Oruch and sifrei musar. Understandibly the success of the student depended on his personal abilities in addition to the teacher.

Secular studies were important as we sometimes had to deal with non-Jews. We learned Russian and to have a beautiful handwriting. Since my father was living in Germany for business I also studied German. I also studied Ivrit and grammar as reading other books. For this I had a separate teacher.

I would write monthly to my father in Konigsberg about my studies and daily schedule. I was fluent in Hebrew, clear in tanach. I knew ahavas tzion, mishnayos Berochos and Shabbos by heart and sufficient Gemorroh.

My father was happy to receive my letters and encouraged me. One time he brought me a Shas, Rom printing with fancy binding.

This is how I and my friends studied six days a week. One-hour secular studies in Hebrew and five times a week one hour in goyish. At the gymnasium we studied Russian, math and geography. Writing in Russian we learned with our Ivrit teacher.

I have pleasant childhood memories. My mother enjoyed hearing the letters that I wrote to my father and his letters to me. I was honored by the whole community like the child of wealthy people. My mother's father paid for the east wall in the shul where he sat in front next to the Holy ark and so I was often honored with maftir. Shabbos mincha I would read and also Shir Hashirim Ruth and Koheles. In the eyes of the people I was the example of a perfect child.

At eleven I entered the local school and learned there two hours each day in the afternoon except Shabbos. We studied Russian subjects, sat without a head covering and I finished the studies before bar-mitzvah with honors. My bar-mitzvah was celebrated with a lot of fanfare with all my relatives, teachers, friends, neighbors and others. I gave a half hour talk on the sugiah of being left handed.

After bar-mitzvah I continued to study by myself in Isserkesses shul. Also at that time I studied with a teacher other subjects. In secret I prepared myself to enter the Gymnazia. My teacher gave me a book to study Slavik which was necessary to get into school. He also gave me a goyish prayer book with pictures of priests. Which had a big cross on the page after the introduction. My mother happened to see the book and shook with fear. She came to me screaming: oy va voi, your teacher wants to bring you to convert and for sure wants you to go to the Gymnazia. Of course, she immediately fired the teacher and told me to forget about Gymnazia.

I loved my mother and her tears touched my heart so I did not think about it any more. She found another private teacher for me.

The name of our family Gluskin comes from the town Hlusk. My grandfather and his grandfather were Rabbis in Hlusk for many generations. They wrote books and we have a few of them like Agudas Eizov and Maros Hatzozvos of the Gaon Rabbi Zev from Bialistok. My father born in Hlusk was the grandson of one of these Rabbis. My name Zev is after the author of Agudas Eizov. It is considered a segula for Torah and good deeds to be called after a grandfather.

My mother born in Slutsk to the Lipshitz family. Her father had a business in Konigsburg but he died there before I was born. Her mother had a big store in Slutsk and after her husband died she lived with my mother. I remember her well. She died when I was five. Her name as Stacy was known and people called my mother Feigel Stacies which is engraved on her tombstone.

My father was called Laizer Stacies and people did not know that his surname is Gluskin, as they knew my mother as Feigel Stacies. In 5633 when I was fourteen I travelled with my father to Konigsburg.

*Zev joined Chovevei Tzion in Warsaw in the 1880's, became a member of Bnei Moshe and one of the founders of Menucha Venachaloh society that established the settlement of Rechovot. He was one of the founders of Achiasaf publishing house. Participated in the establishment of the Carmel society (1896), to sell wine produced in the settlements and was its first director.*

*In 1901 he participated in Chovevei Tzion mission to Baron Edmond de Rothchild to persuade him to continue his settlement activities in Eretz Yisroel. In 1904 he was among the founders of the Geulah company, which was established for the private purchase of land in Eretz Yisroel and was its director from 1925 – 1946. Late in 1905 he took over directorship of Agudas Hakeromim (Vintners association) and its wine cellars in Rishon Letzion and Zichron Yaakov.*

*When world war 1 broke out, he went to Alexandria and helped organize aid for the Jews who remained there and for the refugees from Eretz Yisroel. He supported the volunteer movement for the establishment of a jewish regiment in the British army from among Eretz Yisroel refugees.*

Library in Zev Gluskin house, Tel Aviv 1940.

**Yehoshua Gluskin**

Yehoshua Gluskin a Chabad chossid and grandson of Moshe Zev married the daughter of a Chabad family and became the Rabbi in Loyev/Loev.

The Dnieper River in Loyev

*In Loev 1861 there were 361 farms and 2 Jewish schools. A public college was opened in 1863. It was a town of intellectual Loyev/Chernobel chassidim. In 1861 Mordechai a grandson of Aharon of Chernobel was appointed a Rebbe of the Chernobeler Chassidim in Loyev. Reb Aharon bought land for him and came there for his coronation ceremony.*

The wife of Yehoshua Gluskin, Gita, was the daughter of Don Slonim of Navogorod-Syeversk son of the famous Chabad chossid Isser Kitzes who also originated in Shklov and uncle of Rebbetzin Menucha Rochel and brother of mechutan of the Mittler Rebbe of Lubavitch.

Don had a sister Gutte Esther who married Eliyahu Tumarkin son of Yosef Tumarkin, Rov of Krementchug d. 5639/1879 and Chossid of the Tzemach Tzedek and Maharash. *(The whole family is closely related to the greatest names in Shklov.* ***Yalkut Mishpochos*** *- Belinson. See also* ***Reshimas Devorim*** *p. 419, 420.)*

Yehoshua's wife was a daughter of Don Slonim son of Isser Kises of Shklov son of Eliezer Grayever (b. 9 Teves 5504 d.10 Teves 5591) author of **Mishnas Drebbi Eliezer** son of Yaakov a dayan in Pinsk. His wife was a daughter of Eliezer Lipman of Rozini son of Shimshon of Rozini son of Yisroel Zak who married the daughter of Yosef Yaski from Dubna. Yosef Yaski from Dubna son of Yehuda Yidel of Kavli was an anscestor of Yehoshua Gluskin's grandfather Moshe Zev. Thus Yehoshua and his wife Gita were actually distant cousins.

Yehoshua Gluskin had two sons and three daughters that we know of. His son Ber was buried in Shklov in 1863? ***(Kovetz Ahl Yad)***, Aharon, Chana, Mania and Rochel. Rabbi Yehoshua Gluskin spent time in Shklov possibly because that is where his wife's grandparents and family lived and he had many relatives there as well.

Approximately 358 years ago in the year 5420/1660, two Jews saved the Jews of their village. The Jews of Rozini were falsely accused of killing a non-Jew, after they threw a dead mutilated child into the house of a Jew. They warned the Jews that if they do not hand over the killers the whole community will be wiped out. Two Jews, Yisroel and Tuvia accepted death in order to save the other Jews of the town. The Jewish villagers then made a family tree for these two Jews. Yisroel was a descendant from Rashi (1040 – 1105) and he was an anscestor of Yehoshua Gluskin wife's.

Yisroel had a son Shimon who wrote a special selichos prayer. The prayers are printed in Sefer **Daas Kedoshim** pages 5-8. After that he writes the family lineage. The whole story is written up in Sefer **Daas Kedoshim** from

Yisroel Tuviah Eizenshtadt, Petersburg 5657-5658 and printed here in the Hebrew.

In 1880 *(**Oholei Shem** 5672)* Rabbi Yehoshua Zelig Zak a distant cousin of Yehoshua Gluskins wife was appointed as a Rabbi in Hlusk. He later became Rabbi in Homel. He was also a grandson of the famous Chabad Chossid Boruch Mordechai Ettinger of Bobroysk.

In the **responsa Yad Eliyahu** published Vilna 1905 response 4, 18, we find the name Aryeh Leib who was a Rabbi in Loyev. The Loyever Rebbe Chaim Yitzchok Heshel was born there in 1886. The writer Meir Goldovsky was born there in April 1884.

In 1895 there was a fire in which all four synagogues, and probably any written records, were burnt.

Entrance to the Jewish cemetery in Loyev

The cemetery is an area of two hectares on the northern outskirts of the town, on a hill with a slope to the west. There are no Jewish symbols anywhere. On one side is the Loyevsky electrical networks of Gomelenergo (producing electric and heat energy) and on the other side the educational center of the agriculture and food center of the executive committee of the Loev region. For more detailed information check http://aviv.by/culture/kladbishhe-v-loeve-gde-staryc-pamyatniki/

The western part of the cemetery that is not fenced in and is adjacent to the veterinary-baceriological laboratory is overgrown and has fragments of tombstones. On an undeveloped field there are three stones. The only one that can be read is: An important and modest woman, Mrs Chanin, the daughter of Rabbi Leib Chaim Gluskin, died 23 Kislev 5672/November 11 1911. It is very possible Leib Chaim was a brother of Aharon or Yehoshua Gluskin.

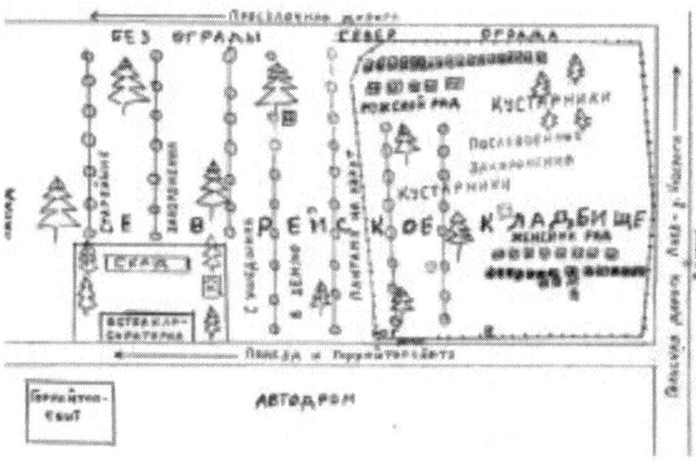

**Lineage of Gita** wife of Yehoshua Gluskin

*Further details of her lineage can be found in* ***Sefer Hatoldos*** *Rabbi Shneur Zalman of Liadi – the Alter Rebbe by Rav Avrohom Chanoch Glitzenshtein. Also see* ***Zichronos Hamaor*** *vol. 2 p. 439.*

**Yisroel** whose anscestor was Rashi had three children

**Generation two**

Menachem Nochum ab"d of Pilo and Polotsk married the daughter of the ab"d of Lutsk, Vilna and Pozna.

**Shimon** passed away before Shabbos in the year 5458, his second wife Esther passed away the 15 of Shvat 5502.

Sholom ab"d of Birz. His wife was the daughter of Meshulam Zalman Mirlas Neimark. The gaon Chacham Tzvi married her sister and so they were brother-in-laws. Passed away approximately in the year 5485.
**Grandchildren**

**Generation three**

Menachem Nochum had a boy and girl

Aharon Avrohom of Tiktin

The Daughter was married to Chaim son of Dovid Sholom.

**Shimon** had four sons

**Tzvi Hirsch Zak.** His wife Dina daughter of Eliezer Lipman ab"d Chelm son of Yisroel Heilprin ab"d Kratashin.

Moshe Zak married the daughter of Shlomo ab"d Zalkava on Tuesday 12 Kislev 5451.

Yechiel dayan in Rozini passed away before the year 5472.

Yishochor Ber passed away 16 Iyar 5517.

Sholom had 2 sons and one daughter

Yisroel Zak ab"d of Zabludovi and Biraz. His wife was the daughter of Yosef Yaski ab"d of Dubno.

Chaim ab"d of Biraz after his older brother passed away.

Daughter wife of Dovid Katzinelinfoigen son of Yechile ab"d of Kidan.

Great grandchildren – generation four

Tzvi Hirsh had 2 sons and one daughter

Chaim dayan in Rozini

**Eliezer Lipman** dayan in Rozini his wife was Nechama.

He passed away the 27 Iyar 5525 and she passed away on the 19 Kislev 5533.

Beila wife of Avrohom son of Aryeh Leib Pollack. She passed away on Thursday the 16 Menachem Av 5519.

Moshe Zak had two sons

Sholom dayan Brazini passed away suddenly on the 22 Teves 5486. His wife Rochel passed away on the 8 Adar 5486.

Yissochor Ber Dayan Brazinai.

Yechiel had two sons
Sholom
Nachmon

Yissochor Ber had one son

Shimon Zak. He passed away on the 27 Adar 5513.

Yiroel Zak had one son and two daughters

Dovid ab"d Amdur

Daughter wife of Tzvi Hirsch Bruda ab"d Zablodovai, Ludai and Horodna

Daughter wife of Meir son of Arye leib ab"d Vitebsk

Chaim Zak had three sons

Yisroel ab"d Birz. Passed away in the year 5535

Yitzchok ab"d Pasval in Zamut

Meshulam Zalman ab"d Pakrai. He left the Rabbinate and moved to live in Vilna. Passed away on the 13 Adar 5560.

Dovid Katzenelinfoigen had five sons

Avrohom Katzenelinfoigen ab"d Slutsk and Brisk. He met the GRA when he was seven years old and took him to his father in Kidan.

Moshe Zalman

Yoel ab"d Shinove, Yartshub and Horobetshub. His wife was the daughter of Chaim Hakohen Rappaport ab"d of Levov.

Yisroel ab"d of Kelavriev, Vilka-Vishk.

Sholom ab"d Ashatiz

**Generation five**

Eliezer Lipman Zak had one son and two daughters.

Yaakov passed away while his father was living on the 12 Kislev 5520

Dina the wife of Yaakov son of Levi baal Chiddushei Mahari. Passed away 6 Nissan 5504.

**Yocheved wife of Yaakov** son of Eliezer scribe and dayan and moreh tzedek in Minsk.

**Generation six**

Yaakov had a son

**Eliezer** author of Mishnas Drebbi (Rabbi Eiezer ben Yaakov from Slonim printed in Shklov 5579/1819) on Shas. Born 7 Teves 5504. In 5534 was given semicha by Rabbi Raphael Hamburger ab"d Pinsk. His first wife was the daughter of Yitzchok Eizik ab"d Pinsk. His second wife was the daughter of Nochum Grayever from Slonim and that is where he lived. He passed away the tenth of Teves 5591.

For more details of anscestory read Toldos Mishpachas Horav Miliadi.

**Generation seven**

Eliezer Grayever had five sons and two daughters.
With his first wife they had a child who was called Yitzchok Eizik.

With his second wife

Moshe Shlomo Zalman Roizis of Shklov

**Isser** from Shklov known as Isser Kises

Tzvi Hirsh of Slonim

Pinchos from Vilkomir

Chaya the wife of Moshe Maizel from Horodok they had a son Eliyohu Chaim Maizlish ab"d of Lodz.

Yocheved wife of Gershon

**Generation eight**

**Isser** married Itke.

Don

Zalman of Shklov

Eliezer Slonim

Gutte Esther married Eliyohu Tumarkin

Chaya d. Friday 27 Tammuz 5595

Isser fasted for forty years except Shabbos and Yom Tov and was a strict vegetarian even as he often travelled for business to Leiptzig. He was constantly studying Torah, was a chossid of The Alter Rebbe Rabbi Shneur Zalman of Liadi. People came to him when they had disagreements in business and followed his advice.

***Kovetz Ahl Yad*** *volume 1 (11) p. 158. List of families in the Pinkas of Shklov. Among the names of the Kitzes family is mentioned Chaya who the author of Daas Kedoshim does not mention.*

**Generation nine**

**Don**
Yitzchok Slonim

Yaakov of North Novogrod

Gita

ספר דעת קדושים מר' ישראל טוביה אייזינשטאט מראזיני פלך הוראדנא, ליטא, נדפס פטרבורג תרנז - תרנח.

גם זו העיר ראזיני לא נחה שקטה מחמת המציק כי יצא השטן ממחבואו להחרידה בלילה אחד בעלילה הבדויה אשר התעללו בנו שונאנו, ובקנאתם השליכו ילד נוצרי מת מושרט בבשרו שריטות הרבה במערת הבית אשר לה"ר ישראל בה"ר שלום (הבית עם המערה אשר בו עודנו עומד על תלו בראזינאי ויהי

למורשה לבית הרה"ג הנודע לתפארת מ' גרשון במ' יעקב ז"ל זאקהיים וצאצאיו, ומפי בנו הישיש מ' אריה ליב נמסר להרה"ג מ' בנימין וואלף אבד"ק יעקאטרינאסלאוו. בו הגאון המפורסם מ' יוסף קאצינעלונבויגען אבד"ק בריסק והגליל בנסעו בכל שנה ליריד זעלווי היה מתכוין לשבות בראזינאי והיה אוכל סעודה שלישית בבית הזה לזכרון המאורע מאבותיו הקדושים זצ"ל.) וממחרת התנפלו על הבית וילכו הלוך וזעוק: הוא הילד אשר שפכו היהודים את דמו ללוש בו את המצות לחגם והתואנה הזאת אשר נעשתה בצדיה מידי חרשי משחית הקמים עלינו, היתה למפץ וכלי זעם לעשות העיר למהפכה, רבים הוגשו לנחושתים ואסורים בזקים ישבו בבית כלא, רק בעלי הכסף עשירי העם הגינו עליהם בכספם לבלתי כרוע תחת אסיר. אבל מה? רכושם היה להם לשלל כמעט באון אומר השב, וכשלוש שנים משנת תי"ז עד שנת ת"ך היתה העיר נצורה במצור ותחת שואה בתגלגלה לרגלי ענוי הדין שנמשך זמן כביר, ומועד מועדים חלפו באין קץ ותקוה לאסירי עני וברזל, והעיר ראזינאי נבוכה.

הימים האלה היו בימי יאהן קאזימיר השני, הוא היה תחלה קארדינאל הפאבסטע ברומי, ומלך על פולין וליטא בשנת ת"ח היא שנת 1648 למספרם עד שנת תכ"ח. בימיו היתה גם גזירת ת"ח ופשטו הקאזאקים על ליטא בשנות תי"ד ותט"ו. והיעזואיטים פרצו בארץ וישלחו חצי קנאתם ביהודים, כהסיתם בם את עמי הארץ בעלילותיהם. וקאזימיר כי אבה ללכת בדרך המלכים אשר לפניו שביו על היהודים למחסה, והאצילים והעם לא שלטו בם שלטת. לא עצר כח, כי בהיותו עוין את קארל מלך שוועדין היו ימיו מכאובים וכעס ולא ידע מנוחה, והיעזואיטים חורשי און וקוצרי עמל, אשר לבם היה רק רע על היהודים הפכו את לב העם מקצה בעלילות הדם אשר הסיתום בם. ולא נתנו גם מדרך כף רגל ליהודים לבוא אל המלך וע"כ בכל משך שלש השנים אשר חפצו בני העיר ראזינאי למצוא משפט בבת המלך מגינם ומשגכם לא יכלו למצוא עזרה בצרה למו. ומאת היעזואיטים היתה נסבה להיות שופטים אכרים מדלת העם ובקנאת הדת ושנאת היהודים הוציאו בחלקלקות והנף משפט כרצונם.

מקץ שנת תי"ט הגיעה השעה לשום קץ ותכלה למשפט עיר האומללה, אשר התפרפרה בין מות לחיים, אז התאספו האכרים מראזינאי וסביבותיה לשבת כסאות למשפט, המונים המונים נהרו אל עמק יהושפט, הוא עומק המשפט אשר יחרוצו על מעשה העלילה אשר היתה עד הנה בלשכת החשאים, השופטים גזרו אומר: „מות יומת הרוצח אשר רצח נפש הילד לו נודע מי הכהו, אך באשר נעלם ולא נודע עפ"י החקירה והדרישה מי הוא יאשם יהודה! כי נחשד בראשונה" וע"כ הוציאו לראש משפט כי יקחו שנים אנשים מראשי עדת ישראל בראזינאי להמיתם והם ישאו את עון כולם (ישנה משפחה בראזינאי אשר אנשיה יקטפו מיד המות בטרם הגיעם לשנת השלשים בערך, והאגדה אומרת כי מוצאם מזרע השופטים שהיו בימים ההם ע"כ לא יחצו ימיהם - והמאמין יאמין.) כה סרו מני דרך , נטו מני אורח השופטים ההם ובמשפטם זה טמנו נאים פח לרגלי טובים השנים מו"ה ישראל ומו"ה טוביה שנאחזו במצודה, כי גדולי העיר וראשיה היו, וכן היו בעיניהם.

הקדושים האלה יצאו כהולך בחליל לקראת גזר דינם וצדקו עליהם דין שמים בשמחה וקבלו וקימו לתת נפשם כופר העם למען הצילו ממהומת מות וכליון חרוץ „האח! הנה מה טוב גורלנו! אף נחלת שפרה לנו" אמרו איש אל אחיו „כופר נפשנו נתן להחיות עם רב" ובלב מלא רצון ורגש קודש הכינו עצמם בקדושה ובטהרה להוציא להורג נפשם להציל העדה מרעתה, לתת חייהם במחיר כל בני העיר, גם נשאו כפיהם השמימה לאל הדורש דמי עשוקים, כי ירצה דמם כקרבן כליל להגן על עיר העלובה, אשר לא תבאנה תואנות שקר ועלילות שוא בשעריה, ולא יוסיפו עוד בני עולה לענותה מעתה ועד עולם.

משפט הנועד על הקדושים הוגבל לעשותו ביום הששי יום שני של ראש השנה שנת ת"ך. ביום הקדוש אשר כל באי עולם יעברו לפני שופט כל בשר כבני מרון, עברו קדושי עליון אלה כשיות נאלמות, לטבח הובלו בידי שופטיהם אחרי שפכם שיחם זו תפלה לה', מה נורה היה המחזה האיומה הזאת? אימה גדולה וחשכה נפלה על פני כל העם, ויחרד לבם לקול יוצא ממעמקי לב, כל קדושי עליון ישמיעו הגיון פרידתם מכל בני חלד, ויציאתם מן העולם להתהלך לפני ה' באור החיים.

הם אך כלו את תפלתם, והשופטים העריצים נגשו אליהם להוציאם להורג, וקול ענות נשמע ממרגיזי אל „הנה בידכם טובכם ואשרכם! שנו דתכם מחיר חייכם ותנצלו" „חלילה! חלילה לנו מבגוד בה' אלקינו ובנחלת קדשנו!" ענו ברגש קודש „סורו! סורו קראו למו טוב לנו להיות קרבן כליל כשה לעולה מהסתפח בנחלת זרים" ויצא הקדוש מו"ה ישראל ראשון לטבח בקדשו שם ה', ובצאת נשמתו באחד אמר לו רעו מו"ה טוביה „אשריך ישראל ! וטוב לך" נשמע בלשון הקודש מ' ישראל לוחכת העפר, כמשיבה ועונה לר' טוביה „גם חלקך בחיים רעי! עמדי לחיי העולם הבא".

אבות לבנים יגידו זקני עירנו יספרו לנו, כי אחרי שמהרגו הקדושים האלה הגיעה פקודת הממשלה העליונה להניחם בחיים. אבל! לא כן חפץ ה', כי יקר בעיניו המותה לחסידיו, וכבר יצא הגזירה מלפניו שיקבלו עליהם את הדין, ורוכב ערבות שש ושמח בבוא אליו נפשות צדיקים אלה לדבקה בו ולזכות את בניהם אחריהם ואת כל יושבי עירם כי יגינו בצדקתם עליהם.

אחר הדברים האלה התעורר הרב הגאון מ' שמעון בן הקדוש מו"ה ישראל הי"ד, ויסדר נוסח סליחות לאמרו בבתי כנסיות דראזינאי ביום הכפורים בכל שנה, ותקן הזכרה לנשמות הקדושים, כי יפקדו בכל שנה בימי הזכרת נשמות המתים שנהגו בכל תפוצות ישראל, ולתקופת השנה למתתם הוא יום השני של ראש השנה, וכן נוהגים בראזינאי עד היום בביהמ"ד לת"ק גחש"א, ובביהמ"ד של ר' גרשון זקהיים שאחד ממשפחת הקדוש יושב על הבימה ומסדר ההזכרה בניגון מיוחד, וביוה"כ יאמרו הסליחות כל המתפללים בביהמ"ד לח"ק גחש"א ובביהמ"ד של ר' גרשון נצר מיוצאי חלצי הקדושים, זכותם תעמוד להציל מכל אסון יהודה וישראל, עד המתים יחיה אל, יקומם בנין אריאל, ובא לציון גואל.

**Aharon Gluskin**

Rabbi Aharon son of Yehoshua Gluskin (1840 – 1908) received semicha from the Tzemach Tzedek (1788 – 1866). Aharon Gluskin became the Rov of Paritch after Reb Hillel who passed away in 1864. This would have made him about 25 years old.

***Oholei Shem*** *by Shmuel Noach Gottleib printed in Pinsk 1912* Rabbi Aharon son of Shmuel Kaminker received smicha - ordination from Rabbi Shmaryohu Noach Schneerson of Bobroysk, Rabbi Moshe Shmuel Shapiro av beis din in Bobroysk and Rabbi Aharon Gluskin of Paritch. *After the passing of the Tzemach Tzedek, his children split up into becoming leaders of specific groups. Shmaryohu Noach was the third son of Yehuda Leib the Rebbe of Kopust who was a son of the Tzemach Tzedek. He studied under the Tzemach Tzedek, his father and his brother Shlomo Zalman. He married his cousin daughter of Yisroel Noach of Nezhin. He became the Rebbe of Kopust for a time and then his brother Sholom Dovber of Retziza took over as Rebbe. In 5641/1881 Rabbi Shapiro was made AB"D.*

Aharon Gluskin's name is mentioned as giving money to help with the printing of Sefer **Pirkei Hanazer** on the laws of Shechita and Bedika published in Lublin 1886 on page 165 with other names of people from Loyev. His name is also mentioned as giving money to print the **Sdei Chemed**, klolim on Shas and Poskim, page 197, published Warsaw 1901 but there is mentioned that he was in Brezhin when he gave the donation.

***M'oros Nosson*** *p.130 chapter 36, Yerushalayim 1998, Rabbi Nosson Nota Alavskaya.* The chossid Rabbi Aharon Gluskin was one of the few remainders who represented the greatness of the faith of the house of Israel. All his days, including when he was in business and a successful businessman, he dwelt in Torah and avodah. He was a famous and precious Chabad chossid. Many cities asked him to become their Rabbi but he refused.

Miriam daughter of Keila Liba Gluskin remembers her uncle Mendel and grandfather Aharon wearing white on special occasions like Pesach Sheni and sukkos. The Tzemach Tzedek also wore white on Shabbos and Yom Tov. She also remembers how they moved during davening with great intensity.

Reb Hillel of Paritch lived in Brahin in his childhood days which is the same town that the Serebryanski family lived. Thus, it seems natural that the child of Shneur Zalman Serebryanski came to study under Reb Hillel. The term for such people was 'yoshvim-zitzers,' meaning they were sitting and constantly studying Torah. *Eliyohu Serebryanski met Aharon Gluskin (called with an endearing term Oreh) when they were both studying under the tutelage of the famous Rabbi Hillel in Paritch, although they probably knew of each other before due to the closeness of people who lived in Brahin and Loyev about 25 miles distance. In fact, the Loyev Rebbe would stay at the Serebryanski house when he visited his followers in Brahin. Reb Zalman Serebryanski remembers how they stayed at their house for a half year and he knew the whole family well. Thus, the families probably knew of each other even before coming to Reb Hillel.*

Reb Aharon worked in the lumber business, but he used all his time to study Torah and Chassidus. Even when he had to travel, he always took along seforim. When they arrived at an inn and the passengers went over to warm the stove, Reb Aharon would sit down with his Gemora and learn with a sweetness that warmed his frozen limbs. One time he was asked why he prays during work, he responded, "Don't you occasionaly think of work during prayers? It is ok for me to be confused and mixed up and pray during work."

After the passing of Rabbi Reb Hillel in 1864, the Chassidic townspeople asked Rabbi Aharon Gluskin to succeed him. He refused, claiming that he was undeserving to fill the place of Reb Hillel and also did not want to support himself through the Rabbinate. He continued working in the lumber business. As the custom was they would buy the lumber rights of a forest, cut the trees and send the logs as rafts down the river to the big lumber fair in Leipzig. He would sometimes sit on a raft and study as the barges of logs floated down the river.

One time when all his money was invested in lumber, a telegram came on Shabbos to where he was staying for business with news that the rafts broke and all the logs were lost and that his house burned. Reb Aharon understood what the telegram meant to convey, but throughout Shabbos refused to look at it and continued to rejoice as if the telegram never came. On Motzei Shabbos and only after Havdalah did he ask his son about the telegram. He said, "Aleh zainen gezunt – everyone is healthy! Nu, now we have to go masser/complain to Reb Hillel."

He saw this as a sign from heaven that he should accept the Rabbinic position in Paritch. He went to the grave of Reb Hillel, asked his forgiveness, and said: If this is your holy will that I take your place then I accept the judgment. *(Yossi - I asked my grandfather Reb Zalman if his grandfather Reb Aharon was able to speak with souls and thus spoke directly with Reb Hillel to hear his response. He thought for a moment and said possibly.)*

Thus, he assumed the position of Rabbi after the famous Chassidic Rabbi Hillel of Paritch passed away in 1864. After taking on the Rabbinical position in 1865, Rabbi Aharon became known as a holy man. He was beloved by all. Once, two men came to him for a din Torah and after giving a verdict, the claimant asked the defendant to shake his hand upon his commitment to pay him by the time they agreed upon.

When the time came, the defendant refused to pay and Rabbi Aharon sent him a summons to come to the court – bais din. The man arrived but refused to pay. Rabbi Aharon told him; "since you obligated yourself with a handshake, if you do not pay – the hand will not be yours!" The man continued to refuse to pay and within a month his hand dried up and was paralyzed for the rest of his life.

Another time two people came to Rabbi Aharon for a din Torah. After Rabbi Aharon gave his psak – ruling, one person did not want to accept it and could not move his hand till he acquiesced.

Reb Mottel Rivkin related that which he heard from Avrohom Itche Glasman who married the youngest daughter of Aharon Gluskin. Once during a din Torah, Reb Aharon felt that one of the sides was not going to fulfill the verdict. Reb Aharon asked the defendant to give a tekias kaf – hand shake. In the end, the man did not fulfill his part of the judgement and his hand got cut off in an accident.

After the passing of the Tzemach Tzedek – Rabbi Menachem Mendel Schneerson, Aharon named his son Menachem Mendel. Another child named after the Tzemach Tzedek was Menachem Mendel Serebryanski who married Nechamah, a daughter of Rabbi Aharon Gluskin.

His daughter Nechama mentioned that kids would come over to their house to play and make a lot of noise. He would sit and learn and never told them to be quiet.

Reb Yehoshua Shneur Zalman Serebryanski son of Menachem Mendel and Nechamah remembers seeing a note written in 1906 from his grandfather Reb Aharon (Ore) to his father sending him 25 rubles for Zalman's opsherenish and noting that he should begin to wear a tallis kotton.

Reb Zalman also related the following story. There was once a wedding of his father's sister and the chosson was a son of a great Rabbi. Many great Rabbis came including Chaim Soloveichik/Brisker. After the wedding my father Mendel Serebryanski took him to the train station. While they were waiting, Reb Chaim said about Aharon Gluskin that he heard that he was a lamdan but did not know how great of a lamdan he was.

**Aharon Gluskin** b. about 1840 (in Garaditch/Haraditch?) – d. 1908 Paritch
m. about 1860 Esther Wolfson b around 1840

1) Keila Leiba b.    d. 27 Tishrei 5698/October 1 1937

2) Ita b. 1868 in Loyev was first wife of Yosef Gutner. She died 1894 and was buried in Loyev.

3) Basya Riva b. 1878 Loyev, died 1944. Married Yosef Gutner who was b. 1864 in Loyev, moved to Moscow 1920's. He served in the Choral Synagogue, was arrested in 1937 and sent to Gulag, d. 1940. Burial place unknown.

4) Baila b. 1872 died 1942, starved during siege and buried in mass grave in Leningrad.

5) Nechamah b. around 1882 d. 1930's

6) Mussia born in Loyev, married Isaac Volovitch. She died 1941 and he died 1942 in Poltava.

7) Rochel Chaya b. Loyev

8) Menachem Mendel b. 1878 Loyev d. 13 Kislev 1936 Leningrad

9) Chana Mira "Mirel" youngest. Married Gluzman. Moved from Khazakstan to Israel in 1948.

**Keila Leiba Gluskin**

Married Rabbi Jacob Yitzchok son of Shneur Zalman Helfgot d. 3 Teves /December 7 1945, eventually moved to Baltimore. Keila was fluent in Russian, Hebrew, Yiddish and German. She arranged private tutoring for her daughter through a Rabbi who came to the house to teach. They had 7 children. Yehoshua, Nathan, Greisha, Hirsh, Rochel, Miriam and Isser.

Yehoshua/Yevsei b. 1898 in Loyev d.1955, physician. Migrated to Moscow in the 1920's, buried in Perlovskoe cemetery in Moscow. His wife Fania Polack b. 1904 d. 1989 Moscow was also a physician. They did not have children together but his wife had a daughter Celia which he adopted as his own.

Nathan b. 1885 (1930 was in Cook, Illinois m. Nettie b. about 1888) physician.

Greisha born in Loyev 1892 d. 1951 moved to Moscow in the 1920's, physician, buried in Perlovskoe cemetery Moscow. He did not have his own family, was a very good doctor and extremely kind person. He loved his patients and they loved him. He was the family doctor for the entire Moscow Gluskin family.

Hirsh/Grigozy died from tuberculosis. Never married.

Rochel born in Loyev 1893. D. 1970 buried in Vostriakovo cemetery Moscow. She was a dental nurse. Married Moshe Minkin b. Gomel 1887 d. 1977 buried same cemetery. In 1920-21 they moved to Moscow. He had a small hardware store, then he worked as a supply officer in state departments. Mark was born in Gomel 1919. Esther born in 1926. Mark m. Ita (Atya Gutner) children Vladimir,

Leonid m. Alla Gurevitch and had a child Elizabeta Minkin. Fira m. Yevesy Gurevitch.

Miriam b.1898 – 13 Shvat /January 20 2000. Miriam Helfgot m. Dr Benjamin Sax Hacohen 1879 – 6 Menachem Av/August 5 1949. Had three children, Albert, Daniel and Ruth. Dr Sax's mother was Sara Levy.

Isser b. November 28 1899 d. August 15 1964

At the time in Russia there were quotas that prevented many Jews from attending medical school. Only the brightest and capable were chosen. In addition to the quotas there was also a lottery system where those accepted by the quota system were allowed to attend medical school only if the lot came up with their name. Greisha and Yevsei both got in this way. Nathan became a doctor in the USA. He helped the Helfgots come to the USA in 1918.

Yaakov Helfgott davened three times a day. He would go to shul early in the morning and return to the home of his daughter Miriam and son-in-law Dr. Benjamin Sax on Kalow Ave at Eutaw place. Apparently, he lived with them. There he would sit in the large library and study from the Holy books with a glass of tea and sugar. The day he died they found him wrapped in tefillin hunched over a sefer. Below photo of (1) Rabbi Yakov Yitchak Helfgott ztsl, (2) Miriam zl and her father Rabbi Helfgott ztsl, and (3) Anna Helfgott

Anna Helfgott, Jacob's youngest sister was a Hebrew teacher in D.C. She was engaged and very much in love at the age of 18. Her fiancé died and she never got over it, remaining single her whole life. She taught Esther Altshul Helfgott the mah nishtana. Jacob passed away when Esther was 3 but she had a picture of him holding her in his lap and although the picture is missing it still lives in her heart and mind, an indelible memory. Below kever of Keila Leiba Gluskin Helfgott zl [mother of Miriam zl] Keila was the oldest daughter of Rabbi Aaron Gluskin of Paritchi and sister of Rav Menachem Mendel Gluskin of Minsk and Leningrad

אמנו היקרה קיילע ליבע
בת הרב ר' אהרן
גלוסקין מפאריטש
ואחות הרב ר' מנחם מענדיל
גלוסקין מלענינגראד
נפ' כז תשרי תרצ"ח
KATE LOVE
HELFGOTT
OCT. 1, 1937
BELOVED MOTHER

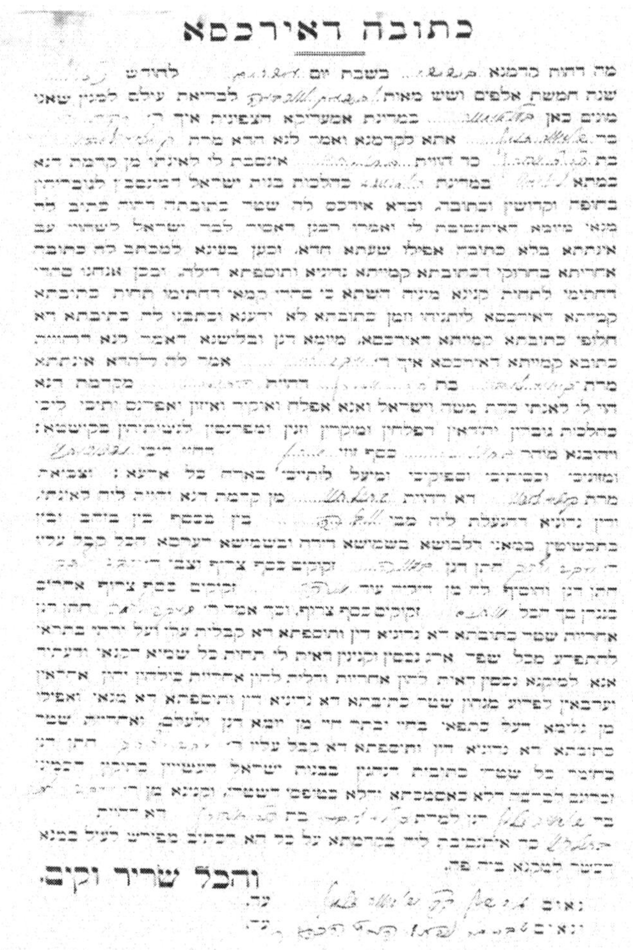

# כתובה דאירכסא

והכל שריר וקים.

Above the second Ketubah from Rabbi Yaakov Helfgott to Keila Lieba copied above.

**Ita** married Yosef Gutner, they had 5 children Luba, Yehoshua, Yevsei, Yaakov and Hertz. When Ita died he married Basya Riva. Yaakov m. Klara they had two children Ita (Atya) and Shura (Alexandra). Luba Gutner m. Yevesy they had a child Ita "beba". Hertz/Girtz arrested 1927, never returned. M. Genia (daughter, Boris, Dusya).

**Basya Riva** married Yosef Gutner and they had a son Avrohom he was a staunch communist and journalist. During Stalin's reign Avrohom was arrested and perished and in 1937 Yosef was imprisoned and killed.

**Baila** married Yitzchok Gurevitch b. Snovsk 1861, they lived in Snovsk. Moved to Leningrad in 1931. She died during the siege and was buried in Peskarevskoe cemetery. He died June 27, 1941. Buried in the Preobragenskoe cemetery. He was in the Lumber trade before the revolution.

Their children were Don, Aharon, Yehoshua, Fradl, Ida, Esther and Perl.

Don who died in WW2 married Manya and they had 2 children Lina and Tamara. Lina got married and had a child Valerig. Aharon also died during WW2. Yehoshua/ Yevesy travelled to America his second marriage to Fira Minkin daughter of Moshe Minkin and Rochel Helfgot. Perl married Yosef Ragilski they had a son Uri.

**Nechama** married around 1899 to Menachem Mendel Serebryanski who died 1941 in Samarkand. Nechama spent a long time each night saying Krias Shema ahl hamita. She had tea glasses with Nechama Serebryanski engraved on them. Was very elegent. Nechama Werdiger has a few objects that belonged to her.

*Serebryanski was also a very meyuchas family as can be seen by the fact that Mendel's sister Taibel married Leib Shneerson son of Dovber of Retzitza. They had a daughter Soro. They divorced after a short marriage. Their daughter Sarah did not get married and died during the siege of Leningrad.*

*In* ***Toldos Mishpachas Horav Miliadi*** *p.105 Leib Schneerson is mentioned but not whom he married. His brother Chaim Yeshaya also served as Rov in Paritch from 1895 -1901 till he got his own place in Roman. (****Yagdil Torah*** *Tishrei-Cheshvan 5748, year 8 #1, volume 38 p.29.)*

They had four children Sarah b. around 1900, Ita Freida born around 1902 died 1927 13th Marcheshvan, Shneur Zalman b. 1904 (Yehoshua was added later due to illness) and another girl who died young.

**Musya** married Isaac Volovitch 4 children Esther, Mera, Aharon, Iliya. Esther had 2 children Zina and Roman.

**Rochel Chaya** married Aharon/Isser Ginsburg three children were killed by the Grermans and a fourth child Aharon survived.

**Beila** married Yitzchok Gurevitz (d. 27 June 1941) and lived in Senobesk, Ukraine and later in Leningrad. 7 children Don (d. WW2), Aharon (d. WW2), Yehoshua (Yevesy-moved from Moscow to USA. In his second marriage he was married to a daughter of Rochel Minkin - Esther), Fraidel, Ita, Esther and Perel. Beila d. during the siege of Leningrad (which was from 8 September 1941 – 18 January 1943.)

**Menachem Mendel** Gluskin b. 1878 Loyev Belarus d. 13 Kislev 1936, married 1909 to Fraidel Rabinovitch – b. 1888 Minsk d. 13 Kislev 1929.

Children – Gita b. July 6 1922 Paritch,

Sonia b. July 10 1917 Paritch,

Leah b. June 27 1914 Minsk married Yosef Amusin 1941,

Esther Chaya b. April 25 1911 in Minsk married Yitzchok Mintz 7 August 1936.

**Chana Mirel**– youngest. Married a man in Khazakstan, Glazman whose wife had died and was Rav in Burzeno, Ukraine.3 children Chana, Mirel and Isser.

**The life of Rabbi Menachem Mendel Gluskin**

HIS FIRST STEPS

"Rabbi Menachem Mendel Gluskin was a young man in a period when it was possible for a Rabbi to work and guide. This was before the Soviet Regime humbled all stature and silenced individual accomplishment. He therefore did not have the opportunity to exhibit the fullness of his capabilities and power of his influence. All that we know of him are his first steps, cautious and slow, due to the afflictions of the time. The beginning of his Rabbinate predicted greatness but due to the oppression, the possibilities did not materialize. His light was extinguished in the darkness of the spiritual drought in the land and he was unable to enlighten the skies of Judaism.

He was also not given the opportunity to publish any of his writings and immortalize himself the way other writers do. This was due not only to the external circumstances but also due to the internal holding back of that which raged within him. It was not natural for him to spread his springs outward. His learning was concealed and closed with seven locks which he only let out in a time of need to teach and guide.

The very existence of his personality and being, his unique existence and movement upon the earth constitute a precious possession. Therefore, that which he inherits to future generations is not attached to a bundle of writings but with a bundle of life. There only remain individuals who conceal within their soul the contact they had with him, and they guard the rays of light of his personality. Come; let us contemplate this extraordinary man and his qualities that gave light into Russian Jewry at a period when it was fading.

LIKE SHIPS IN THE MIDST OF THE SEA

Rav Gluskin embraced his world in one unique point without diffusion or fragmentation. He was whole in his personality as well as in his studies. His focus on the main point allowed him to grasp matters of great scope and to sail great distances. At first glance and reflection he grasped the soul of the matter of that which he learned, the secret of its existence, the very essence and force that gave it life.

Shallow people can incorporate and fill the hollow of their soul with various thoughts and many theories, a little of this and a little of that, and the pit is not filled by its sand. Not so those who prefer the profound, they are of one spirit that conquers their being to the end and completely fills them. Rav Mendel Gluskin was one of these. Torah filled his whole being and from it he was able to look at everything that happened, he observed the manifestations of the world and time, with the changing times and vanishing eras. 1) Particularly in times of emergency there awoke within him amazing powers that he had not previously imagined. Hard times break delicate people and strengthen those are built of steel. Rav Gluskin was a man of steel. Therefore, he shone during that period of darkness like a tower of light to all those who lost the way or were depressed.

1) *Torah and its observance are a base to expand from, observe all and come back to the balance that it holds. Many religious people use religion as a space to hide behind and limit themselves. Those who believe and see*

*the Creator life force in everything, they apply Torah to all life situations and see creation in an expansive way. In this way, they connect directly with the ever-expanding universe that we live in and the source of life.*

He was a man of few words and his main influence was with his personality, aristocratic behavior, refined feelings, and his relationship with people was a wondrous example.

There is no need to stress that in Soviet Russia it was impossible to organize orderly co-operation; the most that was possible was to connect with a hint or with words that hide their meaning and Rav Gluskin was an artist in this field. Thus, he was able to influence brothers in opinion and family in spirit without direct contact or words. Those who left Russia after the Second World War are able to relate about his way of connecting and of the influence of Rav Gluskin from Minsk.

From 1934 he influenced them from distant Leningrad. Even though the connection was weak and the meeting quick and silent, like ships meeting in the middle of a stormy night who hint to each other through flashes of light. Ships that meet in the middle of the sea and neither know what the other is carrying or what their destination is. It is similar for those who have Jewish spirit in the oppressive times of Russia with a tyrannical and hostile police force. But the travelers who came to safe shores know to tell what was hidden on those passing ships and what the hint was. Who knows what happened to them in the storm? A sigh breaks forth from the heart of the lucky story teller, who came to his/her place of safety, regarding those who sank in a drowning world.

This is the meaning of the regards given over by those who escaped Soviet Russia about the fate of the Rav of Leningrad who stood guard during the period of destruction. Even though it is now more than forty years since the Soviet revolution, there still appears some light in the darkness of the Judaism in Russia. There is felt a desire to return to the source. There is no doubt that the seeds that he planted at the beginning with the sweat of his brow and blood of his heart were not swallowed but sprouted and they are growing and giving fruit."

Menachem Mendel son of Aharon and Esther was born into a Chabad Family in the city of Loyev in Belarus/ White Russia in 1878 and was named after the Tzemach Tzedek, Rabbi Menachem Mendel Shneerson. Loyev is where his grandparents Yehoshua Gluskin who was Rabbi and his wife Gita lived. Mendel's parents lived in Paritch where his father was Rabbi. He was born into a distinguished family whose history was filled with Torah giants. Mendel was no different. He was a child prodigy with personal charm that enchanted all those who came in contact with him.

His father and grandfather taught by example. They lived Torah and had no expectations that others should live the same way. They loved each person as being an expression of Hashem and therefore did not judge others. They kept a balance between the world around them and the space their mind and heart were in.

They fully understood about educating each child according to the individuality of the child and not dictating what the child should do or not do. At the same time, they educated each child to have a deep positive feeling to being Jewish and Judaism. Mendel was no different. That which he demanded of himself, he did not demand of anyone else. They were happy to guide people who asked but had no agenda to tell anyone what they should or should not do.

His mother and grandmother were deeply religious and lived as such, being careful with all the details of a Torah way of life. They were in charge of the house. The family lived and behaved with refined expressions of emotions and thought.

Mendel's clarity in what he did was based in his clarity in mind and emotions and understanding of Torah. He embodied the soul and spirit of Torah. He was able to guide people and tell them what Torah wants since he came from a place of purity. He was able to flow with the situation in each moment. As it changed, he was able to pace himself and go with it. He lived fully in each moment, the pain and joy both occupying his being.

Mendel had a brilliant mind not only in Torah and Halacha but also in worldly subjects. When he was young he attempted to receive a graduation certificate from the gymnazia – college/university as an external student. He went for a test to the city of Bobroysk.

In language and Russian history, he received a high grade. The test for mathematics was set for Shabbos. Since there was no pikuach nefesh/danger to life involved he did not go for the test and never received his diploma and remained self-taught. That which he studied remained with him till the end of his life. In the language of our sages *(**Pirkei Ovos** 2:9, **Ovos D'Rabbi Nosson** 14:3)* he was a bor sod she'eino m'abed tipo – a plastered pit that does not lose a drop or to translate the saying in different words - a holder of secrets where no drop goes to waste.

We do not know how often he discussed Torah with Rabbi Rabinowitz, but at some point, he received semicha from Rabbi Eliezer Rabinowitz. He became his son-in-law but we do not know anything about how it came about. It was not strange that a Chabad Chossid married the daughter of Rabbi Rabinowitz since his wife's sister was already married to a Chabad Chossid. Rabbi Zev Wolf Bikhovski son of the famous Chossid Chaim Avrohom Bichofsky, married a daughter of the Minsker Gadol.

In 1909 Menachem Mendel Gluskin married Fradel the daughter of Rabbi Eliezer Rabinowitz of Minsk, granddaughter of the Minsker Gadol Rabbi Yehuda Yerucham Perlman.

Fradel knew French and so in a short time he also learned French. When they did not want the children to understand them, they spoke in French.

Rochel daughter of Keila Leiba Gluskin remembers her uncle Mendel in Paritch wearing white on special occasions like Pesach, Pesach Sheni and Sukkos. *(**Shaarie Torah** 6:11, Warsaw February 1912.)* Rabbi Shlomo Yosef Zevin (at that time was Rabbi in Kazmirov) wrote, "My dear friend Rabbi Menachem Mendel Hluskin ab"d of Paritch noted that according to the Kesef Mishna there is no question etc." *(**Ben Tzion Gershuni, Shaarei Tzion** 5697 Choveres 1-5 p.53)* Mendel became Rav of many communities including Paritch, Prilooki and Nezhin. It would seem that he became Rabbi in Paritch around 1901/1902 and at the same time was responding to Nezhin or other places where there was no Rov at the time. See **Heichal Habesht** volume 30 p. 180-182. Rabbi Menachem Mendel Gluskin was a chossid of the Rebbe Rashab of Lubavitch - **Heichal Habesht** volume 30 p. 182 note 45.

In **Heichal Habesht** vol. 30 p. 181 we find that there were many great Rabbis who wanted to become Rabbi in Paritch at that time. One in particular was the son in law of the Rebbe of Kopust. In the end the Rabbinate went to Rabbi Menachem Mendel Gluskin who was not a follower of Kopust but who got on with everyone.

***Meir Gurkov writes (Sefer Hazichronos-Divrei Huyomim)*** He became Rov in Nezhin (in addition to Paritch) after Mendel Chein died. Mendel Chein was killed by soldiers of Denikin on August 27 1919. ***See about Rabbi Chein and Nezhin in Oholei Shem volume one and responsa Avnei Chein Kehot 2013.***

He lived in a time when there were still pogroms in Russia and when people lived in fear of the Beilis trial (1911-1913) knowing that if he was found guilty it would unleash a terrible destruction of Jews in Europe. When that was over the first World war began and then the Russian revolution.

In **Igeres Kodesh** - letters of the Rebbe Rashab of Lubavitch vol 2 p. 869 dated 2nd of Elul 5677/August 20 1917, Rabbi Menachem Mendel Gluskin is mentioned as being the Rov representing Paritch as part of a commission to help Jewish communities in Russia. See also **Toldos Chabad** in Soviet Russia p. 94 that Rabbi Menachem Mendel Gluskin from Paritch was part of the gathering of Rabbis in Moscow 26-28 Menachem Av 5677/ 14-16 August 1917. It is also mentioned in **Igeres Kodesh** of his son the Rebbe Rayatz vol. 1 p. 545 dated 16 Marcheshvan 5687/October 24 1926 with a few famous names including Rabbi Menachem Mendel Gluskin from Paritch.

After his father Aharon passed away Mendel became Rov in Paritch. It was there that his daughters Sonia and Gita were born.

***Sefer Zikaron*** *Binyomin Eliyahu Gorodetsky p. 339.* After Rabbi Gluskin left and became rov in Minsk, a group of representatives from Paritch came to ask my father to accept the position as rov in Paritch.

Hillel Zaidman describes the difficult situation in Soviet Russia and the fact that Rabbi Mendel Gluskin was able to survive through it for a relatively long time. How his amazing abilities were able to bring clarity by relating to the people and all the changes that created confusion for all.

## Minsk

In 1924 his father-in-law Rabbi Eliezer Rabinovich Chief Rabbi of Minsk passed away and he was invited to become the new Chief Rabbi. Since Rabbi Eliezer Rabinowitz was the son-in-law of the previous Chief Rabbi people joked, saying that the abilities of being a chief rabbi is not inherited from father to son but from father-in-law to son-in-law. Also, since his wife's grandfather was called the Godol of Minsk, it became a term that some used to refer to the chief Rabbi. Although Rabbi Rabinowitz was also called by some the Godol of Minsk, it was not used after he passed away. That is why we find several people writing the Mendel Gluskin was the son-in-law of the Gadol of Minsk but it is a little confusing since the term was really given to his wife's grandfather. *The book **Hagadol of Minsk** was published by Feldheim 1991 and in Russian by Shvut Ami in 2001.*

*(**Shaarei Tzion** year 17 choveres 1-5 Tishrei-Shvat p.53)* Minsk was the metropolis of Torah at that time in Russia and as such was the most important and central city regarding Judaism in Russia. Rabbi Gluskin's role now became central not just to Minsk but to all Russia. This made his work on the Vaad established by the Rebbe Rayatz even more expansive. Thus, his work branched out in a huge way to work for the good of all Jews in Russia. He constantly operated with total self sacrifice during the menacing period of the Yevseksia, to support Torah and religion, to support the Torah institutions, Talmud Torah's and Yeshivah in Minsk, that all operated illegaly, where hundreds of students were educated and he made sure that they were maintained and supported. His heart was open to dealing with all general matters effecting Jews in Russia.

Arriving in Minsk he moved into the residence of his father-in-law. The residence was the whole second floor of the house on Bogodilania Street *(the name was later changed to Komsomoliskaya.)* In the entrance, there was a wide hallway. To the right was the dining room and to the left the bedrooms. Straight, there was a door that opened to a small corridor that contained a large box. Each week at the time of Shalosh Seudas a group of yeshivah boys would sit there and sing melodies.

One boy Yosef Vilkovitz had a better voice than the others. In the 1930's he moved to Leningrad and went to the university to study Hebrew. In 1937 he was arrested and sent to a concentration camp and died.

From the small corridor, a person then entered a large long room and after that was a small room. That was the bedroom of Rabbi Rabinowitch and after he passed his second wife Chana Soroh slept there. She ran the house and after Rabbi Gluskin's wife died the children called her Auntie. Between themselves they spoke Russian but with their father they spoke in Yiddish.

Chana Soro knew how to look after a house and was a wonderful cook. Rabbi Gluskin's daughter Gita was always following her in the kitchen and sometimes helping. This way Gita learned to cook all the Jewish foods, especially the holiday foods. Shtrudel, zemlach, taiglach, eingemachtz, etc. The other girls did not care for house work. They preferred to read books. Gita did not read as much and had to catch up in her later years.

He received a letter from the Rebbe Rayatz *(**Igrot Kodesh** volume one p. 397)* dated first day of Rosh Chodesh Iyar 5684/May 4 1924,

**Horav Hagaon Moreinu Rabbi Menachem Mendel Gluskin**

**In response to your letter of the past 13th of Nissan (April 13 1924), Hashem Yisborech will assist your distinguished presence to sustain and administer your pure congregation with springs of wisdom and all the religious and benevolent organizations should grow in goodness and blessing. And the principals of Torah and those who study it should be raised in the physical and spiritual.**

**There should be blessing and peace** כאו"נ וידידו הדו"ש ומברכו

Rabbi Alter Hilovitz was given to him as a personal secretary. *(**Chikrei Zemanim** by Alter Hilovitz, Mosad Horav Kook, Yerushalayim 5741, vol. 1 p.19, **Sefer Hayovel** for Rabbi Dr Hilovitz, Johanesberg, p.19,21.)* "He knew my fathers house, drew me close to him and showed me how he guides people." Rabbi Gluskin gave him semicha and Rabbi Mordechai Shmuel Krol among others. *(**Hane'emon** 3 Sivan 5705 p.14, Tel Aviv)*

A short time after he became rov in Minsk *(**Sefer Hazichronos Divrei Hayomim** p. 34-37)* Meir Gurkov came into town to sell siddurim that a friend had published but could not sell them. "I went into his house, he received me honorably. I then explained to him the purpose of my coming, to sell the siddurim that were printed in accordance to the guidance of the Rebbe Rayatz. All I need is a place to put the many boxes when they come since everyone is afraid to be found with prayer books, but as a Rov that would not be a problem. I saw that he was unable to refuse me."

In a letter sent from Riga with secret coding ***(Igeres Kodesh** vol. 1 p. 612)* the Rebbe Rayatz writes *(8 Marcheshvan 5688/ November 3 1927)* that Rabbi Menachem Mendel Gluskin is one of the decision makers about how to move forward with the situation of Judaism in Russia.

Dr Hillel Zaidman writes: Rav Gluskin would derive insights into the words of the sages and clarify their opinions through cogent analysis. As he rose to greatness in Torah scholarship, he rose equally in his mastery of Chassidus. His humility resembled that of Moshe Rabbeinu. Although he frequently came up with new interpretations he never claimed any originality for his cutting-edge breakthroughs in Rabbinic thought. Anything he discerned, he attributed to the greatness of former Gedolim, on whose shoulders he stood to glimpse into the Pardes.

His inner light shone from the depths of an elevated soul and in conversation he shared hidden treasures of his vast knowledge and expertise in Halachah in a way that would ignite the other persons understanding. The range of his deep learning was multifaceted and wide. He shunned polemics, with the goal in order to do mitzvoth, realizing that if the Jews were divided through dispute they were vulnerable to their enemies as Haman yemach shemo knew in Megillas Esther.

He penetrated into the depths of Jewish matters in a straight forward manner. He employed objectivity without prior biases or prejudices or preconceived notions or side interests, a requirement of his functioning as Av Bet Din in Minsk. His analysis was like a chisel of logic. His life was one of dedication and self-sacrifice for all Jews with his soul filled with Ahavas Hashem, Ahavas Torah, and Ahavas Yisrael.

Although Rav Gluskin was a Chassid among Misnagdim, a relationship of respect, care, and love was established, for what was common to Chassidim and Misnagdim was respect for greatness in Torah. He did not engage in polemics with the opponents of Chassidim. Instead of saying "Let us go and prove, and argue" he would say, "Let us go and sing." It is impossible not to be enchanted by the grace of his personality and the modesty of his middos tovos.

Dr Saul Lieberman

When his brother-in-law Dr. Saul Lieberman (a nephew of the Chazon Ish who visited the Gluskin's house many times) humorously nudged him with the statement "the Chassidic Shtiebelach are superfluous", Rav Gluskin responded with a smile and laugh saying, "I think every city and shtetl should have Chassidic Shteibelach, so that Jews not become arrogant with the fancy and big architectural synagogues." Hillel Zaidman writes that he added with a smile: "Never-the-less, I think every city should have a Chassidic Shtible. Why? Because then it gives each person a one-time opportunity to enter one, and then they will say to him, what are you and who are you."

The oppression and persecution of Judaism under the Communists in Russia aroused in Rav Gluskin wondrous powers of resistance, courage, resolve, and steadfastness to allow for continuity of Jewish life. Rav Gluskin brought light into the darkness. Numerous letters of the previous Lubavitch Rebbe in Iggerot Kodesh describe Rav Gluskin's efforts to disseminate torah and Yiddishkeit in times of persecution. During communist rule brit milah, shechitah, teaching torah, and even owning a Hebrew book, or writing one Hebrew letter was forbidden. Rav Gluskin's courage and resolve prevented the light of torah and Yiddishkeit from going out under the tyrannical communist regime.

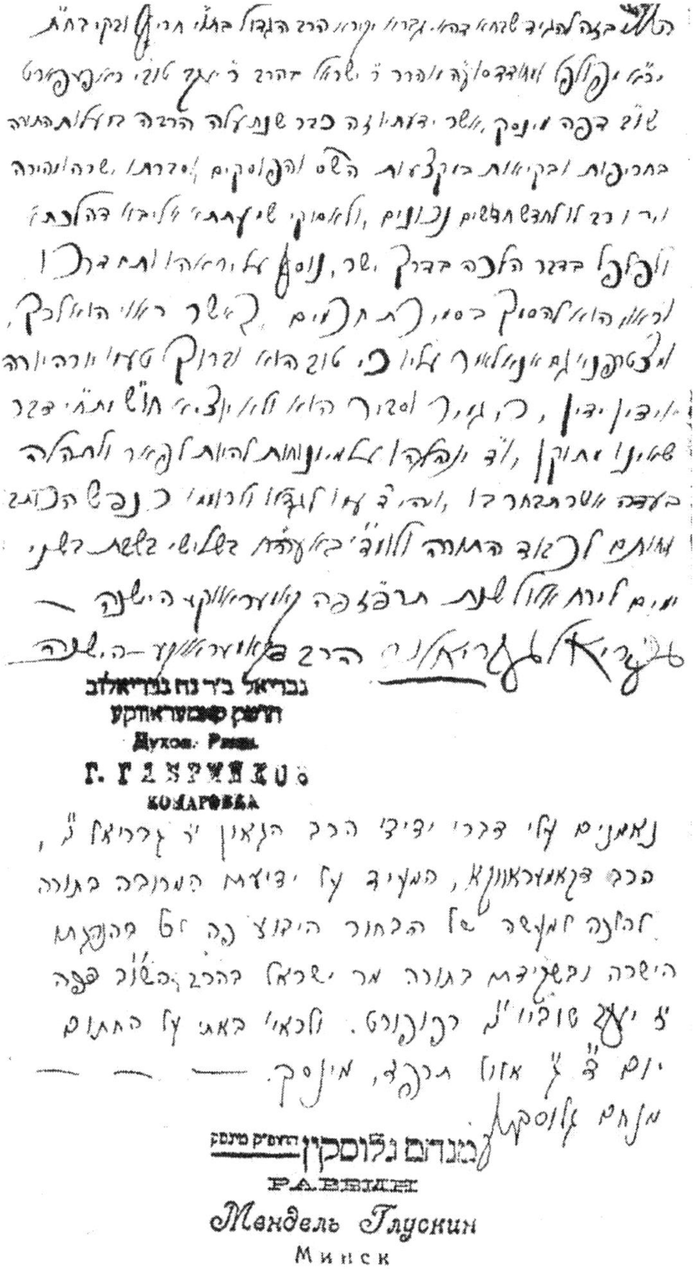

גבריאל ב״ר נח גבריאלוב

[illegible]

Духов. Равв.

Г. [illegible]

Комаровка

מנחם גלוסקין הרה״ק מינסק

РАВВИН

Мендель Глускин

Минск

סמיכה לרבנות מהרב גבריאלוב והרב גלוסקין

This semicha was given to Yisroel son of Yaakov Tuvia Rapaport on Wednesday Elul 3 5687/August 31 1927, printed in **Ner Yisroel** p.19 Tel-Aviv 5758 a sefer Zikaron by Aharon Surski.

Rabbi Mordechai Eliyahu Slushetz (5674/1914 – 5727/1967) mentions something he saw from Rabbi Gluskin. *(**Orchos Vetoldos** revised edition 5771 p. 21 note 18)* When a piece of matzo was found bent over, thus leaving a possibility for some partially unbaked dough Rabbi Slushetz would remove it from the matzo and immediately throw it on the ground. When he was asked, he responded that this is what he saw done by the last chief Rabbi in Minsk the Gaon Rabbi Menachem Mendel Gluskin ob"m. *(**Tevunah** Journal 8, Jerusalem 5708/1948 p.85)* Rabbi Yitzchok Vidler may his blood be avenged was ordained by the Gaon Rabbi Shmaryohu Noach Shneerson of Bobroisk, the Gaon Rabbi Chaim Tzvi Shapiro head of the Beis din of Bobroisk and the Gaon Rabbi Menachem Mendel Gluskin chief Rabbi of Minsk. Rabbi Vidler married the daughter of the Gaon, Rabbi Osher Anshil Rakubchik, who was in charge of kashrus and a member of the Beth Din of Minsk.

When Gita was 6 or 7 years old her mother registered her in a cheder of boys. There she learned the Alef Beis and to read siddur and Chumash. Gita was very proud of herself going to this cheder with her bag.

At some point his daughters Leah and Sonia wanted to go to university but they did not have a high school diploma. Since they did not go to school on Shabbos, they were expelled from school, Leah from sixth grade and Sonia from fifth grade. The school asked Sonia to come on

Shabbos and just sit there without doing any work. Sonia refused to accept any compromise.

Even though he was a Rabbi in a community of Misnagdim, he was a Chosid from birth. He was a Lubavitcher Chossid and a true chossid with all his heart and soul. He was not radical in conduct or dress. He was a happy man, loved jokes, loved melodies and enjoyed singing. He had a knack for good humor and an exceptional ability to listen.

He was not aggressive and did not demand anything specific from his daughters. Even when Esther walked around during the summer sleeveless and no socks or stockings. He may not have liked it and it bothered him but he kept his feelings about it to himself.

The daughter of the shochat who lived in the Polish shul in the same courtyard once asked her father, "Why is the daughter of Rabbi Gluskin allowed walk around sleeveless and without socks and you don't let me do it?" He responded, "Gluskin is the head Rabbi and can allow himself but I cannot."

He loved cleanliness and order. In the morning when he got out of bed he immediately made the bed and told his daughters to do the same. He had a cronic nose drip and he would wash his handkerchief before he gave it to be put in the laundry with the other clothes. During the week he wore black clothing, Shabbos a woolen black coat and on Yom Tov a silk black coat. Underneath he wore a white shirt and had a white scarf.

He used to smoke self-rolled cigarettes. His daughter Gita would often prepare them. He would sit a long time studying and every now and then he would get up and straighten his shoulders moving his arms around. He also made sure that his daughters would do the same. One time Sonia and Gita went to an office where they had wooden boards for benches and the girls lay down on them to straighten their backs. (**Meorei Yisroel** p. 304) One day a woman came to ask a shayla about a chicken. He had just stepped out for a few minutes, leaving in his office a young man Rabbi Hilovitz who was doing shimush with him in addition to being his secretary, and an older rov Rabbi Yechezkiel Abramski from Slutsk who was there for some reason. The visiting rov not wanting to pasken in another Rov's town, turned to Rabbi Hilovitz making light of the question. Not having time to wait he left. The woman decided to wait for Rabbi Gluskin to return, since she always asked him her shaylos.

When he returned, Rabbi Hilovitz told him what happened. Rabbi Gluskin saw that indeed it was a difficult question but he was machshir it. He looked at the chicken, and he thought a bit, looked at it again, thought some more, and finally said "Nu, it's hefsed merubah, we can be meikil", and ruled it kosher.

Later, when they were alone, the assistant asked him why he had relied on hefsed merubeh to permit something he was clearly reluctant to permit otherwise. This woman was far from poor, and could easily afford the loss of one chicken. He replied, "Embarrassing a rov is also a hefsed merubeh". He explained that grief of a great person is equal to hefsed meruba and even more. And if there is a way to be machshir in such a case, then that is how we need to conduct our self. The grief that Rabbi Abramski would have finding out that it was prohibited and that he made a mistake, would have been great and therefore I pronounced it kosher.

In January 1926 a group of shochetim were arrested. In the local newspaper a letter was printed blaming Rabbi Gluskin, although he was not charged or arrested. It was to lay the ground to do more damage to the religious leaders. ***Minsk Ir Vo'aim*** *vol 2 p. 78-81.* A local play was made of the case and included Rabbi Gluskin.

*In* ***Igeres Kodesh*** *of the Rebbe Rayatz vol. 11 p. 73 – 74 a letter dated August 26 1926,* Rabbi Gluskin signed as one of three people representing the Rabbinical assistance committee for Russian Jewry with Rabbi Yaakov Klemes and Rabbi Yosef Yitzchok Shneerson.

***Igros Kodesh*** *Admur Rayatz vol. 15 p. 96, October 25 1927, Riga.* "With this I want to let you my dear friend know that we arrived the previous erev Shabbos, and Hashem should allow that we can hear good news from each other, so please let me know what is good in your life.

With love and love for Torah please give my regards to Rabbi Yehoshua Tzimblist, Rabbi Asher Kirshstein and Rabbi Gavriel Gavrielov, and I will be very thankfull to you for giving them my blessings for strengthening Torah in their area and surrounding areas."

In 1927 they arrested all the Rabbis including Rabbi Gluskin in order to force them to sign that there is no persecution of Jews in Russia. After they signed they were released.

***V'ele Toldos*** *– Sefer Hazikaron for Rabbi Abramski, Moriah 1978, p. 27.* At a certain point he became a member of a special group of four Rabbis who worked using all possible means in public and in secret to strengthen Torah and Judaism throughout Russia. At the head of this group was Rabbi Yosef Yitzchok Schneerson until he left in 1927.

They were in secret contact with people outside Russia who helped them financially.

On these letters the Rabbis did not sign their given names due to the fear of what the Russian sensor and secret police would do to them if caught. Instead they each chose a verse of Torah with which they signed. Rabbi Yaakov Klemes from Moscow signed Hakshivo Lekol Shavii; Rabbi Menachem Mendel Gluskin signed Migdol Yeshuos Malko; Rabbi Shlomo Yosef Zevin signed Shir Hashirim; Rabbi Yechezkiel Abramski signed Yemin Hashem Romemo which is part of the verse that he would say for his name at the end of Shmonei Esrei. *Mentioned also in* ***Melech Beyofyov*** *p. 176.*

***Sefer Hazikoron*** *Binyomin Eliyahu Gorodetsky p. 37.* As long as the Rebbe was in Russia there were famous Rabbis who stood behind him, like Rabbi Milkovsky chief Rabbi of Kharkov, Rabbi Klemes chief Rabbi of Moscow, Rabbi Menachem Mendel Gluskin chief Rabbi of Minsk, Rabbi Yechezkiel Abramski chief Rabbi of Slutsk, and the wealthy Aharon Horenstein of Kiev.

All these people signed that the Lubavitcher Rebbe is the only one who represents Judaism in Russia. They called the paper that they signed "giluy daas'. See details of this in Sefer Hazikoron.

***Toldos Chabad*** *in Soviet Russia p.38.* In 1928 Rabbi Gluskin wrote: "the situation of those in our city who study Torah is fearful and menacing, since the situation with Jews here is hard pressed, even more than the problematic situations in the rest of the jewsih settlements in the country.

***Toldos Chabad*** *in Soviet Russia p.38* – Rabbi M M Gluskin the Moro Dasro of Minsk was involved in strengthening and supporting the study of Torah in Mohilev-Shklov. Rabbi Feinstein from Shklov and Rabbi Galaventz from Mohilev write that they are concerned that with the Rebbe Rayatz leaving Russia, the support will stop.

***Igros Kodesh*** *Admur Rayatz vol. 13 p. 200-201, February 19 1930, Chicago.* "Today I am in great pain, the terrible situation is indescribable, and with all my strength and the power of Holy fathers to their children and grandchildren, I beseech our father in heaven and demand that He should have pity and show mercy for His people and inheritance, as the basket is already overflowing, I shudder and tremble hearing all the news.

For the last two days I am in contact with people to save the Rabbi's of Minsk, Hashem should show mercy, but nothing actual has yet happened, I already have tickets for a boat for my dear friend the tzaddik and Tomim Rabbi Gluskin and I am waiting for a telegram to let me know where they can be sent.

And at this moment the terrible news of the Rabbi and his friends reached me, may Hashem show mercy."

דער

"THE NATIONAL JEWISH DAILY"

פיהרער פון מינסקער קהלה ארעסטירט

רוסלאנד ערקלערט פראטעסט פון דער וועלט-קירכע אלס א קאפיטאליסטישע פארשווערונג

צוויי לאיערס „דיסבארד", אנדערע קריגען לייכטערע שטראף צוליעב האנדלונגען אין עקסידענט-קייסעס

Der Tog – The National Jewish Daily Sunday February 16 1930/18 Shavat 5690, reporting on the arrest.

מארגען זשורנאל-טאגעבי

פּילע רבנים און פיהרער פון דער מינסקער קהלה אונטער ארעסט

5 אראבער פערארורטהיילט פאר איבערפאלען בית יתומים אין צפת

קישינעווער פאליצמייסטער אראפ

Morgen Djournal – Morning journal Sunday February 16 1930 reporting on the arrest.

***Toldos Chabad in Soviet Russia*** *p.111*- on the committee to support Jews of Russia, R. Gluskin representative of Rabbi Zevin. Ibid p.179 – Rabbi Gluskin writes that the conditions here are so difficult that I had to borrow the small sum of 200 rubles to fix the mikvah. Ibid p.196 -

Rabbi Gluskin's house was confiscated by the government as mentioned in ***Yarchon Shaarei Tzion*** *- Yerushalayim shevat-adar sheni 5689 vol 9, no. 5-6-7 p. 15b. In* ***Yarchon Shaarei Tzion*** *Kislev-Teves 5689 vol. 9, no. 3-4 p.15b* is mentioned that he was one of those forced by the Soviet regime to sign that there is no problem with religion in Russia.

There were friends who left Minsk for America or elsewhere who created the opportunity for Rabbi Gluskin to leave and settle elsewhere, even the Russian government would have been happy to get rid of him. But he decided that he has to stay with the people who cannot leave.

*(Letters of the Rebbe Rayatz volume 11 p. 169 in a letter dated 7 Kislev 5792/November 17 1931)* **Regarding the Rabbinate position in Boston with Chevra Shas, it is proper to endeavor that it should be a Rabbi who is fitting for the position. At the moment I do not know anyone in the USA who is fitting for this position. Understandably of the Rabbis who are in Russia I do know who is fitting, i.e. Rabbi Menachem Mendel Gluskin of Minsk and Rabbi Levi Yitzchok Schneerson.**

*(**Minsk Ir Vo'aim** p. 513 – Rochel Chadash)* His daughter Gita would go to her friend's house in Minsk and they would give her flowers to bring home for Shabbos.

In an official document, he is also known as Mendel Aronovich. In a similar vein his daughter is mentioned as Gita Mendelevna.

There was a meeting of about twenty Rabbonim including Rabbi Gluskin. It was decided about what would be included in a siddur Tefillos Yisroel. This was a prototype of the siddur Rinas Yisroel.

In 1927 they began to arrest Rabbis in the big cities. Rabbi Medalia of Moscow was arrested with the claim that he was a counter revolutionary. He was sent to Siberia and what happened with him there was not known. At that time Rabbi Mendel Gluskin disappeared from Minsk and stayed in Moscow, a large mixed city, where there were many non-Jews, making it easier for him to hide since they had no picture of him. *(**Minsk Ir Vo'aim** vol 2 p. 157.)*

In a letter (**Igros kodesh** vol 16, p.207-8) to Chaim Ozer dated August 23 1928 The Rebbe Rayatz writes that Mendel Levin who was a Rabbi in Minsk came here and told me how the Rabbis and Torah scholars are starving. They can only get bread by paying a fortune or stealing. Rabbi Gluskin asked him to publicize the problem. This starvation is different from 1920-21 when everyone was equally starving. Now the Yevseksia are using it in their war to destroy religion. It is a war that they are fighting in many different ways all of which are a shock to anyone who hears of them.

In a letter to Rabbi Kook *(**Igros Leraya** - Avrohom Yitzchok Hakohen Kook, letter 262 p.281-3)* Chaim Ozer writes about the terrible situation in Russia. A week ago, they arrested 25 Rabbis in Minsk including Rabbi Gluskin.

***Rabbi Yehoshua of Horodna**, a Kovetz in his memory p.6, Yerushalayim 5709.* One time they arrested many Rabbis including the head Rabbi M"M Gluskin, my brother-in-law Asher Kirshstein who became a Rabbi in Afula and my brother Mordechai. They wanted to squeez out of the rabbis to sign that the government was protecting the Jewish religion. They came to my father and told him, "you see we have not done any harm to you. We know that you are an upright person but we want you to sign on this paper."

He responded, "first release the Chief Rabbi and then I will discuss it with him." They replied, "we will free Kirshstein and your son as long as you agree to do what we want." He did not budge but said, "it is better that you keep my sons in prison and release the Chief Rabbi, because without him, I will not sign." In the end they released the Rabbi and the others were released after and everything worked out.

In 1927-28 the government began to confiscate all private houses. At first, they only took thirty percent of the house and put another family there. In the Rabbis house, they put three other families. A couple with a ten-year-old child was put in the bedroom of the Rabbi.

The woman saw how they prepared every Friday for Shabbos and how the family conducted themselves on Shabbos. The family was totally free to be themselves and live their life at home. The woman tried to emulate the Gluskin's even though she was a Russian Christian.

After a time, the government took the house away from the owner to be a government house. They did not have any privileges – lishnatzi - to live in a government owned house and so they had to find a private house. This was very difficult to find since most houses were taken over by the government. In the end they found a house but it was being renovated and so they had to wait until it was finished in order to move in.

During the waiting period all the children slept in different places. For example, Gita slept by her aunt Braina

Bichovsky. Leah and Sonia slept by Mr. Zildin, an acquaintance of Rabbi Gluskin. The new place was smaller than the old but it had several rooms, a dining room, bedroom and office for the Rabbi. There was also a small room for (Mumma) Aunt Chana Soro.

The transition happened in the year of 1929 when at the end of the year Rabbi Mendel's wife became sick. The doctors were unable to diagnose the problem. The Rabbi invited doctors and even brought together a council of professors but to no avail. In the end it was found that she had contracted typhus. He invited her brother Meir who lived in Moscow to help her feel a little better. Also, Hirsh Gelfant a nephew who was an excellent doctor looked after her.

Meanwhile their oldest daughter Esther was arrested and sitting in prison. The Rabbi went to the police station to ask that she at least be allowed to visit her mother before she died and that he would be responsible for her return.

The reason she was arrested was because boys were attracted to her and always accompanied her. The boys were Jewish and some belonged to Hashomer Hatzair a Zionist organization. In Russia being a Zionist was enough to be arrested.

Fradel passed away on the 13th of Kislev 5690/December 15 1929. They did not tell her that the house they were in was soon going to be occupied by people the government will put in. They released Esther and she was at her mother's funeral.

The night, when her mother Fradel died, Gita who was seven years old, stayed at her Aunt Braina. In the morning

Meir came and carried Gita home. At home he put her on the ground and said, "Mommy is not here anymore." Gita felt very down and her father said, "Now I will be your mother and father."

Braina and Zev Wolf Bichovsky

The earth at the cemetery was very dry. Fradel was laid to rest in her shrouds and Gita became terrified and started screaming. Later in Leningrad she saw many funerals but the people all had to be in a wooden box since the ground had water.

The stones were moved during the month of Menachem Av 1962 from Minsk to Novoborisov. The middle stone is of Fradel Gluskin. See https://www.geni.com/people/Rabbi-Yerucham-Yehuda-Leib-Perelman-Hagadol-MeMinsk/6000000003239743166

After the funeral the family had to leave the place they were living and find another private house. This was impossible since all houses had been confiscated by the government. Therefore, it was decided to live in the cold shul. Chana Soro had government permission to live in the old apartment. She had a daughter who lived in Moscow while her two sons lived in Poland. Chana Soro died in the ghetto of Minsk.

In Minsk, there was a courtyard of the shul. In the middle of the courtyard there was a building named the cold shul.

From this building there was an entry to the second floor. On the second floor there was a large room maybe one hundred square meters with the ceiling about 15 meters high. One wall was next to the main shul and it had a large tall and wide window. At one time this was an extension of the woman's section that went around the shul. From a nearby window in the wall of thc shul we could watch the men's section.

They gave us the large room to live in. We divided the room into section with wooden boards and so we ended up with a few small rooms. The place was open without doors. In winter it was literarily freezing. The bodies of the family were always frozen. In two corners of the room were a round oven covered with a thin metal sheet that we heated twice a day. Since it was insufficient, they built another cub shaped oven with a clay floor in the middle of the room.

In the middle of the oven there was a floor that made it like all other ovens in White Russia. They could bake bread, challah and put the cholent in it for Shabbos. The oven was called "the Russian oven." On Friday Chana Soro put the cholent in a metal pot full of water and some type of candy in the oven and sealed it with a wet rag. Shabbos morning, they took out the metal pot with metal rods and drank tea with sugar or cake.

One time something unpleasant happened with the oven. During winter they heated the oven with coals not wood. Wood was difficult to come by and it was a job to chop the wood and clean the ashes. Every day as the oven was cooling off Chana put coals in to make sure they were dry for the next day.

One time in the middle of the night a coal came on fire and the oven let out smoke. Since the escape for the smoke was closed the smoke entered the room and went to the ceiling.

As the smoke was pilling up it was becoming lower in the room until it came to the height of a standing person.

A young man Hirshel from the village of Semuchblovitchi also lived there and he would rise at six in the morning to go to work. When he stood up he hit the layer of smoke, fainted and fell to the floor. It woke up the Rabbi, Esther and Gita. They all slept on mattresses on the floor and did not smell the smoke. Now they all felt the pain of the person who fell and got out of bed. The Rabbi went to the big outer window and opened it and then opened the pipe for smoke to leave the oven. The fire in the oven continued for a while and some people came to check the young man but he recovered quickly.

After the death of his wife Rabbi Mendel Gluskin said to his daughter Gita that since they did not have any boys and she is the youngest, she should say Kaddish. *See responsa* ***Chavos Yoir*** *volume 2 chapter 222. Zelda (Miskovsky) only daughter of Sholom Shlomo Schneerson was twelve when her father passed away and she said kaddish the whole year. When Dovid Brevman of Kfar Chabad passed away and he only had daughters they asked the Lubavitcher Rebbe. He said to ask the Rabbonim and Rabbi Garelick of Kfar Chabad said that the daughters can say kaddish. They had a minyan in the house till the shloshim so the daughters can say kaddish.* Gita went three times a day for eleven months as is the custom. Gita stood on the left of the person who led the prayers and prayed with them. She would say kaddish and all the men would answer omain. Thus, she learned to say all the prayers by heart.

On the last day of the eleventh month a strange thing occurred. Gita was playing with her friends and was delayed coming to the shul till after they finished the evening prayers. Upon entering she found the place was empty and 3 or 4 people standing in the dark including her father. She ran towards them and when she came near began to say kaddish. Gita was so emotional that she began to cry and said the kaddish crying. Rabbi Gluskin also began to cry. With this the year of kaddish concluded.

While they lived in the shul, Rabbi Gluskin hired a teacher Mr. Matlitzki to teach Gita. He was short, single and about forty years old. He taught Gita Prophets and the main thing was that she should learn verses by heart. He had a good taste and the first verses he gave Gita to learn by heart were Isaiah 2:2-5 **"And it will be in the end of days, etc."** Isaiah 5:1-7 **"I will sing now, etc."** Isaiah 11:1-10 **"And a staff will emerge from the lineage of Yishai, etc."** Isaiah 40:1-5 **"Comfort me comfort me my people, etc."** Gita remembered these verses the rest of her life. She learned them without translation or explanation. The truth is although she understood she did not know it well since she was eight or nine years old and had not learned the prophets beforehand.

Again, at the beginning of the 1930's they arrested Rabbi Gluskin. The G.P.U. Russian secret police came and made a search. All the walls had shelves filled with books and a ladder to climb up and find books. One of the police climbed a ladder and started looking through the pages of a book. Who knows what he was looking for?

At that moment Meir who helped us in the cold shul walked in. He would come and help a lot under unbearable circumstances. He made life bearable for the family. There was no water or a bathroom in the building. Meir would bring in buckets of clean water and take out buckets of dirty water. It made life easier for the Gluskin family and saved them.

Meir was very poor and unfortunate. He had a sick wife and five children. When his wife died he remarried and the second wife demanded that he buy her a fur coat. Meanwhile Meir was a straight forward man full of energy.

He came in to the room while they were searching and the police did not let him out of the room. But he did not have patience or time to wait, because below in the shul he already put on the fire that was under the floor something he did daily. At that moment the policeman on the ladder jumped down and grabbed Meir. It was funny but painful. Gita who was watching did not know what happened to him after that.

Rabbi Gluskin was taken to prison but was soon released. He was being charged with receiving money from overseas for "mo'os chittim," money to give food to the poor for Pesach. The Rabbi took the whole guilt on himself. After he was released, a Jewish religious person who became a mole for G.P.U. Russian secret police followed him around to report on his activities. This made life very unbearable for him. Each day they looked for ways to make his life unbearable.

He suffered watching the spiritual decline and intense physical problems of the Jewish community in Minsk. Besides being a giant in Torah he was very expansive in general knowledge. At the same time, he was extremely modest. In silence, he carried the suffering of his community that he represented with honor, and the interaction that he had with the anti-religious government.

Before Pesach he kept a large box with matzos to give people. Each person who came received matzo. One time two butchers whose faces made them look like thieves came and asked for matza. Rabbi Gluskin gave each an amount of matza but they wanted more. Rabbi Gluskin said he needs for other people as well so they started showing the Rabbi threatening fists if he does not give them the rest of the matza.

Gita who was watching became afraid and went to the neighbor who was a slaughterer of animals. He lived in the courtyard in the small Polish shul. He was physical very strong and Gita was friendly with his two daughters and visited them many times. Gita asked his help. By the time she came back they had left. Somehow the Rabbi was able to stop them with soft and gentle words. The Rabbis health suffered greatly from his restraint since he internalized everything.

Another time a woman who did not keep mitzvos and ate chometz on Pesach came for matza. He gave her and explained to his children that at least while she is eating matza she will not be eating chometz. Mendel Gluskin taught his daughters to see, first of all, something good in everyone.

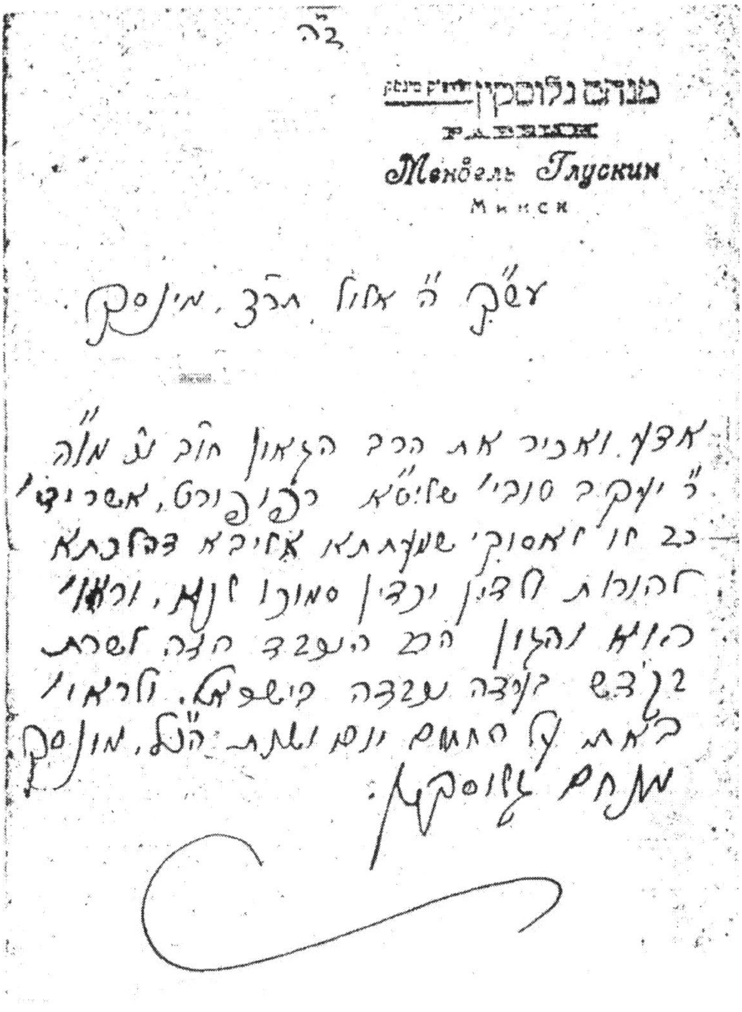

ב"ה

מנחם גלוסקין

Мендель Глускин

Минск

עש"ק ה' אלול תר"צ. מינסק

מנחם גלוסקין

כתב סמיכה לרבנות מהרב גלוסקין

This semicha was given to Yaakov Tuvia Rapaport Elul 5 5690/August 29 1930. *Published in* ***Ner Yisroel, Sefer Zikaron*** *Tel Aviv 5758 p. 72 by Aharon Surski.*

In the book Hagodol of Minsk is mentioned that the Chassidic Rebbe Aharon of Kaidonov would visit the Minsker Godol. There is a letter from Rabbi Menachem

Mendel Gluskin when he was Rov in Minsk 5693/1933 to Shlomo Chaim Perlow son of the Mishmeres Sholom of Kaidonov who was at that time Rav in Brahin, they wrote many times to each other but this is the only letter we have. *(**Yagdil Torah** Adar 1977 5737 p.41 reprinted from sefer **Shono Beshono** 5728 p.126).* Brahin was also where Rabbi Gluskin's sister Nechama lived. She had married Menachem Mendel Serebryanski. It is where Reb Zalman Serebryanski grew up and the Mishmeres Sholom was Rov. Rabbi Perlow was sent from there to Siberia in 5694/1934 and died there, the year that Mendel Gluskin left Minsk. ***Kovetz Shomrei Hagacheles*** *Yerushalayim 1966,* he corresponded with Rabbi Perlow in matters of Ishus, Chalitza and Yibum.

**בכל נפשך ובכל מאודך**

[נדפס בספר **שנה בשנה** תשכ"ח, ע' 621, ונעתק ב**קובץ יגדיל תורה** ע' מא]

ב"ה, בשלושת ימי הגבלה, תרצ"ג לפ"ק.

החוה"ש לידי"נ הרב הג' וו"ח בנש"ק מו"ה שלמה חיים פערלאוו שליט"א, החופ"ק בראהין. [הוגלה לסיביר בשנת תרצ"ד ושם נאסף. בנו של האדמו"ר רבי שלום מקוידנוב.]
ע"ד החדר במינסק הנה כבר מסרתי לו ע"י אנ"ש בהומל. וה' יעזור ע"ד כבוד שמו ואין להאריך, וד"ל.

וע"ד תירו' המפרשים ע"ז שבפ' הראשונה בק"ש נאמר בכל נפשך ובכל מאדך בל' יחיד ובפ' שני' נפשכם בל' רבים ותירוצם משום דבג' מקשים, אם נאמר בכל נפשך, למה נאמר בכל מאדך? אלא יש לך אדם שגופו חביב עליו מממונו לכך נאמר בכל נפשך, ואם יש לך אדם שממונו חביב עליו מגופו לכך נאמר בכל מאדך (ברכות ס"א, יומא פ"ב) אמרו המפר' שתי' זה אפ"ל רק על יחיד, כי נמצאים יחידים כאלה אבל ברבים אי אפשר לומר שממונם חביב עליהם יותר מנפשם, שהלא "כל אשר

לאיש יתן בעד נפשו" ולכן כיון שכתוב "בכל נפשך" למותר לחזור ולכתוב "בכל מאדך".

והנה הקשה מו"ח הגאון הר"א זצ"ל (אליעזר ראבינוביץ) המד"א דמינסק, לפי פירוש מאודך זה ממון, יש לתרץ לפי תירוץ המפרשים הנ"ל אבל לפי הפירוש שבכל מאודך הוה מודה לו בכל מידה ומידה שהוא מודד לך, שוב חוזרת הקושיא, למה נאמר בפ' ראשונה בכל מאודך ובפ' שניה רק נפשכם ולא מאדכם?

ונ"ל לתרץ בעזה"י בטוב טעם, לפי הגמרא (קידושין ל"ט) שכר מצוה בהאי עלמא ליכא. ושם כתב המהרש"א שזה נאמר רק על היחיד המרובה בזכויות, שכרו הוא רק לעולם הבא, אבל לרבים יש שכר בעולם הזה, והלא מצינו כמה יעודים בתורה שאם תשמעו יבואו עליכם כל הברכות הטובות ותשבו על אדמתכם, ולהיפך, אם לא תשמעו יבואו חלילה כל הקללות. ולפי זה מובן שם דברי הגמ' שרבי יעקב ראה מעשה, "ודלמא מהרהר בעבירה"? ואי סלקא דעתך שכר מצוה בהאי עלמא, אמאי לא אגין מצוה עלי'? אנו רואים מכאן שיש שכר מצוה המגינה שלא לבוא לידי עבירה, ולכן לדברי המהרש"א שלרבים כן יש שכר מצוה, כיון שכתוב "בכל נפשכם" נותנים להם גם שכר זה שהמצוה מגינה עליהם שלא יבואו לידי עבירה. ועכשיו בודאי מיותר לכתוב בכל מאודך - בכל מדה ומדה שהוא מודד לך הוי מודה לו, שלא יחטאו לחשוב על הקב"ה רעה, שממילא לא יחטאו, שהמצוה מגינה.

והשי"ת יעזרנו ע"ד שמו ובזכות הפצת התורה במחשכים, מצוות מגינות, והי' ה' לאור עולם וכו' ועמך כולם צדיקים ונירש חיי טובה וברכה.

כנפשו ונפש ידידו באה"ר
מ"מ גלוסקין, החופ"ק

## LENINGRAD

In 1934 a representative from the Jewish community of Leningrad came to Minsk and invited Rabbi Gluskin to accept the position of Chief Rabbi of Leningrad. Rabbi Tuvia Katzenelenboigen their chief Rabbi died 28th of Kislev 5690. In 1932 the community decided they needed a new Rabbi. A sign was posted "city Rabbi needed." It hung in the air for about one and a half years. Then, on November 30 1933 a meeting of 71 members met to decide again that they needed a new Rabbi. They decided to ask Rabbi Gluskin who accepted the position and moved to Leningrad. He became the head of the Choral Synagogue and Chief Rabbi of Leningrad. Gita was twelve when they left Minsk.

***Zichronosai,*** *Yisroel Yehida Levin p. 68.* At that time, they received (according to a directive from the government that there needs to be a Rabbi in such a big city (for show.)

When the new Chief Rabbi, Menachem Mendel Gluskin (someone from the government hinted to take him) arrived, he got up on the bima and said a maamar chassidus.

When he arrived, he was under the constant scrutiny of the KGB and had to report to them twice a day and had someone constantly following him. ***(Leshema Ozen** 2016 p. 294)* At the constant meetings with the KGB they would often tell him that they do not like his kiddushim, meaning the things he said at them. They denied his living in the synagogue saying it was already occupied by three families.

In Leningrad he continued with the work of the Lubavitcher Rebbe in setting up underground schools and other work. He was known by the name "Seder Hadoros" a book written by Rabbi Yechiel Halperin who had been a Rov in Minsk and before that in Hlusk/Glusk.

Esther the oldest daughter was already a kallah and when they came to Leningrad they made the wedding. After the wedding Esther with her husband Yitzchok Mintz returned to Minsk. They were Zionists and members of Hashomer Hatzair. In 1937 they were arrested for their Zionist activities and sent to prison in Ural Mountains for three years. Yitzchok died there but after three years Esther returned.

Finding a place to live in Leningrad was very difficult. The community bought a place for them to live and paid 25,000 rubles. The man who sold it to them tricked them and sold it after to another person. In Russia there is no authority to go to for justice. Thus, they were on the street with no place to go.

It was summer and the community rented a summer house on the outskirts of Leningrad in Poblovski. ***Teshurah*** *from the wedding of Shmuel and Tzivia Greenberg 5761, Masas Binyomin,* ***Teshurah*** *from the bar-mitzvah of Binyomin Yedidyah Ben-Shimon 5761 p.44,* Mendel Gluskin lived in Povlosk and he was very close with Reb Peretz Motchkin. They would study and farbreng together. *(**Eleh Toldos Peretz** p.120)* He would sit with Reb Peretz Motckin, they would farbreng and learn.

Gita remained there for the winter as well. She made a low ceiling room overlooking the garage into a bedroom. After the summer Rabbi Gluskin was given a corner with a bed in the dining room of the son of the previous Rabbi. They put something around it and Rabbi Gluskin slept there.

Leah and Sonia slept in a small laundry room their uncle Dovid Yitzchok found. Gita would regularly visit her father. One time she entered and saw Hertz the owner of the house standing on a table removing a dead bulb from the chandelier. Rabbi Gluskin was standing next to the table and handed him a new bulb. They were both laughing hysterically. Gita found out that they both remembered a story of the Russian writer Chechov.

***Rabbi Shmaryohu Sossonkin*** writes that Rabbi Gluskin was a great lamdan, boki in horaah, knew the Alter Rebbes Shulchan Aruch by heart and a great sage in Chassidus as well as being a good character and a nobleman.

*Rabbi **Aharon Yaakov Diskin*** writes: "He was a pillar of fire in teaching and guiding people in Torah. In all cities they revered him as an angel of G-d. He had an unusual amount of wisdom with an amazing clarity. He was well versed in many areas of science and knowledge and specifically he was an expert and constant flowing spring in Chassidus Chabad. He knew how to express everything in popular terminology with impeccable logic. Misnagdim, intellectuals, scientists, etc, would all come to listen to his chassidic talks."

During spring, the community rented another summer house in Sustrorutsk. In 1935 Rabbi Gluskin had a heart attack but refused to be hospitalized since he would not be able to eat kosher and keep Yiddishkeit there.

In Leningrad, a neurologist told the Rabbi that the Rabbi is very depressed. The Rabbi replied that the people around me are not aware of it. The Doctor said for you that is even worse.

The Rabbi's sister Baila with her husband Dovid Yitzchok Gurevitch, three grown daughters who were students and a student Yehoshua who went to technical school all lived in one room that was a corridor with twenty-four square meters. At night when they put out the beds no-one could get through. On the left wall were two beds for the Baila and Yitzchok. On the right wall was a long thin box where the student Yehoshua slept and at night they unfolded three more beds for the girls.

It was in this room that Rabbi Gluskin had his first heart attack. He went to the public toilet by himself and did not want help. They lay him on the Yitzchok's bed. Where Yitzchok slept is a question but he loved Rabbi Gluskin and was willing to suffer everything for him, even though he was older and around eighty years old at the time.

Through this room the family of their oldest son Dani his wife and two daughters and a nurse would enter the next room. The room was on the fifth floor of a building with no elevator and the place was shared with four or five neighbors.

When Rabbi Gluskin felt better he and Gita were given a place in the dwelling of one of the Chassidim who lived in Leningrad. His name was Mordechai Noseh Chein – Nosichin. Even though the dwelling was in the middle of the city it was dilapidated and unbelievably filthy. The first floor that was almost really a cellar as you had to go down steps into it and through the windows that were street level you could see the feet of pedestrians.

When you enter there is a narrow dark hall and then a large room where the two daughters and son of Mordechai would go. Mordechai's wife was in the mental institution and the whole family had no-one to take care of things. Sometimes on Friday the sister of his wife would come and cook for them for Shabbos.

The two girls were at regular school, Sonia in sixth grade and Malka in third grade. They were inseparable, loved each other and lived cut off from everyone. The family was sustained by the oldest son Chaim Shlomo. He had a store where he took pictures for official documents and for anyone in general. In the evening when he would come home exhausted the two girls, the father and younger brother Ben-Tzion (Benche) would jump on him for money.

Chaim Shlomo was an honest person, pleasant and devoted to the family. He especially loved his mother and brought her back home. He looked after her like a child. He forced her to eat. When he made an omelet with many eggs and a lot of butter she would scream and not want to eat. The sick mother slept in the narrow room with the two daughters. The mother eventually died in an automobile accident and the two brothers and father starved to death in the siege of Leningrad.

Rabbi Gluskin and Gita slept in a large passageway. On the left in the corner was Rabbi Gluskin's bed and in the right-side corner Gita's bed. Gita became very friendly with Sonia who was her age and she got Gita to read Russian and international literature.

The Chassidic community in Leningrad was relatively large and they received their new Rabbi with great enthusiasm. He was invited to all wedding and took his youngest daughter Gita with him. Gita had friends among the daughters of Chassidim.

One time he explained to Gita that they originated in Sefard. The name Mendel was originally Emmanuel and it was put together with Menachem which was a common name at that time period. *(some write that it is a diminutive of the name man, or from Menachem Mendez or from mandelach/ almonds that grow very quickly, thus those with such a name are people who have a nature of zrizus)* Therefore, Gita eventually gave her first born the name Emmanuel after her father. Since Rabbi Gluksin only had daughters, her husband also agreed that he should carry the family name Gluskin.

In general, he did not pray in the Chassidic shul that was in the courtyard of the main shul. He prayed in the community shul since he was head Rabbi. One time he gave a talk in the Chassidic shul. It was on subject of physical and spiritual. Dovid Yitzchok Gurevitch his brother-in-law who would fast every Monday and Thursday came out from the shul saying: "This was something incredible!"

Gita writes: "I would like to write about the human character of my father. He was gentle and polite and in his relationship with people showed great restraint. There was only one time that I saw him become angry and shout. This happened while we were living by Mordechai Nosci Chen. There were many people sitting around the table and my father spoke with anger. It was in regard to one person whose family name was "Bolotnikov". I was very surprised to see my father like this but it may have been because the man was married to a non Jewish woman and had a child with her. This man loved his girl and she loved her father, but with time the mother and grandmother turned the girl against the father calling him a "Jew." Bolotnikov was a watchmaker and honored and respected my father very much."

Shneur Zalman Duchman *(**Leshema Ozen** – 1963 edition p.81; 2016, p.125)* writes that three weeks before he died, "On November 19 1935/23rd of Cheshvan 5696 was the bar-mitzvah of my son Dovber Menachem Mendel may his blood be avenged. Elchonon Morozow sang the tune of the Rebbe Maharash on the words (Psalms 39:5, Sefer Hanigunim song 13) "Hashem let me know my end and the measure of my days what it is, that I may know when I will cease". Rabbi Gluskin sat there and cried uncontrollably."

Leah was not able to enter the university due to her being religious. Therefore, she got a job at a knitting factory. In 1936 a law went into effect that all citizens have equal rights. Leah and Sonia who wanted to go to university had to take special exams for a graduation certificate since they did not graduate from school. Rabbi Mendel Gluskin helped his daughters in all courses including mathematics and physics.

In 1936 on the twelfth of Kislev during the day the Rabbi and Gita went to a Chassidic wedding. It was very joyful and as usual the Rabbi danced with the Choson and maybe said a few l'chaims. They returned at 1am. Rabbi Gluskin exclaimed "ay yai yai" as he remembered that he had not lit a yahrzeit candle. He became very upset that he had forgotten for a while that this was the date his wife had passed away. After she died he did not want to get married again. He lit the candle and Gita lay down to sleep.

At the time they lived in the room by Mordechai Nose Chein. The Rabbi's bed was in one corner and Gita's bed was in the opposite corner. In the third bed slept Bentzy, the young son of Mordechai.

At 5 a.m. he got up and walked around the room in a strange manner. He was coughing which was not strange as he had a node in his throat. He was having pain in his heart. He was having a second heart attack. Gita was in a deep sleep and so he woke up the boy Bentzy. He asked him bring him hot water to wash his feet. He had to make a fire, heated a pot of water and poured it into a glass bottle and then gave it to the Rabbi, all which was a big task. Then he went to get a doctor. Meanwhile Gita woke up and went to her father who was gasping and snorting. Gita did not realize this was his last breath.

The doctor came and pronounced him dead. He died on the same day as his wife's passing seven years later in the early morning about the same time as his wife. They took his body to the big shul and laid it on the ground in front of the omud. He was eulogized and they took him out. The street was packed and the young Chassidim carried him on their shoulders all the way to the cemetery. For the funeral the two brothers of his wife Nachman and Meir came from Moscow. Also, his sisters Basya Riva and Beila were there. For shiva they sat in the room by Mordechai Noseh Chein. They spread out blankets for everyone to sleep on. For the two aunts they put six chairs together three opposite three and put a blanket on them. Gita was constantly worried that at night the chairs would break and the aunt would fall to the floor.

**The grave of Rabbi Menachem-Mendel Gluskin.**

The funeral looked like a huge demonstration. A year later they put up the stone on the grave. After that the Jewish cemetery was closed by the government and they arrested all the leaders of the community. They were sent to concentration camps and the two sons of the previous Rabbi Hertz and Saul Katzenelenboigen were killed there.

Gita went to the small shul to say kaddish. After the first time she said kaddish, a man by the name of Rav Yitzchok came over to her and said that she is now older (fourteen years old) it is not proper for her to say the kaddish. Gita stopped and her father's brother–in-law Yitzchok Gurevitch husband of Baila (Gluskin) said it for eleven months.

His manuscripts were in a wooden box. During the siege of Leningrad, they were in a room with other old things. The temperatures were freezing with no fuel and while they were away, the neighbors burnt everything including the box, to keep warm. Not even one page was left of his manuscripts.

***M'oros Nosson*** *p.130 chapter 36, Yerushalayim 1998, Rabbi Nosson Nota Alavskaya. Excerpt from his eulogy in the Beis Midrash Darbat in Moscow for the Shloshim of Rabbi M.M. Gluskin.*

The Rabbi was a genius, wise in matters of truth and a "chossid" pious with his master in a way that his intelligence and awe worked in tandem, his noble morals and ethics were pure in strict observance of simultaneous Torah and Avodah, an erudite scholar with encyclopedic knowledge, he was humble, bent when he entered and bent when he left, and did not take credit for himself, even though he was extremely talented and had exalted knowledge, and even when he lived in dire straits with many years of pain, suffering and piles of troubles, even then he supported many Torah scholars, because he was merciful and respectful of Rabbis. He had common sense – smooth and sharp. He never wanted to receive payment for weddings, divorces, etc. He walked humbly and was beloved above and charming below in everyone's eyes.

His father the chossid Rabbi Aharon Gluskin was one of the few remainders who represented the greatness of the faith of the house of Israel. All his days, including when he was in business and a successful businessman, he dwelt in Torah and avodah. He was a famous and precious Chabad chossid. Many cities asked him to become their Rabbi but he refused. But Hashem had other plans for him and caused him to lose all his possessions and only then did he accept to become Rabbi in Paritch where he continued on his path in Torah and avodah. Rabbi M.M. Gluskin was his son, a child of a Holy man. It was in this way that he absorbed all the positive traits and manner of conduct, the best of Chassidus.

In Minsk he also received the best from the misnagdim or non-Chassidic world. His father in law Rabbi Rabinowitz was the son in law of the Minsker Godol. He was not just a genius for himself but he was very street smart and knew what was going on. Leningrad has lost its beauty. The anguish that we hear and see in Leningrad from all people of all walks of life tells us how much he achieved in the three years that he lived there. He was honored by all.

Leah enrolled in the Faculty of History at the University. During her first year, Professor Solomon Yakovlevich Lurie noticed her brilliant abilities. She became a favorite student of the Professor, he studied ancient languages and taught them together with ancient history.

Their uncle arranged that for the years that Leah and Sonia went to University they received 500 Rubles monthly. This was sufficient for their expenses. Gita moved in with Leah and Sonia and Leah became her guardian. A representative from the education department came to check on the living conditions and if Gita has her own bed to sleep in. There was no place for a third bed and thus Gita slept in a narrow metal bed with Leah while Sonia slept on a spring mattress that was on a wooden base.

Leah arranged an experienced teacher for Gita to teach her Russian. He also taught her so that she would be able to take the test to finish elementary school. She past the test and made one mistake in Russian, as she did not know that the "Beetle" was the dog's nickname and wrote the B as a small letter. The other areas that they tested her on she was able to prepare herself and passed with excellence, receiving a document that she completed elementary school. For high school (grades 8-10) she went to school for three years and completed it with honors. At that time with good grades they let you into university without question. In 1940 Gita was accepted in the "prestigious" Philology faculty to the romance department where she studied French. She was there until, the great International war as the second World War was called, June 22 1941. She completed her first year with the tests.

Bolotnikov helped us when he could. One time he came and cheked the large breakfront that we had. It was made of dark wood and had three doors and green stained glass. We brought it with us from Minsk. A person gave it to us because he was afraid that the government would take all his furniture for taxes he owed. It was probably used for books and had a printer inside. We got rid of the printer and made it into a place for clothes and pots. On the bottom were three drawers. Bolotnikov took out the middle draw and removed a beam from inside. After a while he returned and put the beam back.

**War Time**

The upper row Sonya on right and Gita on left. Bottom row Leah with her husband – Joseph Amusin – a world-known scientist in the field of Qumran Scrolls. This family photo of the relatively young people is remarkable – all four became outstanding scientists. All four passed through WWII -- the photo was taken in 1941. To all of them Hebrew was a living language. Thanks to it they were able to make amazing scientific discoveries. Hebrew filled their souls with light, and the mind with wisdom, helping them overcome the despair of Soviet life.

In July 1941 at the initiative of Solomon Ya. Lurye, - a world reknown historian and the teacher of Leah, they left Leningrad. Having heard about the advance of the Nazi army, SY, as a historian, well understood the danger. He wanted to save Leah, she was considered to be an extremely talented girl, and so he persuaded her to leave Leningrad for the East. Leah, however, had just had serious surgery where she lost a lot of blood, was very weak and could not travel alone.

Sonia finished the course at the pedagogy institution and remained in the dorm of the institution to continue her studies.

Thus, Gita left her sister Sonya in Leningrad, and traveled with Leah. The ride to Perm (then, Molotov) took 16 days in cattle cars, being arranged on plank-beds in alternating directions, like herrings in barrels. They did not have to eat all the time. From Perm they continued by the river Kama up to Kazan.

Leah's diploma from the Leningrad Pedagogical Institute made a great impression in Tataria, and she was chosen to be the director of the school in the village of Aleksandrovka, which belonged to the Sarma region of Kazan District; 18 km from Sarma. Since all the men had been taken to this very unexpected war, Gita found herself doing various agricultural jobs, as well as being teacher under Leah. Gita had already finished the first course in the Philosophical Faculty in Leningrad and was employed teaching physics and geography. Gita was 18 years old, and in her class, there were 2 boys of 16 or 17 years old, she was very happy that they were reading books during the lessons.

With the outbreak of the war, Sonia Gluskin remained in the besieged Leningrad. KA Mareeva recalls: "In the summer of 1941, shortly after the war began, we went to the barracks as part of the air defense division and started living in a bomb shelter under the institute (LGPI. Herzen. – LK). We were on duty in attics, in hospitals, at dystrophics. We dug trenches under Pulkovo – more precisely, anti-tank ditches. Sometimes unloading at night for Staronevsky coal – crushed stone from the cars and in the morning received a plate of yeast soup...The death before our eyes of our teachers, weakened from hunger. One of them, Sonia and I were carrying on sleds..."

Sonia Mendelevna managed to leave the blockaded Leningrad through the "Road of Life" which opened through Lake Ladoga. Sonya was taken from Leningrad in a state of complete dystrophy. Sonia Mendelevna got to the village in Tataria to where her sisters lived. They saw a cart driven by a horse nearing the house, and something like a corpse lying on the cart. This was Sonya.

After some time, Sonia was able to stand on her legs. Recovering, in 1943 she volunteered for the army and Gita followed her. Gita was the youngest and often did what here her sisters were doing. However, it was not possible for them to be together. In the army Sonya served on an antiaircraft armoured train as a junior sergeant while Gita served in a communications battalion until the end of the war August 1945 and Sonya until October 1945 with the Japanese – in the Far Eastern front.

Later, Sonya, who never married, educated Gita's elder son. As for Leah, she caught a cold in Tataria, and had to undergo a surgery after which she could not give birth to any child.

Gita 9 May 1945. "Я не плачу" (I am not crying) is written in the back-side.

Medal for the victory over Germany in the great Patriotic war of 1941-1945

Military Unit ozenbrp 210 OsMoska PVO, 13 bldg. 3 BELF (210 air defense, 13 corps, 3 BF) Gluskina Sonya Mendeleevna

## Gita - **Post War**

After the war we returned and found the room was clear of all our belongings and only the breakfront was still there. We lived in another place in very confined quarters. Esther generally went to sleep by her close friend Lisa Machlis. One day our uncle Meir from Moscow let us know that Bolotnikov had moved to Israel and died there. Before he died he asked that someone tell us that everything that he hid in the breakfront belonged to us. Gita knew exactly which beam he removed and with a small ax took it out. In it were hidden gold coins each worth ten rubles. Thanks to this they were able to rent a room for Esther.

A few days before the beginning of the new academic year, Gita returned to Leningrad. After a four-year hiatus, Gita was ready for year two at the Philological faculty. She became aware that in 1944 a new faculty was opened, the Eastern faculty and within it was a new chair of Assyriology and semitic languages including Hebrew and Aramaic. This is exactly what Gita wanted and she approached the deacon of the Philological department. He was totally surprised that she would leave her prestigious studies in the university and become involved in such an unpopular study. Yet he gave his ok.

Gita was in her element as this connected to her Jewish roots. Her studies were directed by Professor Isaac Natanovitch Vinnikov – a remarkable scientist, ethnographer and historian of culture, outstanding Semitic and Arabic linguist. She was now able to plunge into the rich history of Jewish culture, the Spanish Golden age of Jewish poetry, its thinkers and philosophers. The theme of her thesis is the writings of the medieval Jewish poet Yehudah Alharizi (1170-1235). The department of hand written works of the Leningrad Public Library kept excerpts of Alcharizi's "Makama." This became the basis for her dissertation and diploma. It also brings her respect and recognition among Hebraist scholars.

In January 1949 she married Aryeh Vilsker who was student in a lower class and finished his studies in 1950. In 1949 Gita finished her studies with distinction. She was now an official Hebraist Philologue. At the end of the year her first son Emanuel is born. It is also a time when an all out anti semitic campaign went into effect. The arrest of Jewish leaders, persecution of the common Jew, the doctor's case – murderers in white coats was being prepared, etc. The wave of oppression did not bypass the Assyriologists and Hebraists of the Leningrad State University; the department was doomed and the academic teachers were waiting for dismissal or arrest. A new anti semitic deacon was appointed who did not care about the past and simply hated Jews. He closed the Semitic faculty and let everyone go, including the famous professor Yitzchok Vinnikov (1897-1973) as well as Claudia Borisovna Starkova (1915-2000) a specialist in medieval Jewish poetry and Igor Mikhailovich Diakonoff (Diakonov) (1915-1999) an expert in the history of Ancient Near East and Assyrian and Babylonian languages.

Meanwhile Gita was pregnant with her first child and worked "hourly" in her department. She taught three beginner students the basis of Hebrew grammar. One day she met Diakonov in the hallway and he said: "Gita, do not teach any classes tomorrow, our department is cancelled and we are fired." She was basically told to go find her own work. Gita's situation was dire and she was facing a ruthless hostile system. She wrote to the education ministry to see if there was any position in her expertise but they responded that it is not needed anywhere in the Soviet Union.

Now the knowledge of Hebrew language and history was a crime and undignified. When her husband finished his degree in 1950 he was accepted as a librarian and paid 8 rubles a month, not nearly enough to survive on. Meanwhile Gita decided to look for a place in the department of Arabic Philology since Arabic was in demand. They responded mocking her and told her to go try Chinese.

Suddenly Gita was summoned to the Great House on Liteiny Prospect. A young man in normal appearance did not shout at her, stamp his feet or swear. On the contrary, the ministry of State security offered her a quiet job to translate letters and documents that were written in Yiddish. Of course refusing meant that she was challenging the system for which she could be punished but she did not agree to accept such work. Gita said: "there must be some misunderstanding here, Yiddish belongs to the German group and it is not my field." "Who is your father?" asked the young man to which Gita replied: "Rabbi." The young man shook his head disapprovingly and said: "Ok, go."

Gita had studied reading and translating German at the University but not speaking it. Thus she now thought maybe she could teach it as a foreign language in school. They gave her grade 5 with children who had no understanding of decent conduct. This in addition to the attitude in those days that foreign languages were not necessary. After the first class she told the principal that she will not come back for this class. Thus Gita concluded that to teach in a school it needs to be a subject that is respected by the students.

In the Pedagogal institute, the faculty of mathematics now had a new student. Since she had a university diploma it was easy for them to accept her. Students of her caliber only had to go twice a year to lectures. This also gave her the right to teach which she did in evening school. This was in 1951, the pay was minimal and it was used to pay for a baby sitter for her new baby. The school was one-hour distance by tram. So, in additional to the school hours she had two hours traveling time.

They lived in a small room with ten other neighbors. They also had to have the baby sitter live with them and officially register her. When Emanuel was four Gita arranged for him to go to kindergarten and the baby sitter left them for other work. After the death of Stalin on March 5 1953, rumors abounded as to what was going to happen or not happen as there was now a major power struggle.

In 1955 the department of Semitology was restored at the Faculty of Oriental studies of the Leningrad State University. Professor Vinikov was reinstated after being out of work for six years. He made sure that Gita was also hired to work there. That happened in 1957 when Gita finished her studies and received her diploma in Mathematics. She began at as an assistant at the University and then as a lecturer and senior lecturer. This was until 1980 when she began to receive pension.

In 1960 Gita met Solomon Lurie. This meeting determined her focus for the next twenty years. Lurie knew about her work on Alharizi and about a medieval treatise in the British Museum. It was a mathematical treatise including calculations from the diurnal mathematical school which was a subject studied by Solomon Lurie. From the scientist's point of view this unique work would be of great interest to the leading expert on medieval Jewish culture Gita Gluskin.

Of course, due to the iron curtain there was no way they could travel to London. Thus Lurie wrote to the British Museums repository of microfilms and gave them to Gita to study. They were printed on sixty-six sheets of photo paper. The quality of the prints from the microfilm left much to be desired and the Hebrew letters written in medieval type were difficult to read. Gita began by composing its own alphabet, corresponding to the $14^{th}$ century letters, to make it easier to read the text.

The manuscript, entitled "Straightening Curvature" contained three and a half chapter instead of the declared five, belonged to the pen of a certain Alfonso. Nobody seemed to know who he was and Gita decided to find out. She devoted all her time to to deciphering the texts. The case moved slowly month by month and year by year. She received advice from specialists in medieval mathematics and linguistics. The book spoke of a new method to measure the area of a circle. The title "straightening out the curvature" was derived from Isaiah, utopically predicting that someday, in light times, the curve will surely become straight.

Gita pours over medieval theorems, tasks and drawings. The manuscript is saturated with characteristic digressions, arguments and vague hints. Errors and mistakes of the copyist makes even more obscure the meaning of the mysterious work of Alfonso. Finally, after suffering from a heart attack in 1975 Gita completed her work. The treatise is translated, studied and commented on. She knows who Alfonso was.

After reading thousands of pages in a variety of languages, Gita found a reference to Alfonso in the collection "Medieval Manuscripts of the Jews." The second breakthrough was when the Israeli historian Yitzchak Bear published a medieval work called the "Gift of Jealousy" in which the author was Avner of Burgos. After comparing the style of Avner and Alfonso and finding that they were identical, Gita concluded that they were the same person. Now Gita had to find out who Avner of Burgos was. In Professors Vinnikov's personal library was the book, "The History of the Jews in Christian Spain." There she finds an article about Avner Burgossy who devoted himself to the study of philosophy, astronomy and astrology. Under the influence of unknown factors, he adopted Christianity and at baptism received a new name; Alfonso of Valladolid. By this name he signed his "Straightening the curvature,"

In 1975 her eldest son Emanuel moved to Israel, worked on a kibbutz, went through army service, and became a professor of electrical engineering. Her youngest son Boris moved to Israel in 1990.

**Dr. Aryeh Leib Vilsker**[1] [1919-1988], son in law of Rav Menachem Mendel Gluskin

Dr. Aryeh (Leib in Yiddish, son of Chaim Vilsker) married Gita who was a daughter of Rav Menachem Mendel Gluskin. Their son Emanuel retained the name Gluskin as Dr. Emanuel Gluskin since Rav Gluskin only had daughters. In order to continue the Gluskin name Dr. Emanuel, an electrical engineer, goes by the surname "Gluskin". A second son of Gita and Aryeh Vilsker is Boris.

According to documents, Vilsker was Leib Haimovich, in Russian Lev Yefimovich, and in Israel, Arie Vilsker. Vilsker was born in 1919 in Shumsk, Vohlyn province, then Poland and now in the Tarnopol region in Ukraine. He also used the pen name Leib Shumsky after the place of his birth. His father was the owner of a seltzer water plant. Lev attended a Chalutzim Zionist school and when a teenager he took hachshara - technical training for Aliyah. He trained to become a mechanic in Eretz Yisrael.[2] Lev continued singing the Chalutznick Zionist songs throughout his life and was known to stroll throughout St. Petersburg singing these songs.

Lev studied with his two grandfathers who were both Talmudic scholars. Later a Talmud teacher was employed but his grandfathers also continued teaching and testing Lev on Friday at the end of the week. Meanwhile his grandmother would invite Leibele to another room where she secretly gave him a small glass of wine and a piece of lekach - honey cake so that he had a good taste with his learning.

While food may have an incentive, he later studied lishma – purely for the sake of learning. His mother would show the Talmud teacher respect and honor, always preparing a glass of tea for the teacher. The Melamed would say, "Gemorah never cools down, yet tea cools down." Di Gemorah vet nit kalt verin, oon dee tay vet kalt vern." The Talmud teacher initiated Vilsker into the rhythms, the warp and woof of the Aramaic of the Talmud Bavli with its sing song cadences of מאי קא משמע לן (what does this mean?) and מנא הני מלי (how do we know this?).

At the age of 20 after the Western Ukraine was annexed by the Soviet Union, Lev was drafted into the army and sent to the Far East. There he suffered from varicose veins and sores and was admitted to a military hospital. When the war broke out he was enlisted as a military railway man, first in Galichi and then in Estonia.

As a perk of military service Lev was able to petition to study in University. Lev thus went to Leningrad to study at the University. First, he entered the French Department of the Institute of Foreign Languages. Eighteen months later Lev transferred to the Department of Assyriology and Ancient Near East at the Institute of Oriental Studies of Leningrad University. And thus, Lev's good foundation of Hebrew and Aramaic from his youth re-entered his life. His student colleagues included Misha, a future professor at Haifa University, Michael Gleltser and Gita Gluskina who wrote her dissertation on the work of Rabbi Yehudah Alharizi, author of Tcchakcmoni and a translation of the Rambam's Moreh HaNevukhim.

In January of 1949 Lev proposed to Gita Gluskina and in December of 1949 their son Emmanuel was born. Emanuel has sons in Kollel in Jerusalem.

In 1950 Lev graduated from the University with a diploma of Linguist-Semitologist. He received a position in the State Public Library named after ME Saltykov Shedrin at the department of Hebrew and Yiddish books.

Above Photo of Saltykov Shedrin Library from Wikopedia Commons

The department was later renamed the Department of literatures of Asia and Africa. There he was renamed Lev Yefimovich by the staff. He was a librarian and advanced to senior editor and senior researcher.
Professor Vinikov wrote a letter of recommendation in Russian. The letter was saved by Dr. Vilsker and later relayed to his son Dr. Emanuel Gluskin.

Letter of Recommendation translated:

> ***Vilsker, L. H, born in 1919, had entered the Oriental Department of Leningrad State University (named after L. A. Zhdanov and awarded the State medal after Lenin) as a second-year student of the Division of Assyriology and Hebraistics in 1946. Before that, Vilsker had attended the Leningrad Pedagogical Institute of Foreign languages. L. H. Vilsker have been seriously studying the Semitic languages of Arabic, ancient Hebrew, Aramaic,***

*Syriac and at the same time devoted a lot of attention to philosophy and history by taking a number of both general and special courses of lectures, and through conducting an extensive review of literature. In addition, comrade Vilsker has been studying independently the recently found Ugarit manuscripts that represent the extremely important cultural monuments. These resulted in his course project, "Laryngeal sounds in Ugarit language," which demonstrates a profoundness of the author's approach to the analysis of the poorly understood and complex linguistic problems.*

*He dedicated his Diploma project to the word-formation in Hebrew language — this is a question of considerable interest for linguistics, which was not explored properly by science. This Diploma project had received the highest praise from the Committee of the Department of Arabic Philology in May of 1950.*
*The solid training received by comrade Vilsker at the University, as well as completion by him, independently, the serious scientific works mentioned above, give reason to believe that he is thoroughly prepared for conducting scientific work and scientific research.*

*Senior researcher of Institute of Oriental Studies of Academy of Sciences, USSR*
*Professor Vinikov*

Despite excellent recommendations, his scholarly life was not easy, particularly with the lack of publishing opportunities in Russia. He was an unknown entity. How could anyone know about the Russian Hebrew philologist

Lev Vilsker if there was nowhere for him to be published? He was known to some extent at the Leningrad State Public Library where Vilsker worked for almost 30 years. Naturally he was admired by other Hebraists and friends including Alex Tarn,[3] James Lieberman,[4] and Eliezer Rabinovitch.[5] Teaching positions were rarer than publishing opportunities, recalling for us Gershom Scholem's assessment of the situation in Germany during his doctoral studies.[6] Clearly the lack of Jewish studies opportunities was much more severe in Communist Russia than in pre-Nazi Gemany.

Dr. Ezra Fleischer, expert in Medieval Hebrew poetry, and pioneer of the Hebrew poems in the Cairo Geniza, memorialized the following about Vilsker in the Yediot Achronot on March 13, 1988:

***"The passing of Leo Vilsker is a great loss. Our world mourns not just the important research of this great man, an aristocrat of spirit, who was a messenger from an unfriendly country that persecuted him and Jewish scholarship. Leo Vilsker was a colleague with a generous and selfless soul. Many Israeli scientists have lost a friend who inspired us from afar (in Leningrad) with his never tiring research and quest for understanding, with his fiery supreme creative passion, and who at the same time astounded us with his knowledge, and rare modesty."***

The scholarly journal Kiryat Sefer, featured Vilsker's photo portrait with a long article by Professor Fleischer dedicated to the Vilsker's discovery of unpublished poems of Rav Yehudah HaLevy and Rav HaLevy's friendship with Rabbi Moshe ibn Ezra. The article had already been sent for printing when a message about the sudden death of Lev Vilsker arrived from Leningrad.

Professor Fleischer hastened to make necessary changes in the introduction, main text, and footnotes from present to past tense. The editors accepted Fleischer's request to include a special page with a photo of Vilsker. The publishing of a photo in Kiryat Sefer was the first time in the 62-year history of the journal since it was first publishcd since 1926. In the photo Vilsker is wearing a white sweater that he inherited from his scholarly brother-in-law Joseph Amusin[7] who married Leah Gluskina Amusin,[8] the sister of Vilsker's wife Gita Gluskina.[9]

In the article by Dr. Fleischer the focus was upon the youthful years of Yehudah HaLevy and the beginning of his friendship with Rabbi Moses ibn Ezra, a venerable poet. The subtitle reads, "according to the research of Arie Vilsker." After Vilsker's passing there was a tidal wave of popular newspaper articles and scholarly publications broadcasting the importance of Vilsker's research.

Articles noting Vilsker's passing in the Jewih press referred to Dr. Vilsker as the "researcher of Leningrad (hahoker miLeningrad). For instance HaDoar ran this headline "Yisrael Leib Vilsker The Mighty Researcher from Leningrad" :

# הדאר

תרבות, ספרות, והגות יהודית

## ישראל לייב וילסקר —

### החוקר הגיבור מלנינגראד

שנה למותו

מאת משה י' נימן

Back in Russia the passing of Vilsker was marked by a number of obituaries that really did not capture the importance of Vilsker's research for Jewish studies. However relatively a more comprehensive acknowledgement of the impact of Vilskers research did appear in Journal "Sovietish Heimland" (Soviet motherland), No 5, May 1988, Translated by L. Belov on July 6th 1988, Jerusalem and reads:

*Obituary for Vilsker*

> ***In the beginning of 70's, there was a publication by a new author in the journal "Sovietish Heimland." The readers were immediately captivated by the unusual character of his materials that were***

*published generally under the rubric "Our announcements." It is possible to recognize the wide diapason of the author's research by mentioning only some titles of his papers: "New materials for the History of Jews in Russia," "Hymn to wisdom: chapter from the unknown book by Said ben Babshad," The unknown selected aphorisms by philosophers," "About the history of printing among Jews," The source of Pushkiniana among Jews," "A recently-found parable of Aesop, a Syrian version written in Jewish script," "The unknown poems by Yehuda Ha-Levi...." The author of these materials was Leib Vilsker, a Leningrad scientist, candidate of philological sciences.*

*Leib Vilsker was born in 1919 in a small town of Shumsk of Tarnopol region in Ukraine. From 1940 and till the end of WWII, he served in the Soviet Army. In 1950, he had completed his studies at the Department of Semitology and Hebraistics of the Leningrad University. For several years he was in charge of the Department of Semitology at the Leningrad Public Library named after M. E. Saltykov-Shedrin. In 1970, he had defended his dissertation, "Samaritan Language" and received a degree of "candidate of philological sciences." When this dissertation was published as a book in 1974, it was highly appreciated as an important study in semitology as well as a significant contribution to research in the history of Samaritans.*

*By dedicating his life to the problems of ancient Hebrew literature, Vilsker chose an unbeaten path. Each of his works, undoubtedly, manifests a unique discovery. Almost all his research papers that were published in the journal "Sovietish Heimland," have been reprinted in Jewish and Hebrew press abroad, particularly his works about Yehuda Ha-Levi.*

*As a scientist, Leib Vilsker accomplished a lot in the field of deciphering unknown ancient Jewish texts that are located in the library archives in our country [Russia] and which nobody but him was able to study with such competence and pedantic attention to details. In this field, his work has the extreme significance for the world culture.*

*Several of Vilskers works were left unfinished, on his desk. A few days before he died, he had sent to the journal an article about the unknown letters of C. N. Bialik, which Vilsker had been working on during last few months of his life.*

*"Sovietish Heimland" has published two collections of L. Vilsker's works, which were added to the journal publications under the name "Discovered Treasures," and which included only some of his research papers; both these small books made a strong impression on readers. One can tell with confidence that there will be in the future no researchers of ancient Jewish literature, who will be able to work without the discoveries made by L. Vilsker. For the history of ancient Jewish literature, his discoveries have made an invaluable contribution.*

*In bright memory of Vilsker*

*Journal "Sovietish Heimland" (Soviet motherland), No 5, May 1988 Translation from Hebrew to Russian by L. Belov July 6th 1988, Jerusalem*

Unfortunately, while Vilsker was alive, his fame in Israel where he had never been able to get a VISA out of Russia to go to, was obscured due to the difficulties of publishing Jewish related subjects in Russia. Such research during Vilsker's lifetime was not a priority and definitely frowned upon.

Vilsker influenced the work of colleagues such as Chaim Ratshabi, Nechemiah Aloni, Yosef Yahalom, Dov Yarden, and of course Ezra Fleischer. Fleischer referred to Vilsker as "the genius" (ha-iluey). Shulamit Shalit refers to Fleischer as Vilsker's "guardian angel" analogously as Dov Boris Gaponova's guardian angel in the area of belles lettres was Abraham Shlionsky who published a translation of the Hebrew Georgian epic, "The Knight in the Panther's skin" of Rustaveli.[10]

Shalit shows how Vilsker was relatively unknown, he faced discrimination in Russia against Jewish scholarly matters in general which trickled down to his workplace the Leningrad State Public Library, named after ME Saltykov -Shedrin. Shalit touches upon the great persecution of Jews under Soviet Hegemony. She writes, "In Leningrad 1962, Vilsker visited a cousin of Gita, an Israeli. Gita says, "Leib went to hold her on the street and they met other people from the Israeli group, one of the KGB photographed them. And for the "communication with foreigners", the head of the library, a hefty anti-Semite removed Vilsker from the department, where he worked in the specialty of Oriental Manuscripts, and was transferred to the acquisitions department.

The discomfort of surveillance [11] under the Communists manifested itself throughout the Vilsker family as it did for many Soviet Jews. Gita Gluskina Vilsker told Shulamith Shalit: "At various times she and Lev were summoned by the authorities. He was "asked" to collect readers' conversations. "What kind of readers?" - He asked in response. - "But there are Jewish elders that visit your library – they dig in the Talmud and other religious literature; they converse..." And then he [the official] added that Vilsker must keep this conversation secret. Vilsker replied: "I have no secrets from my wife." He paused and added: "You know, everyone has his vocation, profession. You cannot do my job, and I cannot do yours." After that, Lev was not summoned anymore.

As for Gita – this is a different story." Gita's sister Esther joined Hashomer Hatzair and was sent to Siberia for her Zionist activities. Although Hashomer Hatzair was a secular Zionist organization, in Russia there was not differentiation, for a Zionist was a Zionist of any political stripe. Thus the Baal Ha Tanya was arrested because of sending funds to Eretz Yisrael and the date of his release is celebrated by Chabad Lubavitch to this day as a national and religious holiday.

The pattern of the Baal Ha Tanya's arrest under the Tsars, repeated itself in a different modality under the communists when Rav Menachem Mendel Gluskin (father of Gita Gluskina Vilsker) and his father-in-law Rabbi Eliezer Rabinowitch were arrested for religious activities. The Rabbis were kept awake for forty-eight hours and then made to sign a false declaration that there is no religious persecution in Russia.

Rav Gluskin's flock tried to bring their Rabbi his tallis and tefillin but the communists would not allow this, as the state was opposed to all religious activities amongst not only Jews but also Christians in their religion less state which Marx had warned against in proclaiming "religion as the opiate of the masses." Marx's vision was that of secular messianism, and as George Orwell shows in *Animal Farm,* and elsewhere, that it is a failed secular messianism. Hobbes had advocated for a large bureaucratic state when he witnessed mob violence in a state of civil war. Thus, the liberal communist state as a Leviathan bureaucracy, an Egyptian bureaucracy of old, was born.

However, persecution of Jews ensued needless to say not from the radical left of Stalinist Russia. Among them were incidents like "the doctor's plot" when Stalin feared Jewish doctors were trying to poison him, and the phenomena of the "Beilis case" which tapped into a 2000-year-old blood libel accusation. Obviously, dangers are documented from the radical right of the Nazi National Socialist party which also was run by a large bureaucratic state that fused the mastery of technology for example in rail transport and construction of crematoria, according to Richard Rubinstein, in the form of "techno-cracy" (technology + bureaucracy).

Even in `exile' working in Acquisitions Leo was able to bring forth invaluable library knowledge. By keeping his thoughts with Judaic, Hebraic and Semitic linguistics, he ordered books from many foreign countries. When the researchers from abroad came to the library, they were stunned by Vilsker's breadth, depth, and genius. [12. He also became acquainted with the scientific avenues in various fields. Thanks to Lev Vilsker the library collection in Jewish subjects in Leningrad turned to be much richer than in Moscow! Moscow also had a great collection known as the Gunzberg collection from which many recent reprints of obscure Rishonim have been made.

Five years later, a new head of the department categorically demanded to bring Vilsker back, for without him, the entire special collection became "stripped."

In 1979 Vilsker enjoyed a banquet in honor of his 60th anniversary. That evening, he heard a lot of good things. The next morning, he was asked to retire. [13] Before his retirements the library celebrated the 200th anniversary of the birth of A.S. Firkowicz. During the conference for the 200th anniversary Vilkser announced and presented the inscription of a slab that was carved in the Samaritan language [14] dating to 383 CE. The slab was collected by Firkowicz. Such contributions however were somewhat forgotten and Vilsker was forced to retire.

He was full of energy, on the wings of love from all people around him. He looked (Gita reiterates) young and very handsome. But here came the hit! While on retirement, he learned that he could get another 12 rubles, in addition to the 120 rubles of pension (SSI), if he gets involved in a manual labor for a few months. He found a job of a simple bookbinder.
Shulamit Shalit further notes, "But then something unforeseen happened. In a talented person, a confluence of bitter circumstances may, often unexpectedly, uncover new hidden properties of the soul, mind, and character."

When Lev Efimovich would "stumble" on a poem, he did not know whether it was known to the world or was it a discovery. It was risky to publicly declare a discovery of the poem, and it was premature to publish about it. What if the poem was already published in some unknown edition?

What did he do? He would write down the first line, only a single line, and send it in a letter to Israel, to Ezra Fleischer; Vilsker knew that prof. Fleischer was the pre-eminent specialist in medieval Hebrew poetry. The venerable professor, extremely excited, would rush, like a high-spirited young man, to Heichal Shlomo in Jerusalem to dig for hours in a huge catalogue containing records of all famous poems of medieval poets, and then send a response to Leningrad.

No! Nope! Unpublished! In this way Vilsker discovers not one or two, but as many as twenty-two completely unknown poems of the great Yehuda ħa-Levy. He analyses them and publishes his findings, with great difficulties, in the "Sovietish Heimland" journal, that is, in Yiddish, while feeling undisguised suspicion towards himself. Gita's reminiscences: "Lev was not a poet, but he was forced by the circumstances to make translations into Yiddish of the words by the great Yehuda ħa-Levy! The journal was terribly afraid of any word in Hebrew.

As an honest researcher, Lev would supplant the translation with a photocopy of an original. An editorial board' footnote would say: "Original photo was omitted because of the lack of space." But there was an instance when, either by mistake or because the superiors were not present, one fragment facsimile in Hebrew was printed in the journal and the happy scientists in Israel, among them Ezra Fleischer, examined and studied every letter in it. What a story!

The first publication of Lev Vilsker's research about the unknown poems of Yehuda ħa-Levy (born not later than 1075 - died in 1141) appeared in the February issue of the "Sovietish Heimland" journal, in 1982. Eight pages altogether. On April 7, there was an announcement about the publication in Israeli newspaper "Maariv". Other publications announced the publication of "unknown poems of Rav Yehudah HaLevi revealed in Leningrad" brought together brought to light by Vilsker:

# שירים לא ידועים של יהודה הלוי התגלו בלנינגרד

מאת חיים נגיד

Among those who first responded to this terrific publication were such connoisseurs of medieval poetry and literary historians and experts in Yiddish and Hebrew as Yosef Chaim Crunch and Nagid, Yeħuda Ratshabi David Yosifon, Dov Yarden and Nechemiah Aloni. The sensation literally rocked the whole scientific world.

Newspapers were first to respond followed by serious journals. The precious treasure was not buried somewhere in a wilderness in a corner of the earth, not in a cave, but in one of the centers of the civilized world. Many rave responses and reviews reached the author. Inspired by them, Vilsker directed his intelligence and passion of a pioneer on the continued search and analysis of the findings. A year later, he published a new and almost twenty-page long article entitled "198 poems of Yehuda ħa-Levy in unknown edition." This is how the term **"Vilsker List"** had appeared in the scientific literature, for among the mentioned 198 "first lines" of the works of Yehuda ħa-Levy, 111 were not mentioned in any other indexes, including the classic catalog by Shmuel David Luzzatto, that had been studied by the scientists for more than 150 years.

Among the first who responded to the first and the second publication of Vilsker in "Sovietish Heimland" was a rabbi and scholar David Yosifon, who, among other things, was the editor of three volumes - the books of Tanakh (Torah, Prophets, Writings) - with a translation into Russian (published by "Mossad ħa-Rav Kook" in 1978). Originally from Poland, David Yosifon knew both Russian and Yiddish. David Yosifon wrote his second article for the newspaper "Hatzofe" on his deathbed. His relatives had sent the article to an editor along with his letter: "I am writing these words in a hospital fortress "Hadassa," after a major surgery. It turned out that while walking on Jaffa Street, I fell and lost consciousness. Even though I cannot yet get out of bed, I think that this is my duty and pleasure to tell you that the scientist Leib Vilsker, from Leningrad, made a new discovery and has written about it in "Sovietish Heimland." I want and must ask for the attention of all the scientists and researchers towards that fact."

It was his last letter, words of greeting from one scientist to another across the Iron Curtain. Of course, they [Vilsker and Yosifon] were not acquaintances. Later on, others referenced the article by David Yosifon. It is intelligent, insightful, and full of light and love.

In the similar way, "while descending to a grave" (in 1983), Professor Nechemiah Aloni had blessed Vilsker and his labors. That was a reaction to the first article by Vilsker. Professor Aloni wrote in a journal "Sinai" (number 93), "We are waiting with great impatience (bekilyon eynaim) a continuation of his [Vilsker's] work in all its brilliance and depth. We learned more from his concise article than from the thick-winded volumes of other valuable authors." After enumerating orderly the seven discoveries of Vilsker in the eight-page article, while giving them a clear scientific analysis, Aloni adds, "... and the most important discovery is the author himself, who, until yesterday, was not listed among the researcher-experts in the works of Yehuda ħa-Levi but who had become the one from today."

A great scientific discovery gives impetus to an entire scientific field and entails an avalanche of new investigations and publications. Lev Vilsker managed to publish three more articles (altogether five), but he had already written the sixth paper that came out after his death. Professor Yosef Yahalom writes: "In the last article, Vilsker presents for the first time the entirely message of ħa-Levy to his great patron in Granada, the poet Moshe Ibn Ezra, but ... in Yiddish. The text of the Hebrew original of this important manuscript was prohibited for printing, and the death of Vilsker had closed the last window through which we looked furtively, almost like thieves, into the world of Hebrew manuscripts in Leningrad, which was unknown to us." I hear in these words both anger and bitterness; don't we completely agree with them, while pondering over the fate of such scholars and heroes as Lev Vilsker, Joseph Amusin,[15] and many others? Once the Iron Curtain fell, the notable Yosef Yahalom hurried to Leningrad; he then told about the trip and about how he was getting acquainted with the "treasure" of Vilsker ("Peamim" journal, number 46-7, 1991).

Now let us turn to Nechemiah Aloni. He named the poem of Yehuda ħa-Levy about pogrom in Toledo in the XII century, the fourth discovery in the first article by Vilsker. Below a photo of an article about the unknown piyyut by Rav HaLevi on the murder of souls:

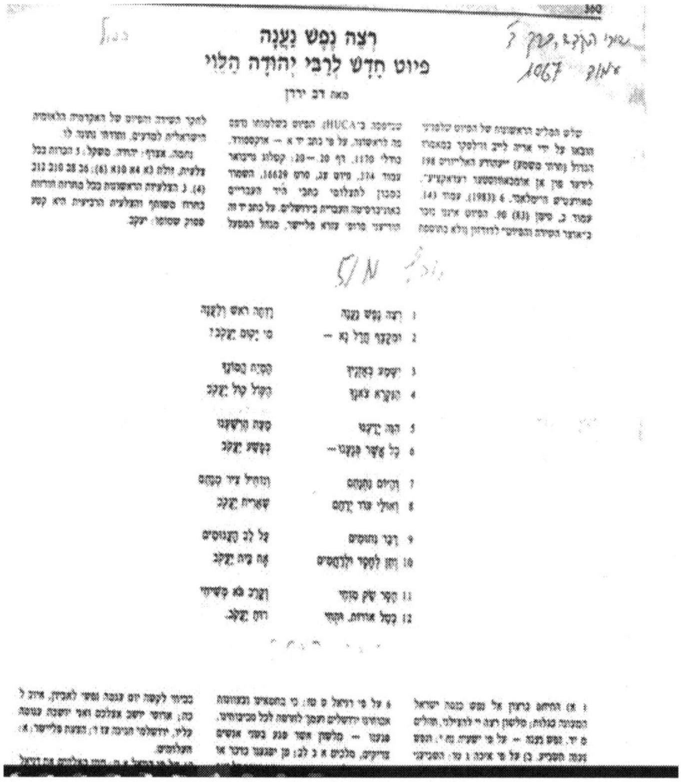

רצה נפש נענה
פיוט חדש לרבי יהודה הלוי
מאת דב ירדן

Aloni writes that the historians knew about the anti-Jewish pogroms perpetrated by Muslims in southern Spain. "I wondered why until now there have been no studies on eulogies (mournful songs) in the works of Yehuda ħa-Levy. And here came Vilsker and presented us with a new poem filled with the clear hints about participation of northern Christians in the pogroms. He presents two expressions that were competently treated by Vilsker: “am seir" (hairy) – most likely that was a nickname for Christians; and "Yad Esau"- the hand of Esau (recalling his hairiness) that could be a hint about Christians as well.

The poem is called "On the pogrom in Toledo." Let me give you a rough translation into Russian, so that the poem content would become clear for the reader. The phonetics of each trop in Hebrew (each stanza ends with the word "day" - yom) is given in the transcription by Shulamith Shalit below.

Да не знать вам, мне внемлющие,/ О горе моем слышащие,/ Живущие в этот День.
Спросите, если не слышали,/ Поведаю, если не знаете,/ Обратите сердца ваши в тот День.
Вам откроется, как пришла беда,/ Как злосчастье на нас обрушилось/ И в чем грех состоял наш – в тот День.
Знают пусть Ариэля изгнанники:/ (то есть, Иерусалима) Вот, еще одно колено Израиля/ Отрублено в тот День.
Госпожой я была, избранницей,/ Средь сестер своих по изгнанию,/ Пока не нагрянул тот День...

Then the poem develops a topic of the former prosperity:  Jews lived in Seira, in Christian Spain, in prosperity and benevolence, their children were counselors for the kings, their elders looked regal and stately, everybody studied Torah, observed the Jewish laws, and lived in peace with the neighbors - "And Esau's hand was with me," but "in his heart, he dreamed about evil deeds, he was thinking about my blood every day."

Here is how Yehuda ħa-Levi sounds in Hebrew:
Lo Aleichem shomey Shimi / ħamitablim al-Nigi / Chaim kulchem ħa-yom.
Shaaltem shmaatem lo / lo agidchem hem yedaatem / sim levavchem minutes ħa-yom.

Ned nirdefa eich kalta / ħa-paa-in BAME Hite / ħachataat ħazot ħa-yom.
Ve-ħodiyu golaten Ariel / ki Shevet E-Israel / Nowhere ħa-yom ...[16]

The fifth discovery, according Aloni, is a song of love "Yonim Yaronu." Here is a brief story. When this song was not known yet in Israel, Vilsker' friend in Leningrad, the composer Hirsch Paikin, created music for the poem, whereas his wife, Clara Yakovlevna, performed the song. At that time, they both started learning Hebrew with Vilsker, secretly. Inspired by the work of the scientist, Paikin wrote a lot of music for the poems by Yehuda ħa-Levy and he even composed an opera about this great poet. They performed this repertoire on many occasions in Israel. But the Paikins are not anymore. Clara Yakovlevna managed to send me from Jerusalem a cassette recording of their songs. I am obliged to simply convey you the words:

Yonim Yaron kamoni kachem / Al Bein MASHAV zaaku Mei Mayhew / Homim al Yamim ħalhu bli chemda / Uzman peerud Chalaf ki bi-Mayhew / (Here performers repeat the first two lines as the chorus).
Ve-ezkor Dodi dadey Yonati / Ki Emergency aloft bosmeychem alai ...

(Doves are cooing, and I am like them /. Here is the watering. And the waters are pure and they murmur like a sea. /Joyless is my wandering. It's time to part. / Doves are cooing. I remember my little dove, the scent of her breasts.[17] /

This is clearly a reference to the metaphor of the beloved [dodi] in the Kabbalah Shabbos hymn, Lechah dodi, which itself refers to Shir Hashirim's numerous allusions to doves (yonim). Rashi follows in the footsteps of Rabbi Akiva who refers to *Shir HaShirim* as a metaphor for the *Kodesh Kodeshim*.[18] In fact Rashi sees the whole poem as a reference for the Beit Hamikash which factors the Song as a metaphor for Hashem's love of his people *Am Yisrael.* Not only does the verse repeat twice *Shuvi Shuvi HaShulamith*[19] an allusion to "if only the Jews would observe two shabbatot according to Hashem's ratzon, then the Mashiach would arrive, but the olfactory metaphors of myrrh, cinnamon, and nerd also evoke the Ketoret ha Samim. Thus, it is not accidental that the Satmar Rav evoking the 3 vows of Shir Ha Shirim cites the verse of the 3 vows, to warn against making aliya en masse, to go up the homah, as forcing the end (dochek et ha-ketz) in reference to eschatological reckoning of the "ingathering of the exiles."

Regarding the image of the "yona" For example (Song of Songs 1:13-17)

יג צְרוֹר הַמֹּר דּוֹדִי לִי, בֵּין שָׁדַי יָלִין.

13 My beloved is unto me as a bag of myrrh, that lies between my breasts. [20]

יד אֶשְׁכֹּל הַכֹּפֶר דּוֹדִי לִי, בְּכַרְמֵי עֵין גֶּדִי.

14 My beloved is unto me as a cluster of henna in the vineyards of Ein-Gedi.

טו הִנָּךְ יָפָה רַעְיָתִי, הִנָּךְ יָפָה עֵינַיִךְ יוֹנִים.

15 Behold, thou art fair, my love; behold, thou art fair; thine eyes are as doves.

טז הִנְּךָ יָפֶה דוֹדִי אַף נָעִים, אַף-עַרְשֵׂנוּ רַעֲנָנָה.

16 Behold, thou art fair, my beloved, yea, pleasant; also, our couch is leafy.

יז קֹרוֹת בָּתֵּינוּ אֲרָזִים, רחיטנו (רַהִיטֵנוּ) בְּרוֹתִים.

17 The beams of our houses are cedars, and our panels are cypresses.

Further in 2: 14 we again encounter the metaphor of the dove, a bird of peace let out by Noach after the flood.

יוֹנָתִי בְּחַגְוֵי הַסֶּלַע, בְּסֵתֶר הַמַּדְרֵגָה, הַרְאִינִי אֶת-מַרְאַיִךְ, הַשְׁמִיעִנִי אֶת-קוֹלֵךְ: כִּי-קוֹלֵךְ עָרֵב, וּמַרְאֵיךְ נָאוֶה.

14 O my dove, that art in the clefts of the rock, in the covert of the cliff, let me see thy countenance, let me hear thy voice; for sweet is thy voice, and thy countenance is comely.

Again in 4:1 the metaphor of the dove is evoked in the Song.

הִנָּךְ יָפָה רַעְיָתִי, הִנָּךְ יָפָה--עֵינַיִךְ יוֹנִים, מִבַּעַד לְצַמָּתֵךְ; שַׂעְרֵךְ כְּעֵדֶר הָעִזִּים, שֶׁגָּלְשׁוּ מֵהַר גִּלְעָד.

1 Behold, thou art fair, my love; behold, thou art fair; **thine eyes are as doves**[21] behind thy veil; thy hair is as a flock of goats, that trail down from mount Gilead.

In Chapter 5 the image of the dove again tropes this time associated with the voice of the beloved knocking (Kol Dodi Dofek) the name of Rav Soloveitchik's famous statement of supporting Medinat Eretz Yisrael as a statement of alliance with the cause of religious Zionism:

אֲנִי יְשֵׁנָה, וְלִבִּי עֵר; קוֹל דּוֹדִי דוֹפֵק, פִּתְחִי-לִי אֲחֹתִי רַעְיָתִי יוֹנָתִי תַמָּתִי--שֶׁרֹּאשִׁי נִמְלָא-טָל, קְוֻצּוֹתַי רְסִיסֵי לָיְלָה.

2 I sleep, but my heart waketh; Hark! My beloved knocketh: 'Open to me, my sister, **my love, my dove,** and my undefiled; for my head is filled with dew, my locks with the drops of the night.'

In chapter 6:9 of Shir HaShirim the dove metaphor appears again:

אַחַת הִיא, יוֹנָתִי תַמָּתִי--אַחַת הִיא לְאִמָּהּ, בָּרָה הִיא לְיוֹלַדְתָּהּ; רָאוּהָ בָנוֹת וַיְאַשְּׁרוּהָ, מְלָכוֹת וּפִילַגְשִׁים וַיְהַלְלוּהָ.

9 **My dove, my undefiled, is but one; she is the only one of her mother**; she is the choice one of her that bore her.

The daughters saw her, and called her happy; yea, the queens and the concubines, and they praised her.

We have already mentioned the name of Abraham Firkowicz.[22] A lover of antiquities, he traveled extensively in different countries of the Middle East. At the end of the XIX century, he sold to the Leningrad (then Imperial Public) Library two collections that were particularly valuable thanks to the manuscripts from the Cairo Geniza. Abraham Harkavi, Paul Kokovtsov, and prof. Khvolson worked with the manuscripts. Scientists from different countries used to come to have a chance to just take a look at the collection.

Now Vilsker decided to "to delve into them." Being free from a job, he directed all his energies to the study of Jewish texts of the collection. He was well versed in different handwritings and fonts and he had a sharp eye for the things that were left unnoticed by others. And his labor was bringing discoveries almost every day. He felt that he had found unknown poetry of the medieval Jewish poets, including poems of Yehuda ħa-Levi, but he could not know that for sure.

Yet Dr. Chaim Vilsker who was the librarian of the St. Petersberg Saltykov Library Jewish division including the Firkovitch[23] and Antonin Judaica Collections, where the scholar/librarian found unpublished poems in manuscript form of Rabbi Yehudah HaLevy which he later annotated and published in Yiddish journals, certainly gave much more than was appreciated by the government library. Dr. Isadore Twerski tried to bring Dr. Vilsker to the Harvard Wiedner collection of Judaica, with a joint appointment to lecture on the holdings of the Saltykov library, but could not secure a visa for the scholar/librarian.

Shulamit Shalit writes of this connection with Harvard by noting:

When E. Fleischer was visiting the United States for his research for a whole year, he decided to organize a trip for Vilsker to the United States. Finally, he would meet with the dear friend, if not in Israel then in the United States, on the neutral ground. Lev Efimovich was delighted with the official invitation from Harvard University to read lectures about the collection of Hebrew manuscripts in the Leningrad Public Library. He decided to tempt the fate. He was redirected from one office to another, and then to another… He came, he wrote, he was refused, and he continued coming again. Oh, dear naive Professor Fleischer! Maybe it was not worth to start this fight, a fight with not the windmills [24] – but with the reinforced-concrete Soviet mills…

On February 12, 1988, Lev Vilsker celebrated his birthday. He turned 69 years old. A few days later he sent his sixth article to Moscow, to the "Sovietish Heimland." On February 19th at 5:00 am, Dr. Vilsker experienced a sharp pain in his chest. A doctor made a direct injection into the heart. But that was wrong. Vilsker managed to say clearly his last words: "Bring a chair for the doctor..."[25]

The earthly life of Leib son of Chaim Vilsker, - Lev Yefimovich in the Soviet Russia, and Arie Vilsker in Israel, - had ended. His eldest son, Emiko, Emmanuel, had been living in Israel for thirteen years already. The younger son, Boris, with his mother Gita, wife Katya and two sons had relocated there in 1990. The grandchildren Misha and Sasha grew up and served in the army. The life of the name - Arie Vilsker – has just begun in Israel, in the world of science.

Vilsker wrote countless items (100 have been identified) in Russian and other European languages on a great breadth and depth of subjects. Vilsker scorned narrow specialization and his knowledge was broad and immense. His works on ancient manuscripts found in the Dead Sea area and the linguistic works on various Semitic languages, as well as his work in lexigraphy were just a few of his accomplishments. A total of 100 scientific papers have been ascribed to Vilsker but he had no place often to publish his findings. Some were published in Yiddish in the journal Sovietish Heimland, but it was not easy for Vilsker to "find a place and forum to share his research."

However RAMBI only retains 2 items relating to Vilskers' work on the Samaritans[26] and their language: "On Leib H. Vilsker Manuel D'arameen Samaritain translated from Russian by J. Margain in Editions du Centre National de la Recherche Sceintifique, 1981, reviewed by Maurice Baillet in Journal of Near Eastern Studies 42, 4 (1983), p. 295-297. Yes, Vilsker taught himself as an auto-didact Samaritan language and Samaritan graphics. The Samaritan language's roots can be traced to the paleo-Jewish alphabet. This subject was not taught in the University where Vilkser studies and thus his auto-didactism is remarkable in that he mastered the language on his own.

Vilsker came to be recognized as a leading Samaratologist. From the abstract of his dissertation ".... Samaritan manuscript collection of the State Public Library consisting of 18,600 sheets of parchment and paper in addition to scrolls as well as inscriptions on stone, silk, and copper." Professor Victor Lebedev the former curator of the Jewish-Arab manuscripts, an area of Vilsker's wife speciality Gita Gluskina, who made Aliyah, wrote in the "Alef-Beit" Magazine that Vilsker studied all 18600 sheets "never missing a single one" out of systematic dedication and diligence. Dr. Gita Gluskin notes in a letter, "In the 1970 Lev had defended his thesis and received the degree of candidate of philological sciences. In 1974 his book Samaritan language was published by a Scientific Research Institute and soon translated into French (Paris 1981). Remarkably while working on the Samaritan manuscripts Lev had completed a detailed catalog of these manuscripts which was published four years after his death in 1992.[27]

Baillet notes that Vilsker was a disciple of I.N. Vinnikov. The review notes that Vilsker's work replaces and trumped that of J. Rosenberg, *Lehrbuch der Samaritanische Sprache und Literatur* (Vienne, 1901). Baillet notes that the origin of that which one calls "Samaritain" is in effect from Occidental Arameen which in historical evolution is successively fused with Hebrew, Greek, and Arabic forms and idioms over the ages. Baillet notes that pages 11-20 give a history of the Samaritans, situated their dialect in the mileau of Arameen, tracing the lines of linguistic evolution. Baillet says the core of the book is pages 21 to 96 focusing on the literature, phonetics, morphology, syntax and lexique of the Samaritan evolved language process. The appendices (p.97-108) give two examples of calligraphic writings and cursive script and two tables of their evolution, with five examples of texts. Pages 111-118 offer a bibliography providing 153 titles and furnishing a list of Samaritan Manuscripts conserved in the Soviet Union. A map is given where these manuscripts are located geographically.

For Vilkser 2 Kings 17:24 is a key text.[28] For Vilsker this verse signifies the arrival of the language of Arameen into Israel. Vilsker (pages 91-92) describes the influence of Hebrew on the Arameen lexicon and their adoption of the "Hebraic law" through their interaction with the Hebrews of the land of Judaea. Baillet writes, "La naissance du Targum est d'ailleurs situee par Vilsker bein avant l'ere chretienne (p.16), ce qui reste surprenant."[29]Vilsker then enumerates the other great sources namely Le Mimar Marqe, the Aramaic liturgical poems, Asatir histories, and inscriptions- about 20 of which are in Arameen. The writing derives from the ancient Hebrew alphabet before the Masoretic script. Baillet notes that Vilsker did a good job on the section on morphology, syntax, and lexigraphical aspects of the Arameen language. Baillet notes that thanks to the work, The Literary and Oral Tradition of Hebrew and Aramaic amongst the Samaritans, vol. 3, pt. 2, The Recitation of Prayers and Hymns (Jerusalem, 1967) of Z. Ben –Hayyim, the phonetical transcription to give the pronunciation of the ancient language for the reader was made possible. Paul Kahle in his Der hebraischer Bibeltext, had raised the question of how the Tiberian masoretes, namely the Ben Asher family arrived at the correct authoritative pronunciation of the biblical text, as opposed to the pronunciations used by the Samaritans.

Kahle writes: Die Samaritaner haben eine Aussprache des Hebraieschen bis auf den heutigen Tag festgehalten, welche die palaestinische Punktation in alten Geniza-Fragmenten einst auch fuer die Aussprache des Hebraischen bei den rabbanitischen juden bezeugt hat. Bei diesen rabbanitischen Juden ist diese Aussprache aber abegloest worden durch eine solche, die von den Masoreten ausgebildet worden ist, die ihren Sitz in Tiberias gehabt haben.[30]

Baillet recognized that Vilsker described correctly the phonetics of the Samaritan language. However, Baillet asks, "Have we truly the words where Quf is pronounced similarly, or is it not in the case where the letter which resembles ayin, has been confounded with it? Baillet is concerned about the true vocalization of the ancient Arameen. Baillet questions the technical reasons from which Vilsker decided to note the pronunciation in the chart of vowels. Baillet notes that the translator from Russian to French adopted the same attitude for the same reasons. Baillet regrets that in the six volumes of Z. Ben Hayyim, this difficulty was not an obstacle. Baillet is not convinced that one word can have two accents on two consecutive syllables, if the first is a secondary accent.

In Baillet's view one is able to say that all words with two syllables carry the accent on the penultimate except if the last syllable is long or very long, which in that case is accented. Baillet feels it is important to thus return on the length of syllables and on the rhythm of the language according to which it is pronounced. With that said the long syllables dominate largely. On these bases Baillet feels that Vilkser and his translator have badly rendered certain pronunciations. They have in effect shadowed (d'innombrables) the long vowels and not noted this in the transcription. Baillet feels that the most severe result is that this negligence is running in the models (paradigms). The same thing is seen in the names of numbers, in pronouns, in names with suffixes, in prepositions, etc. Baillet feels a more serious error still is in the treatment of the term "virgin" pronounced in ancient Arameen as betulti, betultak and not betulti, betulatak (p.53) which correspondes to "mes vierges, tes bierges...." Baillet regrets that certain translation choices of Margain rendered his French edition inferior to the original Russian edition. In the end with all the technicalities aside Baillet admits one must thank Vilkser and Margain as Oriental scholars have need of a grammar of ancient Samaritan and the contribution of Vilsker is a serious progress towards that end.

Baillet concludes by writing :

***Sans doute, les orientalists avaient besoin d'une grammaire de l'arameen samaritain, et celle-ci represente un serieux progress par rapport a ses devancieres. Vilsker et Margain on surement fait tout leur possible, et il fuat les remercier. L'instrument de travail qu'ils nous livrent n'est cependant pas tout a fait au point. N'aurait-il donc pas mieux valu, sur la base de bonnes editions des textes, etudier d'abord a fond la langue de chaque epoque? C'est par une synthese qu'on pourrait arriver a un resultat valable et definitif.***[31]

Today there are about 700 Samaritans still living in Israel. One is named Benjamin Tzedakah whose family served in the Israeli army (IDF). Tzedakah corresponded with Vilsker for many years, as Tzedakah is a scholar of the Samaratin history and language. Second Temple scholars know the Samaritans from Josephus accounts of them.[32]

Rabbinic scholars of the Talmud will recall in tractate Rosh Hashanah the "bad PR" regarding the Samaritans in perek sheni, who were said to have intentionally confused the Rabbinic leadership by making bonfires, to intentionally throw off the accurate reporting of sightings of the new moon as related to Rosh Chodesh.[33] Rabban Gamliel examined witnesses testifying to the new moon whose testimonies risked being confused by the Samaritan sabotage. Before the Samaritan acts of sabotage to new moon sightings the Sanhedrin was more lenient from whom they accepted testimony about the moon's appearance - full, half etc. Beacons used to be lit but after the Samaritans caused harm, they enacted that messengers should go forth. Bonfires were lit by bringing long poles of cedar wood and rushes and pine wood and tow flax tied together. These were lit and waved on top of a hill to and fro so that 3 hills might discern them.[34] The beacons were kindled from Har Ha Zaytim to Sartaba, and from Sartaba to Agrippina and from Agrippina to Hauran and from Hauran to Beth Baltin, so the diaspora appeared as a signal testifying to the new moon.[35] In Jerusalem in a courtyard named Beth Yaazek witnesses assembled for the court to exam them.[36] The court thoroughly examined witness as to how they saw the moon.[37] Rabban Gamliel provided diagrams of the moon in its phases.[38] Rabbi Yehoshua is said to have submitted to Rabban Gamliel's Rosh Hodesh calculations that fell out on Yom Kippur, as opposed to Rabbi Yehoshua's differing calculations, thereby submitting to the authority of the Sanhedrin.[39]

However, Vilsker's works departs from such polemics and scientifically analyzes the language of this sect. Vilsker's work was reviewed in French by Jean-Pierre Rothschild "On Leib H. Vilsker: Manuel d'arameen samaritain trans. From Russian in Revue des Etudes Juives 141, ½ (1982), p. 237-239. Rothschild writes:

***Le present manuel vise, acec success, non al l'exhaustivite, mais a la comodite. On nous fournit (p. 11-20) une introduction rapide a l'histoire samaritaine, a la place de l'arameen samaritain dans sa famille linguistique, a l'histoire de la langue, aux sources samaritaines et a l'histoire de la samaritologie. La partie proprement grammticale est amasee entre les pages 21 et 89 (les neuf pages consacrees a la syntaxe, conre cinque pour les seuls numeraux, sont tout de meme un peu maigres). Le chapitre du lexique (p.91-96) explique plusieurs idiotismes frequents***

*et le calendrier samaritain; l'eppendice 1 (p.97-104) reproduit plusieurs textes tres courts, en respectant le graphisme des scribes, et en donne la transliteration, la transcription phonetique, la traduction et le commentaire; l'appendice 2 presente, d'apres les ketubot de la collection Firkovic, a Leningrad, des specimens d'ecritures echelonnes entre les XVI et XVIII siecles, avecs leurs dates et les noms des copistes. Aux pp. 109-118, une biblioraphie de 153 titres cite les etudes classiques des cent dernieres annees et beaucoup de travaux recents. Bref apercu des manuscrits samaritains, dans les bibliotheques sovietiques pp. 117-118; carte de l'ancienne diaspora samaritaine p.119.*

Vilsker as an autodidact Hebrew philologist focused primarily on the linguistic aspects of the Samaritan language. His scholarly interests included the whole gamut of Jewish studies. He wrote articles on a wide range of topics. The following are the tip of the iceberg of a few of his essays characterized by thoroughness and depth:

1. At the root of Pushkiniana among the Jews
2. Works of Sholem Aleichem translated into Hebrew
3. A review of a bibliography of Mendel Moicher Seforim
4. The Medzibuz tombstone (the kever of the Baal Shem Tov)
5. Unknown letters of Chayim Nachman Bialik

The Saltykov's libraries publication, Oriental Collection, included Vilsker's sole published work that appeared during the years of perestroika, after his passing. This work is called, The Book of Wisdom by Saeed bin Babshada. It became the basis for numerous studies and publications.

Babshad was a philosopher and poet who lived in Babylon. Firkovich obtained this book from a grave in the Jewish cemetery in Egypt. Small fragments of the book were found by different archaeologists in different times and are now located in different libraries of the world. The Israeli Scientist E Shearman who visited the Leningrad library in 1960 mentioned the manuscript. Vilsker gave the name to the manuscript The Book of Wisdom. Vilsker's knowledge of the literature of the Middle Ages and totality of foreign languages allowed Vilsker to establish a genuine name of the author and the time of his life that belonged to the second half of the $10^{th}$ century and first have of the $11^{th}$ century during the bridge between the Geonim and Rishonim.

Vilsker detected a falsification. The poet and philosopher was not a Karaite as was previously assumed. Vilsker did not challenge the editing that someone has "corrected" the original manuscript itself. However, solving the puzzle involved Vilsker to connect the dots. Vilsker read in a Karaite prayer book a liturgical poem that was an acrostic. This acrostic spelled out the author's name of the work Book of Wisdom. David Ben Babshad Ha-Kohen was the name in the decoded encryption. Vilsker argued that "Saed" and "david "are one and the same person. It is well known that adding the Arabic name by non-Arabs in Arabic speaking countries was widespread in those times. By combining disparate excerpts from the books of Saed Ben Babshad and thus restoring the text, the scientist returned a great poetic work of the medieval author to the worlds' consciousness. A.F. Margolin made a poetic translation into Russian of the Book of Wisdom by Saeed ben Babshad. Dr. Fleischer argued that the author was a Persian Jew and wrote a whole book about Saeed Ben Babshad. Vladimir Lazaris made another translation of 37 couplets from this book chapter "Hymn to Wisdom" which was published in Ariel journal number 15, 1993.

The following is a fragment prose translation by Vilsker:

The moon and the sun are shining- these are the greatest of the stars
But in the light of Wisdom, all stars are pale
The tiaras are numerous; the decorations are luxurious
But Before the crown of Wisdom, all tiaras deteriorate
The pure gold is magnificent; the precious stones are splendid

[«Светит Луна, и Солнце – величайшее из светил,/ Но перед светом Мудрости бледнеют все светила./ Многочисленны короны, обильны украшения,/ Но перед венцом Мудрости ветшают все короны./ Прекрасно чистое золото, великолепны драгоценные камни,/ Но перед прелестью Мудрости все они блекнут/».] [40]

In the preface to his book Proverbs of Saeed bin Babshad Dr. Ezra Fleischer[41] wrote that the Vilsker's labor towards rescuing these fragments are simply infinitely invaluable. "I was looking for ways to see Firkowicz manuscripts. Professor Shearman saw them, but did not study them, and I had been waiting for 15 years." In Fleischer's book that numbers over 300 pages, Fleischer constantly refers to the conclusions and findings of Lev Yefimovich as invaluable.

Vilsker's immediate family included an assemblage of a number of scholars. Dr. Vilsker's wife Dr. Gita Gluskina, the daughter of Rav Menachem Mendel Gluskin, was also a medievalist who published a dissertation on the unpublished manuscript of Rabbi Yehudah Al Harizi author of the Takamoni and a translation of Rambam's Moreh HaNevukhim, also found in the St. Petersburg Saltykov library collection. Dr. Vilsker's sister-in-law Dr. Leah Gluskina was a scholar of the period of the second Temple in Jerusalem. Leah's husband was Dr. David Yosef Amusin who published 100s of articles and over 50 books in various languages on Jewish studies on Dead Sea Scrolls, Biblical exegesis, and history of ancient Israel.

---

[1] Where not otherwise noted (for example (1) documents sent by Dr. Emanuel Gluskin) this section is based on a translation from Russian to English by Dr. Marina Korsakova Kreyn of Shulamit Shalit's article appearing online about Dr. Vilsker at article (in Russian) about Vilsker:
http://berkovich-zametki.com/2009/Zametki/Nomer4/Shalit1.php
Papers in which Vilsker is mentioned:
http://www.islamicmanuscripts.info/reference/articles/Vasilyeva-1996--MO-2-2-Oriental.PDF
http://shomron0.tripod.com/articles/howdidabrahamfirkovichacquire.pdf More: http://www.ejwiki.org/wiki/Вильскер,_Лейб_Хаимович

[2] The technical knowledge proved useful and many years later he was able to change the lock all by himself in a cooperative apartment, and this made the whole of his family very proud.

[3] Tarn writes in response to Shulamith Shalit's article on which my section on Vilsker is based on the "intelligence, civilization, and even sense of humor of the Vilsker family": Alex Tarn Beit Aryeh, Israel - at 2013-01-04 12:19:32 EDT. Only now read this article four years ago

and I cannot help but respond. Thanks to his friendship with the son of Lev Yefimovich Vilsker (ז"ל) and Gita Mendelevna Gluskin (תבדל"א), I had the privilege to know both when I still lived in St. Petersburg; I used to visit their apartment on Vasilevsky. And today, Boris and Katia will be visiting me - so that's a coincidence.

All this wonderful family is an example of intelligence [civilized behavior] in the highest sense of the word. They are the scientists, scribes, moneyless that have saved, despite being swept through the Stalinist terror and the war, and the mud and filth of horrific Soviet life, some implausible emotional softness, kindness, and constant unconditional willingness to help, to respond practically to any human need somehow caught up in their sight. I also owe them a lot.

I want to tell a funny story that I heard from Boris. To put it mildly, they [Vilskers] were not rich. When Lev Efimovitch would go out to buy bread, dressed in his threadbare coat and with a red shopping bag in his hand, he was not distinguished from the good-for-nothings that were crowding at the entrance to the grocery store. Hence this important specialist in the field of Jewish medieval poetry would be regularly stopped with a traditional offer "to be the third" [to share a bottle of alcohol]. Once he laughingly told his son about it. – "Well, what do you answer them?" - Boris asked, knowing his father's unwillingness and inability to offend people with the word "no." – "I always tell them the same thing: "Not now ..." - replied Lev Yefimovich. "Not now." This was the essence of Lev Yefimovich. This expression became our proverb.זכרונו צדיק לברכה .

[4] James L. Lieberman

Yekaterinburg, Russia - at 2013-01-04 11:30:38 EDT

Once I was acquainted with Lev Yefimovich and Gita Mendelevna. They were, if I may say so, my "godparents" in medieval Hebrew poetry. And I always remember that and I will always be grateful to them. I am grateful to fate for having brought me to these wonderful people. Meeting and communicating with them was not just pleasant and helpful; this largely changed me and my attitude towards life and people. 4 January 2013.

[5] Eliezer Rabinovich- at 2010-03-02 15:03:12 EDT

Somehow, I missed this great article before and came across it just now. This article is about a dear person with whom we used to be close and whose books, with his inscriptions, are on my bookshelf. Thank you for the article.

[6] Scholem writes, "To be sure the universities did not encourage Jewish studies in those days. Today, when there are hardly any Jews remaining in Germany all the German Universities are eager to establish chairs in Judaica. But in those days when Germany had a lively Jewish population in great ferment, not a single university or provincial ministry would hear of Jewish studies. What Heine wrote is quite true: If there were only one Jew in the world, everyone would come running to have a look at him, but now that there are too many people try to look away.) See: Scholem, Gershom, "How I came to the Kabbalah" in Commentary, May 1980: 69, 005, p. 40.

[7] Amusin published many hundreds of articles in Jewish studies and over 50 books translated in many languages of the world. Yet Rambi lists only the following 4 in English on the DSS:

1 Amusin, I. D. (Iosif Davidovich) 4Q Testimonia, 15-17. Hommages à André Dupont-Sommer (1971) 357-361 1971
2 Amusin, I. D. (Iosif Davidovich) Bemerkungen zu den Qumran-Kommentaren Bibel und Qumran (1968) 9-19 1968
3 Amusin, I. D. (Iosif Davidovich) Un pamphlet antipharisien de Qumran Vestnik Drevnei Istorii 178 (1986) 133-140 1986 4 Amusin, I. D.(Iosif Davidovich) Qumran parallel to Pliny the Elder's account of the Essenes. Qumran Chronicle 2,2 (1993) 113-116 1993 5 Amusin, I. D. (Iosif Davidovich) The reflection of historical events of the first century B.C. in Qumran commentaries (4Q 161 : 4Q 169; 4Q 166) Hebrew Union College Annual 48 (1977) 123-152 1977.

[8] Although Lea Gluskin was also a great Hebraic scholar, Lea's modesty as an Eishet Chayil is seen in her 2 works on behalf of her husband as an Ezer Kinegdo: [1] Gluskina, Lea N. The life and work of Joseph Amussin (1910-1984) Revue de Qumran 14,1 (1989) 109-120 1989 [2] Gluskina, Lea N. The Teacher of Righteousness in Joseph Amussin's studies Mogilany 1989 II (1991) 7-21 1991.

[9] Both Gita and Lea also received doctorates in Jewish studies. Gita published her dissertation on Rav Yehudah Alharizi's work. Lea was a scholar of 2nd Temple Judaism - including the works of Philo, Josephus, Dead Sea Scrolls, and the formation of the Mishnah. Gita and Lea were 2 of 4 sisters. Esther joined Hashomer HaTzair and was punished by Soviet authorities by being sent to harsh conditions in Siberia. Sonia married a man named Minsk, whose son together was the famous ballet dancer Sasha Minsk. I met with Gita in Givatayim around Chanukah of 2004 and interviewed Dr. Gluskina primarily with regards to her father the Av Bet Din of Minsk Rav Menachem

Mendel Gluskin (ztsl) the son in law of Rabbi Eliezer Rabinowitch who was the son in law of the Minsker Gadol, Rabbi Eliyahu Pearlman.

[10] Shalit, Shulamit, "Aryeh Vilsker and his treasures 1919-1988: On the 90th Anniversary of his Birth", accessed 5/12/16 at 12:00 pm. p.2; At URL.

[11] Jonathan Rose writes, "The Soviets as David Fishman illustrates cultivated their own hostility to expressions of Jewish culture, and after the liberation of Nazi occupied territories the Soviets often continued their literary vandalism begun by the Nazis. Before, after and even during the war with Germany, Soviet authorities suppressed reports of Nazi atrocities against the Jews. Russian scholar Arlen Blium draws on the archives of Soviet censors to show that the crescendo of state-enforced anti-Semitism after the war was spearheaded by the suppression of Jewish authors, publishers, and even literary characters, as well as a complete ban on the publication of Yiddish books. There is good reason to believe that shortly before his death in 1953, Stalin was planning to deport the Jews of the USSR to the far reaches of Siberia. The destruction of books may have been once again a first step toward the destruction of Jews" [The Holocaust and the Book, p. 2].

[12] Shalit, Shulamit, p.7

[13] The retirement age in the Soviet Union was 55 for women and 60 for men.

[14] Shulamit Shalit in reference to a criticism of her article with regards to the understanding of the nature of the

“Samaritan language” retorts: Shulamit Shalit Israel - at 2009-02-18 06:12:39 EDT.

An answer to a nameless reader: The reader - at 2009-02-16 04:58:50 EDT article about Vilsker definitely informative and useful, although it is written in a sugary manner similar to other publications of this author. it is not clear why the author and his Samaritan interlocutor do not know that the Samaritans use Aramaic language. Samaritan language does not exist.

If the Samaritans used Aramaic, Leo Vilsker would not call his book "Samaritan language." Dr. Boris Podolsky, an expert in Semitic languages (Tel Aviv University), explains: "The Samaritan Torah was written in the same Hebrew as the Jewish Torah. However, the Samaritans’ pronunciation is very different from our familiar pronunciation in the Hebrew language; this is why the scientists call this version of the Hebrew language the Samaritan language. Besides, the Samaritans, as well as Jews, had translated the Torah into Aramaic (already 2000 years ago); therefore, it is meaningless to speak of Aramaic as the language of Samaritans.”

One can read in the above-mentioned journal "A-B Hadashot ha-Shomron:" “The journal is published in 4 languages: ancient-Samaritan preserved from the time of the First Temple, Arabic, Hebrew, and English. The journal exists from 1935."

More than half of the Samaritans that are living today in Holon, plus another 4 families (in Benjamin, Givat Ada, Ashdod and Matane), speak Hebrew. Before the first intifada, the Samaritans lived in Nablus, in the old town, but then they moved to Kiryat Luza on Mount Gerizim.

This segment of Samaritans speaks Arabic. Take a note that in the presented tables offer Samaritan Alphabet and Written Letter. If desired, the reader could compare them with the Aramaic alphabet and the letter to see that the written letters are completely different.

I have received a call from Dr. David Joffe, a writer and reader of my site, who personally knew L. Vilsker. He thanked me for the publication and said that he found in it the precise description of Vilsker (as Dr. Joffe remembers him): an intelligent and knowledgeable scholar and a very warm person.

[15] As Lea Gluskin notes in her article, "The Life and Works of Joseph Amusin (1910-1984)" which appeared in Revue de Qumrân 14:1, p.109-120.
[16] "This is how my people have perished" – these words will be said another massacre, eight centuries late, by Chaim Nachman Bialik

[17] Notez Bien: play of words in Hebrew: "... ezkor Dodi dadey Yonati" ... which of course is an allusion to Shir HaShirim: See: 1:13-17

[18] See http://databases.jewishlibraries.org/node/17679

[19] שׁוּבִי שׁוּבִי הַשּׁוּלַמִּית, שׁוּבִי שׁוּבִי וְנֶחֱזֶה-בָּךְ; מַה-תֶּחֱזוּ,
בַּשּׁוּלַמִּית, כִּמְחֹלַת, הַמַּחֲנָיִם

[20] Rashi teaches the metaphor of the woman's breast as a reference to the Beit HaMikdash on the pusek:
אִם-חוֹמָה הִיא, נִבְנֶה עָלֶיהָ טִירַת כָּסֶף; וְאִם-דֶּלֶת הִיא, נָצוּר
9 עָלֶיהָ לוּחַ אָרֶז. If she be a wall, we will build upon her a turret of silver; and if she be a door, we will enclose her with boards of cedar. The breast metaphor also figures as

an allusion to the wildlife, flora and fauna of Eretz Yisrael with the "rose (shoshanim) as a symbol of "redemption" (all of Israel is a 3 petalled rose- that informs halachah to hold the Kiddush cup in the palm of the hand
as a rose" when we read שְׁנֵי שָׁדַיִךְ כִּשְׁנֵי עֳפָרִים, תְּאוֹמֵי צְבִיָּה,
5 הָרוֹעִים, בַּשּׁוֹשַׁנִּים. Thy two breasts are like two fawns
that are twins of a gazelle, which feed among the lilies.
י אֲנִי חוֹמָה, וְשָׁדַי כַּמִּגְדָּלוֹת; אָז הָיִיתִי בְעֵינָיו, כְּמוֹצְאֵת
10 שָׁלוֹם. I am a wall, and my breasts like the towers
thereof; then was I in his eyes as one that found peace.
Rashi teaches that the walls refer to the walls of the Beit HaMikdash in Jerusalem and the doors to the doors of the synaogues in Jerusalem.

[21] Perhaps an allusion to the "doe eyes of Leah" who according to rabbinic texts wept when she learned that she was supposed to marry Esav, and then due to the merit of Rochel, Rochel deprived herself to wait another 7 years by letting her sister marry Yakov first.

[22] The earliest Hebrew handmade book pre 1200 from the Sefardic areas is MS Leningrad, Saltykov-Shedrin Public Library, II Firkovitch B 124 Fols. 64-94, a biblical manuscript copied in 946 in Kairouan (Tunisia); MS Leningrad, II Firkovitch Heb.-Ar. I2440 fols 1-9 was written in Valencia in 1119; The third oldest Hebrew book in libraries I at Oxford i.e. Bod Heb.b1, fols 10-20 (Cowley's Catalogue no 2673), a tractate of the BT. Copied in 1123 by a scribe originating in Libya; MS. Leningrad Heb-Ar I4587 fols 1-14is the 4th oldes, copied in Mahdia (Tunisia) in 1125/6; The 5th oldest Hebrew handmade book is in Hamburg: constituting 3 localized manuscripts from Spain dating from the 12th century, the earliest being MS. Hamburg, Staats-und Universitatsbibliothek Cod. Hebr. 19 (Steinschneider's Catalogue no. 165), a Talmudic copy

produced in Gerona in 1184. From Ashkenazic areas only 4 books have survived all of them late 12thcentury and unlocalized. The earliest is dated 1177 (MS Florence, Bibloteca Nazionale Centrale II-I-7 of Talmudic treaties). From Italy 2 manuscripts (written by 8 copyists) have survived from the late 11th century, the oldest dated 1072/73 (MS Vatican Ebr. 31) and 2 from the 1st half of the 12th century. Thus, Leningrad is home to the 2 oldest handmade Hebrew books due to Firkovitch collecting. It is well known that regarding Biblical texts the Leningrad Codex, Allepo Codex, and Vatican recencion are the oldest Biblical texts known to date besides the revolutionary finding s of the DSS. The DSS date to late 2nd temple and thus predate these medieval manuscripts by almost 1000 years. In short, the richest Leningrad collections whose dated manuscripts have been known until recently only from partial catalogues and handlists, references in literature and some microfilms (partly studies by the French team of the SAFR Database Paleoagreaphical Project) may reveal more dated books possibly. It is clear that Vilsker had knowledge of these unknown texts, but circumstance of historical persecution and limits in publishing his findings prevented in some cases "getting the word out" to make these treasures known to the rest of the scholarly community. That is why Vilsker's discovery for instance of 22 unknown poems of Rav Yehudah HaLevy in Vilsker's library is so revolutionary and represents probably even more undiscovered treasures awaiting tro be proclaimed and announced etc.

[23] Much can be said about the Firkovitch collection. One aspect is its copious Karaite materials. For example, the earliest extant example of a tradition of donating privately owned Sifrei Torah and biblical codices to synagogue foundations is documented there. The Karaite custom of

donating biblical ms to synagogue foundations is attested by many inscriptions in biblical codices in the Firkovitch collection of the National Library of Russia in St. Petersburg etc A scribe notes that the Sifrei Torah he was commissioned to transcribe was intended for synagogue use produced for a certain person and his sister so that it be dedicated to a community in a so-far unidentified town in southern Crimea. (MS St. Petersburg, National Library of Russia EBP 1 A 35; see A Harkavy and HL Strack, Katalog der hebraischeen Bibelhandschriften der Kaiserlichen offentlichen Bibliotkek in St. Petersburg (Leipzig, 1875), p. 220. The Sefer Torah was written in Kokoz. The same scribe was active in Crimea later when he inscribed a dedication in a torah scroll donated to the synagogue of the Karaite community in Solkhat (Staryi Krym).

[24] Given Shulamith Shalit's highly cultured background we wonder if the reference to "windmills" is not that of Cervantes in Don Quixote?

[25] Last words are often significant. Consider for example Yakov's blessing to his sons at the end of Bereishit, or Moshe Rabbenu's blessing of the tribes in Zot HaBracha. In rabbinic texts likewise, rabbinic students know that the last words of Rav Yochanan ben Zakai carried immense wisdom even from beyond the veil etc. In secular texts the last words of Socrates have drawn much ink, including Nietzsche's note that "I owe a cock to Aeschlepius" in fact is an allusion to the deity of healing Aechlepias who with Apollo is allied with medicine and refuot etc. Likewise, the reported last words of the poet Goethe were "mehr licht, mehr licht" ambiguously signifying equivocally the uncertainty if the poet was going to a realm where "there was more light that he sensed" or was the poet just

terrified calling for more light, more light? Whatever in limudei Kodesh, the light of the first day according to Rashi is the light stored up for the righteous in olam habah, to which Rambam in Hilchot teshuva elaborates: העולם הבא אין בו גוף וגויה אלא נפשות הצדיקים בלבד בלא גוף כמלאכי השרת. הואיל ואין בו גויות אין בו לא אכילה ולא שתייה ולא דבר מכל הדברים שגופות בני אדם צריכין להן בעולם הזה. ולא יארע דבר בו מן הדברים שמארעין לגופות בעולם הזה. כגון ישיבה ועמידה ושינה ומיתה ועצב ושחוק וכיוצא בהן. כך אמרו חכמים הראשונים העולם הבא אין בו לא אכילה ולא שתיה ולא תשמיש אלא צדיקים יושבים ועטרותיהם בראשיהן ונהנין מזיו השכינה. הרי נתברר לך שאין שם גוף לפי שאין שם אכילה ושתיה. וזה שאמרו צדיקים יושבין דרך חידה אמרו. כלומר הצדיקים מצויין שם בלא עמל ובלא יגיעה. וכן זה שאמרו עטרותיהן בראשיהן כלומר דעת שידעו שבגללה זכו לחיי העולם הבא מצויה עמהן והיא העטרה שלהן כענין שאמר שלמה בעטרה שעטרה לו אמו. והרי הוא אומר ושמחת עולם על ראשם ואין השמחה גוף כדי שתנוח על הראש כך עטרה שאמרו חכמים כאן היא הידיעה. ומהו זהו שאמרו נהנין מזיו שכינה שיודעים ומשיגין מאמתת הקב"ה מה שאינם יודעים והם בגוף האפל השפל:

[26] The article in the EJ by Lidia Domenica Matassa, John Macdonald, Benyamim Tsedaka, Ayala Loewenstamm, Haïm Z'ew Hirschberg and Shlomo Hofman, which cites the work of Benjamin Tzedakah, a Samaritan academic scholar living in Israel who corresponded extensively with Vilsker, recounts the history of the Samaritans by writing: "Samaritanism is related to Judaism in that it accepts the Torah as its holy book. Samaritans consider themselves to be the true followers of the ancient Israelite religious line. The Samaritan temple was on Mt. Gerizim near Shechem (modern Nablus), where dwindling numbers of Samaritans still live and worship today. Passages in the Hebrew Bible indicate that Mt. Gerizim has a legitimate

(albeit obscure) claim to sanctity through its association with those who visited it. Abraham and Joseph both visited Shechem (Gen. 12:6–7, 13:18–20), as did Joseph (Gen. 37:12–14 and Josh. 24:32). In Deuteronomy (11:29 and 27:12), Moses commanded the Israelites to bless Mt. Gerizim when they entered the land of Canaan. When the Israelites crossed the Jordan, they built an altar on Mt. Ebal (opposite Mt. Gerizim), and six of the tribes faced Mt. Gerizim while blessing the people of Israel as Moses commanded (Josh.8:30–33). Throughout Samaritan history, Samaritans have lived near Mt. Gerizim (Pummer 1968, 8).

After the fall of Samaria (724 B.C.E.), the Assyrian conquerors sent much of the population into exile to be resettled in various parts in the Assyrian empire. Towards the end of the seventh century B.C.E., Josiah tried to reform the cult in Jerusalem and, from then on, the stories and laws of the five first books of the Bible (the Torah, or Pentateuch) were at the heart of Jewish monotheism. The Samaritan tradition maintains that its Torah (the Samaritikon) dates to the time of Moses and that it was copied by Abiša ben Phineas shortly after the Israelite entered the land of Canaan. However, modern literary analysis and criticism does not support this position. In describing the origins of the Samaritans, the EJ, continues, "There are a number of theories about the origins of the Samaritans, all of which have in common a tradition that originally the cult of the Hebrew G-d was widespread through the land of Israel. Even so, the origins and early history of the Samaritans are quite problematic because the sources are far removed from the events and because the non-Samaritan sources tend to be hostile.

[27] Alexander Marx as reported by Solomon Goldman encouraged ambitious dissertation seekers to tackle the

Damascus Arabic translation of the Samritan Pentateuch acquired and housed in the JTSA collection.

[28] וַיָּבֵא מֶלֶךְ-אַשּׁוּר מִבָּבֶל וּמִכּוּתָה וּמֵעַוָּא וּמֵחֲמָת, וּסְפַרְוַיִם, וַיֹּשֶׁב בְּעָרֵי שֹׁמְרוֹן, תַּחַת בְּנֵי יִשְׂרָאֵל; וַיִּרְשׁוּ, אֶת-שֹׁמְרוֹן, וַיֵּשְׁבוּ, בְּעָרֶיהָ

[29] Baillet, Maurice, Review, “Manuel d’arameen samaritain, par L.H Vilsker. Traduit du russe par J. Margain. Paris : Editions du Centre Nationale de la Recherche Scientifique, 1981, in Journal of Near Eastern Studies, vol. 42, no.4 (Oct. 1983), University of Chicago Press, p.295.

[30] See: Kahle, Paul, Der hebraische Bibeltext, p. 68.

[31] Baillet, Maurice, Journal of Near Eastern Studies, vol. 42, no.4 (oct. 1983), book review of Manuel d’arameen samaritain. Par L. H. Vilsker. Traduit du russe par J. Margain. Paris: Editions du Centre National de la Recherche Sceintifique, 1981. p. 297.

[32] The EJ writes, “according to Josephus, they once more come into view in Judea, where Manasseh, the brother of the high priest Jaddus, married Nikaso, a daughter of Sanballat III (a descendant of the Sanballat of the time of Nehemiah) (Jos., Ant 11:302–3; Mor 1989, 4). Josephus reports that this Sanballat, like his ancestor a governor of Samaria, hoped that through the marriage of his daughter to the high priest's brother he could establish ties with the Jewish community in Jerusalem. However, Manasseh was offered two choices by the Jerusalem hierarchy: to stay in Jerusalem and divorce his wife, or to leave the city and take his Samaritan wife with him. Manasseh chose the second option, whereupon his father-in-law promised to

build a temple on Mt. Gerizim where Manasseh would be high priest and that, in addition, he would take over civic leadership of Samaria on the death of his father-in-law. According to Josephus, many priests left Jerusalem and followed Manasseh to Samaria (Ant. 11:306–12; Mor 1989, 5). Sanballat III sent 8,000 soldiers to support Alexander's campaigns and also convinced him that it would be to his advantage to allow the Samaritans to build a temple on Mt. Gerizim, where his son-in-law would be high priest. During this period when the Macedonians were consolidating their hold on the region and the Persians were not yet fully vanquished, the Samaritans quickly built their temple (it took less than nine months). The founding of a temple was not unusual; however, this temple was not far from its Jerusalem rival, and from the establishment of this temple the Samaritans and the Jews grew further apart, and it is from this period onwards that much of the anti-Samaritan polemic in the Hebrew Bible and extra-biblical texts (such as Josephus) originates.

The temple was completed around 332 B.C.E., at the time that Alexander finally took control of Gaza (Mor 1989, 7), and was also contemporary with the establishment of a Macedonian colony in the city of Samaria and the rebuilding and resettling of Shechem (Purvis 1968, 105).However, Sanballat III died just two months into Alexander's siege of Gaza (Jos., Ant. 11:325) and, according to the historian Quintus Curtius, after the siege of Gaza Alexander left a Greek official named Andromachus in charge of the region. Despite Sanballat III's promise to his son-in-law, and for the first time since the Persian conquest, a Samaritan was not in charge of Samaria (Mor 1989, 9). The Samaritan leadership reacted strongly to this, rebelled against the Macedonians, captured and burned Andromachus alive, and then fled from Shechem to a cave in the Wadi Daliyeh just north of Jericho (Cross 1985, 7–17). The Macedonians retaliated immediately, with Alexander himself said to have left Jerusalem to punish the Samaritans. All of the rebels were killed, all Samaritans were banished from Samaria, and the city of Samaria was settled with Macedonian veterans (Mor 1989, 10). According to Josephus (Jos., Apion, 2:43), following the post-rebellion massacre, administrative control of the district of Samaria was given to the Jews because of their loyalty to Alexander. The Samaritans who survived the Macedonian massacre, and who had heretofore exercised control and political authority and cultural leadership in Samaria, were now wholly disenfranchised and they could not turn to Jerusalem for help. From the death of Alexander the Great, nothing much is known about the Samaritans until the rise of the Seleucid empire in around 200 B.C.E. From Josephus (Ant. 12:5–10) we know that a number of Samaritans and Jews settled in Egypt and that relations between them were very strained, with each side demanding that sacrifices be directed to their respective sanctuaries. Any grace or favor to one side was seen as detrimental to the other, and so a tit-for-tat hostility developed. In Palestine, the first report of open hostility between Shechemites and Jews in Jerusalem is dated to the time of Ptolemy V (Epiphanes) and Antiochus III in around 200 B.C.E. (Jos., Ant. 12:154–56). According to Josephus, the Jews were being harassed by Samaritans through raids on Jewish land and the capture and sale of Jews into slavery, and the Samaritans found themselves under pressure from Antiochus III, because they had allied themselves with pro-Ptolemaic policy, thinking that they would prevail against the Syrians. This was nothing new. This loyalty dated back to the Persian period when Sanballat the Horonite and Tobiah the Ammonite had allied against Nehemiah, the governor of the province of

Judaea." In 168 B.C.E. the two groups grew still further apart when the Seleucid king (Antiochus IV Epiphanes) ordered the Jews and the Samaritans to rededicate their temples to Zeus. In Judea, *Judah Maccabee organized a rebellion which culminated in the ousting of Zeus from the temple and its subsequent repurification. During this period, both Samaritans and Jews were subject to the persecutions of Antiochus IV Epiphanes (175–164 B.C.E.), as is seen in II Maccabees (5:23; 6:2), even though Samaria did not rebel against Antiochus IV. What had been a religious division now became a political conflict as well. Judea, having fought for its freedom from Seleucid rule, became an independent state, ruled by a line of high priests derived from the Hasmonean dynasty. One of them was John *Hyrcanus (134–104 B.C.E.), whose political program included the expansion of the state along with a campaign of propaganda to advertise itself and, as part of this campaign, Hyrcanus utilized a policy of forced conversion to Judaism. While Antiochus VII (Sidetes) was in the east, John Hyrcanus invaded northern Palestine and Syria.Among the places he captured were Shechem and Mt. Gerizim. Later in his reign, Hyrcanus laid siege to Samaria and after a year's campaign took it (Jos., Wars 1:64ff; Ant. 13:275ff.). The bustling, cosmopolitan, and mainly non-Israelite city of Samaria was utterly destroyed by Hyrcanus (Isser 1999, 571), and in around 128 B.C.E., the sanctuary and temple on Mt. Gerizim were destroyed (Jos., Wars 1:62f.; Ant. 13:254ff.).While the Jewish priesthood ceased to function after 70 C.E., the Samaritans continued to have an active priesthood with a high priest even after the temple on Mt. Gerizim was destroyed (Pummer 1998, 26–27), and whereas the inevitable dispersal of the Samaritans had not yet happened, the process was underway, not least because the Samaritans were now under the economic and political control of

Jerusalem. However, a core group of Samaritans stayed near Mt. Gerizim in the town of Sychar (which may have replaced Shechem as the center of Samaritan religious authority). There are very few sources other than Josephus to help outline the history of the Samaritans in the early Roman period, and those that do exist are often very hostile to their subject. Josephus, for instance, did not even consider the Samaritans to be Jews (Ant. 11:341). Pompey's conquest of Palestine in 63 B.C.E. ended Jewish domination of Samaria (Jos., Wars 1:166). The cities that had been captured by the Hasmoneans were restored to their previous inhabitants. Samaria and other regions were joined to the Roman province of Syria and protected by two full Roman legions. Because so many of the people of Samaria had been killed or were too scattered to bring back together, the Romans repopulated the newly built town of Samaria with new colonists (Jos., Wars 1:169f.; Ant. 14:90f.; Isser 1999, 572). The proconsul of Syria, Aulus Gabinius (57–54 B.C.E.) had to quell an uprising by another Hasmonean, Alexander, son of Aristobulus, during which Roman soldiers sought refuge and came under siege on Mt. Gerizim. (Jos., Wars 1:175ff.; Ant. 14:100). In 43 B.C.E., with Roman backing, *Herod the Great restored order in Samaria (Jos., Wars 1:229; Ant. 14:284; Isser 1999, 572). At the end of the Roman civil war, Herod declared his loyalty to Octavian, who confirmed him as the Jewish king and conferred on him new territories (Jos., Wars 1:396ff.; Ant. 14:217); among these new territories was Samaria. Herod rebuilt and extended the city of Samaria and added a further 6,000 colonists to its population. He renamed the city Sebaste in honor of Octavian (Jos., Wars 1:403; Ant. 14:295ff.; Isser 1999, 573). There are numerous reports of acts of hostility against the Jews by Samaritans. How true these are is unknown, but there does seem to be a prevailing tradition of antagonism between the groups. As an example of the sort of thing reported, Josephus records that during the procuratorship of Coponius (6–9 C.E.) it had been the practice to keep the gates of the Jerusalem temple open after midnight at Passover. On one such occasion, a number of Samaritans are said to have secretly entered and scattered human bones throughout the grounds, rendering them unclean (Ant. 18:29f.). There is another account in Josephus (Ant. 18:85–89) about a massacre of Samaritans during the Procuratorship of Pilate (26–36 C.E.). Josephus reports that a man whom he describes as a rabble-rouser promised to show the Samaritans the sacred vessels of the mishkan (the ancient tabernacle) which, according to Samaritan tradition, Moses had buried in a secret place on Mt. Gerizim. This discovery would signal the Age of Divine Favor (the fulfillment of Samaritan eschatological belief involving Moses, the mishkan and a person (the "rabble-rouser") who was a sort of messianic figure–the "restorer"). A large group gathered in a nearby village with the intention of climbing Mt. Gerizim, but Pilate interpreted this as the prelude to revolt and so the gathered Samaritans were intercepted by Roman troops and killed or captured. The leaders were executed at Pilate's orders. This was too much for the Samaritan council, who complained to Vitellius, the governor of Syria, who accepted their accusations against Pilate and sent Marcellus to take over in Judea and ordered Pilate to return to Rome for trial before the emperor Tiberius. This Pilate did, but Tiberius had died, and we know nothing further about this episode (Grabbe 1994, 424; Isser 1999, 576). An even more serious event occurred during the Procuratorship of Cumanus (48–52 C.E.) at a village named Gema (between Samaria and the Plain of Esdraelon to the north). Josephus reports that some Samaritans attacked a group of Galileans who were on their way to Jerusalem for a festival and killed either many or one (War 2:12:3, 232; Ant. 20, 6:1, 118; Tacitus, Annals XII, 54). When the Jews appealed to Cumanus he did nothing (allegedly because he had been bribed by the Samaritans). A mob of Jews took matters into their own hands and attacked some Samaritan villages. Cumanus then intervened, and both Jews and Samaritans appealed to the Syrian governor, Quadratus. After a preliminary investigation, Quadratus sent Cumanus, the military tribune Celer, some of the Samaritan notables, the high priests Jonathan and Ananias, and other Jewish leaders to Rome for trial before Claudius. Agrippa II petitioned Claudius on behalf of the Jews and Claudius found in their favor, executing the Samaritan delegation and exiling Cumanus. The tribune Celer was taken back to Jerusalem and executed publicly there (Isser 1999, 574–75).

[33] משנה מסכת ראש השנה פרק ב
משנה א אם אינן מכירין אותו משלחין אחר עמו להעידו בראשונה היו מקבלין עדות החדש מכל אדם משקלקלו המינין התקינו שלא יהו מקבלין אלא מן המכירים:
משנה ב בראשונה היו משיאין משואות משקלקלו הכותים התקינו שיהו שלוחין יוצאין:

[34] משנה ג
כיצד היו משיאין משואות מביאין כלונסאות של ארז ארוכין וקנים ועצי שמן ונעורת של פשתן וכורך במשיחה ועולה לראש ההר ומצית בהן את האור ומוליך ומביא ומעלה ומוריד עד שהוא רואה את חברו שהוא עושה כן בראש ההר השני וכן בראש ההר השלישי:

[35]

משנה ד
ומאין היו משיאין משואות מהר המשחה לסרטבא ומסרטבא לגרופינא ומגרופינא לחוורן ומחוורן לבית בלתין ומבית בלתין

לא זזו משם אלא מוליך ומביא ומעלה ומוריד עד שהיה רואה כל הגולה לפניו כמדורת האש

משנה ה [36]
חצר גדולה היתה בירושלים ובית יעזק היתה נקראת ולשם כל העדים מתכנסים ובית דין בודקין אותם שם וסעודות גדולות עושין להם בשביל שיהו רגילין לבא [*] בראשונה לא היו זזין משם כל היום התקין רבן גמליאל הזקן שיהו מהלכין אלפים אמה לכל רוח ולא אלו בלבד אלא אף החכמה הבאה לילד והבא להציל מן הדליקה ומן הגייס ומן הנהר ומן המפולת הרי אלו כאנשי העיר ויש להם אלפים אמה לכל רוח:

[37]
משנה ו כיצד בודקין את העדים זוג שבא ראשון בודקין אותו ראשון ומכניסין את הגדול שבהן ואומרים לו אמור כיצד ראית את
הלבנה לפני החמה או לאחר החמה לצפונה או לדרומה כמה היה גבוה ולאין היה נוטה וכמה היה רחב אם אמר לפני החמה לא אמר כלום ואחר כך היו מכניסים את השני ובודקין אותו אם נמצאו דבריהם מכוונים עדותן קיימת ושאר כל הזוגות שואלין אותם ראשי דברים לא שהיו צריכין להן אלא כדי שלא יצאו בפחי נפש בשביל שיהו רגילים לבא:

משנה ז
ראש בית דין אומר מקודש וכל העם עונין אחריו מקודש מקודש בין שנראה בזמנו בין שלא נראה בזמנו מקדשין אותו ר' אלעזר בר צדוק אומר אם לא נראה בזמנו אין מקדשין אותו שכבר קדשוהו שמים:

משנה ח [38]
דמות צורות לבנות היו לו לרבן גמליאל בטבלא ובכותל בעלייתו שבהן מראה את ההדיוטות ואומר הכזה ראית או כזה מעשה שבאו שנים ואמרו ראינוהו שחרית במזרח וערבית במערב אמר רבי יוחנן בן נורי עדי שקר הם כשבאו ליבנה קיבלן רבן גמליאל ועוד באו שנים ואמרו ראינוהו בזמנו ובליל עבורו לא נראה וקבלן רבן גמליאל אמר רבי דוסא בן הרכינס עדי שקר הן היאך

מעידים על האשה שילדה ולמחר כריסה בין שיניה אמר לו ר' יהושע רואה אני את דבריך:

[39]

משנה ט

שלח לו רבן גמליאל גוזרני עליך שתבא אצלי במקלך ובמעותיך ביום הכפורים שחל להיות בחשבונך הלך ומצאו רבי עקיבא מיצר אמר לו יש לי ללמוד שכל מה שעשה רבן גמליאל עשוי שנאמר (ויקרא כ"ג) אלה מועדי ה' מקראי קודש אשר תקראו אתם בין בזמנן בין שלא בזמנן אין לי מועדות אלא אלו בא לו אצל רבי דוסא בן הרכינס אמר לו אם באין אנו לדון אחר בית דינו של רבן גמליאל צריכין אנו לדון אחר כל בית דין ובית דין שעמד מימות משה ועד עכשיו שנאמר (שמות כ"ד) ויעל משה ואהרן נדב ואביהוא ושבעים מזקני ישראל ולמה לא נתפרשו שמותן של זקנים אלא ללמד שכל שלשה ושלשה שעמדו בית דין על ישראל הרי הוא כבית דינו של משה נטל מקלו ומעותיו בידו והלך ליבנה אצל רבן גמליאל ביום שחל יום הכפורים להיות בחשבונו עמד רבן גמליאל ונשקו על ראשו אמר לו בוא בשלום רבי ותלמידי רבי בחכמה ותלמידי שקבלת דברי:

Dr. Joseph Baumgarten has juxtaposed this famous Mishnah in Maseket RH with the incident conveyed in the DSS whereby the priest of the Dead Sea Qumran sect also arrived at a different Yom Kippur calculation than that of the Sadducee Kohen in Jerusalem. The politics of authority and acknowledge of the "true calendrical reckoning" for Yom Kippur thus not only have a dimension of astronomical precision and accuracy but also a political dimension of "whose authority? Which calendar? Which Yom Kippur calendrical reckoning?"

[40] And here are the translations by V. Lazaris: "Солнце с Луною – их ярче не сыщешь светил,/ Но Мудрости свет все другие светила затмил./ Сверкают короны, алмазный рассыпавши свет,/ Но рядом с короною

Мудрости места им нет./... Забудут героев, забудут отважных бойцов,/ И в памяти высекут лишь имена мудрецов./... Кто деньги добыл, тот богатство свое стережет,/ Кто Мудрость нашел, тот счастливым себя назовет./... На трапезу к Мудрости стоит всегда поспешить/ И есть ее хлеб, и вино ее сладкое пить./... Кто льнет к вам с любовью – в друзья не берите таких,/ Дружите лишь с ней, что вернее и ближе других»...

[41] Dr. Fleischer was the head of the Geniza Hebrew Poetry Institute originally founded by Schocken and transplanted to Israel with the rise of Nazi oppression.

## **THE LIFE AND WORK OF JOSEPH AMUSSIN** (1910 – 1948)

*Note de la rédaction : Comme hommage à la mèmoire du pionnier des ètudes qumrànniennes en Union Soviètique, J. D. Amussin, nous publions ici le texte intègral d'une communication de son èpouse N. L. Gluskina, dans laquelle elle nous donne un rèsumè des contributions qumràniennes de son mari. Dr Z. J. Kapera a annotè le texte et a prèsentè aussi la bibliographie de J. D. Amussin imprimèe aux pp. 121-126.*

By N. Leah Gluskina

Joseph Amussin was born in Vitebsk (Belorussia) on November 29, 1910.[1] In his Jewish family, he was the eldest son and had a brother and two sisters. His father was a leather expert and had to work hard to support the family. Joseph Amussin's childhood coincided with the First World War, the Revolution and the years of civil war. The time was rather hard for the family, but the father, himself uneducated, realized that his son was a gifted boy and tried to give him a good education. Joseph Amussin often remembered his father advising him to learn Hebrew and the history of the Jewish culture while saying that he would be able to learn all other things later, but not these. Luckily the boy encountered a very good teacher, a broad minded and educated man, who trained his pupil for serious studies, developed his intellect and became his first adult deeply esteemed friend.

Amussin read a lot but mainly in Hebrew and according to his account even Tolstoy's "Cossacks" he first read in Hebrew.

At the age of fourteen he left Vitebsk permanently and came to Leningrad. Henceforth, the main events of his life were to be connected with that splendid city.

After many years in search of his true destination Joseph Amussin, on the advice of Academician V. V. Struve,[2] in 1935 entered Leningrad University (Historical Department). While still a student he began his studies in ancient history and prepared a paper, "Pushkin and Tacitus," highly appreciated by specialists and published in 1941 in "Pushkinskiy Vremenik".

When he was taking his final exam at the University the war broke out. Immediately after graduation from the University he enlisted in the army and took part in the war, first as a private soldier and then as lieutenant (1941-1945). During the siege of Leningrad his father like thousands of other inhabitants of the city, died of starvation and Amussin, as the eldest son, felt it his duty to support his mother. Thus, after the war he had to combine his scientific studies with work in order to earn money. He began lecturing in Ancient history and the Leningrad Pedagogic Institute while simultaneously preparing as a post-graduate student of the Institute of Oriental Studies, his first dissertation. It was based on the Emperor Claudius' famous letter to the Alexandrines (P. London 1912) and was devoted to the Emperor's policy towards the Jews.[3]

In 1949 Amussin received his first post-graduate degree. By that time, he had published some papers on his subject in Vestnik Drevney Istorii.[4] In these first papers, he already displayed the characteristic features of his future works: a great interest in philological interpretations of the texts, a careful study of each word and expression; on this basis, he drew historical conclusions which revealed true historic facts.

After getting his degree J. Amussin encountered great difficulties and had a hard time, since he failed to find a job in his field in Leningrad and elsewhere, despite many attempts. At last he left Leningrad for Ulianovsk, Lenin's native city, where he taught ancient history from 1950 till 1954 at the Pedagogic Institute. During that time, he published some papers dealing with the Biblical tradition. Two of them aroused special interest: "The designation of slaves in Hellenistic Egypt according to the Septuagint" (1952)[5] and "The people of the earth (am haaretz)" (1955).[6] Both were translated into other languages (the first into Japanese in 1958, the second into Italian in 1986, posthumously).[7]

In the fall of 1954 Amussin returned to Leningrad very ill after a serious nervous breakdown which he suffered in 1953. He recovered (only partially) several months later and then began to work as an assistant academician of A. I. Tiumenev,[8] continuing till Tiumenev's death in 1959.

From 1960 till the end of his life Amussin was an associate at the Leningrad Department of the Institute of Oriental Studies and the Academy of Sciences in the USSR. Here in 1966 he received his doctor's degree. Only at this institute was he offered the opportunity to devote all his time to scholarly research. These were the happiest years of his hitherto hard life. His work resulted in about 150 publications, including four books: 1) The dead Sea Manuscripts (1960, 1961); 2) The discoveries in the Dead Sea Region (1964, 1965); 3) The Qumran Texts vol. 1. Translation, introduction and Commentary (1971); 4) The Qumran Community (1983). His books and some of his articles were translated into Greek, Japanese, Romanian, Hungarian, Polish, Slovak and Georgian. Some papers were published by Amussin himself in English, German and French (Qumran-Probleme, 1962; Revue de Qumràn, `1963, 1971, 1974; Israel Exploration Journal, 1964; Hommages à André Dupont-Sommer, 1971; Klio, 1981, etc.

All his books and about 65% of his papers dealt with problems connected with the Dead Sea Scrolls.[9] When he came across the first publications of these texts he appreciated in full their immense significance for the history of biblical tradition, of the social and ideological tendencies in pre-Roman and Roman Palestine, of the predecessors of the Christian communities. He was especially interested in the identification of the Qumran community and finally shared the widespread opinion that is had been a branch of the Essene movement.

Much consideration was given by Amussin to the colourful and mysterious image of the Qumran Teacher of Righteousness. He never doubted that the Teacher was not a mythical but a genuine historical personality and might also be the author of some of the Qumran texts. After the Teacher had been prosecuted and put to death by enemies led by the "Impious Priest".

He published on all aspects of the Dead Sea Scrolls including the commentary of Habbakuk, Damascus Document, commentaries on Psalms, as well as Micha, Nachum and the Isaiah scroll. He illuminated how historical events alluded to in the scrolls correlated with ancient historiographical accounts and how the sect, although not Christian, shared some (not all) elements theologically with later Christian developments. He showed how the sects historical allusions are coded in encryptions out of fear of governmental censorship.

He argued that Demetrius is Demetrius 3 Eucairos (95-83 BCE) who had been called upon by the Rabbis in 88 BCE to aid them in their rebellion against Jannaeus (103-76 BCE) until his wife Alexandra Salome (76-67) reinstated the Pharisees to power. He proved that the subsequent struggle between their two sons Aristobulos and Hyrcanus, the first supported by the Sadducees, the second the Pharisees, resulted in the Roman intrusion under Pompeius in 63 B.C. The groups of Pharisees and the Sadducees were both mentioned in a critical manner by the commentator (Ephraim/Manasseh) under various symbolic names. However, he treated them differently. Among the Pharisees he distinguished the leaders from the common adherents and hoped that the rank and file members could be converted and might switch to the side of the Qumranians.

The designations of Alexander Jannaeus as the "Lion of Wrath" and "the Wicked Priest" indicate hostility and Amussin was inclined to identify him with the chief enemy of the Teacher of Righteousness.[10]

Amussin gave special attention to the self-designations of the Qumran community found only in the commentaries and expressive of their social programme and ideology.

Amusin revealed the social conscience of the DSS sect as the poor, ascetic, and simple in phrases such as "the congregation of the poor", "the simple ones of Judah", "the doers of the law", "the elect of G-d", and even "the new covenant" of this sect that held property in common a form of communism *avant la letter* but unlike Marxism that called religion "the opiate of the masses" for the sake of the spiritual religious life as a form of Religious Messianic Utopianism. The Pharisaic Talmudic tradition regarding poverty and wealth as predestined for every individual and existing even after the coming of the messiah differed with the DSS sect who like Christians saw poverty as a virtue. Amusin also dealt with dating of the DSS such as the Manual (1QS) and the Hymns (1QH) being composed earlier than the Commentaries but the Damascus Document (CD)- later. Amusin also traced anti-Talmudic polemic against Qumran theology such as dualism. While DBL has shown that this polemic of the rabbis is against Zorastrianism, Amusin noted that the Qumran sects' designation of "the sons of light" vs. "the sons of darkness" probably was an attack on the Romans. The separate calendar of the DSS sect, their disdain for the corruption in the Jerusalem temple allied with the Roman government, and their otherworldly emphasis on 2 worlds, this and the next, suggested great differences with the Pharisees not to mention the Sadducees. This in part is the subject of DBL's paper delivered at the Cleveland AJL Conference.[11] However, DBL does not focus on the DSS sect's attack on the Jerusalem priesthood during the Roman times whereby the Qumran sect railed against "the priests who have done violence to my torah" evoking out of context Ezekiel 22, 26 and Zephaniah 3,4). In short Amusin's work in part sought to understand the political historical background of corruption from which the DSS sect retreated to the Judean Desert near Ein Gedi. From revealing the historical background of the 'prayer of Nabonidus" who engaged in moon worship, to the historical context of the Nabatean King Aretas called in for help by Hyrcanus, to the Pseudo Cyprian epistle, and the DSS sect as a precursor of Christianity, there was not any aspect of DSS that escaped Amusin's notice or philological and Historical textual analysis. At the end of Amusin's life he followed his social consciousness devoting himself to writing papers on the living conditions of the vulnerable mentioned in the bible such as the poor, widows, and orphans in Ancient Palestine, as well as the legal position of Gerim and toshavim, revealing the policies of the authorities of reigning governments with regards to social help towards the native population. Thus, Mark Cohen in his two-volume set on the _Voice of the Poor_ in the Cairo Geniza that gathers texts that shed light on the Kahal's attention to protecting the vulnerable in medieval society, although a different epoch, also is scholarship motivated by a social conscience, as the Talmud Tractate Maseket Berachot states with regards to when the shema is to be recited at night, "when the poor man returns home (after a hard day of work) to eat his meager dinner of "bread with salt."

*In her original article from p. 112 onwards Leah gives many more details and descriptions of his work.*

For decades Amussin investigated the Qumran texts and other historical sources which could be analyzed in some connection with the Qumran sect. The Qumran studies were for him primarily the investigation of texts. He was both a historian and a philologist. Every paper written by him attracted attention and was much appreciated by other scholars. Unfortunately, only a small part of his writings was translated into European languages whereas many experts in this field have no knowledge of Russian.

Devoting much of his time to Qumran studies, Amussin did not lose his interest in biblical tradition. In the last years of his life he published some papers dealing with the living conditions of the poor including widows and orphans, in ancient Palestine. He was particularly interested in the social and legal position of the non-citizens (gerim and toshavim) trying to elucidate the meaning and differences between the various groups. He also posed the question as to the motives that made people leave their native places and move to foreign lands where they did not obtain equal rights with the native population. Amussin gave much attention to revealing the policy of the authorities towards the newcomers and to explain the causes of social help due to them.

He contradicted the widespread opinion about the identity of the Gerim with the Athenian metics and while recognizing some common features in their status underlined the prevailing significance of obvious differences.[12]

In these papers as well as in his Qumran studies Amussin displayed a scholarly interest in details and at the same time did his best to present a general picture of socio-economic relations. Never did he deviate from the approach he had chosen at the very outset of his research career.

He dreamed of writing a book about the famous anti-Roman revolt of Bar Kochba. But the circumstances of his life were not favourable for carrying out a task. He had a lot of plans and intentions.

On June 12, 1984, his fruitful work and was brought to an end by death. The complete article was published in Revue de Qumran Vol 14 No.1 (53) June 1989 p. 109-120. A bibliography of J.D. Amussin concerning the dead sea scrolls p.121-126, by Zdzislaw J. Kapera.

## Sonia Gluskin

Leah (left), Emik, Sonya, 1960

Sonia on an expedition during Summer 1986 in Panikovichi, Pechora district.

Lisa Ilinichna Volpert (March 30 1926 – October 1 2017) married Pavel Semenovich Reyfman. She graduated literature in S. Petersburg State University, taught at the

Pskov Pedagogel Institute. She won the USSR Women's Chess Championships three times (1954, 1957, 1059) and finished second in Women's World Championship in 1955. She won the title of International Female Grandmaster in 1977. She taught Russian philology and connection of Russian poetry with French literature. Lisa was a good friend of Sonya.

reifman.ru/memoirs/o_pskove/

## CENSORSHIP DURING THE REVOLUTIONARY, SOVIET AND POST-SOVIET RUSSIA

P.S. Reyfman Tales of Pskov

In 1950 the train left Leningrad in the evening, and in the morning arrived in Pskov. In my compartment (I was travelling in a reserved seat), on the opposite bottom shelf was a pretty blonde woman with an intelligent face of 30 years. I talked with her. She lived in Pskov and as it turned out, worked at the Pedagogical Institute in the Russian Language Department.

After learning my story, she said that thre is a small chance to go to work in the institute, because they now have an urgent need for a teacher of methods for teaching literature. They recently refused candidates of science since they were looking for a specialist – methodologist with a science degree. Now, there is no one and they are desperate to take anyone. She offered to introduce me to the head of the literature department.

I told her that I have no idea about methodology on teaching literature, since we did not read such a coure at the university (We read something but did not take it seriously). If I were to be offered to teach such a course I would refuse, but Sonia, who was type of genius, patiently persuaded me. She explained that many begin with this course and then pass it on to the next teacher who came to work. I had a letter of recommendation but after she found out who it was from, advised me not to show it. We talked till 3:00 am.

The next morning, directly from the train, Sonya took me to a teaching hostel in Zapkovka, where she lived. The head of the Department of Literature, Maria Titovna Efimova, came to meet Sonya in shabby appearance and upon seeing me was embarrassed and bothered. Sonya who was friendly with her told her about me, we talked a little, I liked it and we immediately went to the university authorities. The director was not in Pskov at that time. We were recived by his deputy, assistant professor Lygun a pedagogue specialist and thus someone directly interested in teaching the methodology. Maria Titovna recommended me, and he agreed to formalize work for me.

When Sonya went on holidays to Leningrad, she gave me the keys to her room in the hostel.

I became friends with the teachers of the other departments which somehow happened that most of them were Jews. First of all, it is necessary to mention that thanks to Sonya Mendelevna Gluskin, I got to the Pskov Pedagogal Institute. She was a serious researcher, a pupil of the great scientist-linguist Professor Larin, a good teacher, highly intelligent and decent woman, polite and benevolent with the majority of teachers but careful with whom she is close. She was not close to me, although she treated me very well, especially at the beginning. I was too straightforward and "Soviet" for her, and a few instances overshadowed our relationship.

Due to my influence, she applied for membership in the party, and she was refused. She acted with my recommendation and even though the outcome was not my fault some residue remained. After this I somewhat disassociated myself from her and did not express my solidarity with her, creating resentmentabout the decision of the meeting. She had every reason to be accepted. A war veteran who volunteered for the army, an excellent teacher and a principled woman. But, she had something else in her biography, that her father was a Rabbi. Others were accepted even though there were reasons not to, but Sonya was not accepted. I still cannot forgive myself for the stupidity of my advice and misunderstanding the situation.

Recently, Natasha Orlova, a favorite student of Sonya, visited us from Prague. She told me that Sonya was offended because I somehow refused her when she asked me to let her live in my room when I was absent. I was motivated by the fact that this may be misinterpreted by others. Of course this was self-centered behavior, especially for how much she helped me when I first came there. During the difficult times for Sonya, I was somewhat alienated from her, subconsciously afraid of compromising myself. Significantly, in later years Sonya was very close with N. Ya. Mandelstam who worked for several years in the Pskov Pedagogal Institute.

----------

*Source:* http://majmin.pskgu.ru/page/82db1dfb-40b0-4ee8-9352-03d63922688a

*Kostyuchuk L. Teachers of teachers // Pskov Chronicler: Local history almanac. 2010. №3 (4). Pp. 119-124.*

[1] Cf. obituaries in: Vestnik Drevnej Istorii 1984, No. 4 (171), p. 220 and Israel Exploration Journal 35, 1985, p. 76; a bio-bibliographical note in: S. D. Miliband, Biobibliograficeskij slovar' sovelskich vostokovedov, Moskva 1975, Nauka, p. 31f.

[2] One of the most eminent Leningrad scholars of this century; an expert on the ancient Near East. Cf. Miliband, op. cil., pp. 534-536.

[3] Cf. Poslanie imperatora Klavdija k aleksandrijcam (41g. n.e.) kak istocnik dlja social' no-politiceskoj istorii 1 v. n.e., Leningrad 1949, Institut Vostokovedenija Akademii Nauk SSSR, 22 pp. (summary of the dissertation).

[4] Pis'mo i edikt imperatora Klavdja (k voprosu o podlinnosti edikta u Flavija), Vestnik Drevnej Istorii 1949, No. 2, pp. 221-228. Cf. also: K ediklu Tiberija Julija Aleksandra (OGIS 11, 669), Vestnik Drevnej Istorii 1949, No. 1, pp. 73-75.

[5] Terminy oboznacajuscie rabov v ellenisticeskom Egipte po dannym Septuaginty, Vestnik Drevnej Istorii 1952, No. 3, pp. 46-67.

[6] "Narod zemli". (K voprosu o svobodnych zemledel'cach drevnej Azii), Vestnik Drevnej Istorii, No. 2 pp. 14-36.

[7] I termini dsignanti la schia itù dell'Egitto ellenistico in base di storia antica, in: I Biezunska-Malowist (ed)., Problemi e richeche di storia antica, 9. Schiavitù e produzione nella Roma republican, Roma 1986, pp. 107-146.

[8] One of the best Soviet historians of antiquity interested in ancient Near East. Cf. his bibliography in Miliband, op. cit., pp. 560f.

[9] See the Bibliography by Z. J. Kapera, infra, pp. 121-126.

[10] Cf. Kumranskie kommetarii, Vestnik Drevnej Istorii 1968, No.4, pp.91-108 (English summary, p.108); The Qumran Commentaries and their Significance for the History of the Qumran Community, Moscow 1867, xxviith International Congress of Orientalists. Papers Presented by the U.S.S.R. Delegation, 14 pp. (cf. a review by Z.J. Kapera in the Revue de Qumran 6, 1967-1969, pp. 590f); The Reflection of Historical Events of the First Century B.C. in Qumran Commentaries (4Q161; 4Q169; 4Q166) Hebrew Union College Annual 48, 1977, pp. 123-152; and Kumranskie kommentarii, in the book Kumranskaja obscina pp. 74-79 and footnotes on pp. 237f. The full commentaries on the Qumran pesharim can be found in his book: Teksty Kumrana. Vypusk 1, Moskva 1971, pp. 131-314 (cf. reviews by M. Bic in Bibliotheca Orientalis 29, 1972, pp. 335-337 and by A. Zaborski in Zeitschrift fur die alltestamentliche Wissenschaft 85, 1973, p. 117).

[11] http://databases.jewishlibraries.org/node/17674.

[12] Die Gerim in der sozialen Legislatur des Alten Testaments, Klio 63, 1981, pp. 15-23.

**Sonya Mendelevna Gluskina** (1917 - 1997) graduated (1940, 1946-1948) at the **Leningrad Herzen Institute**,

Sonia Mendelevna received an excellent education 1936-1940 then 1946-1948 at the Faculty of Russian Language and Literature of the Leningrad State Pedagogical Herzen Institute. Her work "History of the word red"[1] was recommended by BA Larin for the press (with the efforts of **IS Lutovinova**, one of the last pupils of BA Larin, it was prepared for publication and published).

BA Larin attracted SM Gluskin to work and prepare the **Cardoteki for the "Old Russian Dictionary" (DRS)**: "Sonia was exceptionally capable, intelligent and studied perfectly, especially as she was interested in linguistic subjects. Her abilities and interest in languages was noticed by the head of the Department of Russian language prof. Boris Alexandrovich Larin. He drew her to work on compiling a dictionary of the Old Russian language, "recalls KA Maryeva, a friend of Sophia Mendelevna.

Sonia Mendelevna's vocation for scientific work was remembered by Boris Alexandrovich who wrote to Sophia while she was in the army "...the few days will be gone begore many people are needed for a better job, for which there is no-one to replace you and in which few can compare with you," (What faith in a human and in the triumph of creative work resounds in these words to someone who, having gone through a difficult path of war, must continue what she started in raduate school!).

So, Sonia Mendelevna returned to postgraduate study, and then her appointment to **Pskov**, where the talent of the scientist, the happy gift of the Teacher, was bright and significant for the cause and for the people whom fate had brought with her and whom she had taught.

She worked from February 25, 1948 to June 20, 1992 at the **Russian Language Department of the Pskov Pedagogical Institute**, teaching courses in the Old Slavonic language, the history of the Russian language, introduction in linguistics, general linguistics. Defense of her Ph.D. thesis / under the supervision of **BA Larin** / "Cosmography of **Bogdan Lykov in** 1637 as a Russian revision of the text of the Atlas of **Mercator** " was held in 1949.

During her student years and post-graduate studies (pre-war 1940, post-war 1946-1948) Sonya Mendelevna went with BA Larin every year on dialectological expeditions: there was a collection of dialects for **Dialectological Atlas of the Russian Language (DARYA)**. And in the summer, on vacation, *BA Larin* included *SM Gluskin and K. A. Mareyev* in the various expeditions to study the dialect of local, rural residents of the **Leningrad and Kalinin regions**. We went there after the first, second and third courses. " It was a good school for gaining experience in conducting conversations with dialects, recording, processing recorded. This acquired ability Sofia Mendelevna taught her students and colleagues.

From 1957 to 1987 Sonia Mendelevna directly supervised the collection of dialectal materials for **the Pskov regional dictionary with historical data**: the organization of the dialectological expeditions of students headed by teachers to collect in field conditions the materials of unique Pskov dialects for replenishment of the **Card indexes of the Pskov Regional Dictionary (KPOS)** ; she constantly led the vocabulary seminar; worked as an author and as an editor of articles for the "Pskov Regional Dictionary".

The material of the Card indexes of the modern Pskov dialects and the Historical files of the Pskov monuments for the Dictionary enabled Sofia Mendelevna to systematically and purposefully engage in intensive scientific work.

It is true that much in a person is laid in childhood, comes from the family. I will quote the lines of **E. Gluskin**, the nephew of Sonia Mendelevna, whom she helped to raise for her sister Gita from five to seventeen years of age: "... the fundamental nature that was typical of Sonya as a person comes not only from her talent, but also from the education she received. Here, in the first place, one should keep in mind the family from which Sonya came from. Both on the paternal and maternal line Sonya comes from the family of great Rabbis. Her father was the chief Rabbi of Minsk, and then of Leningrad - two cities with large Jewish communities.

A somewhat unusual feature of her father was his interest in secular sciences; in this area he showed great abilities and accordingly brought up his daughters. "

Of course, the personal desire of Sonia Mendelevna to engage in research work was of no small importance, especially to carry out the work that had been begun until the end. She "was a single-minded, receptive person with original and deep thinking. Of course, such factors as scientific work under the leadership of Boris Aleksandrovich Larin, his personal example, ... a remarkable scientific school, as well as favorable living conditions in Pskov (which she loved and appreciated) also played a very important role and could put on a par with the education received in childhood. "

So, the life and work of Sonia Mendelevna for many decades was connected with Pskov. "Fate led S.M. Gluskin to Pskov because in connection with the campaign against cosmopolitanism, despite the voluntary participation in the Great Patriotic War, despite the brilliant graduation from the post-graduate school, because of "the fifth point" they could not live in Leningrad, no matter how they tried. The Chair of the Russian language at the Herzen Institute, **Nadezhda Pavlova Grinkova**, was a brave and honest man. But we can say that Pskov was lucky: Sonia Mendelevna, who closely linked her fate with the Pskov Pedagogical Institute, her scientific activity - with Pskov dialects, with the Pskov regional dictionary, all these decades was the backbone of the department, the leading teacher, the organizer of the best, first of all scientific, the department of the Russian language ... A mature scientist has already come to the chair of the Russian language of our institute."

And time was far from easy ... Not everyone can now understand how important it was, besides all, to stand without betraying one's principles and the main features of one's personality: "The courage and wisdom of Sophia Mendelevna affected everything. In an autobiography, in a personal sheet on the accounting of cadres - everywhere Sonia Mendelevna wrote that she is the daughter of a Rabbi (This is respect for her parents, a debt to those worthy people who gave life to children!) Friends know how much hardship had to be borne the whole family because of this social origin ...). And in the fact that in the early 1950s it was precisely Gluskin who stood up in all the tests concerning the quality of the teaching of theoretical disciplines in the light of Stalin's teaching about the languages (and it was about her, about her professionalism, the positive lines in the conclusion of the commission!), and in the fact that in the future it was Sonia Mendelevna who came to the aid of those who needed support ( **Nadezhda Yakovlevna Mandelstam,** thanks to Sonya Mendelevna and at the support of the rector of the Institute **Ivan Vasilievich Kovalev,** was able to come to work in Pskov in the early 60's, it was Sofia Mendelevna who accepted **Alexander Solzhenitsyn** and **I. Brodsky** who came to visit N.Ya. Mandelstam ...)".

The relentless work on the Pskov dialects, local monuments, primarily in connection with the creation of the "Pskov regional dictionary with historical data" allowed SM Gluskina to make serious scientific discoveries recognized in the scientific world: about the sound [ch] in the Pskov dialects; on special phenomena of morphology in the Pskov dialects. In connection with the work of SM Gluskin who dealt with morphological features in the Pskov dialects, **Yu. S. Maslov**, a **professor at the Leningrad University**, a scientific consultant at the **Faculty of Advanced Studies** in general linguistics, in 1967 he wrote in his review: "In addition to a very well-written review of the most important problems in this young field of linguistic science, a number of original ideas of scientific interest were expressed, as well as facts from dialectological material. The corresponding part of the essay by SM Gluskina was recommended by the head of the seminar for publication in the press."

Gluskin's valuable discovery was the proof of the absence of a second palatalization of the back-lingual consonants in the Pskov dialects in the past and of the traces of it at the present time. For example, in the words of the following roots: "kep" instead of "chain", "kedit" instead of "set", "kevka" intead of tsetka". Theoretical conclusions from this phenomenon, supported by archeological data, allow both linguists, archeologists and historians to make assumptions about the ethnogenesis of the Slavs – in particular, Krivichi. This discovery was recognized and supported by the Polish Scientist **S. Stieber.** The domestic scientist and academian **A A Zaliznyak**, who himself came to the same observations many years later, suggested calling it "A Gluskina effect". Such a vivid ancient feature of the Pskov dialects was one of the defining in the theory of the ancient Pskov-Novogrod dialect created by AA Zaliznyak. Nikita Ilyich Tolstoy always showed sincere interest in the research of the Pskov people's speech.

SM Gluskin was a skillful leader, since the talent of a scientist, teacher and a woman allowed her to make the necessary decisions and act in such a way that everything was done for the sake of the person: In fact, Gluskina was the undisputed deputy head of the department. Even under **Ivan Terentievich Gomonov,** this was a remarkable collaboration in academic and scientific work. Pskov regional dictionary, conferences on Pskov dialects, collections on the results of conferences, etc.; creative friendship of the department with BA Larin; joint work with colleagues from the Leningrad University, from other scientific institutions ... It so happened that Sonya Mendelevne Gluskina was not offered a department chair even when there was no manager ("fifth point"!), but in that short time when she was (February 1949 – July 20 1949; September 10 1956 – August 1 1957), Sonia Mendelevna managed to do many good and sensible things. For many, she herself, SM Gluskina knew how to attract colleagues and organize work."

Talented in everything, Sonia Mendelevna released into a great life of knowledgeable teachers of the Russian language, good researchers (even if someone did not go exactly along the scientific path), who with reverence and gratitude remember Sonia Mendelevna.

D. f.c. Prof. L.Ya Kostyuchuk

Emmanuel Gluskin wrote:

Abram Davidovich Duvidovich who was in Pskov is truly unforgettable. Each time he met me -- he very painfully pinched my cheek, in order to express his love, which I naturally hated. Once he rode a bus with his wife, Evelina

Israilevna -- a quiet and nice woman, heroically tolerating her "crazy" husband. As usual, they were loudly and impressively speaking Yiddish, not paying any attention to the public around. "Are you husband and wife? How long are you married?" asked a Russian man sitting near them -- "50 years". "Счастливые люди!"

Sonya was an exceptional person. In Russia times were difficult for everyone and the memories of these times also brought the sisters together. Sonia always knew what she was doing, and in what she did, she invested all her soul and energy.

She was stubborn with perseverance and purposefulness. She was an independent thinker, which may be one reason that she did not marry. When Emanuel asked her why she wrote articles alone, she replied that "it is difficult to write together with another person, I have to think."

Sonia was a single minded, receptive person with original and deep thinking. Thus, in addition to her father and family other factors helped her develop. Such as scientific work under the leadership of Boris Aleksandrovich Larin, his personal example, a remarkable scientific school as well as favorable living conditions in Pskov that she loved and appreciated. Sonia was involved in many scientific discoveries.

Sonia had to combine the ability to live in a relatively simple environment, that is the ability to gather good friends and like-minded people around her (sometimes not even at the academic level) with her penchant for intense and focused scientific work. Her activity and exclusive responsibility in relations with friends replaced her personal and family relations.

She did not like to depend on anyone and in all the forced circumstances she tried to "manage" herself. She was a woman of rare courage and despite inherent sensitivity, perceived the difficulties of life with the firmness of a peasant woman. In her daily behavior there was nothing to indicate that she was an outstanding scientist. Modesty was instilled in her from childhood, and she retained this feature at all stages of life. The Russian environment that she lived in nourished her for many years. She had a very friendly and cordial association with Prakovia Ivanovna.

Sonia had a constant continuos and intense mental process with inner concentration making it difficult for many to have a relationship with her. Emanuel had a very strong spiritual connection with her. It manifested itself in the fact that they understood each other instantly and deeply. It was organic, in addition to years of familiarity.

Sonia visiting with son and daughter of Emmanuel 1989. Judean Desert

Sonia and Emik in Israel

Emmanuel Gluskin

After her arrival in Israel in 1992 she moved in with Emanuel Gluskin who lived then in Beersheva. One time when Emanuel came home from work he saw her profile in the window. And climbing the stairs he wrote a quatrain. She liked it because it was dedicated to her and therefore wrote it down and saved it.

I see a proud nose in the window,
Like an eagle on the throne.
The soup is cooked, its clear to me.
And in the cabin – Sonya.

After when we moved to Kfar Saba, every Shabbos at sunset we went for a walk to the local water tower, sat down on a bench and started talking about various philosophical, pshycological and other topics, connected with our daily life or intelellectual interests. Her fighting zeal in defending her point of view never faded. At a time when she could no longer think about scientific work, her intellectual insistence remained, always keeping her banner high.

She was highly organized and efficient. As part of her daily routine she came to Emanuels house every morning and helped clean the beds and wash the dishes after breakfast. This gave her meaning in her late years.

She volunteered free of charge to help beginners who came to Israel, learn Hebrew. Among her students was one girl who had no chance to seriously advance in the language due to a defect. Nevertheless, the lessons were always on time, without omissions and indulgences. Among her papers there were a huge number of extracts – all kinds of words and expressions in Hebrew. She taught this language with exceptional diligence and conscientiousness. She kept a separate list of proverbs.

She once said that sometimes scientific work exhausted her so much that she had to give up for a while, because she was no longer able to even look at another manuscript.

In the last years of her life, Sonya devoted much time and effort to editing translations from Hebrew to Russian. The translation of a guidebook on Israel, or artistic, historical and religious books that were being prepared for publication. She never stopped working and was frustrated by her limitations in old age. Yet, even in the hospital, already knowing the full severity of her condition, she continued to read and work as much as possible. Two days before her death she asked for a volume of Pushkins poems.

One day three months before her death, she realized from her conversation with the doctors that she had cancer. As she exited the hospital, Emmanuel saw in her glance to him a guilty smile. Outwardly calm but full recognition that she was soon to depart. Beyond this there were never any signs of complaint about it.

Her nature showed itself in her last days with the peace of mind that she manifested in her hopeless condition. At one point her head began to tremble violently. She said briefly and simply, "well, when the head shakes all sorts of new things appear." It was said with the same calm with which she said, "well its already getting colder."

During her stay in hospital many friends and relatives visited. Bracha Argaman is the wife of Sonia's cousin, a nurse by profession, at night on duty in the ward and helped physically. Her childhood friend Nechama Cohen with her daughters constanly surrounded her with care and financial help without her knowing while she lived in Kfar Saba. Exceptional respect and attention was shown to Sonia by her new, devoted friends: Grigory Kanovich, a well-known writer, and in particular his wife Olga, which during the illness of Sonya brought to the hospital a real mors made from frozen Lithuanian cranberries - the only drink that the patient did not refuse to drink. Victor Gin and his wife Ella, the artist Tanya Kafyan, very young Masha Fingert from the Raanan Symphony Orchestra. Masha came three times to Sonia in the ward and played the viola. Visiting the patient were classmates from the ulpan where the newcomers learn the basics of Hebrew, giving Sonia warmth and attention. Old friends who lived in Jerusalem, the Mayor and Lisa, who are already feeling unwell, came. Old friends came also, very busy doctors from Beersheva – Ilya and lilya Ovschyshory.

Sonia and Gita Gluskin in the hospital during the last days of Sonia

Sonia and Gita (with a paralyzed hand) discussing - about one and a half months before Sonia's death – Gita's translation from Hebrew to Russian, edited by Sonya.

1 Another important work in this area is Gershom Scholem's essay, "Colors and their Symbolism in Jewish Tradition and Mysticism" [Seven papers originally delivered at the annual Eranos conference in Ascona, Switzerland, August 1972. in Spring Publications; edited by Klauss Ottmann, Color Symbolism: The Eranos Lectures (May 1, 2005)].

**Esther Gluskin**

Esther was the oldest daughter of Menachem Mendel and Fraidel Gluskin. At the age of eighteen she was imprisoned for taking part in a Zionist youth group, Hashomer Hatzair. In 1934 when Rabbi Gluskin moved to Leningrad, Esther was already engaged to Isaac Mintz. He was from an assimilated family far from Zionism and religion. They made a kosher wedding in Leningrad and returned to Minsk.

The first child a boy died before he was a year old. In the communal apartment, where the Mintz's lived before the war, lived a government informant who began to admonish Emma. Encountering resistance from Esther, she was taken to jail. In 1938 they were arrested for their Zionist activities. As a result of the beatings she received in prison a dead girl was born. She was returned to the prison cell from the hospital and from there they were exiled to Solikmask in the Nothern Ural Mountains for three years.
Esther was sitting in a large cell, where under the floor was a room for interrogations: there they "knocked out" gold from dentists. From day to day screams ran from under the floor. But with Esther nothing terrible happened.

One night they all woke up from a noise. In the barred prison window, they saw that the prison yard was full of "pipes", where men were being pushed out of the prison. While there some prison criminals decided to kill Esther. But she had a fan, a Russian thief called Ivan Afanasyev. He reported the criminals to his superiors. Those criminals were taken to other prisons.

Her marriage with Isaac Mintz had fallen apart and since he saved her from death they became close and she finally gave birth to a baby. Despite that Isaac Mintz allowed the baby to use his name.

Sasha was born with a softened spine (you can imagine what she ate in prison during her pregnacy). Esther put the newborn child to sleep on the straw so that the back strengthened. Looking at the straight back of an adult Sasha, it was hard to imagine all this. Soon Esther was safely released from prison. Her husband did not accept her with the baby, and she settled with her sister.

Esther said that a few years later she received a letter from Ivan Afanasyev where he wrote to her that he was at large and loves her as before, but he has one road in life: back to prison, so he cannot connect his life with Esther. Sasha inherited his patronymic and surname from Esther's husband, and from Afanasyev the Russian soft nose, thus Sasha himself called: valenochek.

Thus, the future dancer of the Kirov and Ballet Theater Alexander Isaakovitch Mintz was born. After the release she moved close to her sisters and settled in Borovichi near Leningrad since there was a ban on who could live in Leningrad. At the beginning of the war, the Germans began to bomb Borovitchi. Esther moved with her one-year old son who had rickets, a vitamin D definiency, to Tataria where Leah and Gita lived. They all adored the child with such beautiful eyes, clear, open to the world and surprised. Food was scarce but he received semolina porridge with butter. He barely survived. Esther devoted herself to raising Shurik till he was tall and slender, endowed with special grace, good manners and kind character.

# Минц-Глускина Эстер Менделеевна (I9II)

**Дата рождения:** 1911 г.

**Место рождения:** г. Минск

**Пол:** женщина

**Национальность:** еврей

**Образование:** среднее

**Профессия / место работы:** служащая, Магазин Минвоенторг

**Место проживания:** Минск, 3-я линия, Комаровка 23а, кв. 5

**Дата ареста:** 8 марта 1938 г.

**Обвинение:** 76, 72 - К/рев. агитация

**Осуждение:** 10 октября 1938 г.

**Осудивший орган:** ОСО

**Приговор:** 3 года ИТЛ, отбыв.: г.Соликамск Усольлаг МВД, освоб. 03.1941

**Дата реабилитации:** 27 октября 1955 г.

**Реабилитирующий орган:** Верховный суд СССР

**Архивное дело:** КГБ БССР - 5697-с

**Источники данных:** БД "Жертвы политического террора в СССР"; Белорусский "Мемориал"

# Mints-Gluskina Esther Mendeleevna (I9II)

**Date of birth:** 1911

**Place of birth:** Minsk

**Sex:** woman

**Nationality:** Hebrew

**Education:** secondary

**Profession / place of work:** office worker, Shop Minventorg

**Place of residence:** Minsk, 3rd line, Komarovka 23a, ap. 5

**Date of arrest:** March 8, 1938.

**Charge:** 76, 72 - K / roar. agitation

**Condemnation:** October 10, 1938

**Tho condemned body:** CCA

**Verdict:** 3 years ITL, departure: Solikamsk Usollag Ministry of Internal Affairs, oshib. 03.1941

**Rehabilitation Date:** October 27, 1955

**Rehabilitation body:** Supreme Court of the USSR

**Archival business:** KGB BSSR - 5697-s

**Sources of data:** DB "Victims of political terror in the USSR"; Belarusian "Memorial"

Esther returned from the exile with Shurik who often requested "сЮп!". Her official husband, Isaak Minz did not want to take her back with the son. Isaak went to his relatives in Tashkent and remarried.

They lived 6 people in a 16-square meter room, obviously not a space to grow up as a ballet dancer. Nevertheless, his father once visited and saw him in the narrow corridor of the communal flat, small Shurik staying on tiptoe with a leg thrown behind -- and the family "allowed" this unusual Jewish boy to learn ballet.

Once the sister of Ivanov came to Leningrad to see Shurik as the family called him. Gita was at home. To Gita's question why the dad did not come, the sister responded that the latter is sure that his road is back to prison, and he does not want to spoil the life of the child.

It is very easy to explain this whole story by one word -- Russia! Indeed -- why, in fact, a daughter of the chief Rabbi of Leningrad and a simple Russian criminal cannot accept each other in the country that it is anyway impossible to understand by human mind?! ("Умом Россию не понять ...").

In 1972 they left the Soviet Union together and eventually settled in the US.

When she passed away Rabbi Jacobson who was in charge of the Chevra Kadisha buried her in the section that only had people who were very religious, who kept Torah and mitzvos their whole life. He was asked why he buried her there? His response was; a child of Mendel! it cannot be that she did not do teshuva before she died.

**Alexander, Esther's son.**

Alexander Mintz born 1941 in Minsk – April 30 1992. He was knicknamed Shurik.

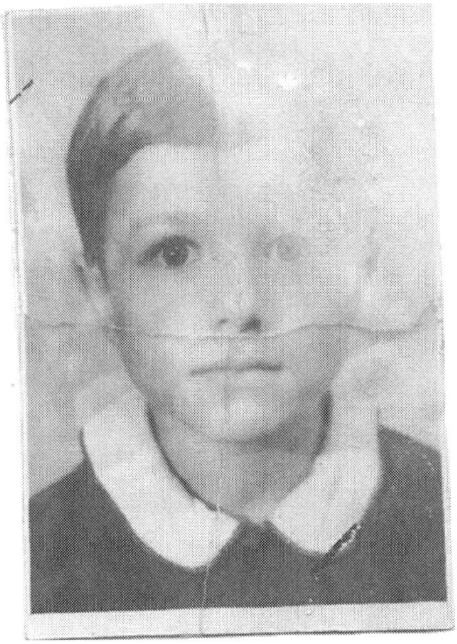

His best friend was Nikita Dolgushin, another ballet pupil. Together they once cornered and caught a hooligan on a porch. The time came, and once, when Shurik came to visit Nikina, Nikita's mother did not let him in, because Nikita (who started to be a soloist) was resting before a theater performance. This was the first blow that separated him from others. From then on, the difficulties of Shurik's life continued to grow.

He danced with the Petrozavodsk Ballet Company and the Maly Theater and Kirov Ballet in Leningrad. He also taught at the Vaganova Institute in Leningrad, where he trained. In 1972 he moved to Italy, where he taught at the

Center of Dance in Rome and at La Scala in Milan. He joined the Ballet Theater School faculty in 1973 and performed acting roles in six works. Among them he is known for his work on The Nutcracker (1977), The Turning Point (1977) and Live from Lincoln Center (1976). Mr. Minz also performed with Pearl Lang and with the Los Angeles Ballet in Alexandra Danilova's production of "Coppelia." He also appeared on television in the series "Hart to Hart."

He died of a heart attack in NY. He was a ballet master and character dancer with the American Ballet Theatre.

*The Encyclopedia of Ballet and Dance edited by Mary Clarke and David Vaughan published by G.P. Putnam's sons NY. The New York Times Obituaries May 1 and 2, 1992.* http://www.nytimes.com/.../alexander-minz-dies-ballet-master-...

In the first picture, you see M.B. watching Shurik dancing with Natasha Makarova, in a studio. In the nutcracker, Shurik is dancing there the Educator of the Girl.

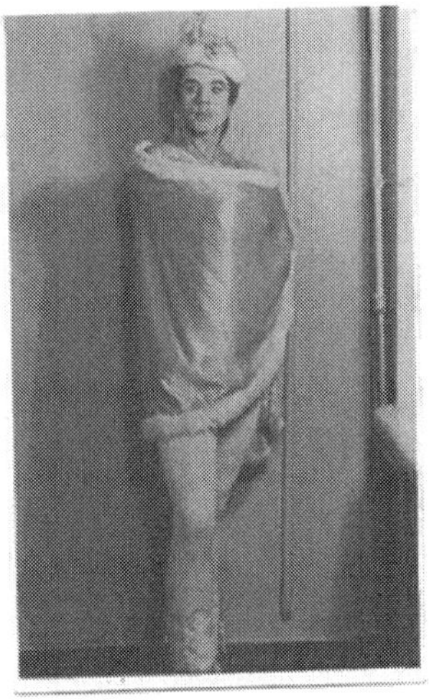

Esther and Shurik

Alexander Mintz – Golden heart

No. 46 (394)
*Nina Alovert*

The name of Alexander Mintz, the ballet artist, constantly arose in my stories about the St. Petersburg ballet. My dear and unforgettable friend was a friend of Natalia Makarova, Mikhail Baryshnikov, Alla Osipenko, Nikita Dolgushin, as well as other people of art not associated with the ballet, including all those who met with him and fell under the spell of his extraordinary personality. Therefore, when I talk about Mintz, naturally, I will also touch on the fate of his friends when Sasha was involved in their life's vicissitudes.

Once, when I came to Petersburg in the late 1980s, I was at the concert of Mikhail Zhvanetsky. After the concert, sitting in his make-up room, I listened to interviews, although he did not remember the name of the interviewers. He was asked how he came to St. Petersburg and how he feels in this city today. Zhvanetsky replied that he missed those true Petersburgers who had left for the West, and the first name he mentioned was Sasha Mintz.

Sasha Mintz really looked like a true Petersburger. Tall, leggy, elegant, he held himself like a real dandy, although in the Russian period of his life he was poor and the tailcoat was only worn on stage. Above all else, or first of all, he was a man of honor, who had a holy respect for friendly ties. In the late 1970s, Makarova asked him to help her rebuild the ballet La Bayadère, which was performed at the Marinsky Theater, for the American Ballet Theater (ABT). Makarova created her version of the ballet on the basis of the editors M. Petipa, V. Ponomarev, V. Chabukiani.

Mintz by this time received an invitation to appear in the film about the criminal world of Chicago in the 30s. Mintz was offered the role of one of the famous leaders of this world. Sasha refused because the shooting coincided with the period of the production of "La Bayadere". He really wanted to act, but Natasha, who he literally worshiped all his life and was his old school friend, had asked! In the play he had one of the main pantomime roles: Brahmin. Mintz was a gifted artist.

In America, I almost did not see him dancing, but in pantomime and dance roles, he is unforgettable. In my entire life I almost did not see equal ballet artists. When he had already left ABT, I could definitely determine which of the performers of his roles saw him on stage and who did not.

Sasha was one of the first friends in our company who emigrated. Naturally he left together with his mother. When they began to make out the documents, it was then that Sasha's fantastic details about the pedigree became clear.

I do not remember how I met Alexander Isaakovich-Ivanovich Mintz-Afanasyev. But when he graduated from the Choreography School, I was already worried about his fate. He graduated from high school as a typical dancer, but after graduating from school for some reason they did not take him to the theater Kirov, although he already stood out with his nobility of execution. Sasha was not a real classical dancer, but his role was clearly much wider than the role of a typical dancer. I think it was this unconventionality of Sasha's obviously uncommon personality that confused the leaders of the theater. Even at the final performance his talent was noted by the venerable critic Yu.I. Slonimsky, who was indignant that such an original dancer was not taken to the Kirov Theater.

Mintz went to work in Petrozavodsk for two years. I visited Sasha, went to see him in the plays. It's unlikely that I will ever see Hans, such a touching and in love, in "Giselle" as Mintz was. He was younger than Giselle and Albert, and this gave a different color to what is happening on stage. It seemed that Hans' gentle heart was broken after Giselle's death ... And in all the roles that he danced, he immediately stood out on stage among the other performers: plastic, musical, expressive ... Sasha danced and Makko in "The Path of Thunder," and a romantic Espadu in Don Quixote, keen on the elements of dance, and an eccentric artist in the opera The Ball-Masquerade.

Two years later, Mintz was taken to the Kirov Theater. He performed Spanish dances, secondary mimic roles, he was occupied in his works by beginning choreographers. But his talent in Russia was not fully revealed. Perhaps, if he had got into a new troupe by L. V. Yakobson ... However, what to wonder. Mintz did not take foreign trips, which, according to the concepts of that time, made him a dancer and second-class citizen. Sasha reacted painfully to this injustice. In a word, in 1971 Mintz gathered in exile, in 1972 he and his mother were released.

At first Sasha taught in the ballet troupe of the Milan Opera, was pleased with life, but missed his friends in Russia. Constantly calling me from Italy: "How is the Little Prince?" "Little Prince" friends called Misha Baryshnikov, so he went under this "code" name for conspiracy. Oh, those secrets of the time! We are wise when talking about the simplest things, the Russian agent who listens to us, has long been aware of what is being said, and a transatlantic friend will long puzzle his head trying to understand what you wanted to tell him.

In the fate of Baryshnikov, Sasha Mintz played an important role. When in 1974 Baryshnikov came with a tour group from Russia to Canada, Sasha already worked at the American Ballet Theater (ABT). He immediately flew to Toronto, but not only to see dear friend Misha. Sasha had a secret task for Misha: in New York he was instructed to give Baryshnikov an invitation to stay in the West. Sasha told me about this and I did not inquire who specifically entrusted him with this mission.

In any case, Natasha Makarova, the closest friend and Mintza and Baryshnikova, who also worked at ABT and was already a famous ballerina, asked me to tell Misha that Lucia Chase, the director of ABT, is ready to take him into the troupe and that she, Makarova, will dance with him the first performances. Sasha took on this assignment with one condition:

Misha was happy to meet his old friend. Despite his vigilant surveillance, he was not afraid of anything and went with him to visit Canadian friends of Mintz. Baryshnikov made his choice, he was prepared for this decision by the whole situation at the Kirov Theater, conservatism, stagnation, lack of prospects for interesting work. And yet the decision to break for good with Russian ballet and friends was given to Baryshnikov with great difficulty. Deciding finally, Misha allowed Sasha to arrange his escape. Sasha called New York ...

On June 28 or 29, 1974, Baryshnikov asked for political asylum in Canada. Then he left for America. July 28 was his triumphant debut on the stage of the Metropolitan Opera, where he and Makarova danced Giselle.

When I came to America in 1977, I felt that Misha was still sensitive to the past, I did not question him about escaping to Canada. Now Baryshnikov calmly talks about his past life. In particular, he talked about the events in Toronto in an interview given to Olga Khrustaleva during her tour in Riga in 1979. By the way, Khrustaleva, a talented Moscow journalist, publisher of the magazine, is the wife of another friend of Baryshnikov and Mintz, Andrei Kuznetsov.

Andrei - the son of the premiere of the Kirov Theater, Tatyana Vecheslova and Svyatoslav Kuznetsov, danced at the Kirov Theater. When Baryshnikov did not return from Canada, several young dancers from the theater were taken into the army, including Andrei Kuznetsov. Since the ballet dancers relied on the reservation, they began talking, asking inappropriate questions ...

On the draftee's question, why they were taken into the army, a military person answered: "So you will not run like Baryshnikov." The answer was instantly widely known and the boys were returned to the theatre. Having arrived to dance in Riga, Misha gave an interview to the only Russian journalist - the wife of his Leningrad friend, she published this interview in Riga and Moscow.

So, Baryshnikov told Olga Khrustaleva that after the farewell performance of Russian dancers in Canada, he went out and began to give autographs to the fans who were waiting for him at the actor's entrance. Having signed a large number of programs, Baryshnikov said: "Sorry, I need to leave for a few minutes, I'll be back." And he ran, and the fans ran after him. It all looked comical, Misha began to laugh. He had to stop and give a few more autographs.

Then he ran across the square to where his black car was waiting around the corner. One of the informers rushed after him. As Sasha told me, Baryshnikov ran so fast (and this was a terrible moment as they had to catch up with him) that he overtook the car. The car started after him ... In the car, Misha was waiting for Mintz, an Englishwoman, Mishina, a friend who flew to his performances in Toronto, one of the officials. Misha was brought to a farm, where they all spent the first night without sleep. Misha was terribly nervous and drank. In the morning they began to act on a sober head ...

Baryshnikov and Mintz worked together for several years in the ABT. Still living in Russia, I heard that Baryshnikov staged the ballet The Nutcracker to the music of PI Tchaikovsky, while Sasha Mintz danced Drosselmeyer. When Baryshnikov called me again from America, I said to him: "Misha, we all, Sasha's friends, are very grateful to you for giving Sasha a role in your performance." Baryshnikov responded, "I am grateful to Sasha, he contributed to my ballet by his participation."

When in 1977, my mother and children, in turn, flew across the ocean and left the plane at Kennedy airport, we were met by Mintz and Baryshnikov. On the very first evening at the apartment of Baryshnikov I saw a film shot on his ballet. The film began with a prologue, where Mintz-Drosselmeier with the help of dolls tells a fairy tale, decides the fate of the heroes of The Nutcracker. Then I saw this ballet on stage with Baryshnikov and Mintz, but from that first evening in America I remember only the significant, in my own beautiful, tragic face Mintz-Drosselmeyer and flying through the whole screen in the weightless jump of the great dancer, Little Prince-Baryshnikov.

Mintz-Drosselmeyer in the ballet is in fact the most important character. In the entire plot of this ballet, only two characters - Drosselmeyer and Clara - are living people in the world of dolls. Nutcracker-Prince - a phantom, revived the Drosselmeier doll. Between Clara and Drosselmeier, the abyss is not even years, but the experience of life. Did Mintz give his hero love for a girl like Lewis Carol's love for Alice? This could only be guessed. In any case, Drosselmeyer Mintz loved Clara not with the fatherly love of a good godfather, his love was excruciating. And it was impossible not to follow Mintz during the entire performance, trying to penetrate into the mysterious world of his hero. Presenting Klara an ugly Nutcracker doll, he insistently, at first as if quite innocently with the excitement of the player and at the same time lovingly drawn Clara into the story with the Nutcracker,

Baryshnikov is one of the very few choreographers who "heard" the tragic music of the famous adagio from the second act (usually the directors under the "sobbing" of violins compose just another difficult support) and put not a serene children's fairy tale, but a ballet about lost dreams. The idyllic love of Clara and Prince ends tragically. To the music of Adagio Baryshnikov composed a trio: Clara, Prince and Drosselmeier. Drosselmeyer tries to lead Clara away, tear her away from the Prince.

The reasons, like all true feelings of Drosselmeyer-Mintz, were unsaid in the ballet. We felt only the mental pain of Drosselmeyer and the perseverance with which he sought to destroy the illusion created by him. What was it? Jealousy? Pity for a girl whose love test has gone too far? Scared in desperation, Clara, running past the Nutcracker, who could no longer see in the dying kingdom of dolls, rushed with a childlike hope to a clever, omnipotent adult: "Give it back to me!" "No, it's just a dream," as if Drosselmeier answered with his hands spread and the sad and lonely, in all of his wisdom and love.

Of course, the action was set by Baryshnikov, but Mintz filled the image of Drosselmeyer with a special meaning. All that he did, every movement, dance or pantomime, every mental nuance produced the impression of instant improvisation, the birth of the image before our eyes. The ballet was shot on videocassette quite successfully. action was set Baryshnikov, but Mintz filled the image of Drosselmeyer with a special meaning. All that he did, every movement, dance or pantomime, every mental nuance produced the impression of instant improvisation, the birth of the image before our eyes.

Mintz left ABT and returned, he did more than one significant actor's work. You cannot talk about everyone in the article. But there is one unusual among them: in 1983, Mintz starred in the film-ballet "Obsessed". The plot was based on the classical Jewish play by Sh. Anski "Dibuk". She staged the ballet and shot a film commissioned by American TV Pearl Lang, a famous American contemporary dancer, she also danced the main role.

The play was written based on the ancient Hasidic tradition, the genre of ballet is a mystical drama about two lovers, Leah and Hannan. Father Leah Sender forcibly extradites his daughter to marry the son of wealthy parents. Hannan dies of a heart rupture. But even after the death of Hannan, his spirit - the dibbuk - continues to pursue the girl with his love. Poor Leah only finds death in death from both the hateful bridegroom and the enamored spirit. Mintz danced the role of Sender. I have not seen the film as it was shot for over one year: constantly there was not enough money to finish shooting. But I was present at the shooting and I can say that Mintz in the ballet was the most significant figure in plastic, expressiveness, significance of the created image, the artist naturally combined irony and tragic origin.

Mintz traveled a lot, taught in different theaters and different schools in the world. I've been to his lessons. Always fit, correct, he combined rigid demands with a joke and love for everyone in the class, the dancers looked at him with adoration. Mintz was one of those adult children in our harsh world who only know how to love and does not know how to handle money. Under his big salary he opened a line of credit with the banks and immediately he spent money on his friends, books and records (Sasha loved the opera). So, for example, when he came to work in San Francisco, he wrote to me: "Come, I finished the room specially for you, you'll like it." So, when he died, the banks were left with what he owed them.

Towards the end, Mintz taught in Italy, where he was supposed to have a heart operation - to replace the valve. Before the operation, he came to New York, which he was very fond of. By coincidence, I never saw him before his death: my Petersburg friends were visiting.

Mintz was very busy on the last day before his departure and did not come to the place of the scheduled meeting. The last evening, he spent in the Russian Samovar, where his friends, mostly Americans, came. He looked young, was handsome, merry ... Dancing, I even drank a little.

The rest is known from the words of an Italian dancer who accompanied him on a trip. Hearing that Sasha returned home, Enrico went to his room: Sasha walked around the room, pressing his hands to his heart. "It hurts," he said, "but nothing, nothing." When Enrico looked at him again, Sasha was kneeling on the floor, blood gushed from his mouth. As they explained later, the aorta ruptured.

At about the same time, on the night of April 29th (April 1992), in Rome, our mutual friend, former premier of the Kirov Theater Svyatoslav Kuznetsov, came to himself from anesthesia after heart surgery, smiled at his nurse, joked about his condition and died at the beginning of the fifth heart attack.

We buried Sasha in a Jewish cemetery in New York near the grave of Emma/Esther Mendelevna. At parting in the funeral home were Makarova and Baryshnikov. At the funeral, unknown relatives from Australia came to visit me. The few went to the cemetery. When the coffin was lowered into the ground, my friend Zoya Lymar-Krasnovskaya, with whom Sasha was still studying at the ballet school, was the first to throw the earth and even flowers on the lid of the coffin, despite the indignation of the relatives: they were supposed to throw the earth in first according to Jewish custom. I hope that God forgave us, Sasha was to me in America as a brother, one of my closest friends, my unforgettable Sasha Mintz - a golden heart.

*Shulamit Shalit in the "Seven arts": http://7iskusstv.com/2010/Nomer6/Shalit1.php*

From Eliezer Rabinovich

A wonderful article about a man I knew from another, family, side - his mother (who was called Esther in the family, not Emma) was my cousin. And with Mrs. Alovert we were together at the funeral, but there was no living Sasha to introduce us to each other. My wife and I sometimes go to the cemetery.

**Yosef Gutner**

He was responsible for collecting donations at the Moscow synagogue and distributed them among jewish people in need. He barely spoke any Russian, didn't work in Soviet Russia, was kind, religious, law abiding man. His spent his time taking care of his family - his sick wife and their sick (retarded) granddaughter whose name was Inka. They lived in a very small room in the same apartment building where Aleksandra lived.

In 1938 at the age of 75 he was arrested and accusted of collaborating with Polish Jews. He died in the Gulag at the age of 75. When he was arrested, Inka who was about 12 years old was sent to a mental facility where she died in a year or so. He died in less than a year in a camp. His wife, Ita, was left by herself.

**Aleksandra Krupenina**

Aleksandra Krupenina was born in 1926 in Moscow to the family of a doctor. Her father Yaakov Gutner was a highly experienced specialist who taught in the medical university and worked in the city hospital. Her mother, Klara Mironova did not work. The family was not religious, spoke Russian in the house and did not keep any Jewish traditions. Her grandparents Yosef and Basya Gutner were religious and observed everything according to Orthodox tradition. In the 1930's Aleksandra saw them praying at home. She had no clue if there was an active synagogue in the city. As a little girl, she often watched them with interest. They celebrated all the holidays and Aleksandra especially remembers Passover when all the relatives would gather and eat delicious food on beautiful dishes. They would sing Jewish songs that were all beautiful.

Jews were persecuted in Russia as long as she remembers. From her early childhood, she felt like an outcast, different from everyone else. This was a constant feeling as long as she lived in Russia. Many Jews took part in the Communist revolution, and many Jews occupied high positions in the Communist Party and government. In 1937-1938 Stalin executed most of them. The Inteligentsia (artists, writers, etc) was decimated and humiliated in 1949 and the government knicknamed the Jews, "Bezrodnye Kosmopolity" – people without heritage and no allegiance to any country. Jews were removed from any supervisory/managerial positions and publicly humiliated. Her father also suffered as he was fired from all places of teaching and practicing and was forced to retire. Article 5 in any government application (ethnicity) became like a yellow Magen David for Jews.

Aleksandra left for America in 1997 after the fall of the Soviet Union when Russia became democratic, but Article 5 remained. She watched Russian television and how in the government and parliament, the governers and senators are represented by all possible ethnicities but not the Jews. Thus, it appears that little has changed with regard to anti-semitism. Although synagogues are being opened and Jewish religion has made some comebacks, the underlying hate for Jews remains and they are still outcasts in many ways.

Alex Krupenin writes:

She is not happy telling her story since it is extremely sad and painful including death, war, uncertainty, hunger/starvation, poverty, difficult living, freedom-less life in general and under high security clearance she had all her life. Without proper education, missing a lot of living conditions, normal food supply, complicated housing - she struggled most of her life. Basically, until she left the country in 1997, her life was "miserable" and "hopeless". Growing older, seeing no "light at the end of the tunnel", I can't even imagine what would it be if they would have stay in Russia. You can't even imagine what people are going through in simple situations back in Russia. They get used to it but I can guarantee you - it would be clearly abnormal, sick, unjust, inhuman, non-civilized, and stupid - if you try to get roots of these behavioral styles. They live in it and get used to it. Every reasonable person from free world would be outraged in most of their acts. 70% are animals, 20% are sick, and the rest 10% can't affect anything on that sinking ship called "Russian society".

She lives in her own container, somewhat connected to real life and somewhat not really. She is a product of brainwashed Russian population. For example, she still thinks that Crimea annexation by Russia in 2014 was a "right thing to do". And many other, large and small tales are sitting firm in her head - creating blind spots, shadowing normal human reaction to outrageous human rights violations that used to be, happen current, and will always stay the essence of that land people living style.

It is impossible to grasp the whole picture of living hell and viciousness. The communists destroyed life of the whole family - based on what? Just their mid-century style rancor to humanity... I have a scan of the great-grandfather case documents from KGB archive (sent by same Grisha we are collecting money for). It's a shame what has been done. To complete the picture, they did the same to their own people, too. It's a fact that almost 100 million people lives were destroyed by these communists-animals. They are worse than animals because animals never kill or eradicate similar ones...

Trust me, it's a cursed land and cursed people inhabit it. Nothing teaches them, nothing scares them, nothing normal grows there. It looks normal in micro scale, but it's a monster altogether. Vicious, hateful, and malicious monster that doesn't live normal life itself, and not letting others to have a life granted by G-d.

The story of her family is less tragic than many others. Still, if we record it then it will give people an understanding how millions of intelligent, peaceful, hardworking, professional people were forced to live, struggle, meet their grief and sorrow, day-in and day-out, year-after-year, hoping for better but always getting the worth. Only coming here and looking around I was just amazed how many things we were deprived back in Russia FOR NO REASON! Simple things, like dishwasher or cream cheese. Why were we held miserable? Everybody has his own theory/answer to that question. Me, too...

**Miriam Helfgott Gluskin Sax**

Miriam was born in Lviv. The family moved to Gomel then Yekatrinislaw and Moscow.

My (DBL) grandmother reports that there was a pogrom in Gomel. She said the family survived by hiding in an attic. She mentioned that Bialik's poem "On the City of Slaughter" in response to the Kishnev pogrom, which calls for fighting back and militarizing the Jews to resist such acts of pogrom violence was not feasible. Bialik deplores how the Jews hid like mice and did not fight back. She preferred Agnon's model in the story "Ma'aseh Ha-Ez". In Agnon's short story there is a very poor family which depends on a goat for food and clothing. Even the son's bar mitzvah tallit is knit out of the goat's hair and the goat provided milk and cheese for the family to eat. One day there is a pogrom. The father sacrifices the goat. Agnon evokes images of the ketonet passim in the Yosef novella of Genesis. The father then hangs the tallit of the bar mitzvah son on the porch after dipping the tallit in the blood of the goat. In this way the thugs assume that the violence has already hit that house and the thugs proceed on to another victim. Thus Agnon's Midrash of "Ma'aseh ha-ez" is a response to Bialik's "on the city of slaughter." Agnon sees the goat as symbol of redemption as in the Pesach Haggadah with the song Chad Gad Yah. Yet the goat also has allusions to the scapegoat pushed off a cliff in the ritual of Yom Kippur described in Maseket Yoma. Whatever one's position believing with Bialik in *Muscle Judaism* [*Muskeljudentum*) a term coined by Max Nordau or with Agnon in Outsmarting Judaism, my grandmother gave thanks that the family was spared in Gomel from the pogrom.

They were in Moscow for a short time. Since Jews were not allowed to live in Moscow they received special permission to do so. She remembers how the family would walk to shul every Shabbos and Yomtov and how joyful Yomtov was. Miriam's three brothers, Nathan, Yivesay, and Griesha were all physicians. Nathan practiced in Baltimore and supplied affidavits for the family to come to Baltimore.

However, Yivesay and Griesha practiced medicine in Russia. One brother was captured by the Nazis in WWII as a physician but managed to escape with the luck of Hashem. Another brother physician was implicated later in Stalin's "doctor's plot" where the paranoid Stalin accused certain Jewish doctors of trying to poison him.[1]

Each Shabbos the Helfgotts after davening had guests who came for the meal and words of Torah. Keila Leiba's shabbos table and later Miriam's own Shabbos table, and later Ruth S. Levy's was always open and Rabbis, intellectuals, and all in need were welcome. For example, intellectuals such as Israeli Dr. Yoel Wachtel (PhD Hebrew University of Jerusalem and PhD Medieval Jewish Philosophy), opera singer Sivia Stuck, Holocaust survivor Leo Bretholz [see, *Leap into Darkness*, which tells a chilling and nail biting story about a young Jewish boy and his ventures escaping across Europe], Jewish undergrad students at Hopkins from abroad and Hopkins medical students, and the Eisenberg family were frequent guests of the Ruth S Levy family on Yom Tov and Shabbos.

Picture of Miriam as a young lady:

Miriam lived to 105 years and was the oldest surviving nurse of Sinai Hospital. Dr. Robert I Levy and Ruth S Levy held a birthday party for Miriam at 100 years of age. At this party many speeches and presentations were given but Miriam said she cherished most of all her grandson David's dedication of a ring of trees planted in Hadassah Forest in Eretz Yisrael in her honor the most.

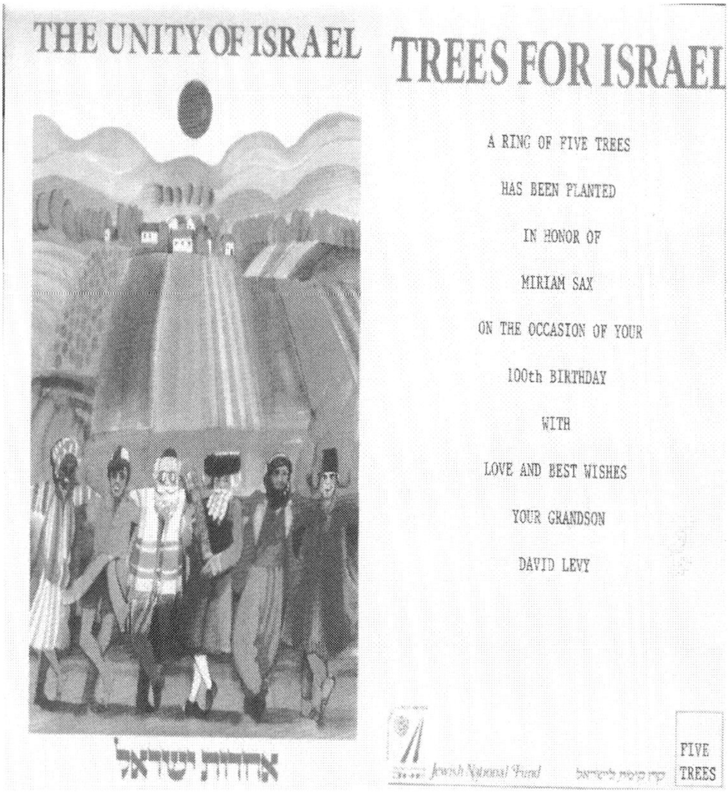

THE UNITY OF ISRAEL
TREES FOR ISRAEL
A RING OF FIVE TREES
HAS BEEN PLANTED
IN HONOR OF
MIRIAM SAX
ON THE OCCASION OF YOUR
100th BIRTHDAY
WITH
LOVE AND BEST WISHES
YOUR GRANDSON
DAVID LEVY
אחדות ישראל
Jewish National Fund
FIVE
TREES


Above Receipt of ring of trees planted in Hadasah forest for Miriam Sax.

David planted the trees himself and cited the statement of Rabbi Yochanan ben Zakkai, "if someone tells you the mashiach has come, go and plant a tree" along with the aggadata of Choni the Master of the circle who in Avoth de Rabbi Nathan is said to have planted a fruit tree, went to sleep like Rip Van Winkle (lehavdil) and woke up many generations later to see his great great great great great grandchildren enjoying the fruits. David later wonders if there are coincidences regarding David's gift to his grandmother of trees in Israel and the fact that Miriam's yahrzeit is on Tu b'shevat - the new year for trees?

Coincidences are the yad Hashem in Megilat Esther. What if the King was not sleepless that night(?), what if Mordechai did not hear the plot to destroy the Jews(?), "what if Ether had not been chosen as the beauty queen for Achashverosh beauty contest?" etc.). Miriam later passed on Tu b'shevat at the age of 105. David always felt uncanny coincidences sometimes can mean something as in Megillat Esther?

Above David planting trees in Hadasah Forest below. Sign welcoming tree planters in multiple modern languages.

Miriam came to Baltimore in 1917 with her parents, supported by the affidavit of physician Dr. Nathan Helfgott. Miriam studied to become a nurse because the US would not accept the dental degree which Miriam earned in Russia. Miriam then worked at Sinai Hospital in the maternity ward.

Miriam was fluent in Yiddish, Russian, and later English. She was a Tehillim zoger as well as recited Techinos (prayers) in Yiddish. She kissed the mezuzah every time walking through a doorway and was a very pious emunadik person who always saw the bright side of things, the glass half full, and was an eternal optimist.

While working in the maternity ward of Sinai Hospital in Baltimore she met Dr. Benjamin Sax a radiologist. At that time Doctors were not allowed to fraternize or date nurses. Therefore, the two eloped in Philadelphia and were married by two Chabad Rabbis in Philadelphia.

יתן ה' את האשה הבאה אל ביתך כרחל וכלאה אשר בנו שתיהם את

בית ישראל.

וְהַכֹּל שָׁרִיר וְקַיָּם.

Photo of The Ketubah between Miriam and Benjamin Sax.

Dr. Benjamin Sax was the son of Sara Levi Sax and Jacob Sax from Poland. The Sax family had ties to the antique business and went into business with Levy (Sara's family), Ginzberg selling precious rare works of art and antiques. Till this day in the upper East side this antique dealer has a store Bernard & S. Dean Levy, Inc. The Levy family has been active in the field of fine Americana since the founding of Ginsburg & Levy, Inc., in 1901 and spanning four generations. See https://www.levygalleries.com/w/history/

Dr. Benjamin Sax's house on Callow Avenue in Baltimore was therefore filled with precious antiques, including 18th century French clocks, American Eagle mirrors, Oriental Rugs, and rare 19th century famous French paintings, etc.

In 1948 Miriam's husband Dr. Benjamin Sax was tragically killed in a car crash on 5th of Av while Miriam was driving on the New Jersey Turnpike. A sleep deprived (or drunk?) truck driver hit the car from behind killing Dr. Benjamin Sax. Miriam was seriously hurt needing hip, knee, shoulder, and teeth replaced. They said Miriam would never walk again but she defied the odds and walked with a cane.

Miriam had no way to support the family (3 children) so all the antiques in the Callow Ave home were sold for pittance. The antique dealers took advantage of Miriam's financial desperate situation and finagled priceless antiques such as eagle mirrors and rare 18th century French paintings, and clocks.

The family of 4 (Miriam, Albert, Daniel, and Ruth) were forced to move into a very small apartment. Even though the doctors said Miriam would never walk after the car accident that killed her husband she proved them wrong. Due to her strong nature, courage, and perseverance she walked with a cane and got a job as a nurse in a public school, since it entailed less standing than at the maternity ward at Sinai. The school was closed on Shabbos which was important.

My mother Ruth remembers missing her father, and how during the Chagim it was particularly sad to be at a seder table of friends and not at her own father's seder table. My mother recalled to me how very religious Pesach was, with discussion around the seder table regarding the issur of eating kitniyot. My mother wondered why she could not eat peanuts during Passover and why her mother and the children had to do major cleaning, and bring separate Pesach dishes for eating on Pesach. Miriam herself recalled to me how her father Rabbi Yakov Yitchak Helfgott wore his kittel at the seder table and spoke about how wonderful Pesach was in the "old country". Rabbi Yitchak Helfgott gave silver dollars as the afikoman present in exchange for the matzah absconded with at the Pesach seder. My mother recalls how her own father when alive would shake the table so that the cup of Eliyahu HaNavi shook, and made it seem as if a mystical process was occurring.

After the car accident Miriam's daughter Ruth Sax Levy devotedly took care of her mother, even like Rabbi Tarfon putting on Miriam's slippers so that her mother's feet not touch the cold floor. Ruth did all she could to assure the comfort and wellbeing of her mother, even making possible her stay in a nice retirement community next to the Ner Israel Yeshivah (financially supported with help by Dr. Robert I Levy who economically helped both his own mother and Miriam in nice retirement communities. Dr. Robert I Levy also has the zekut of financially supporting all his 3 children by paying for their schooling from kindergarten to graduate school, as well as his 5 grandchildren, from kindergarten to grad school. Robert also helped finance the houses in which his children

Elizabeth, Kathy, and David live in Baltimore, Kansas, and NY.

At the retirement community of North Oaks in Baltimore, Rabbi Oberstein became Miriam's rabbi, and was present at the Levaya. The Eishet Chayil was sung at Miriam's kever.

Ruth bat Miriam exceptionally fulfilled the virtue of honoring her parents כַּבֵּד אֶת-אָבִיךָ, וְאֶת-אִמֶּךָ – [*Kavod et avikhah vet imekhah]*. There was not a more devoted daughter than Ruth who carried on the simple Emunah peshuta of her mother. Miriam displayed eternal optimism and love for all despite immense physical medical challenges in life after the car crash. The intellectual nature and love of books of Ruth's father, so tragically killed in a car crash in 1949, ensured that the family possess a magnificent library in their home on Callow Avenue, in Baltimore. After the car accident although the family was forced to move into a small apartment because of the limits of their economic standard of living. It was not easy for Miriam raising 3 children alone.

While most of the possessions in the house were sold Ruth and her two brother's clung to their father's books as a kesher with his devotion to learning, and respect for the life of the mind and intellectual activities. Miriam especially prized the siddurim, Tehillim texts, and techinos genre (Yiddish prayers written by women). Miriam was a Tehillim zoger her whole life and sat in "an Archie Bunker chair" and recited Tehillim. Albert got he Heinrich Graetz history set and Daniel the Jewish Encyclopedia.

Rabbi Bass, the shamash of Chizuk Amuna Congregation which was orthodox at the time the Sax family belonged to Chizuk Amuna, also gave Miriam a number of sefarim that she learned from.

Photo of Ruth S Sax on bima for Confirmation class at Chizuk Amuna.

Coincidentally while Rabbi Bass made Aliyah, his grandson married one of Rabbi Dovid Katz" daughter's[?]. Rabbi Katz was a mentor of David. Coincidentally, Rabbi Dovid's father Rabbi Moshe Katz from Mintz received semichah from Rabbi Eliezer Rabinowitch who was the father in law of Miriam's uncle Rav Menachem Mendel Gluskin ztsl. David spent close to a decade in the house of Rabbi Dovid Katz on Friday nights learning Midrash Rabbah on the parasha and in shiurim at Beth Avraham Congregation, formerly Rabbi Elimelech Hertzberg (zl) a Belzer Chasid who reportedly gave shoah survivors the shirt off his back and his own bed to sleep in. Memorably David also learned Rabbi Yonatan Eyebeshutz Zevat

Devash with Rabbi Katz in a small group. David also was lucky to be in an academic havruta with Rabbi Katz at the apartment of Gershon Greenberg near Washington DC also attended by Arthur Lesley, Morris Faierstein, Bernard Cooperman (UMCP), Charles Manekin, and other academics. David's father Robert lemeah ve-ezreim also was invited to attend one of these havruta sessions, where medieval charters against the Jews and other anti-Jewish legislation was lectured on. One unforgettable shiur was given by Rabbi Katz with a close reading of the sheolot ve-teshuvot of the Nodah BiYehudah. One was on the Nodah biYehuda's question of how the Nodah biYedah's niece could consummate the wedding night if she had a bleeding problem as a niddah.

Rabbi Katz was able to share with David the illustrious lineage of Rav Gluskin's father in law Rabbi Rabinowitz and Rabbi Rabinowitz own father in law Rabbi Eliyahu Pearlman, the Minsker Gadol and how Rav Gluskin "like an exotic plant" (expression of Dr. Saul Lieberman in Minsk Yizkor book) fit into this family of Mitnagdim in Minsk. Miriam had different kinds of memories of her illustrious uncle Rav Menachem ztsl. The memories of Miriam as a woman also were of how her own Mother Keila Leiba Gluskin Helfgott (zl) made candies out of radishes, turning the bitter into the sweet. Miriam's father Rabbi Helfgott recalled that radishes, a delicacy in tannaitic times, were always on the table of Rabbi Yehudah Hanasi. Rav Yehudah HaNasi (Rebbi) when he was on his death bed, had all his disciples praying for him. It was when his maidservant interrupted the prayers that his soul was freed to heaven.

Miriam's last moments were when her son-in-law, Dr. Robert I Levy, who supported her, came to make a bikur holim visit. Dr. Levy recalls that Miriam's last words were "abba" apparently mistaking her son in law Dr. Robert I

Levy for her father Rabbi Yakov Yitchak Helfgott. Dr. Robert I Levy visited his own mother (Ruth Bear Levy) and mother in law every day when they were elderly to check in and make sure they were all right (all medicines lined up and propertly administered) and say hi. Ruth made sure Miriam's favorite foods were available from 7 Mile Kosher market, as well as many other details. Ruth's brothers Albert and Daniel were very busy with their carriers as physicians and resided in NYC and Boston, so all the responsibility for taking care of Miriam was on Ruth and Robert who saw to Miriam's every need and probably are reasons that Miriam defied statistics and lived to the ripe age of 105 years given the good care showered upon her by her immediate family in Baltimore.

---

1 https://www.chabad.org/library/article_cdo/aid/2995708/jewish/The-Beginning-of-the-Doctors-Plot.htm

**Ruth S. Levy (zl)**

Like the Biblical Ruth, Ruth S. Levy manifested virtues of faith in the God of Israel, obedience to His Will, courage, humility, strength of character, virtue, excellence, hard work, diligence, concientioussness, and perseverance, kindness, moral and intellectual integrity, and mercy. Like Esther, who also has a whole section of Tanakh named after her, Ruth is a strong women who ensures the continuance of her people and makes hard decisions in tough times always acting out of magnanimous greatness of soul and gemilut hasidim. And Naomi said to her daughter-in-law, 'blessed be he of the Lord, who has not left off his kindness [hesed] from the living and from the dead'" Ruth 2:20. As Maimonides puts it, the concept of hesed: "Includes two notions, one of them consisting in the exercise of beneficence toward one who deserves it, but in a greater measure than he deserves it. In most cases, the prophetic books use the word hesed in the sense of practicing beneficence toward one who has no right at all to claim this from you" [Guide for the Perplexed] Ruth's mode is not only the first but the second, to practice benevolence toward people who even have no claim on her for it. Ruth

S. Levy did this in countless ways always acting selflessly sacrificing for others. Ruth, in spite of the dissuasion of Naomi, accompanied her mother-in-law to Bethlehem, and cast in her lot with the people of Judah, despite the reversal of fortune how she had been raised as a Moabite princess and due to misfortune became destitute as was the case in part with Ruth S. Levy after loosing her father in the car accident. Dr. Robert I Levy a successful brilliant physician and scientist became Ruth's Go'el and like Boaz (Robert's nick name is Bob) eventually named their male offspring David whose middle name is Benjamin after his maternal grandfather killed in the car accident, thereby redeeming the estate like the biblical Boaz. Although the biblical text states two interceding generations between Boaz and David, our family history proceeds over Oved and Jesse right to David so that the interest in the genealogy of David (iv. 20 et seq.) is thought to indicate a date when David had become a messianic scion of the nation. The difference in the Biblical book of Ruth and Ruth S. Levy is that Ruth S. Levy was no Moabitess and in fact stems from a venerable blood line of rabbinic dynasties of Chabad, Shklov, and Slonnim. As our opening dedication holds we wish Ruth Joy Levy to carry on in the footsteps fo Ruth S Levy growing in torah, reach the chuppah and do acts of loving kindness (gemilut Hasidim), and understand that you stem from reiner khsidische idene fun khsidim kodoshim shtam.

Ruth's tznius, which reflected her aristocratic bearing, was evident in her dress and her mannerisms and continued into her final days, even when she could hardly communicate due to lung cancer. Ruth grew up without a father most of her life because her father was killed in 1949 in a car accident.

Ruth was precocious as a child and went to Bryn Mawr College in Philadelphia on a scholarship at the age of 15, three years before most teenagers go to College. Ruth knew Yiddish, Hebrew, and English from her mother but the standards at Bryn Mawr College at that time required that ruth pass a German, ancient attic Greek, and French exam. The BA Ruth obtained from Bryn Mawr might be considered a PhD requirement today. Ruth recalls that she had to translate a passage of Kant's *Kritik der Reinen Vernunft,* KrV for the German exam, a passage from Plato's dialogues and the presocratics in Greek (Her teachers included Drs Richard Lattimore and Gregory Nagy who at that time taught at Bryn Mawr and is famous for his translation of Homer), and the fable of LaFontaine's the Ant and the Grasshopper (*La Cigale et la Fourmi*) for a Frenh exam. Ruth enjoyed philosophy and comparative literature classes and later went on to teach in an all-girls Jewish high school English literature once she married Dr Robert I Levy, on top of raising a family and devotedly taking care of her mother Miriam who was injured in the car crash, who she visited every day and cared for. Ruth met Robert at a classical music concert.

A gift Ruth bestowed on her family was the lesson she gave them in *kibud av va'eim.* Ruth treated her parents and her in-laws like the royalty they were: serving them, caring for them, waiting on them hand and foot fulfilling the mitzvah of *kavod et avikhah ve-eimekhah.* Ruth made sure Miriam not only had her all the needs and comforts in life lined up and was comfortable in North Oaks retirement community where Rabbi Oberstein gave lectures/shiurim, but also brought kosher dainties from afar for her mother who like rogelach, tzimmus, gefilta fish, and kreplach that Ruth made herself learned from her mother Miriam. הָיְתָה כָּאֳנִיּוֹת סוֹחֵר, מִמֶּרְחָק תָּבִיא לַחְמָהּ

Miriam also liked bagels and lox but the salt in the lox was not really the most healthy food for Miriam. The family secret however in the culinary arts was handed down from

Keila Leiba Gluskin who made sweet candies out of radishes changing the bitter into the sweet. It is said that Rav Yehudah HANasi's household always had radishes on its table, a delicacy in Tannaitic times.

When discussing the eishes chayil, Shlomo Hamelech writes:*"Oz vehadar levusha vatischak leyom acharon* – Strength and majesty are her raiment, and she joyfully awaits the last day. Oz vehadar, strength and majesty, are also accurate descriptions for her dignified levaya of Ruth zl. The funeral home was packed, with over 1,000 people in attendance, as David's having previously served in the Ner Israel High school motivated Rabbi Yakov Schuchman to have the whole Ner Israel Israel Henry Beren HS attend the funeral at Levinsons down the street (Yeshiva Lane) from Ner.

Furthermore, in the shiva house on 6248 Woodcrest Ave a Sefer Torah was supplied by Rabbi Dovid Katz, from which David B. Levy leyned during shiva on Monday and Thursday and the house never missed a minyan for Schaharit, minchah, and ma'ariv. At the levaya David wanted to give over a hesped about the illustrious Rabbinic stock and history from which Ruth zl and Miriam stemmed but did not due to the custom of not giving a hesped on Rosh Hodesh Nisan as per advice of Rabbi Yochanan Stengel who along with Rabbi Aaron Levine of the Agudah taught David Daf Yomi many years.

However, the pusek that illustrates Ruth (zl) the most is *"pihah patchah bichochmah ve-torah chesed al leshona"*. Ruth was full of wisdom (chokmah) and binah (understanding) both practical and more theoretical whether it be recognizing a conflict of interest of a lawyer who posed as buyer and seller in a business deal of real estate Ruth was orchestrating זָמְמָה שָׂדֶה וַתִּקָּחֵהוּ, מִפְּרִי כַפֶּיהָ נָטְעָה כָּרֶם , or her vast knowledge of literature and philosophy etc. which she loved and cherished because her father's library was stocked not only with sefarim but many sets of first editions of Comparative literature.

Ruth's BA at Bryn Mawr College was the equivalent today to a PHD as she passed an exam in Greek given by Gregory Nagy and Richard Latimore requiring translation of pre-Socratic fragments, translation of a portion in German of Kant's *Kritik der reinen Vernunft* KrV (Ruth was worried about passing this exam as she knew Yiddish from her Mother Miriam but German was required for the BA requirement at Bryn Mawr), a French exam translating a section of Lafontaine's Les Fables, and explication de text of Old English from Beowulf and Chaucer. Such were the standards then for a BA with majors in philosophy & English / comparative literature.

However, Ruth's knowledge of secular literature was largely self-taught and continued throughout her life as an autodidact where she explored works in Hebrew literature and Religious Zionism. Ruth regularly attended lectures at the Baltimore Hebrew University and enrolled for classes in Israeli History, Israeli politics, Hebrew literature, Tanakh, Biblical Archeology, Jewish philosophy, Jewish history etc. Yet Ruth, who had a modest job teaching literature in a HS, was very active in practical matters always sacrificing for others, and never indulged in luxuries for herself, was never lazy, never idle, distinguishing between needs and wants צוֹפִיָּה הֲלִיכוֹת בֵּיתָהּ, וְלֶחֶם עַצְלוּת לֹא תֹאכֵל

Ruth is now joyfully reaping the rewards for all the selfless acts in her lifetime, we, those left behind, are bereft and forlorn — without her help, without her wisdom, without her cheer, without her laugh. Ruth planned for the future of the well being of her children and thus did not fear the snowy days of the future "because all her household was dressed in royality" לֹא תִירָא לְבֵיתָהּ מִשָּׁלֶג, כִּי כָל־בֵּיתָהּ לָבֻשׁ שָׁנִים Ruth planned for the future financially of her children and grandchildren investing and sacrificing everything for them. עוֹז וְהָדָר לְבוּשָׁהּ, וַתִּשְׂחַק לְיוֹם אַחֲרוֹן

May we find joy in emulating her special graceful and magnanimous ways, and may we soon be zocheh (merit) to the fulfillment of: "Az yimalei schok pinu uleshoneinu rina – Then our mouth will be filled with laughter and our tongue with glad song." Ruth along with Robert played the piano and made sure her 3 children received piano and music lessons (see Intro in vol. *Music and Medicine* by Robert I Levy).

May we never forget Ruth's encouragement of all her children's educational pursuits. After each day of school Ruth asked, "did you learn anything important that transformed you for the better morally, spiritually, and intellectually? More importantly it is not the score you won on your quiz but did you ask a thoughtful penetrating question that makes the examined life worth living?" Ruth was an excellent teacher full of patience and love when she helped her children with homework. She knew the best teaching methods to reach each particular child with their own learning styles חֲנֹךְ לַנַּעַר, עַל-פִּי דַרְכּוֹ. Ruth's 3 children never had anxiety about scoring high academically (although they did) because Ruth instilled a true love for learning lishmah and the joy of intellectual contemplation and understanding. In helping with home work she instilled calm, quietude, and reassurance of the big picture and what ultimately matters and is redemptive in life. Ruth had a vision of philosophy of education.

Ruth's three children attained advanced degrees. The son in Jewish studies and two daughters at Hopkins in Creative Writing under playwright Edward Albee and the middle daughter a degree in Chinese philosophy and

Mandarin Language at Princeton magna cum laude. The Middle child was also the valedictorian of her competitive High school class and was accepted not only at Princeton but Harvard and Yale. Ruth is the one who should take credit for the academic achievements.

All three children knew that really these attainments were Ruth's who encouraged and nourished the intellectual quest and life of the mind in all her family from an early age by reading to her children first children's books like *the Little Midrash* says and then classics for the teenage years like James Michener's *the Source,* Chaim Grade's *My Mother's Sabbath Days,* Leon Uris' *Exodus.* Vacations revolved around reading. Ruth gathered her children all around the table in an inexpensive cabin that the family rented for vacations in the remote mountains of Western Maryland and West Virginia. These were not fancy vacations at hotels. Rather they revolved around learning, quality time, reading and sitting on the porch watching the birds fly overhead, the deer in the meadows, and sound of acorns off of trees, and excursions to the lake for a row boat ride. They were not vacations filled with glitz of minature golf, amusement park rides, and the sickness of constantly needing to be "entertained" in vanity of vanities. Ruth spent nothing on herself. Rather everything was for the wellbeing of her children and mother and mother in law. In this way Ruth sacrificed for others, and was always concerned and devoted to the needs of others. Ruth gave much Tzedakah and participated in many worthwhile projects such as sending monies to orphans in Israel, supporting soup kitchens in Israel like Penai Meir, and projects like Leket Israel which gathers left over food from simchot to share with people that need the food to survive. כַּפָּהּ פָּרְשָׂה לֶעָנִי, וְיָדֶיהָ שִׁלְּחָה לָאֶבְיוֹן Ruth also greatly patronized the arts supporting the Baltimore symphony, Shakespeare Folger Theater, and many museums across the world. David's memorable trips with his two parents include one to Amsterdam where the family stayed for a Shabbat with a shomer shabbos former colleague of Dr. Robert Levy's in Amsterdam. Robert's cousin Flora Aitkin was descended from the Rabbi Hartegensis family of Amsterdam. The second major trip David remembers with Ruth and Robert I Levy is a trip to Greece and Turkey where particularly Jewish historical sites were sought out. David remembers how anti-Semitic some of the Greek people were. In Turkey in Istanbul David remembers a remarkable meal on the Bosporus hosted by a Jewish family whose son had frequently been hosted by the Levy family for Shabbos while attending Johns Hopkins University in Baltimore.

Ruth valued memory and understood the importance of remembrance. She devotedly attended Yizkor for her father who was killed in a car crash in 1949. Ruth visited his kever between Rosh Hoshanah and Yom Kippur every year. Ruth also drove and accompanied her mother Miriam to the kever of her grandparents Keila Leiba Gluskin Helfgott and Rabbi Yaakov Helfgott in Rosedale cemetery in Baltimore where Rabbi Katz' parents are also buried.

Thus David's genealogical research was really begun by Ruth and continued by David who visited various members of the Gluskin family in Eretz Yisrael in 2005 where David interviewed Dr. Gita Gluskina in Givatayim, and 2017 meeting with Dr. Emmanuel Gluskin. Photo in Jerusalem below of Dr. Emmanuel Gluskin, David, and Yosi Dr. Gluskin's son:

Ruth's interest in remembering the past is also seen in her contact with Debbie Nussbaum. Ruth placed an ad in the Algemeiner Journal to trace and be put in contact with her Russian Gluskin cousins. Thus this genealogical research was really begun by Ruth. Ruth was an avid reader of Jewish history. Her learning about the past was not sufficient for Ruth who wanted to not only remember the past, live in the present, and trust the future. One must learn from the past. And that sent Ruth into her living Zionist commitment. Besides charitable work on behalf of Israel Ruth was an avid follower of Israeli life, culture, and politics as well as Jewish history & philosophy

In her later years Ruth pursued much intellectual exploration in Zionist thought and ideology on the history of Eretz Yisrael from antiquity to the present vibrant political dynamics. From Arthur Hertzberg's The Zionist Idea, to writings by Chaim Weizman, Menachem Begin (White Nights), to early Hebrew literature such as works by Agnon, Bialik, Brenner, Tchernikovsky, to the poetry of Rachel, Uri Tzvi Greenberg, to recent writers such as A.B. Yehoshua, Amichai, Amos Oz, etc. There was not any area extraneous to Eretz Yisrael and its life that did not escape the cognition of Ruth who as with Yehudah HaLevi felt very strongly the Hibat Zion illustrated in the verse, "Ani bi Ma'ariv ve lebi bi-mizrah (אני במערב ולבי במזרח)"

Ruth's ahavat Yisrael for every Jew was a manifestation of her love for the land of Israel the ultimate home of the Jewish spirit and the unfolding of the Jewish destiny upon the stage of history. This is why Ruth's funeral was somewhat of a paradox. At Sol Levinson thousands of students from Ner Yisrael attended the funeral and even Rabbi Dovid Katz, a Kohen attended in a special outside area designated for Kohanim.

These various types of Talmud scholars that attended the levaya speak to the eternal Jewish spark that remains alive in the exile, but ironically Ruth's whole later life was a longing for the negation of the exile (shallal ha-galut) to come closer to the eternal homeland of the Jews by understanding not only the forms of Zionism as political (Herzl), cultural (Ahad HA'am), linguistic (Eliezer ben

Yehudah), and religious (Rav Kook, etc.) but appreciating EY pioneers, builders, and still today its torchbearers. Ruth sought to understand Israel today, its achievements, and challenges then, now, and in the future. Ruth's pride and respect for the early halutzim who came to the land "livnot u le hibanot bah" (to build and be personally rebuilt" to reading the works of female Zionists like Henrietta Szold the organizer, Rachel Bluwstein the poet, Rahel ben Zvi the pioneer, and Gold Meir the leader. This interest in women Zionists extended to female voices today such as those of Ruth Wisse although a Yiddishist by profession a true lover of Israel as illustrated in her book on Jewish power. It included women Zionists of all political spectrums such as Letty Pogrebin, Anne Roiphe, Rose Halperin, Blu Greenberg, Tael Tamir, Anita Shapira, Ruth Gavison, Ayelet Shaked, Rachel Danzinger, Einat Ramon, Sharon Shalom, Ellin Willis, and Esther Jungreis. Ruth also read widely and enjoyed encountering people of Mizrahi backgrounds or Jews from Arab Speaking lands including Moracco, Syria, Iraq, etc. Ruth also was thankful for non-Jewish Zionist voices as illustrated by Martin Luther King, Robert Kennedy, Patrick Moynahan who gave an important speech at the UN in favor of Israel when it was not popular to do so. When the Durban conference occurred branding Zionism as Racism, Ruth was not afraid to speak up, reject, and condemn such liberal political correctness in the name of anti-Semitism. Ruth condemned BDS and her roots with her mother who escaped communist Russia while many of her cousins did not, never forgot how communism persecuted the Jews, how her mother's brother was one of the physicians condemned in Stalin's Doctor's plot persecutions, and how even her mother's uncle Rav Gluskin was imprisoned for religious activity 2x in communist Russia. Ruth was cognizant however not only of Stalinist cleansing of Jewish communists, but daily she remembered the Churban

Europa that came from the fascist right of the Nazi totalitarians and their allies such as the Hungarian Arrow Cross. Thus politically Ruth did not tend towards extremes of the right or left, but rather encouraged her children to think critically and realize that much of politics is corruption especially after what Leo Strauss identified as Machiavelli as the teacher of evil when he said "the ends justify the means." Ruth's greatest virtue was seeing every person as a kingly end rather than a means only respecting everyone as *Bitzelem Elokim*. She saw the dignity in all, respecting political differences but at the same time according respect, dignity, and love of each person as a child of G-d because all are *BiTzelem Elokim*. She did not understand being in the image of G-d literally as anthropomorphic resemblance but rather the divine spark to strive for moral, spiritual, and intellectual virtue, living a life of the mind, a thoughtful life, a life of questioning and Emunah with deep ahavat Hashem, ahavat Torah, and ahavat Yisrael. David never saw Ruth angry and never heard Ruth speak loshon harah.

Ruth's respect for elders was exemplary in the way she cared for both her mother and mother in law. Ruth's life was a *kiddush Ha-shem* or sanctification of G-d's name, and the difficult illness with cancer at the end of her stay in olam ha zeh should only be a kappara and yisurin shel ahava, in a life dedicated to the needs of others, where she always put herself last and habitually acted *lifnim mishurat ha-din*, giving tzedakah generously, ensuring her children's love of learning lishma, caring for others, etc. As the Mishnah in Peah 1:1 states and Ruth fulfilled, "

> These are the precepts that have no prescribed measure, the corner of the field (left for the poor, i.e. support of Leket Israel), the first fruit offering (bikurim in parasha Ki Savo, which Ruth heard David layn on Shabbos),

> acts of gemilut hasidim (loving kindness), and talmud Torah.

This Mishnah is recapitulated in Talmud Bavli Shabbos 127a which Ruth also fulfilled as best possible for a woman:

> These are the precepts whose fruits a person enjoys in this world but whose principle remains intact in olam habah. They are the honor and devotion due mother and father, acts of gemilut chasadim, early attendance at the house of study morning and evening (Ruth encouraged David to attend Shacharit and Maariv every day and David also daavened Minchah at Ner Israel when he worked there as a HS teacher and librarian, hospitality (hachnoset orchim), bikur holim, dowering the bride, escorting the dead, kavanah in tefillah (which she learned from Miriam the Tehillim and Techinus sager), bringing peace between man and his fellow (Aaron's virtue), vetalmud Torah kineged kulam.

Ruth's life is an example of self-sacrifice for others and her presence blessed all who circulated in her orbit. May Ruth's memory be for a blessing and her soul caught up in the bundle of life like a shining name in Gan Eden zl.

David Levy sitting with his grandmothers Miriam Gluskin Helfgott Sax and Ruth Bear Levy learning mishnayos.

**Yehoshua Shneur Zalman Serebryanski**

Born in Bragin/Brahin Belarus, his approximate birthday is 8 Teves 5664/December 27 1903 (January 10 1904) - 3 Tammuz 5751/June 15 1991. Official birth document in those days did not always indicate exact day of birth, just when the day of birth was registered. It was not a custom in many Jewish communities to celebrate birthdays and even the exact day of a bar mitzvah was not a big matter and so he did not remember the exact day when he became thirteen. In Russia, they changed from the Julian calendar to the Gregorian calendar in 1918. Thus January 31 1918 was followed by February 14 1918. So he decided on an approximate birthday.

He was named after his great grandfather Shneur Zalman who was named after the first Chabad Rebbe. The name Yehoshua was added later due to illness. He was an only son with three older sisters. *Russian newspapers of Rechitsa area has names and other details about people from Bragin and Loyev. Zalman's grandfather Eliyahu, a burgher, son of Zalman, is mentioned as being called up for Jury duty for the year 1901 by the Rechitsa district court as well as Sholom Schneerson, a descendant of an honored citizen, from Lubavitch. Published in the Minsk bi-monthly newspaper Vedomosti (1838-1917) 23 September 1900 issue number 74 page 1. Also names of people in Bragin and Loyev are in "Vsay Russia" an all-Russian industrial address book.*

https://archive.org/details/1895VsayRossiya
*Some of the names and details in English*
https://www.jewishgen.org/belarus/lists/albell_minsk_records.html?fbclid=IwAR3KjuLZbrkXYhPmA1Inw7AQeNbeoyamFE-kXMIChw9aaVX_Nwx_LOzVsM

For Zalman's third birthday they received a letter from his grandfather Rabbi Aharon Gluskin that from the age of three the child should constantly wear a tallis kotton and included was a gift 25 rubles. At the time there were about 400 Jewish families in Brahin living in a separate area from the non Jews.

Cheder was from 9 am and some days 10 am, till 10 pm. They had long breaks to play, swim, go row boating or horseback riding. Before the revolution most Jewish children had no secular education. He remembers his grandfather constantly learning Gemorah. The majority of the Jews in the town were Chassidim of Chernobel.

His family was wealthy and therefore had a large house with a large courtyard and garden. Visiting Jewish dignitaries would stay at their house. During the summer of 5596/1836 the third Chabad Rebbe known as the Tzemack Tzedek stopped in Brahin on the way to visit the grave of his grandfather in Haditch and probably stayed at the Serebryanski house who were the only Lubavitch Chassidim in that town.

The Loyev-Chernobel Rebbe would stay at the Serebryanski house when he visited his followers in Brahin. Reb Zalman remembered when they stayed at the Serebryanski house for a half year and thus he got to know the whole family well.

1910 Cast Portrait: Brahin children's production of the play Birchas Yankev (Jacob's blessing). Yiddish inscription: me (Mottel Levin, dressed as a woman), and my friends right to left, top: Meyer, Meyer; bottom: Chaim, Yankl, Avrohom, Chaim Zushe. Yivo1000towns.cjh.org

From 1911 – 1914 a Jewish children's weekly magazine named He'och (The Brother) was published in Lubavitch Russia. Many boys pre bar-mitzvah age were subscribed to it. In two 1911 editions, February 5 and 11 the names of 59 boys who subscribed are mentioned. Zalman who was much younger is not mentioned, yet he was definitely aware of magazine.

His father Menachem Mendel was a chossid internally and externally. He had a good and kind heart and helped many people. Even though he was busy and of high status, he was kind and friendly to all, including non-Jews. He had a large business. Before the revolution he worked far from home with Zalman's uncles, supplying and building parts for the Russian railroad. He would come home for Jewish holidays. His mother never let people know her pain and problems whether personal or due to communal issues, she always smiled. At home she never sighed.

His factory employed many people, yet each one felt a personal connection with Reb Mendel. The love and respect for him came to the fore during times of hardship for the entire population, whether during pogroms or when the communists came into power.

During the Beilis blood libel trials, the Jewish community lived in constant fear that any day could bring a new progrom. This was from September 23 1911 until his equital on October 28 1913. Zalman was a young boy 8-10 years old during that time. Then World War 1 began July 28 1914 when he was eleven and finished November 11 1918 when he was 15 years old. In 1917 the Russian revolution erupted. There was civil war and struggle for power that continued for a long time.

During this time the Navardok yeshiva sent small groups of students to study in various towns and one of them was Brahin. (*Mosdos Torah in Europe bebinyonon ubechurbonom N.Y. 1956, p.256.)* Zalman remembers them well. He studied in the shul below while they studied upstairs. They were there for approximately two years. He went in to the yeshiva to observe them and got to know the way they learn and perspectives in learning and life.

During the turmoil of the first world war and its aftermath with the communist revolution, there were many criminal gangs that took advantage of the situation to plunder, murder and destroy. When these gangs approached Brahin many of Reb Mendel's workers came to his defense. They gathered him and all the other Jews into his house and formed a human wall around the house in order to protect them.

Under the Tsar the Jews felt oppression, not having equal rights, fear of pogroms, especially during the beilis blood libel and terror. There was WW1 and then the revolution, the civil war with reds and whites, bandits and murderers who roamed. It was dangerous to travel from town to town.

One time they attacked a nearby village and murdered all the Jews. The next day, forty bodies were brought to Brahin for burial. Subsequently they organized self defense in Brahin. About fifty boys organized themselves with rifles and a machine gun and used a synagogue as their base. Guards were posted on all the roads but thank G-d their service was never called for.

Growing up, Zalman had complete freedom, no-one told him what to do, he read many Russian books, he was immersed in his week and had deep feelings for yidishkeit. He felt that communism was wrong even though he could not explain what was wrong besides atheism. But there were problems due to the books that he read as they gave him thoughts not in accordance with Torah or that communism was a nice idea. People asked questions against religion which he could not answer as he did not have enough knowledge to answer the questions. But deep in his heart he felt that it was wrong and that yiddishkeit was correct but he could not explain it to himself.

He read the books that were part of the Russian culture and revolution. Many of the Jewish people in the area became communists. All of his friends became part of the communist party. They tried to convince him to join but he would not and so he remained alone learning in shul daily and when the Rabbi came in he would learn with him. One day an old friend came to convince him to join the communist party and he responded, (Isaiah 48:22) "There is no peace, says Hashem, to the wicked."

One day Zalman came into shul and Reb Shimon Zelichover (who stayed in Brahin for a period of time) told him that he has a headache. Zalman asked him how he could help him. Reb Shimon said, "farher (test) me on shas." Zalman asked, "how?" Reb Shimon said, "open the Rambam and read and I will tell where it is from in shas." Reb Zalman said that the way he learned Gemorah and Rashi was with a simplicity that answered all the questions of Tosfos and the commentaries.

*Reb Shimon also known as Shimele of Zelichov, his full name was Avrohom Shimon Halevi Engel-Horowitz. He was a chossid of Ger and Koznitz. For a period of time, he was a Mashgiach Ruchni in the famous Yeshiva of Chachmei Lublin. Afterwards he taught Torah in Krakow and was murdered during WW2. He told over a story that he read among the hand written papers of the Baal Hatanaya that were in the possession of the Rabbi in Brahin, the Mishmeres Sholom. He also visited the Rebbe Rayatz*

*of Lubavitch several times. The Imrei Emes said that he has the most organized memory in all Poland. Rabbi Yosef Yitzchok of Lubavitch said that for hundreds of years there has not been a person with a memory like his. Reb Beirish Veidenfeld of Tshebin said that he has a unique ability to remember besides for the Rogatchover Gaon. He prayed nusach Chabad but after prayers said the ani maamin since they are not part of the prayers.*

Zalman studied with the young son of the Mishmeres Sholom (Sholom son of Boruch Mordechai of Kaidinov). He said that when the boy was eleven years old he would come to shul Friday afternoon after the mikvah to say Posach Eliyohu and his face would be shining.
In 1919 towards the end of WW1 a typhus epidemic spread across Europe killing many people. Zalman contracted the disease. His sister stayed home to care for him as he had fever and was weak. At one point the front door was opened by a passing soldier. Seeing a young woman there with no-one to stop him he knew that he could do whatever he desired with the woman. Zalman garnered his strength, sat up in bed, and said to the soldier, "come in, come in, I have typhus." The soldier turned and left.

In 1920, life became a little bit more stable even though it was still very difficult. A new economical policy was introduced that allowed private enterprise. Life improved a little but due to the difficult time people did not know what was really going on other cities. In 5680/1920 there was a pogrom in Chernobel and Shlomo Ben-Tzion from Chernobel came to stay in Brahin for a few weeks.

In approximately 1919 His sister Ita Fraida married Elazar Gurevitch and they lived in a nearby town Yanovitch. In 5683/1922 they had a baby girl named Esther. She was named after two great grandmothers, the mother of Nechama Gluskin and wife of Aharon Gluskin and the mother of Miriam Chaikin mother of Elazar Gurevitch. She then had a second girl. (***Sefer Zikaron*** *of Rabbi Binyamin Eliyahu Gorodetsky p.57*) "I ate the sedorim at the home of Reb Boruch who was a shochet in Brahin. He was a lamdan and Chernobeler Chossid. All his son-in-laws were Lubavitch Chassidim."

After the Communist Revolution, the government confiscated all the Serebryanski wealth. All that remained was his house with a large garden and a cow. Having no choice, Reb Zalman's father began working as a simple woodchopper in order to provide for his family. Zalman also chopped wood and they supplied the wood for the shul.

He found it difficult getting used to the new circumstances, with his father earning a paltry salary from the government. He was 17 years old and considered going to work to help his family. However, when he told his father about his intentions, his father adamantly opposed it and said that until his wedding, his head should be solely involved in learning Torah and not in work.

Despite the difficult spiritual circumstances and war that the government waged against anything religious, his father was able to maintain a Chassidic lifestyle and was even able to raise his children in the spirit of pure yiras shomayim.

A student from the yeshiva Lubavitch Yeshiva Tomchei Tmimim in Rostov traveled through Brahin. He told them about the yeshiva where time had stopped, the progressive atmosphere of "progress" did not penetrate the walls of the beis midrash, and the talmidim conducted themselves as G-d fearing individuals.

Reb Menachem Mendel was eager to register his son in the yeshiva in Rostov which was also the seat of Lubavitch at the time. When he told Zalman that he wanted him to go, Zalman responded that the economic conditions are very difficult and that he is able to work to help his parents. His father said, "Hashem will help me, I want you to learn and be a Yid."

Before sending his son to a distant city, he went to consult with his friend and relative, Reb Sholom Perlov (grandson of the Tzemach Tzedek and author of *Mishmeres Shalom*). At first he said no, apparently because he wanted Zalman to continue learning with his young son. However, after a while he realized that it was in Zalman's best interests to go and learn in Yeshivas Tomchei Temimim. He gave the young man a letter of recommendation for the Rebbe Rayatz as well as a sum of money for a *pidyon nefesh*.

Reb Menachem Mendel's financial state in those days was so poor that he did not even have the money for the trip to Rostov. He borrowed 100 rubles and had to sell the few silver items in his possession, and with the money that he received, was able to buy tickets for himself and his son to Rostov. It was a long journey to Rostov, first by steamer to Kiev and then from Kiev by train to Rostov.

This was in the early years of the Rebbe Rayatz's leadership. The previous Rebbe was still there but getting ready to move to Leningrad. Upon their arrival after Pesach 1924, they had yechidus. In the yechidus the Rebbe asked him if he could read Russian. He responded that he can read the large letters on the front page of a newspaper. The Rebbe smiled, apparently the Yeshiva did not accept anyone who could read Russian since that would mean that his mind could have been corrupted in some way, but in this case he was not concerned. After the yechidus he instructed the administration to accept Yehoshua Shneur Zalman into the yeshiva.

He was tested by Yehuda Eber; after a day or two he was told to go to Kharkov with about 10 students since the Yeshiva in Rostov had to disband while most students went to other cities. The initial appearance of the yeshiva students was strange to Zalman, young men with beards and long coats and he said to his father that he does not know if he wants to stay there. His father told his to try it out. After a few days he found that they do not care about communism at all and were in fact very intelligent and focused on their ideals. They kept Judaism with complete self sacrifice.

In Kharkov, they sat down and learned but there were no facilities for food. They lived on dry food buying vegetables, eggs that they ate raw since they had nowhere to cook them and bread. They spent their time learning 8 am – 11pm and were happy in the yeshiva. Zalman felt solid and that all the questions that he used to have were gone, He was at peace, sleeping on a wooden bench with his jacket as a pillow. During the summer they studied in the woman's gallery in shul and although there was not enough light or air, they felt good.

Reb Yehoshua Shneur Zalman, who had never learned in a formal yeshiva, found it hard at first to get used to the yeshiva schedule. In his town of Brahin, he was known as a bachur with a particularly active nature. So for example, during the transition between the government of the Czar and the takeover by the communists, when bands of murderers travelled through the towns and sowed fear among the Jewish communities, Zalman was one of the leaders of the defence force. Now he found it difficult when he was expected to sit most of the day and learn.

Within a short time, he became acquainted with the special character of the talmidim of the yeshiva, and learned to recognize them internally, the penimius that burned with a fire of love and fear of Hashem. Chassidus, which he learned for the first time in an organized way, had its effect on him and began changing his middos.

He became friendly with the best of the Temimim at that time. He learned Nigleh with Reb Zalman Kurenitzer and Chassidus with Reb Nachum Goldschmid. As he learned, he discovered the tremendous wisdom and rare cleverness of his friends and his admiration for them grew from day to day. Each night after they finished learning at 11pm he would sit for an hour or more with his friend Nochum and discuss his thoughts and what he had learned that day. He was not used to studying Tanya and learning Chassidus and it took him about one year till it was able to penetrate him.

For Tishrei several boys went to the Rebbe in Leningrad, but since Zalman was not brought up with travelling to the Rebbe he did not feel a need to go. How to pay for the travel tickets was an issue for many of the boys and

Nochum needed money to travel so Zalman gave him the money to travel.

Before Purim, Reb Chatche Feigin said to Zalman, "since you did not go for Tishrei I will take you with me for Purim." Zalman and one of his friends Leibel Neuschuler went. For Zalman this was the first time that he travelled to the Rebbe and he did not know that people come and have a private audience with the Rebbe. He listened to the maamorim that the Rebbe said and studied Chassidus for a few weeks. It was winter time and very cold. Then he returned to Kharkov where he received permission to go home for Pesach. For the next three months he felt like he was somewhere between heaven and earth from his experience being at the Rebbe.

He continued going to the Rebbe until the Rebbe left in 1927. It was there that he met Reb Levik's sons, Menachem Mendel who later became the Lubavitcher Rebbe, Berel and Laibel. Menachem Mendel spoke with him about analysis of Rashi on the portion of the week.

Reb Yehoshua Shneur Zalman, who in the not-too-distant past had been a child of a well-to-do family, still had some items of clothing from those better days and he came to yeshiva with a fine fur coat. Within a short time, he noticed a bachur who suffered greatly from the cold and fell ill. He did not think twice but gave the bachur his coat. After a few more incidents in which he helped needy bachurim, he became known as "Zalman der gutter."

In accordance with the yeshiva's schedule, his day began with two hours of Chassidus as a preparation for davening. After the davening they learned Nigleh for eight hours, and then another two hours of Chassidus. During the Chassidus sedarim they mainly learned the maamarim of the Rebbe Rashab and the Rebbe Rayatz. However, the packed day did not suffice for him. Once he had gotten a taste of the sweetness of Chassidus, he wanted to learn more and more. When the day of learning was over, he remained for another two hours in which he studied the Chassidic teachings of the Rebbeim.

*The yeshiva in Rostov that had come from the town of Lubavitch lasted for nearly a year. At the end of the winter of 5681, the Yevsektzia began persecuting the Chabad Chassidim in Rostov. They held a public trial that led to the closing of the yeshiva. The talmidim had to move and they travelled to Tomchei T'mimim in Poltava. They did not last long there either. Within two years, the yeshiva in Poltava was closed and due to the sensitive situation, it was decided to split the yeshiva into two outposts, one in Nevel and one in Charkov.*

*In Tishrei 5684/1923, the Rebbe Rayatz decided to bring the yeshiva back to Rostov so that it would once again be close by and under his direct supervision. The talmidim were close to the Rebbe and could attend his farbrengens, have yechidus, and receive instructions in avodas Hashem. They were able to see the Rebbe often. During the winter of 5684, the Rebbe urged Anash to be moser nefesh in support of Judaism. At the 19 Kislev farbrengen that took place in Rostov, the Rebbe made a covenant with some Chassidim who committed to taking care of Jewish matters in their city. A short time later, on a visit to Moscow, the Rebbe made the famous covenant with nine T'mimim (with the Rebbe as the tenth) who swore to go in the path of the Rebbe and be moser nefesh for the dissemination of Torah till their last drop of blood.*

*These actions of the Rebbe became known to the GPU and they waited for him at his house in Rostov in order to arrest him. He found out about this as he was on his way home from Moscow, and he turned back around and settled in a village near Moscow for several weeks. The GPU was determined to arrest him and when Pesach approached and the Rebbe decided to return home, the GPU came to arrest him. It was only after much political manoeuvring that they came to an agreement with the GPU. If the Rebbe would leave Rostov, they would leave him alone.*

*A few weeks after Pesach and after Zalman arrived, the Rebbe Rayatz left Rostov and moved to Leningrad. The yeshiva was closed.*

In the meantime, the yeshiva in Charkov, which had begun with a small group of talmidim from Rostov, flourished. Within a year, the yeshiva grew even more when a group of bachurim including Mendel Futerfass and Ben Tzion Shemtov came from Kremenchug.

Reb Zalman was one of the older bachurim and he soon became an active part of the administration of the yeshiva. Chassidim who learned in Kharkov in those days remember him as a "good mother of the bachurim." He was unusually goodhearted and took care of all the bachurim's needs. When a bachur fell sick, he would visit him and take care of him. In one instance he took care of a bochur for three months.

Reb Yechezkel (Chatshe) Feigin, was the general menahel of all branches of Tomchei T'mimim. For a short period Zalman was his secretary. His friends found it frustrating since he never gave them the slightest hint of the work that he did. When Chatshe left to work for the Rebbe in Leningrad, he put Zalman in charge of administration. He came occasionally to Kharkov in order to personally oversee the development of the yeshiva and assess its needs. Reb Feigin would occasionally deliver instructions and missions to Reb Zalman from the Rebbe Rayatz in connection with the running of the yeshiva in Charkov.

For the most part, these were the most secret of matters, and years later, Reb Zalman said that he often received instructions in writing from the Rebbe and on the letter it said "top secret, to be burned after reading." Until the end of his life, he was pained about having to burn the Rebbe's writing, but there was no alternative in those terrible days.

Reb Yehoshua Shneur Zalman would go to Leningrad, where the Rebbe was, for Tishrei. Aside from the zechus of being in the Rebbe's presence, he was a partner in the Rebbe's holy work when Reb Chatshe Feigin asked for his help in the many administrative and secretarial duties the Rebbe had given him that included copying the Rebbes letters.

One of the obstacles that stood in the way of the Temimim who wanted to learn was being drafted into the Red Army. If it was hard to live a religiously observant life as a civilian, in the army it was nearly impossible. Not surprisingly, the bachurim did all they could to gain an exemption.

At the end of 5685/1925, Reb Yehoshua Shneur Zalman and his friend Reb Aharon Yosef Blinitzky had to present themselves to the enlistment office. For Tishrei 5686, the mashgiach Reb Chatshe went with the two of them to the Rebbe in Leningrad to obtain his bracha that they succeed in avoiding the draft. Before hakafos, a time considered especially auspicious, Reb Chatshe took the two bachurim for yechidus and pleaded on their behalf. The Rebbe's response was: They must serve G-d rather than serve in the army.

With that answer, they were confident that they would be exempt and indeed, when it was their turn, they miraculously received the "white card," which meant they were exempt from military service.

In the commission were all types of people; doctors, military personel and others. One of them said to Zalman, "what do you do?" Zalman responded, "I study Talmud." He said, "Bring us a note signed by an official recognized signature that you are studying and you will be free." Zalman got such a letter and was not accepted into the army. He was given a little book that said he was free from the army and the reason that he is not allowed to defend the mother land with a weapon in his hand is because he is not to be trusted. Zalman did not care what it said as long as he was free from serving in the army.

When he visited Brahin next his sister was sick. In 1927 his sister Ita Fraida tragically passed away. While many Jews became staunch communists' others remained faithful to Torah. One day a Jewish taylor and shoemaker who had become caught up in the communist fervor came to argue with Reb Elazar. They argued and began to fight, Ita who was pregnant got caught in the middle. She was hurt and passed away shortly later. Her sister Sarah Simcha then married Elazar in order to raise the two children.

As the years passed, Reb Chatshe Feigin got to know Reb Zalman's tremendous qualities and his abilities in leadership and organization. When he had to leave Russia, he gave Reb Zalman the responsibility of the physical running of the yeshiva in Kharkov. The spiritual running of the yeshiva was given to Reb Yehoshua Korf who was the mashgiach of the yeshiva. The two of them together ran the yeshiva in the face of communist persecution.

In letters that Reb Zalman wrote to his friend, Reb Eliyahu Sklar, he hinted at the state of the yeshiva. This is what he wrote in a letter dated 3 Seitzei 5687/1927:

"I am working at the factory [=yeshiva] here in the department that was previously in Szedrin. My friends Yeshua Korf and L. N. [Leibe Neuschuler] are here too."

On 2 Teves 5688 he wrote: "The factory [=yeshiva] that was previously in Szedrin is now here and has expanded in numbers. There are 25 workers [=students].

After the Rebbe left in 1927 things became worse and they changed their policies again. After a number of years in which the yeshiva was in the shul in Charkov, the GPU decided to put an end to the learning taking place there. Since all the talmidim were over 18 and their learning did not constitute a violation of the law, the GPU decided to use fear tactics.

On the morning of a wintry day in 5688, a representative of the GPU appeared at the shul. With him was the representative of the Cultural Department and they found the talmidim in the midst of their learning. There were twenty-five talmidim there, but most of them managed to immediately slip out when they realized what was going on. The GPU agent was only able to write down information on eight boys.

The two agents spoke to one of the gabbaim, Reb Moshe Meir, and told him that the gabbaim of the shul were accused of opening an educational institute on the premises without permission from the Cultural Department. They instructed him to sign that this was in fact the case.

Reb Zalman, who was present, tried to explain to the gabbai that he could avoid signing the incriminating document by claiming that it wasn't a formal institution, but individual bachurim who gathered to learn in the shul. However, the gabbai was scared and signed.

When they finished writing up a report of their visit, they told the gabbai that he had to get the names of the other boys who were learning there and had slipped out. They threatened him and said that if he did not come the next day to the offices of the GPU with a complete list, they would work on getting the shul closed down with the accusation that illegal activities had taken place there.

It was only after the two men left that the gabbai calmed down and began to think clearly about what had happened. He realized that Reb Zalman was right, that they had no legal reason to close the shul and they certainly couldn't demand that he bring the names of all the talmidim. He wrote a letter in which he said he did not know the national language well and that his signature on the document was merely due to pressure. He wrote that after thinking it over, he had concluded that the report wasn't at all correct, since there had been nothing illegal going on in the shul, just individual bachurim who had come, each one separately, in order to learn in the shul.

The next day, Reb Moshe Meir the gabbai went with the other gabbaim to the Cultural Department of Kharkov and presented his letter of protest. The clerk took it but repeated his demand that the gabbaim must produce a list of the names of talmidim who had slipped out.

Although officially the law was on their side, the gabbaim knew that if they aroused the ire of the GPU they could pay dearly. They had no doubt that the GPU could carry out their threat and close the shul. They told Reb Zalman that they could not take on the great responsibility of having the shul closed, and so they wanted the talmidim to stop visiting the shul and find somewhere else to learn.

Reb Zalman understood the feelings of the gabbaim but he had an idea. "I have a simple suggestion. Let us arrange new elections for gabbaim and we will ask one of the senior Chassidim to run against you. We will make sure this old Chassid is elected as gabbai and the GPU will surely not bother him."

They accepted Reb Zalman's idea and within a short time an old Chassid of the Tzemach Tzedek was elected gabbai. The yeshiva continued to operate in the shul and the GPU realized that a man of his age was not afraid that they would undermine his livelihood etc. and they left him alone.

The Rebbe Rayatz received a detailed report about the visit of the GPU at the shul in Kharkov and in a letter dated 8 Nissan 5688 to Professor Chavkin, he wrote (in German): "In Kharkov the following took place. Religious classes were held in the shul for adults (over 18), which is permissible according to Soviet law. Nevertheless, special action was taken against them. Not only did they not allow them to continue, they even went to people who hosted them and forbade them from letting the talmidim into their homes at night, in order to force them to leave."

Reb Zalman's tactic succeeded in maintaining the yeshiva for nearly a year and a half, until the summer of 5689, when at a certain point the GPU ran out of patience. They personally made sure to maintain a presence in the shul, until the talmidim saw they could no longer have a yeshiva there.

The bochurim learned for a short time in a village near Kharkov where they rented a house from a gentile. They learned with Reb Yehoshua Korf, but the yeshiva in

Kharkov was soon disbanded. Some of the bachurim went to Nevel and some went to Yekaterinoslav.

The big yeshivah moved to Nevel. Reb Chatche asked Zalman to stay in Kharkov and organize a farzich meaning students who studied on their own and did not need help. Zalman's brother-in-law Ben Tzion Shemtov was also involved. Before that there was a yeshiva for boys of 14-16 known as chadorim, where they had someone come and teach a few times a week. They were taught in small numbers and in various places so that the government does not notice. Zalman said there is a lot to tell about it but he did not go into details.

Before the bachurim went to Yekaterinoslav, Reb Zalman went there for two weeks to set up the infrastructure for the new secret yeshiva. During his short visit he visited the home of the rav, Rabbi Levi Yitzchok Schneersohn, father of the Rebbe MH"M, with whom he discussed communal matters. Before he left he went into Reb Levik who said a two-hour discourse to him in Kabbalah and Chassidus. He visited Reb Levik Schneerson in Yakatrinislav several times, but never saw Reb Levik's sons there. On one visit they gave Reb Levik a hard time about his study of Kabbalah but he did not react to them.

In the summer of 1928 he wrote to his parents that he found a woman suitable to be his wife. His mother immediately travelled to Kharkov. After meeting everyone, she said that she cannot afford to pay for a second trip so they should make the wedding while she was there. He married Brocha Futerfass on Friday August 17, 1928/2nd day Rosh Chodesh 1st of Elul 5688. Since neither side had money people said, two dead people are going dancing."

Brocha later remarked that she saw in him a father figure for her children to admire and emulate. Meanwhile the Yeshiva was dispersed and Zalman started to look for work. Brocha's sister Esther Golda married Bentzion Shemtov.

After their wedding Zalman and Brocha lived in inner room of Maryasha Badana Futerfas's (Brocha's mother) two room apartment. Maryasha moved there from Pleshnitz after her wedding. Her oldest son Hendel Futerfas (Lieberman) captured a view of the village Pleshnitz in his painting of Kiddush levono. Brocha was born in that apartment. Her father Menachem Mendel set up a business that his wife Maryasha took over after he passed away. The Chassidic community had been there since the time of the Rebbe Maharash.

There was a stove to cook and heat the apartment and a machine to make raincoats out of canvas. Free enterprise was still allowed and so Zalman took Brocha's grandmother's small old wine press and began to make wine. To make wine they used raisins since fresh grapes were not available. Since Jews only bought for Shabbos or another occassion they sold wine to non-Jews as well. Thus the following year when Chaim was born they were able to celeberate without financial worries.

However, the regime was known to make sudden changes in policy as part of their tactics in creating fear and having control among people. Suddenly free enterprise was no longer permitted. Thus they began to make flower designs for brooches at home for a government industry. They slept by day and worked by night. No matter the circumstances Zalman and Brocha always had a smile for others. This was the happiest time for the Brocha as she was working together at home with her husband.

As circumstances changed Zalman became a partner with a non-Jew in a government kiosk. Working long hours, he only saw his son on Shabbos. Therefore, each night he left a candy – tzukerke under his son's pillow, to let him know that his father is thinking of him and loves him.

One time in shul Itche the Masmid was daaving late and Reb Zalman was leading the farbrengen. Reb Itche asked that they be quiet as they were disturbing his daavening. Reb Zalman admonished Reb Itche for putting his personal avoda before a Chassidishe farbrengen. When Reb Zalman came home after Shabbos he found that his young son Chaim had suddenly become sick with high temperature. As he was thinking of calling the doctor someone told him to ask forgiveness from Reb Itche (who stayed with Reb Mendel Deitsch) which he did and the infant instantly became better.

In general Reb Itche would drink a lot of maske at the farbrengens. One time at the end of a farbrengen his walking was very staggered and so Reb Zalman held him as he walked home. Reb Itche kept saying, "Oy, ich hob im lib – I love him," Reb Zalman said, "vemen - who Reb Iche?" Reb Itche replied, "Der Oibershter, Der Oibershter."

Reb Zalman visited his parents several times while living in Kharkov. He would take the train from Kharkov to Homel and from Homel to Khoyanky and then take a wagon for about 25 kilometers to Brahin. He took his son Chaim with him a few times. In the summer of 1932/33, Chaim noticed a wagon coming from the opposite direction, full of hay with an elderly Jew sitting on top saying something (possibly Tehillim) to himself. Reb Zalman said that he is a Lubavitcher Chossid who lives in Brahin.

When the children were born, Zalman and Brocha were of the same mind not to send them to a government school. Therefore, they hired a teacher and closed the doors and windows when he came so that no-one should detect their illegal activity. Zalman paid him all his official earnings and so had to earn money besides that to live on. The legal age to begin school was six. Therefore, they bought bags for the children and sent them out of the house at the same time as all other children went to school. When neighbours inquired as to which school they went to, Zalman and Brocha mentioned a distant school. They thought it strange but said nothing.

After Lenin's death, a power struggle ensued between Stalin and Trotsky. In October 1927, Trotsy was removed from the central committee and in November expelled from the communist party, exiled to Alma-Ata in January and expelled from the Soviet Union in 1929. It was during this time that Stalin took control of the ruling party. In a bid to control everything they forced farmers to form collectives, creating a famine in the breadbasket of Russia. Manufacturing belonged to the people making bribery and corruption the norm of life. The secret police were everywhere causing fear to rule the land. Alchoholism replaced ambition and hope. Propaganda blinded the people to the reality of life.

In 1930 after Chaim was born a new issue arose. The government decided that those who were not accepted into the army because they were clerics and untrustworthy to serve the motherland, instead they shall do some other service for three months. It was before Rosh Hashono when they called Zalman and his friend Yankel Gurkov to come. After Yom Kippur they presented themselves and were sent to a town to build a military factory. There were barracks for about four hundred people there. Thus was created a labor battalion.

As Shabbos approached they submitted an application to those in charge to be released from work on Shabbos. Zalman told them that if they are released from work on Shabbos they will be more productive the rest of the week.

When Shabbos came, even though they had not received a reply, they did not go out to work. When their immediate supervisor asked them why? They said that they had already applied to rest on Shabbos.

They did not know what the result of their action would bring as they could have easily been sent to Siberia for ten years. Meanwhile they said their prayers and Tehillim. Suddenly a person from another barrack came in and told them that there is a paper for them in his barrack. They went to look at it and saw that on it was written that it is ok for them not to work on Shabbos.

At the end of three months the government decided that the terms of service will be three years. Zalman's wife Brocha could not tolerate the new edict and went to the various agencies involved seeking a deferment for her husband.

Finally, she discovered that only clergy could be imprisoned and sent to the labor division. Her husband had only been a student and should not be in the labor corp. An application was made for Zalman's release based on this law. Obviously the head of the unit paid no attention to it. Meanwhile a neighbor of Zalman's was on the local council overseeing such matters. He sent a letter to Zalman's commander, informing him that Zalman was obligated to serve in the army and not in the labor corp. A struggle ensued over which corp Zalman should serve and eventually an order was obtained from the governer and Zalman was released to the regular army.

Once he was freed, he immediately set to work to get the release of his friend Yaakov Gurkov and his brother-in-law Mendel Futerfass. It took a few months and finally they too were free.

But in the Russia of those days, these legal proofs could last only a short time. A few years later, the military officials decided that they could draft Reb Zalman and his friends anyway. Once again, they were called every year to present themselves for training exercises in the rear guard army.

After this Zalman and his brother-in-law were both called up for reserve duty. Zalman watched as his brother-in-law played the fool. Mendel had filled his pockets with papers from work. When they asked for his call up papers, he pulled out one paper and said here it is. They looked at it and said, it is a bill. He then pulled out another paper and so on, each one was some other business paper. They saw how disorganized he was and having no need for a scatterbrain decided to send him home.

In the army Zalman kept Judaism as best as he could. Since regulations were that you cannot have a beard, he told the barber that he has sensitive skin and cannot have his hair cut with a razor. At mealtime, he offered his bowl of soup to the non-Jew sitting next to him, which he happily accepted. Zalman thought that this would go unnoticed. Within half an hour he was called to the commander. "Why didn't you eat your soup?" He replied, "I am not used to such food, coffee and bread are sufficient for me." The officer accepted his words and dismissed him.

A short while later the political officer attached to the group called Zalman to his office. He screamed saying, "I know why you don't want to eat, you are trying to weaken yourself so that you will be discharged. Your trick will not work with me. If in twenty-four hours you do not start eating properly, I will send you to the canals." People working on the canals were known to die in great numbers.

Zalman continued eating only kosher and a few days passed and nothing happened. Then the official called Zalman in and of course he was prepared for the worst.

"Do you play chess?" "yes I do" Zalman replied. "Good, then you will play with me whenever I call you." Nothing more was said. He was left alone to eat and daaven discreetly. During the cold winter he used his tallis to wrap himself as well. Since it was made with thick wool it protected him from the cold and probably saved him from freezing. He had his tefillin with him and daavened under his covers early in the morning and sometimes in the short break they had in the afternoon.

When Brocha was pregnant with their third child she was bleeding early in her pregnancy. When she consulted the doctor, he told her to abort the child. She came home and cried to her mother, who told her to go to bed and stay there till the baby was born. This is how she succeeded in giving birth to her daughter.

In 1937 the KGB were able to plant an informer among the Lubavitchers. By the time they realized it, it was too late. The KGB would usually come to arrest people at midnight. Reb Zalman did not sleep nights at home. It was known that the KGB was looking for Reb Zalman. Reb Zalman once related the fact that he was fleeing from the KGB day and night. Many times he did not eat or sleep for long periods of time.

(Hamashpiah Shlomo Chaim Kesselman vol. 1 p.46) Once in the middle of the night Reb Zalman arrived at the dilapidated home of Reb Shlomo Chaim Kesselman. He was received with a smiling face and was given rice with milk to eat. He was given a corner to sleep, where the rain did not leak through the roof. In the morning he saw that Reb Shlomo Chaim had slept on the chair with his head resting on the table. When he stopped at his next place of refuge, which was a Lubavitcher house, they told him that it was possible that Reb Shlomo Chaim had given him the only food in the house.

Since some Lubavitchers were guards in or had their own factories, he eventually located places to sleep. One of those places was a factory where they dyed textile. Since they needed to cook the dyes and kept the fires burning it was warm the entire winter. Afterwards Reb Zalman was conscripted into the army. In the summer he was required to go for one-month training.

During the years 1937-39 the KGB arrested many Chassidim, four of whom were; Reb Avrohom Boruch Pevzner, Reb Nochum Pinson, Tzemach Gurevitch and Rabbi Shmuel Katzman. For one entire year Reb Pevzner did not have tefillin, until his wife was able to bring him a pair. When he saw the tefillin he fainted. Eventually he passed away in prison. There were other Chassidim who were taken away and either disappeared, were shot or sent to Siberia.

In 1938 Zalman's father and sisters arrived from Brahin and lived out of town in a house at the top of a hill. The family went to them during the summer and Zalman went there during the summer when he was not on duty in the army.

World War II began in late Elul 5699/1939. The Germans air bombed Poland and then sent in their soldiers and swiftly conquered the country. The Soviet Union, which bordered on Poland, quickly sent large numbers of soldiers in the direction of the new front and simultaneously began calling up reserves. One of the reserve soldiers who received a notice to report was Reb Zalman.

Reb Zalman first became acquainted with the military establishment about ten years earlier, in 5689/1929. The "white card" that he managed to obtain in 5685/1925 through the bracha of the Rebbe Rayatz saved him for four years, but later he was called up.

However, since he had been marked down as someone unfaithful to communist ideals, they were afraid to send him to the front, lest he become a spy for the west. For those unreliable citizens like him they had a special department called the "rear guard army," in which they had to do hard labor for the military.

In these military camps, the communists in charge did their best to instill communist values. Until the communist era, most citizens, even gentiles, were simple people who believed in G-d. When they were asked, "How are you?" they would reply, "Thank G-d." Their faith was superficial though, and the communist lecturers were able to confuse them with so-called proofs to the non-existence of G-d, G-d forbid.

Reb Zalman stood out among the boorish gentiles. As a clever and learned Chassid, he was able to respond to all the questions of the communist lecturers and to make a mockery of their so-called proofs. The gentiles who worked with him in the labor camp rejoiced to hear his clever responses and when he would finish, they would applaud, "Bravo Zalman."

It was only in the early years that a soldier could contradict the communist leader. As time went by, the communists intensified their religious persecution and whoever dared to contradict them, could expect to be sentenced to jail and exile for the crime of undermining the government.

In the summer of 5697, after the communist regime succeeded in imposing absolute terror over the citizens in the Soviet Union, they began drafting into the regular army even those who were marked as disloyal to communism. Terror of the government was so great that they no longer feared that the soldiers would try and spy for the west.

Reb Zalman was among those who were drafted. After undergoing fitness and aptitude tests, they decided to train him as a sapper who could blow up bridges and such during a war. Every summer, Reb Zalman had to show up for the reserves for several weeks in which he trained as a sapper.

As mentioned, when the war broke out, Reb Zalman was drafted and he began a round of intensive training for his mission to the front. In Reb Zalman's division, as in the rest of the Russian army's divisions, there were two commanders, a military commander and a political commander. This latter commander was called a *politruk* whose job was to oversee the soldiers' loyalty to communist ideals. This politruk dogged Zalman's steps when he discovered that Reb Zalman did not eat from the mess hall. He said that Zalman refrained from eating so that he would become weak and be sent home. However, Zalman, who was a physically strong man,

On Erev Yom Kippur, Reb Zalman asked the commander to exempt him from military training the next day and offered to do guard duty instead. The commander agreed, but emphasized that Reb Zalman also needed the permission of the politruk. Reb Zalman approached the politruk apprehensively. People said he was a Jew who had abandoned religion, and surely he would figure out why Reb Zalman was asking for guard duty.

To Reb Zalman's surprise, the politruk approved his request, but before signing it he said, "Zalman, I know the reason for your request. Tomorrow is Yom Kippur!" Then in an emotional voice he said, "Pray for me too."

Reb Zalman was going to be sent to the front two weeks later, the night of Simchas Torah. Whoever was sent to the front was very likely to be killed. Fortunately for him, a big miracle occurred. The plan was to send Reb Zalman's division, along with a large shipment of weapons, to the front. By mistake, the weapons were sent before the division was ready. At precisely that time, there was a lull in the fighting and the commanders at the front said there was no need for additional soldiers, and the weapons that had been sent would suffice for the soldiers who were already there.

This wonderful news arrived the night of Simchas Torah, shortly before Reb Zalman was supposed to board a train for the front. The commander announced that everyone was free to go home for the time being. Reb Zalman immediately walked to the big shul for hakafos. His older son Chaim, who was standing on the steps of the shul, was surprised to see his father in the distance.

After Yom Tov they heard that the Russians had signed an agreement with the Germans to divide Poland, and so Russia stayed out of the hostilities for the meantime. A short while later, Reb Zalman was informed by the army that they had decided to transfer him from the sappers' unit to the rear air defence unit. This unit was enlarged after the Russians saw the devastation the Germans inflicted on Poland, when they sent dozens of planes over Warsaw and bombed the city. The Russians decided to train thousands of soldiers for anti-aircraft defence in order to defend the cities in the rear during the war.

In the summer of 5700, when it came time for reserve duty, Reb Zalman was trained in anti-aircraft artillery fire. He also underwent training for fire containment, in case of fires that might result from aerial attack.

In the summer of 5701/1941, the Germans violated the agreement they had signed with the Russians and they launched a large scale attack against the Russians. Russia, once again, joined the countries that were fighting the Germans, and all those subject to the draft were told to quickly report to their units.

Reb Zalman was in bed with a fever after coming down with severe pneumonia. Reb Yaakov Gansburg, a young bachur at the time, was staying in his house. When Reb Zalman heard on the radio about the outbreak of war, he begged him to run. Reb Yaakov listened to him and immediately travelled to Samarkand where he stayed for the duration of the war. Afterward, he obtained a polish passport and was able to leave Russia.

Reb Zalman could not flee both due to his health and because he held a red draft card that listed him as a soldier in the Russian army. The law said that all men from 18-40 had to have either a white draft card that indicated exemption from military duty or a red one that indicated that the carrier was an army draftee.

News about the Germans' approach to Charkov was heard before Rosh HaShana 5702/1941. Reb Zalman and his family deliberated about whether to remain or run. In those days, Russians did not know that Germans were massacring Jews in the lands that they conquered and many Jews, who remembered the German soldiers in World War I, thought it was better to be subject to German rule than to remain under the Soviets.

In the meantime, Reb Zalman received notice from the army that as a soldier, his family was permitted, for free, to board a train travelling to the interior of the country, far from the front. After Yom Kippur, Reb Zalman consulted with three friends and they decided that Reb Zalman should remain and his family would leave.

Reb Zalman's wife went with her mother and her three children, Chaim, Aharon and Nechama, on a train arranged by the army, and travelled to Saratov. It was a freight train and several families squeezed into each compartment.

German planes occasionally flew over and bombed the railroad tracks. This is why the trip that should have taken two days took eighteen days, and the food they had taken with them was not enough for the trip.

Reb Zalman's son Chaim showed initiative and after discovering that one of the gentile families on board had a basket full of eggs, he bartered and took one hundred eggs in exchange for some items they had. Thus they were nourished by raw eggs for the remainder of the journey.

Reb Zalman's father, his sister, and her two daughters, remained for a short time with Reb Zalman, but after a few days they also decided to flee. They paid a lot of money for places on a passenger train and also arrived in Saratov.

From Saratov, Reb Zalman's family continued to travel on in the direction of Tashkent, where they stayed with their uncle Reb Benzion Shemtov. While there, his daughter became sick and could not continue travelling. She remained with her uncle, while her mother and brothers continued to Samarkand.

Shortly after they arrived, Chaim became sick with pneumonia that infected both lungs, and he was taken to the hospital. He saw the people around him dying like flies. There were so many dead that the hospital staff had no time to bury them all and the stench of the bodies wafted in the air. He realized that if he wanted to live, he had to get out of there quickly, but his temperature was very high and the doctors did not allow him to leave.

What did Chaim do? When the nurses came to take his temperature, he put the thermometer under the blanket where he shook it down, and then he gave it back to the nurse. After a few times that he returned the thermometer with reasonable temperatures, the doctors released him. He happily returned home where his family cared for him until he miraculously recovered. The one who helped him was Mrs. Sarah Kievman, who used her connections and obtained medications from America.

In the meantime, Reb Zalman remained alone, burning with fever, in his home in Kharkov. On Shabbos Breishis, he felt stronger and he decided to go to shul. That day, the army had distributed the monthly salary to the soldiers and although he needed that money very much, he did not consider desecrating Shabbos for it and he remained in shul.

In the following days, as the German forces approached very close to Kharkov, the Russian commanders realized that they would be unable to withstand the Germans and they told the soldiers to run away. Many of the gentile soldiers, who were unafraid of the Germans, did not flee but removed their uniforms and went back to civilian life. Although the Jewish soldiers had yet to hear of the German atrocities against their brethren, most preferred to flee and join their families in the interior.

The winter began and it was bitter cold outside. Reb Zalman, who was still sick, took along with him a handmade woollen tallis that was very thick and wrapped himself in it to protect himself from the cold. He fled Kharkov through the forests that surrounded the city.

On his way out of the city, he met two Jews, relatives of his, who had connections in high places in the communist party. They told him that they had a horse and wagon with a large amount of food, mostly butter, which they had planned on selling on the black market. However, now they saw that the roads were full of mud and it was hard to travel in a wagon, and they preferred leaving quickly by train. They had gotten tickets from their friends in the party. They asked him to take the horse and wagon till Saratov and in exchange, he could eat from the food on the wagon.

Reb Zalman agreed and considered this outstanding divine providence. He travelled with the horse and wagon for two weeks and at night he stopped in villages along the way where he slept at the homes of the villagers and paid them with merchandise from the wagon. He ate a lot of butter, which greatly helped his infected lungs so that by the time he reached Saratov, he was completely healed.

After bringing the horse and wagon to the owners, Reb Zalman made inquiries about his family. He fortuitously met his aunt, Hinda Deitsch, the wife of Reb Menachem Mendel. She had been in Samarkand already and had returned to Saratov in order to take her daughter, Mirel Kugel, to Samarkand. She told Reb Zalman that his daughter Nechama was with the Shemtov family in Tashkent and his wife and sons were living in Samarkand.

As soon as he heard this, Reb Zalman set forth for Tashkent. He spent time in Tashkent until his daughter fully recovered and then took her with him to Samarkand.

Reb Zalman still wore his army uniform and held on to the document that stated that he was a soldier on leave and he had the right to travel throughout the country. After he settled in Samarkand, he was supposed to report to the military command in the district where they would certainly send him to the front. Most of the soldiers who had been sent to the front had been killed, and Reb Zalman did not know which was preferable – to go to the army or to remain in Samarkand and be in danger of being caught as a military deserter.

He consulted with a friend. The friend had experience and he wanted to absolve Reb Zalman of any doubt. He asked to see the red document and when Reb Zalman gave it to him, he ripped it. Now, said his friend, you have no choice. You are a deserter.

In order not to be caught in random identity checks carried out by the police, Reb Zalman grew his hair to give himself an older look and he added twenty years to his ID card. As a man of sixty, he was exempt from the army. A policeman once stopped him and after seeing his papers suspected they were forged, and ordered him to come to the police station. Reb Zalman bribed the cop who then released him.

When he had first arrived in Samarkand, he became sick again and was unable to work for a living. Having no other choice, his son Chaim went to the market and tried his luck at business. He was able to bring some bread home and mainly, products with fat that could heal Reb Zalman's lungs.

Even during these difficult times, Reb Zalman ensured that Chaim learned Torah. He would get up at six in the morning in order to learn Gemara with a neighbour, Reb Eliyahu Chaim Roitblatt. It was very cold at that hour of the morning, even the water prepared for negel vasser was frozen, but nothing stopped them from learning.

Reb Zalman recovered half a year later and found work as a watchman in a factory. At that time, Yeshivas Tomchei Temimim had opened a branch in Samarkand. Reb Zalman told his son Chaim to stop working and he sent him to yeshiva.

During the war, thousands of Jewish refugees from Poland stayed in Samarkand and the Russian authorities turned a blind eye to their religious practices. Those were years of relief, relative to the terrible years of persecution that the Chassidim suffered at the end of the 1930's. Reb Zalman's sons Chaim and Aharon learned with Reb Roitblatt and with Reb Moshe Robinson. Then Chaim went to yeshiva where he learned Talmud with Reb Zalman Shimon

Dworkin and Reb Eliyahu Plotkin, and Chassidus with the mashpia, Reb Nissan Nemanov.

After a while, Reb Zalman began to work in textiles in partnership with his friend Reb Naftali Junik. Like many Lubavitchers, they set aside large sums to support the Talmud Torah and yeshivah Tomchei Temimim, which operated in Samarkand and where hundreds of refugee children were educated.

At the end of World War II, in 1945, an agreement was signed by Russia and Poland in which all Polish citizens who fled to Russia during the war were permitted to leave Russia and return to their homeland. The Russian government provided freight cars, known as *eshalons,* to transport the hundreds of thousands of Polish refugees.

You had to sign up before a certain date to be included on the train. Yet the Chabad chassidim in Samarkand did not sign up as they were not sure what the Rebbe Rayatz wanted them to do. They also did not trust the Russians who could have stopped the train on the three-week journey to check people's papers and many Chabad chassidim were wanted men by the Russian secret police. When they saw that Reb Nissan decided to leave they followed but it was too late to sign up as Polish citizens for the train.

Since many of the refugees had not taken their passports or any official identifying documents with them, the Russians allowed anyone who had any sort of paper that testified that he was a Polish citizen to cross the border.

When Chabad askanim found out that there was a way of leaving Russia, Reb Leibel Mochkin was sent to Lvov (Lemberg), the border city between Russia and Poland, to check out the opportunity for escape. Upon his arrival there, he learned that the emigration of Polish citizens had ended. However, he made connections in the right places by giving handsome bribes, and managed to have the border opened again. He then travelled to Samarkand and Tashkent, and urged Anash to take advantage of this one-time opportunity.

Among the hundreds of Lubavitchers to leave Samarkand for Lvov were Reb Zalman and his family. Upon arriving in Lvov, the Chassidim asked him to take a position in the special committee that had been formed to arrange the mass flight. The committee was responsible for obtaining the large amounts of money needed to procure Polish documents, as well as to bribe border officials and NKVD agents. Reb Zalman, who was a reliable and organized person, was appointed as treasurer of the committee.

After they successfully enabled hundreds of Lubavitchers to leave, the money in the fund was used up. In a most unusual move, the committee formed a beis din of 23 rabbis, which has the power to judge issues of life and death, which ruled that whoever crossed the border had to leave all his money with the members of the committee so that they could continue to finance their holy work.

Anash acceeded to this psak din and left their silver and jewellery (excluding marriage bands) with the committee. However, this wasn't enough. Reb Zalman's brother-in-law, Reb Benzion Shemtov, who came to Poland at the end of Kislev 5707, wrote a letter on 2 Teves to his friend, Reb Sholom Mendel Kalmanson (who was in Prague and who frequently sent letters to the Rebbe Rayatz), and asked him to send them money:

**I just received a letter from Lvov from the people involved in the move, Reb Menachem Mendel ben Mariasha (Futerfas), Yehoshua Shneur Zalman ben Nechama (Serebryanski), Yehuda Leib ben Henya (Mochkin), Moshe Chaim Dubrawski (I don't know his mother's name), whose work conditions have worsened**

**due to the impending danger and they request that the Rebbe remember them for good literally every day.**

**In brief, the message in their letters is that if the means are not sent to them at the earliest possible opportunity, they are in absolute danger, r"l. They request to first pay offtwo thousand dollars ... In our camp they established a beis din of 23 and everyone gave whatever they had, down to the last penny.**

Reb Zalman threw himself into the communal work. When necessary, he included his son Chaim who was a young bachur at the time, to carry out errands for the committee. Chaim would meet up with Polish citizens in bars and would get their Polish documentation in exchange for money that he had been given by the committee.

He would often go to Reb Mendel Garelik, who was an expert at forging documents, and give and take documents to and from him. Lubavitcher rabbanim, who considered these activities *hatzolas nefashos* and *pikuach nefesh,* allowed them to work on Shabbos when necessary. It sometimes happened that Chaim had to carry documents on Shabbos. As the rabbanim told him, he would put the papers under his yarmulke so he would be carrying in an unusual way.

Many of the details of what went on and Reb Zalman's involvement are printed in the book Peilos Chutzah Gevulos by Sholom Ber Friedland based in the detailed papers that Reb Sholom Mendel Kalmanson kept. At one point the KGB was searching to arrest Reb Zalman so he left for a few months to Moscow and visited his cousins from the Gluskin family who lived there.

Reb Zalman and his family were in the last group that was able to leave Russia for Poland, on 9 Teves 5707. Hundreds of people crowded onto this train into two compartments. Lubavitchers were afraid to remain on this train until its intended destination and they paid the conductor so that he would stop for a few minutes in Krakow. He stopped and within a few minutes, they had all alighted from the train.

Anash went from Krakow to Lodz. From there, they continued their long, indirect journey until they arrived in free countries. At this time, there were a number of incidents of pogroms against Jews returning to Poland and it was dangerous to remain in Poland. It was even more dangerous for Anash who had left Russia, since the Polish government was under Soviet rule and they feared having their forged documentation exposed and being sent back to Russia. They tried leaving Poland as fast as they could.

In Lodz, there were only a few Lubavitchers who were Polish citizens. They had businesses there. The only one who remained of the Lubavitcher refugees was Reb Yitzchok Goldin. He stayed in Poland in order to help the Lubavitchers coming from Lvov, and from there he was also in touch with Anash in Lvov. Reb Goldin remained in Lodz for nearly a year, and he helped many Lubavitchers.

In Kislev-Teves 5707, Mrs. Hadassah Perman joined him and was a big help. Within a short time though, she was arrested. After being miraculously released, she was smuggled out to Prague. Reb Goldin then asked Reb Zalman to stay and help him in his holy work.

Reb Zalman, who was a member of the committee, decided to remain with his wife and daughter (Nechama) in Poland. He sent his mother-in-law and two sons with a group of Lubavitchers, who crossed the border with the help of the Bricha, to Austria and from there to Paris.

While his wife and daughter stayed in Bitom, Reb Zalman would travel to the border town of Premishlan and bribe the train officials there so they would give envelopes to members of the committee who remained in Lvov. Money was placed in these envelopes as well as documents, along with passports of Polish citizens who had already crossed the border that would be reused.

The members of the committee that remained in Lvov also conveyed messages via the train employees. They employed secret codes used by Anash in Russia. Reb Mendel Futerfas, for example, would sign his name with the words *Chema Chavis* which means "butter barrel" and translates into Yiddish as "Futerfas."

Staying in the border town was very dangerous, especially for someone like Reb Zalman who looked obviously Jewish with his beard. Nevertheless, he was committed to his goal and relied on the brachos of the Rebbe Rayatz for those involved in holy work.

After a short time, the Soviet police discovered the smuggling operation and began a large scale hunt for the Lubavitchers remaining in Lvov. After hearing of their arrest, Reb Zalman wondered whether he should continue endangering his life by remaining in Poland to help the few Lubavitchers still in Lvov. He asked the Rebbe through Reb Sholom Mendel Kalmanson in Prague who conveyed the question.

The Rebbe's response was:

**Regarding your letter of 27 Nissan about the Tamim Zalman Serebryanski, to whatever degree possible it would be good if he still remains where he is and helps his brethren. As far as his health, efforts should be made that he not lack any of his bodily needs, and may Hashem strengthen him and be of help to him in everything he needs, materially and spiritually.**

Reb Zalman remained in Poland for another few months. He moved between Lodz, Krakow, and Bitom. In Bitom there was an orphanage run by the Vaad Hatzalah and Reb

Zalman worked to transfer these children to western countries.

On 10 Elul 5707, he asked the Rebbe again, through Rabbi Kalmanson, whether he could go to Paris and join his family. The Rebbe's response, dated 25 Elul, said:

**If the place is dangerous, it is proper that he move to Paris [it should be] in success. However, it is necessary to try to find a way, even after he travels, to remain in contact with our friends Anash in the homeland, and may Hashem help him materially and spiritually.**

Reb Zalman, together with his wife and daughter, traveled from Poland to Paris at the beginning of the winter of 5708. His sons were learning in Yeshivas Tomchei Temimim in Brunoy. Upon arriving in Paris, he was happy to see his sons learning without the constant fear that had been their lot in Russia. However, he was sad to see the financial state of the yeshiva, which was terrible to the point that the bachurim did not have anything to eat.

His brother-in-law, Reb Bentzion Shemtov, asked him to join the yeshiva's vaad to help out with his organizational abilities. He agreed, and even attended some meetings, but after seeing no results from these meetings, he decided to work alone. He spoke to some Lubavitchers and suggested that they fundraise for the yeshiva in exchange for a percentage of what they raised. They began visiting Jewish homes in Paris and were able to bring home nice sums of money.

Along with Reb Zalman's concern for the financial state of the yeshiva, he was also concerned about the spiritual state of the Jews of Paris. The lives of Anash in Paris were Chassidish with farbrengens etc. and their children attended the yeshiva in Brunoy, but hardly anything was going on for other Jews.

One can defend Anash who were weary from all the suffering they had undergone, living with the status of refugees with temporary visas for France. This is why they did not do enough to spread Judaism and Chassidus outside of their own community.

Reb Zalman, who was moser nefesh in Russia and Poland to fulfill the Rebbe's wishes, did the same in Paris and began spreading Torah and Chassidus among non-Lubavitchers.

He began with house calls, and he tried to convince the parents to send their children to a Talmud Torah he would start. At first, the parents were unwilling to take their children out of school. They told him they would be happy if someone came to their home to teach their children in the afternoon, after they came home from school.

Reb Zalman quickly took them up on their offers. Most Lubavitchers in Paris were unemployed at the time since their stay in France was only temporary, with no work permits.

The Joint arranged apartments for them and provided a monthly stipend for food and sustenance, but other than that, there was no income. Reb Zalman easily found ten men and arranged for them to learn with the children in exchange for a monthly salary.

Reb Zalman went from house to house and announced the new plan that would instill Torah and its values in Jewish children. He also placed a pushka in every home and from these pushkas he was able to cover the ten salaries.

After forming a large group of children who learned in the afternoon. he was able to convince the parents to send them to learn in the mornings too. That is how the first Lubavitcher Talmud Torah was established in Paris.

Within a few months it grew, with dozens of children in attendance. Reb Zalman supported the Talmud Torah throughout the time he spent in Paris. When he received the Rebbe Rayatz's bracha to move to Australia, he transferred the responsibility for the school to Reb Hillel Azimov.

**Chaim Serebryanski**

Chaim was born to Yehoshua Shneur Zalman and Brocha on the sixth of Iyar in the year 5689/1929 in the city of Kharkov in the Ukraine. He passed away in Brooklyn, New York on the sixth of Nissan in the year 5775/2015.

Chaim was named after his mother's grandfather Chaim Futerfas who passed away shortly before little Chaim was born. Before he passed away, Chaim Futerfas gathered everyone and said a maamar. This tradition was passed down. Prior to his passing, Chaim Serebryanski left instructions to have a maamar recited in his memory on the occasion of his Sheloshim.

To better understand Chaim it is important to know the circumstances surrounding his childhood and early development. The family home was Chassidic in all senses. Beyond their doors the world was comprised of the anti-religious, anti-G-d and intensely anti-Semitic. Communism reigned supreme and thus the physical and spiritual condition of the country's inhabitants was continuously deteriorating.

The government nationalized everything, stripping the people of their possessions leaving them with only the minimal on which to subside. They designed everything to destroy religion and belief in G-d. As a result, being a Lubavitcher was a serious crime since Lubavitchers were engaged in doing things to support and spread belief in G-d and religion. A person who did not work or chose to do as he or she wished was considered a parasite and was to be eliminated. The only books that were available were about Stalin and Communist or Marxist idealism.

No-one had any incentive to grow food or raise animals since it all belonged to the government. Food became extremely scarce. Thus, there flourished a black market for everything. Obtaining even a small amount of the limited food became a major focus of all people. The black market worked in the following way. A baker was allowed x amount of flour, a clothing store x amount of clothes. The person running the store would sell part in accordance with government law. The rest would be sold on the black market at twenty to one hundred times the legal price. Long lines of people waiting for food to be available became the norm.

The next year when their first child Chaim was born they were able to celebrate without financial worries. Yehudah Chitrik a cousin of Reb Zalman recalled that he was at Chaim's bris. Members of the Chabad community and relatives were there. He was born in the eighth month and the bris was a nidche. It was common for a child to die from some disease. Therefore, Brocha was meticulous about keeping the bed of her child sanitized. No-one was allowed to sit on it, although one time a cousin came from Moscow and sat on the bed.

Three years after Chaim was born his brother Aharon came into this world. He was named after his great grandfather, his father's mother's father Rabbi Aharon Gluskin who was the Rabbi in Paritch after Reb Hillel. Three years later his sister Nechamah was born. She was named after Reb Zalman's mother who was a daughter of Reb Aharon Gluskin. Nechamah Gluskin was very intelligent and well versed in Torah. Her brother Menachem Mendel was Rov in Paritch, Minsk and then Leningrad. The Rebbe Rayatz wrote in a letter that he knows of two special Rabbis one is Rabbi Levi Yitzchok Schneerson and the other is Rabbi Menachem Mendel Gluskin.

While Chaim was four, his brother Aharon was very sick and in hospital for about half a year. His father Reb Zalman sent a letter after Shabbos parshas tzav to Reb Yechezkiel (Chatche) Feigin for the Rebbe Rayatz in Warsaw that was received 23 of Nissan. Reb Zalman mentioned that Chaim will be five in the summer and that he can almost read the whole daavening from the siddur by himself and that he has been teaching him.

The Korf family (that lived in Kharkov) had three children who were born at about the same time as the Serebryanski children. Gedaliah Korf was the same age as Chaim. Even before they became married, Rabbi Shea Korf was responsible for the ruchniyos of the underground yeshivah while Reb Zalman was in charge of the gashmiyus.

Chaim's earliest memory was dancing with Reb Itche the Masmid. Another of Chaim's early memories was when, at three years of age, he saw something that left an indelible memory in his mind. He saw a wagon loaded high with hay and on top of the hay sat a simple Jew reciting Tehillim. A few times he visited the town of Brahin (Bragin) where his father's parents lived.

As a child he was told stories from Midrash. One story that he heard many times was about the two brothers who were concerned for each other and met on top of a mountain and that is why Hashem chose to build the Bais Hamikdosh on that spot. The lesson from the story left an indelible impression on him. His grandfather came to live in Charkov at some point after his wife passed away but I do not know when exactly.

From approximately 1934 or 1935 Chaim lived with his parents in Kharkov in a one room apartment on the second floor of the building at 7 Katsaska Uletza. The second room of that apartment had been taken away by the government. There was an iron staircase that resounded loudly with each step taken by those ascending or descending the stairs. Rats were abundant but they did not disturb the family. The room had a kerosene stove that kept the room warm and was used to cook water and food, in addition to having a table and beds in the room.

The apartments were in a building built around a small courtyard with ten other tenant families residing in those rooms. There was a communal toilet in the courtyard. There was no light and newspaper was used for toilet paper, the ink of the paper then had to be washed off. The toilet was maintained and cleaned by a man who came with a horse and wagon to remove the human waste. A foul odor permeated the area, and they always poured – kartolivka – chlorine over the whole place.

Chaim's great grandmother Rochel Leah, helped her widowed daughter Maryasha Badana raise her children. They were both strong opinionated women. She maintained a special Chassidic atmosphere that she instilled within them, also giving a firm spiritual foundation upon which they could grow. She raised the mashpia Mendel Futerfas who claimed that of all his chassidus came from her. Rochel Leah was also instrumental in the raising of Chaim.

Mendel Futerfas and his wife lived with Maryasha for the first two years of their marriage. The room was partitioned into sleeping areas. The apartment had no hot water. Sometimes they went to the local bathhouse to bathe. Other times they used water heated at home in a pot on the stove.

Hinda Deitsch with her daughter lived some distance away in Afkona but came to visit her mother many times. She had to travel by the tramway to get there. In the last year of her life Rochel Leah was not well. That year she moved to her bed that was at her daughter Hinda's house. Without even one word of complaint, Hinda took care of her mother until she passed away.

Chaim's opsheren was on Lag B'omer. Itche the Masmid (Gurevich) was there with others and they had a farbrengen.

The shul on Meshchansky Street was burned with over 400 Jews inside, by the Germans. See details in the following article.
https://www.shukach.com/ru/node/42923?fbclid=IwAR39MuZQR11bhcHzrA9ADggLe2MezNqfIl68OOMDz55Ke97Lo69tj9tL89U

Every Shabbos from the time Chaim was three years old he would go with his father for the half hour walk to shul. Each Shabbos there was a farbrengen and so they stayed in shul for the entire day. Avrohom Boruch Pewzner and Reb Itche the Masmid would farbreng. Reb Itche was a half Rebbe who daavened most of the time and would eat very little.

During the farbrengens they spoke about topics that would strengthen their mesiras nefesh in keeping Shabbos and educating children as well as for each mitzvah.

A chossid by the name of Shifman who was an engineer had to go to work on Shabbos. When he was at work, Shifman did not write even though this was a crime that could have cost him his life. However, he had a brilliant mind which the officials needed, so they left him alone. At farbrengens the men imbibed a lot of alcohol which helped to raise people's spirits.

Reb Zalman took his three-year-old Chaim to Hakafos on Simchas Torah night in Kharkov. He was the only child in attendance. Itche the Masmid danced Hakafos with Chaim while the Chasidim stood around and clapped. Chaim remembered Itche the Masmid sitting in the women's gallery learning, his feet soaking in a bucket of water to keep himself awake to learn. He also remembered Itche daavening in the women's gallery. According to Hershel Chitrik, Itche also used a small room off the woman's section for daavening. When Chaim was five, Itche the Masmid left Kharkov.

Sometimes Chaim would go to the market place with his grandmother when she went to buy a chicken. They would take it to a shed behind the shul and pay the shochet. He was usually there on Wednesdays or Thursdays. He would shecht chickens for the thirty Lubavitch families (and maybe a few others) that lived in Kharkov and kept kosher. Chaim did not taste meat till he was fourteen years old in Samarkand.

For Chanukah they would buy a fat goose and render the schmaltz for use on Pesach. They baked matzos at home. They bought flour in the store and kashered the oven. They had rolling pins and used clock gears as a tool to make holes in the matza. For sukkos they never had the arba minim in Kharkov. There was an old Jew in Kharkov who had the only sukkah in their area and they would go in to make Kiddush and eat bread, there was no special challah. Fish, fruit and vegetables were then eaten at home.

By the age of six Chaim knew all the combinations of the sefiras for counting the Omer baal peh– by heart taught to him by his dedicated great grandmother Rochel Leah. She tested him on what he learned. Chaim related that his Bobbe taught him all the sefiros of sefiras haomer according to chassidus.

His grandmothers from both sides of the family were very learned and special people. He felt especially close to Rochel Leah. Thus at only six year of age he travelled by public transportation, a tram, to her levaya - funeral. Public transportation in Kharkov was either a tram or a bus.

Chaim both fought and played soccer and boxing with the goyim. Catching flies was another distraction. When his teacher arrived, the goyish kids would note the event by saying, "Feema (that is the name they knew him with) your teacher is here." Thankfully they were old and trusty neighbors who never reported the teacher's arrival to the authorities.

During the summer Chaim went to a country house – dutche, where Reb Zalman's sister lived. There he enjoyed the animals, swimming, and other activities. Every morning Zalman's sister would wake Chaim to open the gate and let out the cow to the person who would collect people's animals and take them out to pasture. One morning she did not wake him and he was very upset. His father was working and only came to be with them for Shabbos. One year he came every day, which meant that there was cleaning to do when they got back to their apartment in town.

There were over one hundred thousand Jews and more than twenty shuls in Kharkov. The communists closed all shuls except one, the "Mashenska shul." It was a very large shul that had five thousand seats. (Later on the shul was destroyed by the Germans.) The people who attended the shul were mainly elderly. For the most part the young people had become communists which prohibited religion. At the same time the communists promoted the respect of elders and left them alone to live as they desired as they did not constitute any real challenge to communism.

Upstairs in the shul there was a nusach Ari minyan with about 500 people. Downstairs there was a smaller shul that had a nusach Ashkenaz minyan. Adjoining the shul there was a shteeble that had room for 70-80 people. It was in that room that the Lubavitcher Chassidim daavened. On Rosh Hashono and Yom Kippur the street was full of Jews as they all tried to attend even if they could not get into the packed shul. On Yomim Tovim about 2000 people would come to hear the famous chazonim who officiated on the holidays.

The shul had a mikvah in the basement. It was heated by wood and coal. The water came from an underground source. Shlomo der geller (due to his red beard or Shlomo der bedder) and his wife looked after the mikvah. It was the only one in Kharkov. No-one paid any attention to the mikvah or to anyone who went there since it was in the basement. On Shabbos after going to the mikvah, the Chassidim would learn chassidus. They began shacharis at about 11:00 am ended at about 2:00 pm. At seudah shlishis Reb Itche would review a maamor.

There were people who spied on other people and would report to the Russian secret police. Children could not come to shul as they had to be in school. If a young person attended the shul it could be considered to be a crime as it meant they were not working for, or supporting, the communist ideals.

Chaim's uncle, Rabbi Ben-Tzion Shemtov, was sent to Siberia for three years. Chaim's parents sent him a shofar which he returned to them when he returned. The shofar had cracks with holes in it but it was still halachically kosher. Chaim kept that shofar in his home in Australia.

Rabbi Zalman Shimon Dvorkin came to Kharkov as the KGB was after him. He was in hiding at Reb Zalman's house for about three quarters of a year.

Rashi (Reb Shmuel Yitzchok) Raices was living at the time in Moscow. He had lived before near Minsk but the Rayatz told him to sell his house and move near the capital. They made a lottery for someone to go to the kever in Haditch. Raices was chosen and after Haditch he visited Kharkov that is nearby. He stayed at Reb Zalman's home. The wife of Chanoch Hendel Kugel who was the mashpiah in Lubavitch had a sister Gita, who was the grandmother of Raices. In this way there was a family connection to Brocha Serebryanski (Futerfas.)

When he returned to Moscow he told his son Yosef that he met a boy Chaim and he is zeir a gutte – a very good person. Chaim was about 8 years old at the time. Later they met in Samarkand and learned together.

In the schools, officials did all that they could to remove any connection with religion from children, belief in G-d was prohibited. That is why they made a six-day week so there would not be Shabbos or Sunday. There were five work days and the sixth day was a day of rest.

Compulsory school for children began at eight years of age. School hours were 8 am till 12 noon. The rest of the day they had homework to do. There was no full day school or cheder. At the beginning of communism there were Chadorim in a variety of places but then they cracked down on them. The Yeshivah's were hidden in a variety of areas to teach boys of 14 and 15 years of age. When they were discovered, the teachers and students were arrested.

Chaim did not have any yeshivah or cheder when he was a child. In Gruzia and Kutais there was a yeshivah. Although there was no formal cheder or school, sometimes 4 or 5 boys were able to be brought together to study (until 1941.) The home of Mendel and Hinda Deitch housed an Aron Hakodesh, a table, benches and beds on the side in which bochurim slept. It was known as "the zal."

Each building was assigned a watchman to keep account of the number of people who lived there. He was a communist goy who was paid to turn a blind eye regarding the bochurim. There was an elderly Jew in that neighborhood who built a sukkah each year.

Chaim's parents hired a teacher who taught him to daaven etc. At five years of age he was able to daaven fluently from Hodu till Shmonei Esrei. His father taught him when he was able to so. Each Shabbos in shul they learned chassidus before daavening and following the daavening there was a farbrengen. Unobtrusively about thirty Lubavitch families or forty men came together in the shteeble adjoining the shul. Later the farbrengens were held in homes in honor of a special day. The big farbrengen like Yud Tes Kislev was held in shul all night and in the morning everyone went to work.

The fact that people had to work Shabbos was a big problem. The Lubavitchers attempted to take jobs as watchmen in factories. That job was to ensure that no-one stole from the factory. In that work there was no chilul Shabbos. For a period of time Chaim's father, Reb Zalman also worked as a watchman all night. Also there were factories that gave people work to take home. That allowed Chaim's parents and others to take home work and bring it back without working on Shabbos. The work and jobs went through many changes and availability of work for Reb Zalman and other Lubavitchers caused many extreme hardships.

Lubavitchers had great mesiras nefesh in avoiding the sending of their children to school, following the guidance of the Rebbe Rayatz. In school they taught kefirah - heresy and there was a problem when it came to observing Shabbos. The government schools were propaganda centers for atheism, communism and the cult of the great leader "Father Stalin." The government was set up to make everyone report about anything irregular with regard to other citizens, such as the case of a child not going to school. The police would then come and take the child away. The child was put in a boarding school where he/ she would be taught communist beliefs.

Reb Zalman also received support from a cousin Sarah Schneerson who was considered one of the greatest mathematicians in Leningrad. She never got married as it was almost impossible to find a suitable spouse for her since she was frum. Chaim saw her several times when she came to visit the family. Later when he saw a picture of the Rebbe Rayatz, he said that her facial features were like the Rayatz. She was the daughter of Reb Zalman's mother's sister Taibel, who married Rabbi Yehudah Leib Schneerson, son of Rabbi Sholom Dov Ber of Retzitza, and who was a grandson of the TzemachTzedek. They became divorced and so their marriage is not mentioned in books.

Chaim's grandmother Maryasha had very strong opinions. She told him that marozhene – ice cream, is traif. At some point during his childhood he went to see the Russian circus.

Reb Zalman told Hershel Broncher, "I fixed my sons." As children Chaim and Arel used to fight a lot. Once in the middle of a Russian winter he sent them both out into the cold saying, "you are not allowed to come back into the house until after you agree never to fight again." It was several hours before they came back.

Chaim's parents hired a Jewish woman who was a retired teacher to give him private lessons. Each morning at 8am Chaim left the house like all other children. Instead of going to school, Chaim went to his teacher. He learned all that was taught in a regular school and left for home at 12 noon.

At 3 pm an elderly Jew who was a good teacher would arrive at the apartment. The family made sure all the windows were covered by the curtains so that no-one could look in. He was just called the rebbe – teacher. At eight years old Chaim began to learn Bobo Kama and it took three years, from 1937 to 1939 to finish. He learned Hebrew grammar, writing, tanach, and at ten years old he was studying Mishlei.

His uncle Mendel Futerfas urged him to learn Tanya by heart. He memorized the chapters of the first part of Tanya before bar-mitzvah. The rest he continued memorizing by heart after bar-mitzvah. Chaim once said that in Russia they lived with the maamar Ein Hakodosh Boruch Hu Boh

Bitruniah – 5685 and it gave them the strength to keep on going with mesirus nefesh.

In 1938 his grandfather with his father's sisters and the two children moved from Brahin to Kharkov.

In 1939 a new neighbor, who was a communist teacher, moved in. As soon as she realized that he did not go school, she warned Zalman and Brocha that they had better send their two sons to school or she would report them to the authorities. At that point they had no choice but to enroll Chaim and his brother Aharon in the local school. There were about twenty students in the class.

During the school year 1939 - 40 he did not go on Shabbos. Since they had a six day week it was not easily discernable that he did not go on Shabbos. Each week was another excuse. At the end of the year, someone probably with a Jewish background realized that he did not go on Shabbos. His brother Aharon (Arel) was very weak anyway and so was away from school a lot for health reasons. At times Chaim stood by Arel's side to protect him from bullies.

They knew he was different anyway. He went to school with a cap on but removed it when he sat in class. They all wore a red tie except Chaim. His father told him that a red tie is like a cross, so he did not wear it. His mother Brocha was asked to come to see the principal. When she arrived at the school the principal had to go to the toilet. She told the secretary that if she waited she would be late for work and left. In Russia if you were late for work it was considered a criminal offense.

At the end of the year the principal came to their home with one of the teachers. The principal told them that they knew what was going on. They threatened to report the family to the KGB if they did not send Chaim to school every day the following year. Reb Zalman and Brocha understood the consequences but the Second World War started in June and so the whole matter became a non-issue.

Chaim often had to stand in line – otchara - for food as that was the order of the day with the limited food supplies. There was a major preoccupation with procuring food to eat. This only worsened with the outbreak of World War Two when starvation became an expected part of everyday life.

One-time Chaim went to the black market to sell a piece of leather in order to have money to buy food. He was caught by the police. They took him to the station and locked him up for the night. As soon as Mendel Deitsch heard about it he went to the police station and paid them money to let him out.

World War 2 began in 1939. Reb Zalman was supposed to be sent to the front lines with Poland on Simchas Torah night. A miracle occurred and he was allowed to go home instead of getting on the train. Chaim, who was standing on the steps of the shul, was surprised to see his father come to shul. That night his father danced hakofos in army uniform.

In the summer of 1941 after the Germans broke their agreement with Russia a call-up was announced. Chaim's father was in bed with severe lung infection, burning with fever. Rabbi Yaakov Ginsburg was then a bochur serving as the shochet for the Lubavitch community. He was living in the Serebryanski home. Reb Zalman urged him to leave immediately to Samarkand, which he did.

Nochum Sternberg was born on the 17th of Elul 5701/1941. His bris was held in the Serebryanski home eight days later, the third day of the week, Elul 25 5701/September 16

1941. The hospital was bombed by the Germans and Reb Zalman took Mrs Sternberg and her family into his home.

Nechama Serebryanski with two Sternberg girls.

In order to escape the approaching Germans, before Rosh Hashono of 5702/1941, Chaim left by train to the interior of the country. The army arranged for families of soldiers to leave. He escaped with his grandmother, mother, brother and sister. His father remained in Kharkov. It was a freight train and several families squeezed into each compartment. They travelled to Saratov. Due to the frequent bombing, the two-day trip took eighteen days.

Although food was short, Chaim found a way to get some. He discovered that one non-Jewish family had hundreds of eggs. He bartered and took one hundred eggs that sustained them for the rest of the trip.

From Saratov, Chaim travelled with his family to Tashkent, where they stayed with his uncle Reb Bentzion Shemtov. His sister Nechamah became sick and stayed there while Chaim, Arel and their mother Brocha continued travelling to Samarkand.

## SAMARKAND

Shortly after arriving in Samarkand, Chaim became sick with pneumonia that infected both lungs, and he was taken to the hospital. He saw people around him dying like flies. There were so many dead that the hospital staff had no time to bury them. The stench and energy of the dead bodies was in the air and Chaim realized that if he wanted to live he had to get out of the hospital. However, his temperature was very high and the doctors would not allow him to leave.

What did Chaim do? When the nurses came to take his temperature, he put the thermometer under the blanket where he shook it down, and then gave it back to the nurse. After a few times of returning the thermometer to them with reasonable temperatures, the doctors were happy release him. He happily returned home where his family cared for him until he miraculously recovered. Mrs Sarah Kievman used her connections and obtained medications for him from America.

Meanwhile Reb Zalman had arrived in Saratov to look for his family and met Muma Hinda Deitsch who was there shopping. She told him where the family was. He first went to Tashkent and once Nechamah had fully recovered took her with him to Samarkand.

When he arrived in Samarkand he became sick again. He had TB (tuberculosis) and smoked a lot. He was unable to work for a living. His son Chaim went to the market place to do business. He was able to bring home bread and fatty products to help heal his father.

He would buy a sack of salt and carry it to the market. Then he divided it into small cups and made enough money to buy a loaf of bread. At times you could only get a half or third of a loaf. This was all they had to eat.

At six o'clock each morning, Chaim would get up to learn Gemoro with his neighbor, Rabbi Eliyahu Chaim Roitblat. In winter it was still cold at that time and the water that he prepared for negel vasser was frozen. By candlelight they would sit and learn together. Later Chaim went out to earn money. (Machteres Samarkand p. 467 has a picture of Hillel and Berel Zaltzman in the yard where Chaim and his family lived.)

While Reb Zalman was sick, Chaim went out to do business, earn money and buy food. Half a year after he arrived, Reb Zalman was feeling a little better and felt that was able to earn money. He told Chaim that he wants him to be a yid and he needs to go to yeshivah. These were the same words that Reb Zalman's father said to him before he took him to the Yeshiva in Rostov.

The poverty was very intense. Brocha used shoelaces around her feet to walk as she could not afford shoes. Mendel Deitsch would cook a big pot of water and put in whatever he could find in order to feed as many people as possible.

Chaim's father's father, Menachem Mendel ben Eliyohu passed away the 8th of Elul 5702 and is buried in Samarkand. His grandfather died of starvation. Chaim remembers that he gave him the little food he had. He always saw his grandfather constantly studying Torah or saying Tehillim by heart.

For his bar-mitzvah they had a loaf of black bread, a piece of dried herring and samargon- home brewed alchohol. In

Samarkand we learned like in Lubavitch. The best years were when he was 15, 16 and 17.

On Yud Tes Kislev they held a special farbrengen. Mendel Deitsch would cook kasha and Avrohom Zaltzman would bring a barrel of sauerkraut. Due to extreme poverty they did not have eating utensils, so they had to take knives and carve spoons out of wood. Avrohom Zaltzman would play violin and the boys would use wooden clappers and bang on the tables.

In 5703 was the first time he made a blessing on the Lulav and esrog. Lulovim, haddasim and arovos were plentiful. Someone managed to bring one single esrog to Samarkand. Since everyone used it the color changed on the outside till it became a question if it can be used. A response of the Chasam Sofer was found stating that such a change is the best change, it is mehudar, since it shows how much everyone loves the mitzvahs of Hashem and it can therefore be used.

Chaim first learned in the Talmud Torah from Rabbi Eliyohu Chaim Roitblat and Rabbi Moshe Rubinson (Karlevitcher.) Later he learned in the Yeshivah, Reb Zalman Shimon Dvorkin and Reb Avrohom Eliyohu Plotkin taught him nigleh, while Reb Nissan Nemenov taught him Chassidus.

Reb Chaim related how it was a great pleasure to listen to the lectures of Rav Avrohom Elya as he was known. He had an amazing order to his learning. Approaching each subject from all possible angles he would bring out many fine line logics, "Er hot aroom genumen dem inyan – he encompassed the matter."

During his lessons he would say that when an Amora gave an opinion it was after taking into account all possibilities as well as his opponent's opinion. The same is with the Amorah who gave a different opinion. Since they both held their ground we need to understand what is hidden in their opinions. There are some very fine logics that divide them and he would then explain them in a deep and detailed manner.

One-time Chaim with a group of friends were returned home from their studies late at night. A band of ruffians met them. Yehoshua (Heishka) Dubrawsky held a guy from behind while Chaim kicked him in the front between his legs sending him to hospital. That person was the leader of the group and they never bothered the boys again.

One-time Chaim and Yossel Reices were walking together and thought someone was following so they walked all over till they felt it was safe. Another time they were asked to follow someone to see if he was a spy for the secret police. They followed and saw that he went to the old part of the city and not the new and so they decided he was probably not a spy. They were such close friends that sometimes they were called Chaim Yossels as if it was one name.

Another time in class Moshe Gurkov was playing or throwing stones and Chaim got a slap for it. When he went to Reb Nissan to say that it was not fair since he did not do it, Reb Nissan said you probably deserve it for something else.

Mottel Kozliner mentioned that when he came to Samarkand his father told him, "I will show you a bochur who sits a whole day by a sefer and doesn't even stop to go to the bathroom." He showed him Chaim Serebryanski.

At farbrengens it was very packed and the mashpiah would talk in a low voice. This caused a lot of pushing to be able to hear. One time a mashpiah said, "what are you pushing for? If you are supposed to hear you will hear!"

As a bochur in Tomchei Tmimim of Samarkand he began Chazering maamorim by heart. His bobbe Maryasha would occasionally tell him 'zog chassidus' and Chaim would chazer a maamor. After being up learning or farbrenging all Thursday night he would lay down Friday afternoon. When looking closely one could see that his eyes were closed but that his mouth was moving reviewing chassidus by heart.

Rabbi Yehoshua Dubrawsky wrote that Chaim was a rarity. He was a Chassidishe beindel from birth. By nature, such a person has middos of gold, healthy bittul, and emes. Regarding some like this it would be ludicrous to call him a yesh or a baal gaava since that was far from him as east and west. He was a real penimi.

Chaim has a good heart and Chassidishe middos, and is filled with flavor. It is worth mentioning that when he was fifteen, he learned only half a day. During the second half he dealt in business in the Samarkand market to help support his family. His father, the warm hearted Chossid Reb Zalman, was unable to work due to poor health. Certain talmidim said that Chaim was more successful in his half day of learning than those who learned all day.

He would go with Heishka Dubrawsky to learn with his Zaide Mendel Dubrawsky who would teach them maamarim of the Rebbe Maharash. He told them a story that happened with him when he was Rosh Yeshivah in Lubavitch giving a shiur. The Frierdiker Rebbe as Menahel came in to observe the shiur, after the shiur Reb Mendel walked over to the Frierdiker Rebbe and sighed. The Rebbe asked, why the sigh? He responded that he has no koach. The Rebbe then quoted the verse (Yeshayo - Isaiah 40:31) **"vikovei Hashem yachalifu koach"** we exchange our worn out koach with Hashem who in turn gives us his refreshed koach.

In Tiferes Hayehudi p.149 (Chiddushei Torah and stories note 11) the Holy Yid of Peshischa once told his son a Torah thought as they were travelling to Rimanov. The verse (Deuteronomy 25:18) says **"You are tired and exhausted"** after prayers because **"you do not fear Hashem."** He then quoted the above verse from Isaiah – **"vekovei Hashem yachalifu koach"** and explained; when you are tired and exhausted after prayers it means that you do not have to be afraid of judgments since they were sweetened in their source.

## LVOV – LEMBERG

At the end of the war in 1945 Leibel Mochkin was sent to Lvov (Lemberg) to find a way for anash to leave Russia. Chaim with many other Lubavitch families left Samarkand and travelled to Lvov. Reb Zalman was appointed treasurer of the committee that was overseeing the mass evacuation of Chassidim from Russia.

He included his son Chaim who was a young bachur–seventeen at the time and did not yet have a beard, to carry out errands for the committee. Chaim would meet up with Polish citizens in bars and would buy their Polish documentation in exchange for money that he had been given by the committee.

He would often go to Reb Mendel Garelik, who was an expert at forging documents, to give and receive documents from him. Lubavitcher rabbanim, who considered these activities *hatzolas nefashos* and *pikuach nefesh,* allowed them to work on Shabbos when necessary. It sometimes happened that Chaim had to carry documents on Shabbos. As the Rabbanim told him, he would put the papers under his cap so he would be carrying in an unusual way.

His sister Nechama remembers going with him to pay smugglers on Shabbos, and as she was the youngest, she had to carry the money in a belt. In order to give money to help some people he would go to the theater with his sister Nechama. He would enter the front and go to the rear exit, pass the money and go back into the theater. Later he would leave the front of the theater, thus he used the place as a cover for his meeting with the person he gave the money.

During this time in Russia all persons had to carry identity documents on them at all times. Chaim did not have proper documents to be in Lvov. He also carried identification of another person who was fourteen years old. One day the police surrounded the market when Chaim was there and started checking everyone's documents. Chaim was standing next to a bookshop. In a loud voice he asked the shopkeeper if he had certain school books. The policeman therefore thought he was a student and thus did not check his identification. He was stopped at other times and escaped only by miracles.

Anash were living in many places around the city. In order to get them to the echelon - train that took them over the border it needed a vehicle. All vehicles were all in the hands of the government and to get a truck Chaim borrowed from people in the army. He would drink with them and borrow their truck to pick up the Chassidim and take them to the train.

Chaim Ber Wilshansky said one of the activities Reb Chaim did in helping anash escape Russia was getting trucks to drive the families to the train station. As the only trucks available were military trucks he had to get military trucks to transport the families. Once he stopped a truck and he saw that in the truck was sitting a high ranking general, he quickly ran away.

The last group left on the ninth of Teves 5707. The next train that left was stopped and the people arrested. Chaim was supposed to be on that train but by a miracle left on the ninth of Teves. He had just dropped a group of people of at the train and as he was about to leave saw an elderly Jew who needed assistance. He immediately went to help and as he was at the train the whistle blew that it was leaving. He jumped on the train and thus escaped with that train.

Hundreds of people crowded onto this train into two compartments. Lubavitchers were afraid to remain on this train until its intended destination and they paid the conductor so that he would stop for a few minutes in Krakow. He stopped and within a few minutes, they had all alighted from the train.

## FRANCE

Reb Zalman, who was a member of the committee, decided to remain with his wife and daughter Nechama in Poland. He sent his mother-in-law Maryasha, Chaim and Aharon with a group of Lubavitchers, who crossed the border with the help of the Breicha, to Austria and from there to Paris.

On the way to Paris Chaim stopped in Vienna to visit a doctor. He had a lump on his hand that the doctors in Russia said to leave alone. The doctors in Vienna did not know what it was and decided to cut it out. Chaim almost died from that procedure.

In Russia there were very few seforim. To learn chassidus he copied hemshechim by handwriting chassidus and learned from his handwritten copy. When he left Russia on the way to France he was in a place that had seforim. He asked the Rabbi if he could have the set of Pnei Yehoshua. The Rabbi said that if he can tell him something from the Pnei Yehoshua he can have it. Chaim quoted a Pnei Yehoshua that he had learned in Samarkand and was given the set.

Chaim's father only arrived in Paris at the beginning of the winter of 5708. Chaim was learning in Yeshivas Tomchei T'mimim in Brunoy. Chaim sent a note to the Rebbe Rayatz asking for a blessing for his brother Aharon to have a complete recovery and for his friend Mordechai ben Tzippah who was on the other side of the border that his health should be strengthened and be able to leave.

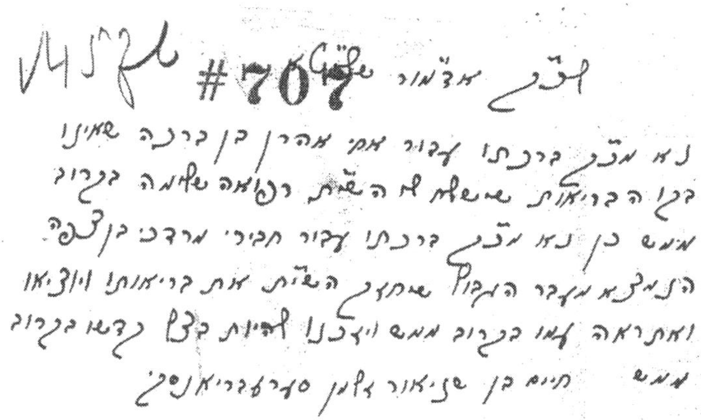


The Yeshivah was at the top of a hill. There was a pool of water at the bottom of the hill that was used as a mikvah. Chaim went every morning with a few of his friends. He said the water was cooler in summer and warmer in winter.

Chaim was known as a 'big masmid' and was a close disciple – a mekabel penimi of Reb Nissan Nemenov originating from their days in Samarkand. He learned dozens of maamarim by heart and accustomed himself to daaven at length with deep contemplation of Chassidic maamarim. He also studied Nigleh assiduously. His love for learning made him forget his physical needs and he hardly ate or slept. At farbrengens, he drank a lot of mashke, which did not help his precarious health.

Chaim's thin body did not withstand the burden he placed upon it and one day, he lost sensation in his hands. A few hours later, he lost sensation in his legs and could not walk. It was also hard for him to speak. He felt paralyzed. He was brought to the hospital, where the doctors declared that his body had broken down due to his poor eating and sleeping habits. They were unable to improve his condition. The heads of The Joint in Paris, who took responsibility for the refugees, brought him the best doctors, but to no avail.

Reb Zalman sent off a letter to the Rebbe Rayatz asking for a brocha. Within a short time, he received a letter with a brocha for a refuah shleima. When a few months went by without improvement, Reb Zalman sent a request for another brocha. The Rebbe wrote that he should make sure to have good doctors, and that there would be a complete recovery.

Meanwhile, Chaim was still in yeshiva almost completely paralyzed. Reb Zalman wrote to the Rebbe once again with the news that the doctors were unable to heal his son, and he asked for recovery without the doctors. The Rebbe's response was: *It is written in the Torah "verapo yirapeh." Since the Torah says to consult with a doctor, they should go to once more to doctors and there would be a complete recovery.*

When Reb Nissan Nemenov saw the Rebbe's answer, he said to Reb Zalman, "You have the Rebbe's promise for a refua shleima. You just need to make a vessel for the blessing by calling a top doctor." A top doctor was called. After he visited Chaim over a period of days and brought various medications, the long-awaited miracle occurred and Chaim began to heal. In fact, the doctor, who was very surprised by the speed of the recovery, said in amazement, "You have big *protektzia* in heaven."

Reb Zalman quickly informed the Rebbe that his son was no longer in danger, and the Rebbe thanked him for the good news. In the following months, Chaim slowly recovered, spending a long time in bed to regain his strength. He was not able to concentrate on learning as he had been used to doing until then, and could not learn in depth for more than ten minutes at a time. He spent most hours of the day resting and occasionally he would review Gemara or maamarim on a superficial level.

His grandmother Maryahsa said to him, "now you are not able to learn, but it is better to have a great desire to learn when you cannot than learn too much now and be turned off later.

It was only in Sivan 5709 that Chaim was able to write his own letter to the Rebbe about the improvement in his health. The Rebbe thanked him and blessed him with physical and spiritual health. Later on, Reb Nissan Nemanov received a letter from the Rebbe Rayatz rebuking him for allowing Chaim to do avoda beyond his physical capabilities, damaging his health.

As many anash families were on temporary resident permits, many began to travel to other countries. Reb Zalman received a letter from the Rebbe Rayatz dated 7 Tammuz 5709/1949 to move to Australia with his family. Chaim like everyone else had to undergo an extensive medical examination. Chaim had wanted to stay in the Yeshivah in Brunoy studying and later travel together with some of his friends to the Rebbe in New York.

After his father received a reply from the Rebbe about his trip with his family, daughter and two sons who are students in Tomchei Temimim Lubavitch, Chaim understood that it was also the Rebbe's response to his question and that he needs to go with his family to Australia. The visas were obtained through the support of Reb Moshe Zalman Feiglin.

They travelled by train to the harbor city of Genoa, Italy with Rabbi Abba Pliskin and his family. From there they embarked on a boat for their trip to Australia. The trip took a full month. On the boat they had a Sefer Torah and minyan.

## THE TOWN OF HLUSK/GLUSK

Since towns did not change too much over the centuries we are including a description of the town from the end of nineteenth century as part of a backdrop. Most of the information was taken from **"Memories of Hlusk"** by Yaakov Lipshitz and **"Self Defence in Hlusk"** by Shmuel Leif both originally in Yiddish and translated by Sol Krongelb.
https://dbs.bh.org.il/place/glusk

Jews settled in Glusk in the third quarter of the 17th century. Yechile B. Solomon Heilprin was the Rabbi there and compiled the regulations of its Chevra Kadisha. In 1717 the Jews paid 600 Zloty poll tax. In 1847 the town had a Jewish population of 3,148. In 1897 1,801 (71% of the total population) and in 1926 2,581 (58.3%). Glusk hd no industry. Some of the Jews produced a special kind of tea (called Glusk tea), but most were gardners, carpenters, horse merchants and small traders. The community came to an end under the Nazi occupation. Most were sent to their death but entire families fled to the forest where many of them fought in partisan units.

Hlusk is part of the area of Bobroysk, and at the time that our story begins it was called Novogrodek district. Over the centuries, the town and area came under various different owners. According to the 1897 Russian census, Hlusk had a population of 5,328 people of which 3,801 were Jews. The houses were crooked and the streets were dirty and unpaved. It was at the edge of the woods, yet it had picturesque landscapes, blossoming meadows, rich with mushrooms and berries.

Map of Hlusk

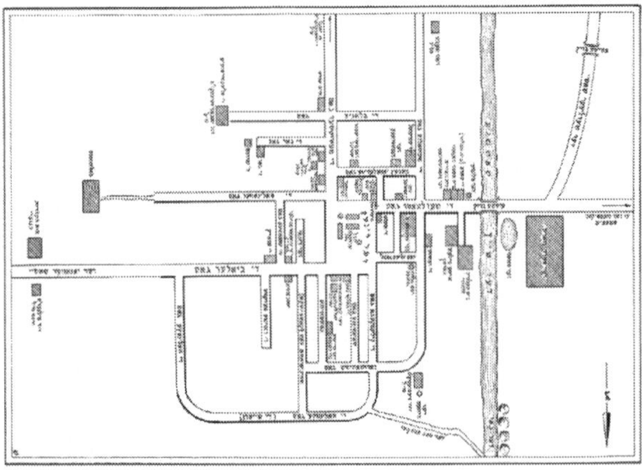

https://digitalcollections.nypl.org/items/966adea0-6630-0133-49b4-00505686a51c#/?uuid=981c8d40-6630-0133-2df9-00505686a51c

The village communication with the outside world was through wagon drivers. One type was those who transported heavy cargo known as *lomovikes*. The other type transported people in coaches and were known as *leygkovikes*. The *lomovikes* travelled twice a week to and from Bobroysk, while *lomovikes* took *parshoinen* - passengers three times a week. The people were crammed into the carriages like herring in a barrel, and if one came out alive from such a trip he/she could say the blessing hagomel.

It was approximately forty-five kilometers to the highway and about fifty kilometers to the railroad in Bobroysk or twenty-nine miles south west of Bobroysk. The road was sandy and the heavy loads made it through with much difficulty. There were two routes. The road that passed through Horodok (Gorodok) was shorter. There they made a rest stop for the horses and went into the inn for a plate of cooked beans with meat and a samovar of tea. During the summer monts they used the longer route through Ladvike and came out to the highway at Bagoshovke.

There was no industry in Hlusk. People engaged in gardening or renting out orchards. There were peddlers, carpenters, tailors, brick layers, horse traders and butcher among the populance. Every Sunday they would head out to the surrounding hamlets and would return home Friday in time for Shabbos. The majority of Hlusker Jews were shopkeepers.

The town center was a marketplace with four rows of shops consisting a total of 120 small stores all facing one another and ten stores in a side street. There were also wholesale stores on one side of the market which sold merchandise to the small shopkeepers. The small shopkeepers would sit a whole week without earning a penny and wait for Sunday, when peasants would come to the shtetl. A few poor farmers would sometimes come during the week.

On Sunday, the peasants brought their products like wood, poultry, calves, flax, dried pelts` from all sorts of animals, cheese, butter, etc. to sell and bought all their household needs from the town's storekeepers. With any leftover money, they would stop into a tavern, order a platter of *taranes (flat dried and salted fish)* and tea, and top it off with a flask of whiskey.

Quite often, they would become drunk and make a little pogrom in the market place. Then the storekeepers would close their shops, and, out of nowhere, there would suddenly appear our esteemed butchers — Pinyeh Tamara's, Motel Elyeh Nachum's, Mayer Noah Lapate's — along with a couple of Hlusker *Chonyokhes* [horse traders]. And if these men were not sufficient to quiet the drunkards, Motke Ayzers the *Chonyokh* would also be called. And this Motkeh, a broad-boned, tall, fine Jewish giant of a man, before whom the whole neighborhood shuddered, would come with his studded whip stick, give a shout *"razoydis!"* ["be gone!"], and start cracking skulls. The gentiles would quickly harness their horses, and in ten minutes there was not a trace left of them.

A story about Motkeh's prowess needs to be told. He was a quiet person. At one sitting, he could eat a small goose with a pound of *gribenes* which are crisp, chicken or goose skin along with a loaf of bread and a quart of whiskey and also drink down the contents of a samovar holding twenty-two glasses of tea. He dealt in horses, would carry sums of cash as he traveled alone at night from hamlet to hamlet, and no one bothered him.

Once he came to a *poritz* [landowner], Dashkevitch, to buy horses. When the *poritz* saw Motkeh, he said to him, "I'm not selling any horses. However, I have a Belgian workhorse. You are reputed to be a strong person, so if you will lift up the horse, I'll give him to you free." A lot of peasants and farm-hands happened to be standing around. Motkeh thought a moment, went over to the horse, put his head between the horse's forelegs, gave a grunt and lifted up the horse. The *poritz* kept his word and gave him the horse. However, Motkeh had ruptured himself and wound up with a hernia, but no one knew of this. The entire countryside feared him.

There was great competition in all aspects of earning a living. The shopkeepers would drag the peasants by their garments into their own shops. Even the cheder teachers competed in the tuition fee and in their flattery of the *balebatim*. Only one person in the shtetl had no competition – Reb Noah Itche Chloneh's. He was the only candle maker in the shtetl and surrounding region, and therefore he was also called Reb Noah Licht macher [Candle maker].

Reb Noah was one of the most pious and respected *balebatim* in Hlusk. True, he was not wealthy. In winter, when a lot of slaughtering was done and there was enough tallow to make candles with an excess to send to the soap factories in Bobruisk, there was an income. But when the summer arrived, it was not so good because practically no slaughtering was done, and Reb Noah, along with the *shochtim* and butchers, had no livelihood. So in the summer, Reb Noah became a *sodovnik,* that is, he rented a fruit-orchard from a *poritz* [land owner] and, if G-d helped, and the trees were not overrun with worms, and there was not too much rain and hail, they got by till winter.

There were two Rabbis one Chassidic and the other a misnaged. There were also separate shochatim for the Chassidim and misnagdim. There were five shuls in the synagogue yard; the great shul, the alte shul, the aristrokatishe shul, a Chassidic shtibel at the old dirt road to Slabodka and a small tailor's shul.

A small river, Ptich, flowed through Hlusk. Nearly all the villagers knew how to swim. On Friday, practically the whole town came out to the river to bathe. The wagon drivers would even bring their horses and bathe themselves together with the horses. There was also a bathhouse in Hlusk. The bathhouse attendants were Itsche *der beder* [literally, Itsche, the bathhouse attendant] and his brother Motel, a Jew with a straggly beard. Every Friday, the entire town went to the bathhouse to wash away the week's accumulation of dirt. The bathhouse was a primitive one with a single oven, which consisted of piled up stones. Hot water would be poured on the stones. A thick steam would rise up, and people would sit on the floor and brush themselves, or one would brush the other, accompanied by shouts, moans and groans.

Hlusk was known for its two klezmer bands. The ordinary people would hire Maishkeh because he was more available and less expensive.

Reb Yoske's band was renowned throughout the entire region from Hlusk to Bobruisk and to Slutsk. People spoke of his playing with reverence. He did not simply play to provide music — his playing was heavenly. He composed a melody which he would play before music connoisseurs at weddings. He did not graduate from a conservatory, but had the ability to play with such power and sweetness. He had complete mastery of his instrument and could bring out tones such as few musicians could achieve.

He was a small, thin Jew with a little beard and with a growth on his forehead which was covered with hair. He lived on the old dirt road in a small, old house. His first wife died young and left him with five or six children. He also had four or five children with his second wife, so that altogether they were a family of ten to twelve people. It should be understood that he was desperately poor despite the fact that he had many students and his wife had small store.

Reb Yoske's band consisted of Reb Yoske himself, first violin; his son Itche, second violin; his son Shlomkeh, violoncello; his son Shneur, trombone and coronet; Laizer the bagel baker, flute; Mendel the tailor, clarinet; and Reb Avraham the wagon driver, double base and drum. This same Reb Avraham also filled in as *badchin* [a jocular entertainer at a wedding]. He would call to the "*dobridziens*" [welcoming of the guests], to the first dance, to the blessing of the groom before the ceremony. During the playing at the evening meal, he was the one who asked the assembled guests to be quiet and so on.

Reb Avraham the drummer, a wagon driver, with a thick beard and blind in the right eye, was blessed with perfect pitch and had a good feel for the music. One nod from Yoske was enough for him to know when to play forte or pianissimo. When he was playing his double bass at a *poritz's* ball to accompany the waltz *"Na Sopki Manchuria,"* ("On the Hills of Manchuria") he did not take his eyes off Yoskeh. And if all went well without any disapproving glances, a smile of satisfaction would spread across his face.

A wedding in Hlusk was an important event. In keeping with the custom, the wedding ceremony took place in the synagogue yard, and the bride and groom were escorted with music to and from the wedding canopy. Everyone in the town, young and old, would trail after. Before the ceremony, when they would play a *dobridzien* [a welcoming musical selection] for the bride and for the groom, Reb Avraham would close his one eye and would call out, "A beautiful *dobridzien* for our dear bride with the dear in-laws, relatives and neighbors! Klezmer, take the instruments in your hands, and sound forth!" And here the klezmer would play forth with a beautiful *volachel* [a kind of dance] which warmed the heart. Warm tears would overwhelm the bride as well as the mothers of the bride and the groom; even the fathers with strong nerves would inconspicuously wipe away a tear.

The main attraction, however, came during the wedding meal. If Yoske knew that there was a music connoisseur among the attendees, he would let his long, thin fingers dance over the strings and began to bring forth touchingly warm tones. The violin would begin to cry and speak compassionately to the heart. All held their breath as they listened to the trills, which were far more beautiful than a nightingale's. I don't think that any bird could emulate his playing. It is said that this plain Jew and great artist was left without any means to support himself in his old age. His children later brought him to America, where he died.

Hlusk was mired in mud for three-quarters of the year. Only one street was paved, and people called it *"Die shosaynegass"* [the highway street]. This street was the setting for the activities of town life, both on Friday and holiday nights as well as throughout the year. Here was the meeting place for couples in love, for friends and group meetings.

Hlusk was not blessed like other towns with many fairs. However, one fair did take place during the year on a Friday before Shavuot which lasted, all told, a half day. This annual market was called *"Piatzinkeh"* and would assemble five *kilometers* from the town beyond Slabodeh – the long road. Preparation for the fair would go on during the whole week. Peasants from the region and also from Hlusk would arrive on Thursday evening to set up their tents and to sleep the night there because the trading would begin before daybreak. People would begin to leave by midday because of the Shabbat.

It is important to mention the military conscripts from Hlusk. Each year after Succoth all the recruits in Hlusk had to come to the *volost* (county office building where doctors examined recruits) in Hlusk to stand before a committee which determined if they were fit for military service. In one respect, it [the military conscription] was good. There would be revenue from the *novobrantzes* - draftees, but often they would instigate a little pogrom and help themselves to something from the shops. Then the Jewish conscripts would "step up to the job" — With special, thick sticks they would crack a few Gentile heads, order would be restored [and] the Gentile *novobrantzes* would be afraid to even stick forth their noses.

The Jewish conscripts engaged in another activity besides restoring order. They would go to the rejected recruits who happened to receive white slips (certificate excusing the individual from military service) and demand money from them for liquor under the pretext that they [the conscripts] were serving in the Czar's army in place of this one or that one [of the rejected recruits].

They would drink away the accumulated money at the place of Reb Itche Fishman the matchmaker's daughter-in-law, Liebe the widow. She used to have good roast goose, stuffed derma, gizzards and other delicacies. It was a private home, but one could always get a good supply of liquor.

The horse-traders from Hlusk were a unique group. They could be spotted a mile away — long hair down to the neck, like the Russian peasants, and clean-shaven. A horse trader always carried a whip with a good, oaken whip handle (useful in case of any trouble.)

All week, except for Sunday, they would go around without any work, and the "trading" was at the inn of *Liebe die kop.* There they got a drink of whiskey along with a portion of fish and a good, fresh roll. They also played cards there. Liebe would extend credit and would write it down in the ledger.

The horse-trader's language was comprehensible only to them: an old woman, an eagle, a bridegroom, a bride — these were categories of horses. The trading was done with the peasants from the surrounding region. Every Sunday the peasants would come to trade horses, and in the exchange, the peasant would always pay a few rubles, and these few rubles were pure profit. Peasants love to trade horses. Indeed, it would very often happen that after five or six exchanges, the peasant would end up with his own horse.

The traders were great experts in preparing the horses for sale: dressing them up, washing them spotless, braiding the tail in a knot and tying it fast with a cord, combing out the mane and weaving in pieces of red material, washing the eyes with vinegar mixed with water. The main task was to make the teeth look right, for the teeth in an old horse had already become worn down and smooth. When an expert comes to evaluate a horse, he pulls out the tongue from the horse's mouth and feels the teeth with his finger. If he finds that the teeth are smooth, it's a sign that the horse is old.

But the horse traders had a "partner" — the *mufker* [literally, an immoral person] or as they called him, the "tooth-doctor." The *mufker* would take a small, triangular file which is used to sharpen a saw and would make notches in the horse's teeth such that one could not distinguish between the altered teeth and genuine teeth. The poor horse would be so beaten under his belly with the whip-stick (so that the signs of his age would not be apparent), that he would jump out of his battered skin. In addition, they would pour a flask of whiskey into the water to intoxicate the horse.

Then, when he was brought to the market, the horse trader would hold his bridle with the left hand and give him a couple of good jabs from time to time with the right hand so that, at the time of evaluation, the horse would really fly like an arrow from a bow, and the deal would be completed in ten minutes. Only when the peasant returned home did he first see what a bargain he snared. A few weeks later, the peasant returned to the market and approached the horse trader: *"Hey, chonyokh, davai pobitaiemkonyi,"* i.e., "Hey, horse trader, let's trade horses again."

In Hlusk there were a variety of Rabbis over the centuries. Rabbi Yechiel Halperin the author of the Seder Hadoros was a Rov in Hlusk. He established the Takanot, the rules and customs of the town and wrote them down. Most of his writings were burned in a fire but a few pieces were saved. He left the town in 5471/1711 before Shavuos to settle in Minsk.

*Responsa* ***Bais Ov Chamishoee*** *by Avrohom Aharon Yudelevitz 1850- 1930, published in NY 5679 Yoreh Deah chapter 229 part 6.*

The wife of Shraga travelled with her brother-in-law to a non-Jew who practices witchcraft near the city of Hlusk, in order to help her become pregnant. He told me that when they came to the village, the Jew who ran the hotel said to them that the custom is to bring the sorcerer a bottle of spirits and place it on the table, he looks at it and tells the reason you came for. Therefore, go buy some and put it in a glass bottle. They did so and after putting it on the table the non-Jew looked at it and it immediately began to bubble and look like there was a fire under it. He said this man here is not your husband and your husband spends time away from home. Her husband was a prikaschik on a boat that sailed the Dnieper river. Then he said that your house is near the river and told how many windows and doors there are. He continued that you do not have children because of the bad thoughts that the musician had while playing at your wedding. It appears like ayin horo. I will give you some grass to drink and you will have a child but the child will be plemished, so you decide. The woman decided to take the grass and a week after the child was born it became blind in one eye. The response continues with discussing the prohibition of doing such a thing.

***Doros Hoacharonim*** *book 1 p. 203* Rabbi Yisroel Lyubov ab"d of Starodov was born in Hlusk in 5602 d.erev Shabbos 28th Adar Sheni 5670. His father Shneur Yaakov was a rosh mesivtah for Reb Hillel of Paritch in Bobroysk and passed away when he was 7 in the year 5609.

***Sefer Hasichos Toras Shmuel*** *p.2 from* ***Sefer Hasichos 5703*** For Rosh Hashono 5627 the Chossid Reb Pesach from Hlusk travelled with other Chassidim, led by Reb Mordechai Yoel, to my grandfather in Lubavitch. In the paper that he gave my grandfather, Reb Pesach wrote about his livelihood and noted that he personally travels with a wagon of wares.

**הלוסק**

לקוטי תורה ברשימת הכתבי יד פ' חוקת. הנחת ר' הלל מפאריטש, מה שדרש אדמו"ר נ"ע (צ"צ) בפ' חוקת בק' הלוסק תקצ"ו 1837 לפ"ק וביאור ע"ז מש"א אדמו"ר נבג"ם במלון הסמוך לק' פאריטש.

נפלאות השם – דף 24 – 21 מעשה שאירע בעיר הלוסק. שו"ת גליא מסכת שאלה ו

## Family Descendants

### Lists of Family Members in Generations

**First Generation**
Moshe Zev
**Second Generation**
**Third Generation**
Yehoshua Gluskin
Eliezer Gluskin
**Fourth Generation**
Aharon Gluskin
Zev Gluskin
**Fifth Generation**
Children of Aharon Gluskin
**Sixth Generation**
Grandchildren of Aharon Gluskin
**Seventh Generation**
Grandchildren of Jacob and Kayle Helfgott
Grandchildren of Ita and Yosef Gutner
Grandchildren of Basya Riva and Yosef Gutner
Grandchildren of Baila and Isaac Gurevitch
Grandchildren of Musia and Isaac Volovitch
Grandchildren of Rochel Chaya and Isser Ginsburg
Grandchildren of Menachem Mendel and Fraidel Gluskin
Grandchildren of Nechama and Menachem Mendel Serebryanski
**Eighth Generation**
**Grandchildren of Nochum and Rose Helfgott**
Children of Aharon and Esther Rose Helfgott
Children of Doris and Milton Rosenfeld
**Grandchildren of Moshe and Rachel Minkin**
Children of Mark and Ita Minkin
**Grandchildren of Benjamin and Miriam Sax**
Children of Albert and Irene Sax
Children of Daniel and Joan Sax

Children of Ruth and Robert Levy
**Grandchildren of Isser and Ana Helfgott**
Children of Leonard Michael and Katherine Helfgott
Children of Esther Wilma Helfgott and Oscar Lee Feit
Children of Dorothy and Mark Lazarus
Children of Leah and Robert Naiman
**Grandchildren of Yaakov and Klara Gutner**
Children of Ita and Mark Minkin
Children of Alexandra and Zinovy Krupenin
**Grandchildren of Hertz and Eugine Gertner**
Children of Lucia and Boris Turetsky
Children of Boris Gutner and Rimma
**Grandchildren of Yevsey and Lubov Gutner**
Children of Ida and Noi Grobshteyn
**Grandchildren of Fraidel and Solomon**
Children of Michael Gurevitz m. Gita
Children of Chaya and Savva Sagir
**Grandchildren of Don and Mania Gurevitch**
Children of Lina Gurevitch m. Vereschagin
**Grandchildren of Aharon and Lyuba Gurevitch**
Children of Nona and Igor Maloy
**Grandchildren of Pearl and Yosef Raginsky**
Children of Yuri and Margarita Raginsky
**Grandchildren of Yevsey Gurevitch and Channa**
Children of Bella and Oleg Drozdov
Children of Alla m. Leonid Minkin
**Grandchildren of Esther and Gafan Nazirov**
Children of Roman and Tamara
**Grandchildren of Mira Volovich/Gefter**
Children of Victor and Nella Gefter
**Grandchildren of Aron Volovitch**
Children of Emma and Semen Vershlovsky
**Grandchildren of Hillel Volovitch**
Children of Elena and Uri Futritcky
**Grandchildren of Aharon and Vera Ginzburg**
Children of Irina and Vitaly Grobshteyn

Children of Margarita and Eugene Grobshteyn
**Grandchildren of Gita Gluskin and Lev Vilsker**
Children of Emanuel and Shlomit Shalom Gluskin
Children of Boruch and Katia Vilsker
**Grandchildren of Elozor and Ita Freida Gorowitz**
Children of Esther and Shmuel Gorowitz
Children of Yaakov and Rochel Edelstein
**Grandchildren of Zalman and Brocha Serebryanski**
Children of Chaim and Esther Serebryanski
Children of Aharon and Zlata Serebryanski
Children of Nechama and Nosson Werdiger

**Ninth Generation**
Children of Vladimir and Ludmila Minkin
Children of Leonid and Alla Minkin
Children of Ben Sax
Children of Karen and Michael McLoughlin
Children of Diana and Darik Corzine
Children of David and Ariella Levy
Children of Isser Helfgott
Children of Jacquie and Zack Cook
Children of Ian and Susan Helfgott
Children of Scott Helfgott
Children of Erik and Anna Naiman
Children of Vladimir and Lumila Minkin
Children of Leonid and Alla Minkin
Children of Svetlana and Timur Kirgizbayev
Children of Alex and Marina Krupeniv
Children of Alex and Olga Krupeniv
Children of Maria and Slava Sukharev
Children of Gregory and Ulyana Gutner
Children of Vitaly and Irina Grobshteyn / Ginsburg
Children of Eugene and Margarita Grobshteyn
Children of Lyuba and Victor Tretyakov
Children of Ludmila and Vladimir Garnik
Children of Alla and Valery Polyakov

Children of Lyuba Kiryanov
Children of Boris and Svetlana Raginsky
Children of Anna and Alex Sorokin
Children of Irina and Maxim Levit
Children of Edward and Korina Nazirov
Children of Galina Vershlovsky
Children of Victoria Futritckly
Children of Vladim and Arina Ginsburg
Children of Natalie and Dmitry Gershman
Children of Roman and Lena Grobshteyn
Children of Reut Esther and Ariel Golan Cohen Gabay
Children of Eitan Chaim and Ayala Gluskin
Children of Gili Fradel Chemda and Avishai Aharoni
Children of Shira Rachel and Omer
Children of Michael and Vered Vilsker
Children of Yossi and Rochie Serebryanski
Children of Menachem Mendel and Channa Serebryanski
Children of Basya and Chaim Dalfin
Children of Binyomin and Chana Serebryanski
Children of Eli and Chana Serebryanski
Children of Chana and Sholom Raichik
Children of Moshe and Bluma Serebryanski
Children of Nechama Dina and Yoske Mishulovin
Children of Miriam and Mendel Simon
Children of Levi and Leah Serebryanski
Children of Yosef and Chana Serebryanski
Children of Rochel and Mendel Lipsker
Children of Mendel and Chomie Serebryanski
Children of Hendel and Shoshi Serebryanski
Children of Debbie and Robbie Nussbaum
Children of Shlomo and Shyrla Werdiger
Children of Michelle and Yitzchok Feiglin
Children of Miriam and Yirmi Goldshmidt
Children of David and Adira Werdiger
Children of Yitzchok and Chana Gorowitz
Children of Ita and Mendel Chanzin

Children of Fruma and Dovid Teichtel
Children of Eliezer and Zissel Gurevitz
Children of Nechama Miriam and Mordechai Tzivin
Children of Sima and Avrohom Chazan
Children of Mendel and Taibel Gurevitch

**Tenth Generation**
**Grandchildren of Vladimir and Ludmila**
Children of Sergey and Tatiana Minkin
Children of Catherine and Denis Zaharov
**Grandchildren of Svetlana and Timur Kirgizbayev**
Children Amir and Luba Kirgiz
Children of Marat and Asya Kirgiz
**Grandchildren of Alex Krupenin and Marina**
Children of Michael and Elena Krupenin
Children of Roman and Natasha Krupenin
**Grandchildren of Vitaly and Irina Ginzburg**
Children of Vadim and Arina Ginzburg
Children of Natalie and Dmitry Gershman
**Grandchildren of Eugene and Margarita Grobshteyn**
Children of Roman and Lena Grobshteyn
**Grandchildren of Yitzchok and Chana Gorowitz**
Children of Menachem Mendel and Chana Rochel Gorowitz
Children of Shaina Basha and Efraim Shmuel Mintz
Children of Nechama Dina and Yehuda Leib Kantor
Children of Hinda and Yosef Hakohen Friedman
Children of Zelda Rochel and Mendy Greenbaum
Children of Risha Brocha and Levi Gurevitch
Children of Sholom Dov Ber and Mushky Gorowitz
Children of Elka and Levi Yitzchok Kaplan
Children of Sara Alta and Moshe Lieberman
Children of Baila Rivka and Chaim Fischer
Children of Yosef and Chana Devorah Gorowitz
Children of Chaya Mushka and Dovber Wolvovsky
**Grandchildren of Yossi and Rochie Serebryanski**

Children of Shmuel Sholom and Feige Rivka Serebryanski

**Grandchildren of Mendel and Chana Serebryanski**

Children of Moshe Mordechai and Sheina Mushka Serebryanski

Children of Yosef Shmuel and Raizel Serebryanski

**Grandchildren of Bashi and Chaim Dalfin**

Children of Menachem Mendel and Dassi Dalfin

Children of Shterna Soro and Eliyohu Naiditch

Children of Brocha and Yossi Feiner

**Grandchildren of Binyomin and Chana Serebryanski**

Children of Bina and Yitzchok Lerman

Children of Chaya and Bentzy Chesney

Children of Brocha Menachem Mendel Wilshanski

**Grandchildren of Chana and Sholom Raichik**

Children of Levi Yitzchok Halevi and Rishi Raichik

Children of Avrohom Aba Halevi and Chaya Mushka Raichik

**Grandchildren of Debbie and Robbie Nossbaum**

Children of Lia and Sholom Meir Pesach "Shmop" Weisbord

Children of Eli and Tammy Nossbaum

Children of Sari and Yair Givati

Children of Tali and Zalman Ainsworth

**Grandchildren of Shlomie and Shyrla Werdiger**

Children of Dov and Devorah Leah "Devi" Werdiger

Children of Maaryasha Bahdanna and Shaya Rubinstein

Children of Itta Rochel and Mattisyahu Roth

Children of Esther Chana and Marcus Silverman

Children of Freeda and Brendon Rothschild

Children of Boruch Yehuda Aryeh "Boz" and Chaya Werdiger

Children of Yehoshua Shneur Zalman and Mushky Werdiger

**Grandchildren of Chaya Malka and Yitzchok Feiglin**

Children of Haddassa and Shimon Kessler

Children of Yehudit and Binyomin "Bennie" Kazatsky

Children of Moshe Hendel and Adena Feiglin
Children of Avital and Gideon Harkhan
Children of Bracha and Avraham Yitzchok "Avreme" Cohney

**Grandchildren of Miriam and Yirmi Goldschmiedt**

Children of Yossi and Shaina Gittel "Gitty" Goldschmiedt
Children of Dvora and Zvi "Zviki" Ebert
Children of Yehuda and Toby Goldschmiedt
Children of Ori and Sari Goldschmiedt
Children of Benyomin and Sari Goldschmiedt
Children of Brocha and Simcha Shreiber

**First Generation**

Moshe Zev lived from1767 – 1829

**Second generation**

Son last name Gluskin lived in Hlusk. We do not know how many children he had.

**Third generation**

Yehoshua Gluskin

--------------

Eliezer Gluskin was born in Hlusk

**Fourth generation**
Yehoshua Gluskin lived in Loyev married Gita daughter of Don Slonim (uncle of Rebbetzin Menucha Rochel and brother of mechutan of Mittler Rebbe)
Aharon b. approximately 1840 in Garaditch or Horoditch d. 1920 in Paritch
Ber buried in Shklov Monday February 9 1863/20 Shvat 5623
Chana
Mania
Rochel
------------------
Zev Gluskin b. in Slutsk on the ninth of Elul 5619/ September 8 1859 son of Eliezer Gluskin. He is named after his ancestor Moshe Zev. No children. He had four older sisters and two younger brothers.
**Fifth generation**
Aharon Gluskin m. Esther (Wolfson) b. approx. 1840
Kayla Leiba b. 1860's d. 27 Tishrei 5698/October 1 1937
Ita b. 1868 in Loyev – 1894
Basya Riva 1878 in Loyev - 1944
Baila 1872 – 1942
Menachem Mendel b. 1878 Loyev Belarus d. 13 Kislev 1936
Nechama born approx. 1882 – 1930's
Musia born in Loyev d. 1941
Rochel Chaya d. 1941
Chana Mirel
---------
**Sixth generation**
**Grandchildren of Aharon Gluskin**
**Kayla Leiba** lived in Moscow m. Yaakov/Jacob Yitzchok Helfgott in Lvov and eventually moved to Baltimore, d. 3 Teves 5706/December 7 1945. Came to Baltimore also with help of her brother Nathan who vouched for family
Nochum d. 1949
Grisha 1893 – 1951 physician

Rachel 1893 – 1970
Miriam 1898 – 13 Shvat 5760/January 20 2000
Yevsey (Yehoshua) 1898 – 1958 Moscow physician m. Fania Polak 1904 - 1989
Isser November 28 1899 – August 15 1964
Nathan b. 1885 - 1930 physician Cook Illinois m. Nettie b. 1888
Dr. Hirsh (Grigozy, never married) d. from Tuberculosis

Gresha and Yivsei were geniuses. Jews were not allowed to go to medical school in Russia but Grisha and Yevsei were so bright exceptions were made. Both were in the Russian military to fight the Nazis. They were caught and miraculously escaped from the Nazis who would murder them immediately if they found out these" Russian military doctors" were Jews etc.
(db.yadvashem.org) Avrohom Gluskin b. 1914 Zelig Gluskin b. 1913 were both conscripted into the Russian military and killed in WW11.

**Ita** married Yosef Gutner 1864 - 1939
Yehoshua/Yevsey 1894 - 1978
Yaakov 1889 - 1974
Hertz 1891 - 1949
When Ita died Yosef married Basya Riva.
**Basya Riva m. Yosef**
Avrohom 1900 – 1941 he was a staunch communist. During Stalin's reign Avrohom was arrested and perished and in 1937 Yosef was imprisoned and killed.
**Baila** m. Yitzchok/Isaac Gurevitch 1861 – 1941 lived in Senobesk, Ukraine and later in Leningrad. Beila d. during the siege of Leningrad (which was from 8 September 1941 – 18 January 1943.)
Fraidel 1903 – 1985
Ita 1905 – 1975
Don 1907 – 1944

Esther 1908 – 1978
Aharon 1909 – 1945
Pearl 1912 – 1991
Yevsey 1916 – 1993 Yehoshua (Yevesy-moved from Moscow to USA. In his second marriage, he was married to a daughter of Rochel Minkin - Esther)
**Menachem Mendel** Gluskin m. 1909 Fraidel Rabinovitch 1888 - 13 Kislev 1929

Esther Chaya b. April 25 1911 Minsk – 30 Shevat 5775/ February 11 1975
Leah b. June 27 1914 Minsk – 1991
Sonia b. 20 Tammuz 5677/July 10 1917 – 10 Tishrei 5758/ October 11 1997

Gita b. July 6 1922 Paritch - 2014
was a scholar in Second Temple Judaism and classical Greek and Roman

**Nechama** Gluskin m. approximately 1899 to Menachem Mendel Serebryanski born approx. 1882 and died 1941 in Samarkand.
Sarah Simcha b. around 1900 d. Iyar 13 5737/May 1 1977 Munich Germany

Ita Freida 1902 - 13 Marcheshvan 5688/November 8 1927

Yehoshua Shneur Zalman (Yehoshua was added later due to illness) b. approximately 8 Teves 5664/December 27 1903 (January 10 1904) – 3 Tammuz 5751/June 15 1991
girl who died young.
M. M. Serebryanski tombstone in Samarkand

**Musya** m. Isaac Volovitch
Esther 1907
Mera
Aharon
Gitel
**Rochel Chaya** m. Isser Ginsburg d. 1941
Jacob d. 1941
Yevsey d. 1941
Gita d.1941

Aaron 1911 – 1978
**Chana Mirel** m. Avrohom Itche Glazman whose wife had died and was Rav in Burzeno, Ukraine. Step children
Chava
Eizer ?
Isser

**Seventh Generation**
**Grandchildren of Kayla Leiba and Jacob Helfgott**
Children of Nochum Helfgott m. Rose Phillips – 1974
Aaron Harry Helfgott 1910 – 1988
Doris Helfgott
------
Children of Rachel m. Moshe Minkin 1887 – 1977
Mark Minkin 1919 – 1993
Esther Minkin 1923 -1992
--------
Children of Miriam m. Benjamin Sax 1879 – 1949
Albert Sax 1931
Daniel Sax 1935 – 2016
Ruth Sax 1935 – 2007
-----------
Children of Isser Helfgott m. Anna Altshul 1899 – 1996
Leah Helfgott 1923
Leonard Michael Helfgott 1937
Esther Wilma Helfgott 1941
Dorothy Helfgott 1944 -2004

**Grandchildren of Ita and Yosef Gutner**
Children of Yaakov Gutner m. Klara Ravikovitch 1896 – 1976
Ita 1921 – 1993
Aleksandra Gutner 1926
-------
Children of Hertz Gutner m. Eugine Sverdlova 1899 – 1981
Lucia Gutner 1924

Boris Gutner 1932

--------------

Children of Yevsey Gutner m. Lubov Shneider d. 1975
Ita Gutner 1921 – 2003

**Grandchildren of Basya Riva m. Yosef Gutner**
Children of Avrohom Gutner m. Lucia Dashevski 1906 – 1996
Natalie Gutner 1930 - 1971

**Grandchildren of Baila and Isaac Gurevitch**
Children of Fraidel m. Solomon
Gita 1924 – 1989
Chaya 1926

---------

Children of Don Gurevitch m. Mania Shuler 1908 – 1978
Tamara Gurevitch 1929
Lina Gurevitch 1934

--------

Children of Aharon Gurevitch m. Lyuba Harlamova
Nona 1937 – 2016

----------

Children of Pearl Gurevitch m. Yosef Raginsky 1912 – 2002
Yuri Raginsky 1940

-------------

Children of Yevsey Gurevitch m. Chana Roberman 1921 – 1969
Baila Gurevitch 1946
Alla Gurevitch 1951

**Grandchildren of Musia and Isaac Volovitch**
Children of Esther Volovitch m. Gafan Nazirov d. 1938
Roman Nazirov 1934 – 2004

---------

Children of Mira Volovitch m. Gifter
Victor Gifter 1932

------------

Children of Aharon Volovich
Emma Volovich 1933

-------------

Children of Gitel Volovich
Elena Volovich 1938

**Grandchildren of Rochel Chaya and Isser Ginzburg**
Children of Aaron Ginsburg m. Vera Bobrik 1920 – 1994
Irina 1948
Margarita 1955

**Grandchildren of Menachem Mendel and Fraidel Gluskin**
Children of Esther Chaya m. 7 August 1936 Yitzchok Mintz 1914 -
Alexander Mintz 1940 -1992

-------

Leah m. married 1941Yosef Amusin November 29 1910 Vitebsk – June 12 1984

-----------------

Children of Gita m. Lev Vilsker 1919 - 1988 Shumsk
Menachem Mendel Emanuel Gluskin 1949 uses surname Gluskin to honor his mother's family. Electrical engineer.
Chaim Boruch Vilsker 1957 Leningrad

**Grandchildren of Nechama and Menachem Mendel Serebryanski**
Children of Ita Freida m. Elozor Noach Gorowitz b.1900 in Urovitch d. Nissan 2 1930.

Esther b. January 10 or Sukkos 5683/1922 in Urevichi (Esther was 13 when her father passed)
Zelda Rochel b. 1924 m. Yaakov Edelstein.
A boy who died at the age of 8.

Sarah Gorowitz and Zelda Rochel Edelstein buried on Mount Olives. On the stone of Sarah is written that she is a daughter of Menachem Mendel (Serebryanski) and great grandaughter of Aharon Gluskin Rabbi of Paritch.

Sarah on left, Esther on right at Zelda Rochel's wedding

Children of Yehoshua Shneur Zalman m. 1 Elul 5688/ August 17 1928 Brocha Futerfas Adar/March 1904 – 8 Teves 5749/December 16 1988

Chaim 6 Iyar 5689 / May 16 1929 – 6 Nissan 5775 / March 26 2015
Aharon "Arel" 8 Tammuz 5692 / July 12 1932
Nechama 20 Iyar 5695 / May 23 1935

**Eighth Generation**
**Grandchildren of Nochum and Rose Helfgott**
Children of Aaron Harry Helfgott m. Esther Rose Goldberg 1916 – 1991
Elen Lee Helfgott
Nora Helfgott
--------
Children of Doris Helfgott m. Milton Rosenfeld
Lisa Hillman
Boy? Hillman
-----------
**Grandchildren of Moshe and Rachel Minkin**
Children of Mark Minkin m. Ita Gutner 1921 – 1993
Vladimir Minkin 1946
Leonid Minkin 1952

**Grandchildren of Benjamin and Miriam Sax**
Children of Albert Sax m. Irene
Ben

Paul
Candy
------------
Children of Ruth Sax m. Robert I Levy 1926
Elizabeth Levy
David Bennet Levy 1967
Kathy

**Grandchildren of Isser and Ana Helfgott**
Children of Leonard Michael Helfgott m. Katherine Anderson
Isser Helfgott
Alexander
Johnathan
-----------
Children of Esther Wilma Helfgott m. Oscar Lee Feit d. 2011 n.c.
Jacqie 1963
Ian Helfgott 1964
Scott 1968
---------
Children of Dorothy Helfgott m. Mark Lazarus
Steven
Joyce
---------
Children of Leah Helfgott m. Robert Naiman
Erik
child
child

**Grandchildren of Yaakov and Klara Gutner**
Children of Ita m. Mark Minkin 1919 – 1985
Vladimir 1946
Leonid 1952
-----------
Children of Alexandra m. Zinovy Krupenin 1924 – 2007

Svetlana 1953
Alex 1956

**Grandchildren of Hertz and Eugine Gertner**
Children of Lucia Gutner m. Boris Turetsky 1928 – 1997
Maria Turetsky 1960
----------------
Children of Boris Gutner m. Rimma Potapova b. 1934
Gregory Gutner 1960

**Grandchildren of Yevsey and Lubov Gutner**
Children of Ida Gutner m. Noi Grobshteyn 1907 – 1982
Vitaly Grobshteyn 1947
Eugene Grobshteyn 1955

**Grandchildren of Fraidel and Solomon**
Children of Michael Gurevitz m. Gita 1924 - 1989
Lyuba Gurevitch 1949
-----------
Children of Chaya and Savva Sagir
Ludmila Sagir b. 1953
Alla Sagir b. 1957
--------------

**Grandchildren of Don and Mania Gurevitch**
Children of Lina Gurevitch m. Vereschagin
Valery Vereschagin
---------------

**Grandchildren of Aharon and Lyuba Gurevitch**
Children of Nona Gurevitch m. Igor Maloy 1937 – 2004
Lyuba Maloy
------------

**Grandchildren of Pearl and Yosef Raginsky**
Children of Yuri Raginsky m. Margarita Michlina b. 1946
Boris 1970
Mariya 1983
------------------

**Grandchildren of Yevsey Gurevitch and Channa**
Children of Bella m. Oleg Drozdov 1943
Anna 1973
Irina Drozdov 1978
----------------
Children of Alla m. Leonid Minkin b.1952
Natalie Minkin 1976 – 1989
Yelizaveta 1991

**Grandchildren of Esther and Gafan Nazirov**
Children of Roman m. Tamara Barishnikova
Edward Nazirov 1963
Stanislov Nazirov
----------
**Grandchildren of Mira Volovich/Gefter**
Children of Victor Gefter m. Nella
Irina Gefter 1964
-------------
**Grandchildren of Aron Volovitch**
Children of Emma m. Semen Vershlovsky
Galina Vershlovsky
---------------
**Grandchildren of Hillel Volovitch**
Children of Elena m. Uri Futritcky b. 1939
Victoria Futritcky
------------------
**Grandchildren of Aharon and Vera Ginzburg**
Children of Irina m. Vitaly Grobshtyn b. 1947
Vadim b. 1972
Natalia b. 1977
----------------
Children of Margarita m. Eugene Grobshteyn b. 1955
Roman b. 1977

**Grandchildren of Gita Gluskin and Lev Vilsker**
Children of Emanuel m. Shlomit Shalom b. 1952

Reut Esther 1982
Eitan Chaim 1985
Gili Fradel Chemda 1989
Shira Rachel 1990
---------------
Chaim Boruch Vilsker m. Katia Nimanova 1957
Michael 1984
Alexander 1985

**Grandchildren of Elozor Noach Gorowitz and Ita Freida**
Children of Esther m.1944 to Shmuel Gorowitz b. January 8 1917 in Kherson

Yitchok b. January 31 1946, Samarkand, Uzbekistan, he married Chana Devorah Rivkin b. 1947,
Ita b. 1947 the 17th of Av in Poking Germany, she married M. M. Chanzin b. 1944
Fruma b. 1949 5/6 Teves in Israel, married Dovid Teichtel

Elazar b. 10/51 Israel m. Zissel Shusterman
Nechama Miriam b. 1953 Israel m. Mordechai Tzivin
Sima Yocheved b. 1955 m. Avrohom Chazan b. 1955
Menachem Mendel Hillel b. 1961 Israel m. Taibel Gopin b.1963
Yosef Boruch 1966
-------
Children of Yaakov and Rochel Edelstein
Lozor
Faige (Sirota)
Boy d. 8 years old

**Grandchildren of Zalman and Brocha Serebryanski**
Children of Chaim Serebryanski m. 13 Sivan 5719/June 19 1959 Esther Magnes b. 17 Av 5689/August 23 1929
Yosef Yitzchok "Yossi" 3 Elul 5720/August 25 1960
Menachem Mendel 23 Tishrei 5722/October 3 1961
Basya "Bashi" 28 Menachem Av 5722/August 28 1962
Binyomin Gershon 26 Menachem Av 5723/August 15 1963
Eliyohu 24 Kislev 5725/November 29 1964
Chana Hinda 20 Menachem Av 5726/August 6 1966
Moshe Mordechai 13 Iyar 5730/May 29 1970
Nechama Dina "Doonie" 26 Iyar 5733/May 28 1973
Miriam Leah Rechel 29 Nissan 5735/April 9 1975
------------------
Children of Aharon Serebryanski m. 28 Adar 5722/April 3 1962 Zlata Skolnick b. 30 Nissan 5698/May 1 1938
Zev Wolf "Velvel" 2 Nissan 5764/March 15 1964
Levi Yitzchok 21 Av 5727/August 26 1967
Yosef "Yossi" 27 Elul 5728/September 20 1968
Rochel Leah 2 Shvat 5731/January 28 1971
Menachem Mendel 16 Iyar 5733/May 18 1973
Chanoch Hendel 2 Kislev 5740/November 22 1979
-----------------------

Children of **Nechama** Serebryanski m. 5 Kislev 5713/ November 23 1952 Nosson/Nathan Werdiger 15 Teves 5683/January 3 1923 – 15 Teves 5766/December 27 2015
Devorah "Debbie" 28 Tishrei 5714/October 7 1953
Shlomo Elimelech 6 Adar 5715/February 27 1955
Chaya Malka "Michelle" 25 Cheshvan 5717/October 30 1956
Maryasha Miriam Badana 5 Nissan 5719/April 13 1959
Menachem David 25 Tammuz 5724/July 4 1964

**Ninth Generation**
**Grandchildren of Mark and Ita Minkin**
Children of Vladimir Minkin m. Ludmila Dobriakov 1945
Sergey Minkin 1968
Catherine Minkin 1972
Nadia Minkin 1983
----------------
Children of Leonid Minkin m. Alla Gurevitch 1951
Natalie 1976 – 1989
Yelizaveta Minkin 1991

**Grandchildren of Albert and Irene Sax**
Children of Ben Sax
Boy?
Matt

**Grandchildren of Robert and Ruth Levy**
Child of David Levy (and Ariella Hasida)
Rut Gila 3 Iyar 5778/April 17 2018

**Grandchildren of Leonard and Katherine Helfgott**
Children of Isser Helfgott
Rubi Helfgott
David Helfgott

**Grandchildren of Esther Wilma and Oscar**

Children of Jacquie Helfgott and Zack Cook
Zelia Ann Cook 1998
------------------------
Children of Ian Helfgott and Susan Holmuller
Hunter Hercules Helfgott 1998
Aaron Shane Helfgott 2001
-------------------------
Children of Scott Helfgott and Bernard
Zack

**Grandchildren of Robert and Liah Naiman**
Children of Erik and Anna Naiman
Fira

**Grandchildren of Ita and Mark Minkin**
Children of Vladimir and Ludmila Dobriakov 1945
Sergey Minkin 1968
Catherine Minkin 1972
Nadia Minkin 1983
-----------------------
Children of Leonid Minkin and Alla Gurevitch 1951
Natalie Minkin 1976 – 1989
Yelizabeta Minkin 1991

**Grandchildren of Alexandra and Zinovy Krupenin**
Children of Svetlana Krupenin m. Timur Kirgizbayev 1952
Amir Kirgiz 1975
Marat Kirgiz 1977
Karim Kirgiz 1984
------------
Children of Alex Krupenin m. Marina Kovalevsky 1957
Jana Kovalevsky
------------------------
Children of Alex Krupenin m. Olga Sudakova 1957
Michael Krupenin 1981
Roman Krupenin 1984

**Grandchildren of Boris and Lucia Turetsky**
Children of Maria Turetsky and Slava Sukharev
Stanislav Sukharev 1982
Eugenia Sukharev 1988

**Grandchildren of Boris and Rimma Gutner**
Children of Gregory Gutner and Ulyana Rozhnova 1969
Sophia 2000
Jacob 2004

**Grandchildren of Ida and Noi Grobshteyn**
Children of Vitaly Grobshteyn and Irina Ginsburg 1948
Vadim Ginsburg 1972
Natalia Ginsburg 1977

------------------------

Children of Eugene Grobshteyn and Margarita Ginzburg 1955
Roman Grobshteyn 1977

**Grandchildren of Michael and Gita Gurevitch**
Children of Lyuba Gurevitch and Victor Tretyakov
Aleksey 1974

**Grandchildren of Savvita and Chaya Sagir**
Children of Ludmila Sagir and Vladimir Garnik
Iliya Garnik 1978

----------------

Children of Alla Sagir and Valery Polyakov

Yuriy Polyakov 1980
Lyuba Polyakov 1985

**Grandchildren of Nona and Igor Maloy**
Children of Lyuba Maloy and Kiryanov
Alexandra Kiryanov 1997

Gleb Kiryanov 2005

**Grandchildren of Yuriy and Margarita Raginsky**
Children of Boris Raginsky and Svetlana Gofman 1972
Michael 2000
Alex 2002
David 2008

**Grandchildren of Bella and Oleg Drozdov**
Children of Anna Drozdov and Alex Sorokin 1959
Grisha Sorokin 1991
Tania Sorokin 1999
------------------------
Children of Irina Drozdova and Maxim Levit 1976
Izabella Demy Drozdov Levit 2012

**Grandchildren of Roman and Tamara Nazirov**
Children of Edward Nazirov and Korina Zonth 1973
Lana Nazirov 2007

**Grandchildren of Emma and Semen Vershlovsky**
Children of Galina Vershlovsky
Rashel Vershlovsky

**Grandchildren of Uriy and Elena Futritckly**
Children of Victoria Futritckly
Alisa
Boy

**Grandchildren of Irina Ginsburg and Vitaly Grobshteyn**
Children of Vladim Ginsburg and Arina Abdurakhmanova
Artur Ginsburg 2002
------------------------
Children of Natalie Ginsburg and Dmitry Gershman
Matvei Gershman 2002
Sonia Gershman 2013

**Grandchildren of Eugene and Margarita Grobshteyn**
Children of Roman Grobshteyn and Lena
Anastasia Grobshteyn 2004
Eugenia Grobshteyn 2010

**Grandchildren of Emanuel and Shlomit Gluskin**
Children of Reut Esther and Ariel Golan Cohen Gabay
Tehila Mazal Cohen-Gabay 2014
Shlomo Cohen-Gabay 2016
------------------
Children of Eitan Chaim Gluskin and Ayala Raz
Naomi Gluskin 2012
Akiva Gluskin 2014
Boy 17 Cheshvan 5779 / October 26 2018
------------------
Children of Gili Fradel Chemda and Avishai Aharoni
Yadidya Aharoni 2015
------------------
Children of Shira Rachel and Omer
Lavi 2014

**Grandchildren of Chaim Boruch and Katia Vilsker**
Children of Michael Vilsker and Vered Alon 1984
Natali Alon Vilsker 2017

**Grandchildren of Chaim and Esther Serebryanski**
Children of Yosef Yitzchok Serebryanski m. Rosh Chodesh Elul 5743 / August 10 1983 Rochel Winter 7 Tammuz 5720 / July 2 1960
Shmuel Sholom 11 Menachem Av 5744 / August 10 1984
Brocha Miriam Malka 23 Iyar 5751 / May 7 1991
Chaya Mushka 6 Shvat 5753 / January 28 1993
Menachem Mendel 14 Tammuz 5755 / July 12 1995

Yosef Yitzchok second marriage 23 Elul 5767/September 6 2007 Perel Dina Winter 7 Tammuz 5712/June 30 1952

-------------

Children of Menachem Mendel Serebryanski m. 16 Sivan 5745/June 5 1985 Channa Turk 3 Teves 5725/December 8 1964

Moshe Mordechai 9 Av 5746/August 14 1986
Yosef Shmuel "Yosele" 25 Tammuz 5747/July 22 1987
Levi Yitzchok "levikle" 2 Av 5749/August 3 1989
Brocha 27 Adar 2 5752/April 1 1992
Shneur Zalman 2 Adar 5758/February 28 1998
Sholom Dov Ber 23 Sivan 5760/June 26 2000
Chanoch 11 Av 5765/August 16 2005

-------------

Children of Basya Serebryanski m. 13 Adar 1 5744/ February 16 1984 Chaim Yaakov Dalfin 19 Teves 5721/ January 7 1961

Menachem Mendel 5 Teves 5746/December 17 1985
Shterna Sara 17 Cheshvan 5748/November 9 1987
Brocha 10 Tammuz 5750/July 2 1990
Hinda Fraida 24 Shvat 5753/February 15 1993
Chaya Mushka 10 Elul 5755/September 5 1995
Baila 28 Av 5758/August 19 1998
Devorah Leah 17 Elul 5762/August 25 2002

--------------

Children of Binyomin Gershon Serebryanski m. 21 Elul 5746/September 25 1986 Chana Gorman 22 Tammuz 5727/ July 30 1967

Bina Rechel 17 Elul 5747/September 11 1987
Chaya 1 Cheshvan 5749 /October 12 1988
Brocha Soro Yehudis 26 Teves 5751/January 12 1991
Bas Sheva "Shevi" 17 Kislev 5754/December 1 1993
Nechama 20 Cheshvan 5757/November 2 1996
Menachem Mendel 30 Kislev 5763/December 4 2002

Shmuel Avrohom Zev "Shmulik" 30 Kislev 5763/ December 4 2002
Yehoshua Shneur Zalman 1 Adar 1 5760/March 8 2000
----------
Children of Eliyahu Serebryanski m. 26 Tishrei 5751/ October 16 1990 Chana Raices 5th Tishrei 5730/ Sept 17 1969
Yehoshua Shneur Zalman 10 Elul 5751/ August 20 1991
Menachem Mendel 12 Kislev 5754/November 26 1993
Shmuel Yitzchok 30 Sivan 5757/May 7 1997
Moshe Mordechai 22 Sivan 5759/June 6 1999
Nochum Aharon 13 Adar 1 5763/February 15 2003
Sholom Dovber 29 Cheshvan 5767/November 20 2006
Chanoch Hendel 5 Adar 5772/ February 28 2012
--------------
Children of Chana Hinda Serebryanski m. 7 Adar 5748/ February 25 1988 Sholom Halevi Raichik 9 Kislev 5724/ November 25 1963
Levi 21 Iyar 5749 /May 26 1989
Avrohom Abba 26 Cheshvan 5751/November 14 1990
Yehoshua Shneur Zalman 12 Adar 5754/February 23 1994
Mendel 4 Adar 5756/February 24 1996
Shmuel Dovid 6 Iyar 5758/ May 2 1998
Moshe 19 Nissan 5761/ April 12 2001
Brocha 21 Nissan 5763/April 23 2003
Chaya 27 Adar 1 5765 /March 7 2005
----------
Children of Moshe Mordechai Serebryanski m. 28 Sivan 5754/June 7 1994 Bluma Edelman 25 Adar 5732//March 11 1972
Yoel 27 Kislev 5756/December 20 1995
Yehoshua Shneur Zalman 16 Adar 2 5763/March 20 2003
Eliyohu 12 Sivan 5770/May 25 2010
Lea 7 Shvat 5775/January 27 2015
--------

Children of Nechama Dina Serebryanski m. 11 Adar 2 5755/March 13 1995 Yosef Yitzchok "Yoske" Mishulovin 6 Shvat 5729/January 25 1969
Basya "Bassie" 17 Shvat 5756/February 6 1996
Brocha 19 Kislev 5759/December 8 1999
Chaya Aidel "Aidy" 27 Av 5765/September 1 2005
--------
Children of Miriam Serebryanski m. 28 Tishrei 5756/ October 22 1995 Yaakov Menachem Mendel Simon 13 Adar 1 5730/February 19 1970
Yehoshua Shneur Zalman 16 Elul 5756/August 31 1966
Chaya Henya 25 Teves 5758/January 22 1998
Moshe 11 Cheshvan 5760/October 21 1999
Boruch Shloma Yehuda 23 Elul 5761/September 11 2001
Basya 5 Tishrei 5766/October 8 2005
Levi Yitzchok 6 Tishrei 5768/September 18 2007
Brocha 5 Adar 1 5771/February 9 2011
Chaim 11 Tishrei 5776/September 24 2015

**Grandchildren of Arel and Zlata Serebryanski**
Children of Levi Yitzchok Serebryanski m. 17 Kislev 5760/ November 25 1999 Chaya Leah 7 Nissan 5728/April 5 1968
Shira Devorah 11 Shvat 5761/February 4 2001
Yehoshua Shneur Zalman 8 Elul 5763/September 5 2003
Rivka Sara 22Tishrei 5766/October 25 2005
Menachem Mendel 28 Tishrei 5770/October 16 2009
Shimon 23 Iyar 5773/May 3 2013
------------
Children of Yosef "Yossi" Serebryanski m. 15 Shvat 5752 Chana Rochel Krinsky 16 Tishrei 5731/October 16 1970
Menachem Mendel 27 Tammuz 5761/July 18 2001
Perel 8 Cheshvan 5770/October 26 2009
Shaina Brocha 8 Cheshvan 5770/October 26 2009
Chaya Mushka 18 Adar 5773/February 28 2013
---------------

Children of Rochel Leah Serebryanski m. 11 Adar 5754/ February 22 1994 Menachem Mendel Lipsker 9 Av
Yosef Yitzchok 6 Shvat 5755/January 7 1995
Chaya Mushka 20 Kislev 5760/November 29 1999
Yisroel Aryeh Leib "Leiby" 14 Tishrei 5763/September 20 2002
Shmuel 20 Cheshvan 5764/November 5 2003
Yehoshua Shneur Zalman 27 Elul 5766/September 20 2006
Yaakov Yehuda "Yanki" 2 Shvat 5773/January 13 2013
Brocha 6 Sivan 5776/June 12 2016

------------

Children of Menachem Mendel Serebryanski m. 21 Elul 5759/September 2 1999 Nechama Dina "Chomie" Bernstein 14 Cheshvan 5737/November 7 1976
Chaya Mushka 3 Tammuz 5761/June 24 2001
Brocha Rivka 21 Elul 5762/August 29 2002
Raizel 6 Teves 5764/December 31 2003
Zalman 14 Tishrei 5766/October 17 2005
Levi Yitzchok "Yitzi" 24 Cheshvan 5768/November 5 2007
Freida 4 Sivan 5769/May 26 2009
Yisroel Aryeh Leib "Leibel" 4 Shvat 5773/January 15 2013
Avrohom Efrayim "Avi" 7 Cheshvan 5776/October 20 2015

------

Children of Chanoch Hendel Serebryanski m. 27 Tishrei 5765/October 12 2004 Shoshana Esther "Shoshi" 24 Tammuz
Chaya Mushka 14 Adar 5766/March 14 2006
Baila 2 Elul
Brocha Simcha 14 Tishrei
Rochel Leah Sivan 5769/2016

**Grandchildren of Nechama and Nosson Werdiger**

Children of Devorah "Debbie" Werdiger m. 14 Av 5733/ August 1 1973 Robert "Robbie" Nossbaum 18 Tammuz 5712/July 11 1952
Lia 11Elul 5736/September 6 1976

Eli 6 Av 5738 / August 9 1978
Sari 25 Adar 1 5741 / March 1 1981
Tali 29 Elul 5744 / September 26 1984
------
Children of Shlomo Elimelech Werdiger m. 22 Adar 5740 / March 10 1980 Shyrla Pakula 19 Cheshvan 5716 / November 4 1955
Maaryasha Bahdanna 15 Teves 5741 / December 22 1980
Dov 15 Teves 5741 / December 22 1980
Itta Rochel 26 Adar 5742 / March 21 1982
Esther Chana 4 Adar 2 5744 / March 8 1984
Freda 29 Adar 1 5746 / March 10 1986
Boruch Yehuda Aryeh "Boz" 29 Adar 5748 / March 18 1988
Yehoshua Shneur Zalman 4 Elul 5751 / August 14 1991
-----
Children of Michelle Werdiger m. 4 Teves 5736 / December 8 1975 Yitzchok Feiglin 13 Elul 5712 / September 3 1952
Haddassa 7 Adar 5739 / March 6 1979
Yehudit 11 Tammuz 5741 / July 13 1981
Moshe Hendel 13 Teves 5744 / December 19 1983
Avital 18 Kislev 5746 / December 1 1986
Bracha 4 Tammuz 5750 / June 27 1990
Yehoshua Shneur Zalman 24 Kislev 5756 / December 17 1995
-------
Children of Maryasha Miriam Badana Werdiger m. 13 Elul 5739 / September 5 1979 Yirmiyahu "Yirmi" Goldshmiedt 2 Teves 5718 / December 24 1957
Yossi 11 Tammuz 5741 / July 13 1981
Dvora 26 Tishrei 5743 / October 13 1982
Yehuda 10 Menachem Av 5744 / August 8 1984
Ori 22 Adar 2 5746 / April 2 1986
Benyomin 3 Tammuz 5750 / June 26 1990
Brocha 6 Shvat 5754 / January 18 1994
-----

Children of David Werdiger m. 26 Kislev 5750/December 24 1989 Adira Kaploun 8 Av 5732/July 19 1972
Shua 14 Teves 5752/December 21 1991
Caylee 24 Kislev 5754/December 8 1993
Aharon Moshe Yitzchok "Ari" 22 Shvat 5754/February 2 1994
Aliza Devorah 2 Teves 5760/December 11 1999
Sarah Bailey 29 Av 5762/July 29 2002
Raphael Shlomo Elimelech "Rafi" 18 Teves 5768/December 27 2007

**Grandchildren of Esther and Shmuel Halevi Gorowitz**
Children of Yitzchok "Itche" Halevi m. Chana Devorah Rivkin b. 1947
Shaina Basha
Menachem Mendel
Nechama Dina
Hinda
Zelda Rochel
Risha Brocha
Elka
Sara Alta
Sholom Dov Ber
Baila Rivka
Yosef

Children of Ita and Menachem Mendel Chanzin
-------------
Children of Fruma and Dovid Teichtel b. 1948
Yudi
Yitzchok
Nechama Brod
Eschnat Elka Teichtel
Sarah Deutsch
Osnat Brod
----------------

Children of Elozor Gurevitch m. Zissel Shusterman
Yitzchok
Zushe
Shneur Zalman
Yisroel
Yosef
Eli
--------------
Children of Nechama Miriam m. Mordechai "Motti" Tzivin
------------------
Children of Sima Yocheved and Avrohom Yehuda Chazan b. 1955 Moscow
Levi Yitzchok Chazan b. January 10 1979 Lod Israel m. Aidy
Sholom Dovber November 14 2002
Ita March 1 2005
Shneur Zalman Eliezer January 19 2008
Menachem Mendel
----------------------
Children of Racheli b. April 5 1980 m. Yossi Klein
Mendy May 11 2003
Moti January 1 2006
Aharon April 10 2009
Rivka November 23 2001
Rikki
---------------------------
Children of Sholom Ber Chazan b. 1981 m. Henia Naparstek
Reuven Meir
Esther
Chaya Mushka
Hillel
Leizer July 25 1985
Yisrolik
Chani m. Lishner

Chaya Mushka m. Kuperman
Sarah m. Kastel
Motti Chazan
---------------
Children of Menachem Mendel Hillel Gurevitch m. Taibel Gopin b. 1963
Baila m. Shmulik Shaikevitz
Levi Yitzchok
Chaya Mushka

**Tenth generation**
**Grandchildren of Vladimir and Ludmila**
Children of Sergey Minkin m. Tatiana Bondarenko b.1977
Maximilian Minkin 2009
Yelizaveta Minkin 2012
------------------
Children of Catherine Minkin m. Denis Zaharov
Konstantin Zaharov 2007
---------------------------
**Grandchildren of Svetlana and Timur Kirgizbayev**
Children Amir Kirgiz m. Luba Khomskaya
Alisa Kirgiz 2001
Maya Kirgiz 2009
Leana Kirgiz 2012
---------------------------
Children of Marat Kirgiz m. Asya Marchak
Nicole Kirgiz 2003
Veniamin Kirgiz 2005
Eli Kirgiz 2008
Zalman Kirgiz 2010
Meir Shaya 22 Kislev 5779 / November 29 2018
----------------------------
**Grandchildren of Alex Krupenin and Marina**
Children of Michael Krupenin m. Elena Evtyukhina b. 1982
Oleg Krupenin 2003
--------------------

Children of Roman Krupenin m. Natasha
Vasily Krupenin 2012
Peter Krupenin 2014
-----------------------

**Grandchildren of Vitaly and Irina Ginzburg**
Children of Vadim Ginzburg m. Arina Abdurakhmano
Artur Ginzburg 2002
------------------

Children of Natalie Ginzburg m. Dmitry Gershman
Matvei Gershman 2002
Sonia Gershman 2013
-----------------

**Grandchildren of Eugene and Margarita Grobshteyn**
Children of Roman Grobshteyn and Lena
Anastasia Grobshteyn 2004
Euginia Grobshteyn 2004
----------------

**Grandchildren of Yitzchok and Chana Gorowitz**
Children of Menachem Mendel Gorowitz m. Chana Rochel
Yehoshua
Avrohom Dovid
Yekusiel "Kushe"
Shneur Zalman
Sholom
Chaya Mushka
Aryeh Leib
--------------

Children of Shaina Basha m. Efraim Shmuel Mintz
Avremi
Levi
Isaac
Sholom
Chaya
Yosef
Mendel
Shua

--------------

Children of Nechama Dina m. Yehuda Leib Kantor
Mussie
Rivka
Liba
Mendy
Hindy
Miriam
Moshe Pinchas
Esty
Shayna Shulamis

-----------------------

Children of Hinda m. Yosef Hakohen Friedman
Chaya Mushka
Menachem Mendel
Shaina Gittel
Faiga Elka
Meir
Rochel Leah
Mordechai
Shmuel
Breina

---------------------

Children of Zelda Rochel m. Mendy Greenbaum
Yosef
Chaya S.
Shneur Zalman
Levi
Mushka

--------------------

Children of Risha Brocha m. Levi Gurevitch
Menachem Mendel
Esther
Chaya Mushka

--------------------

Children of Sholom Dov Ber Gurevitch m.Mushky

Rashi
Esther
----------------------
Children of Elka m. Levi Yitzchok Kaplan
Mendel
Shraga
Mussie
Boruch Sholom
Yehudis
Sarah
-------------------------
Children of Children of Sara Alta m. Moshe Lieberman
Levi
Chaya
Mendel
Shua
Esther
------------------------
Children of Baila Rivka m. Chaim Fischer
Pessy
Mendel
Chaya
Shayna
Esther
-------------------
Children of Yosef Gorowitz m. Chana Devorah
Estee
Elka
Mushka
Tzivi
Chaim
Hudi
Hinda
------------------------
Children of Chaya Mushka m. Dovber Wolvovsky
Hinda

Dovid
Mendel
------------

**Grandchildren of Yossi and Rochie Serebryanski**
Children of Shmuel Sholom Serebryanski m. 14 Sivan 5768/June 17 2008 Faige Rivka Borenstein 28 Elul 5744/ September 25 1984
Menachem Mendel 2 Iyar 5769/April 25 2009
Chaya Mushka "Musya" 26 Adar 2 5771/April 1 2011
Aizik 6 Adar 5773/February 16 2013
Chana 17 Sivan 5775/June 4 2015
Devorah Leah 7 Nissan 5778/March 22 2018
----------------
Chaya Mushka Serebryanski m. Cheshvan 9 5777/ November 10 2016 Shlomo Willick Nissan 17 5746/April 26 1986
------------------
**Grandchildren of Mendel and Chana Serebryanski**
Children of Moshe Mordechai Serebryanski m. 24 Sivan 5769/June 16 2009 Sheina Mushka Raskin b. 23 Nissan 5748/April 10 1988
Shimon 21 Nissan 5770/April 5 2010
Yehoshua Shneur Zalman 15 Kislev 5772/December 11 2011
Bluma 16 Av 5773/July 23 2013
----------
Yosef Shmuel Serebryanski m. 26 Menachem Av 5772/ August 14 2012 Raizel Aber 17 Nissan 5750/April 12 1990
Nechama 15 Av 5773/July 22 2013
Meir 2 Shvat 5775/January 22 2015
Devorah Leah 9 Shvat 5778/January 25 2018
------------------
Levi Yitzchok m. 7 Kislev 5779/November 15 2018 Rochel Ulanovsky 25 Kislev 5752/December 2 1991
-----------

Brocha m. 12 Kislev 5779/November 20 2018 Zev Akiva Aron 11 Shvat 5751/January 26 1991

-----------

**Grandchildren of Bashi and Chaim Dalfin**

Children of Menachem Mendel Dalfin m. 5 Tammuz 5768/July 8 2008 Dassi Katz 10 Adar 5747/March 11 1987

Yeshaya 13 Nissan 5769/April 7 2009

Miriam 28 Adar 2 5771/March 27 2011

Yehoshua Shneur Zalman "Zalmy" 20 Teves 5773/January 2 2013

Chaya 1 Sivan 5776/June 7 2016

Geula Brocha Sheina 3 Shvat 5779/January 9 2019

-----

Children of Shterna Soro Dalfin m. 17 Sivan 5769/June 9 2009 Eliyohu Naiditch 24 Kislev 5747/December 26 1986

Miriam "Maya" 8 Nissan 5771/April 12 2011

Yehoshua Sholom "Shua" 22 Adar 5774/February 22 2014

Shlomo 6 Iyar 5777/May 2 2017

-------

Children of Brocha Dalfin m. 12 Teves 5774/December 15 2013 Yossi Feiner 4 Shvat 5745/January 26 1985

Mina 27 Nissan 5776/April 5 2016

Moshe 27 Nissan 5776/April 5 2016

Yitzchok Shlomo 5 Av 5778/July 17 2018

----------------

Chaya Mushka m. 26 Adar 1 5779/March 3 2019 Yeshaya Hakohen Katz 25 Shvat 5752/January 30 1992

--------------------

**Grandchildren of Binyomin and Chana**

Children of Bina Serebryanski m. 5 Teves 5770/December 22 2009 Yitzchok Lerman 25 Teves 5747/January 26 1987

Devorah Leah 1 Cheshvan 5771/October 9 2010

Tzivia 6 Sivan 5772/May 27 2012

Aron 28 Sivan 5774/June 25 2014

Menucha 20 Av 5777/August 12 2017

-----------

Children of Chaya Serebryanski m. 9 Shvat 5776/January 19 2016 Bentzy Chesney 3 Elul 5747/August 28 1987
Leiba 6 Cheshvan 5777/November 7 2016
Chaim 26 Teves 5778/January 13 2018
---------
Children of Brocha Serebryanski m. 15 Shvat 5776/January 25 2016 Menachem Mendel Wilshanski 12 Av 5751/July 23 1991
Goldy 10 Cheshvan 5777/November 10 2016
Basya 27 Av 5778/August 8 2018
-------------------
**Granchildren of Eli and Chana Serebryanski**
Menachem Mendel m. 12 Kislev 5777December 12 2016 Shaina Nechama Gammal 26 Shvat 5755/January 25 1995
Chaim 7 Cheshvan 5778/October 26 2017
-----------------
**Grandchildren of Chana and Sholom Raichik**
Children of Levi Yitzchok Halevi Raichik m. 3 Nissan 5772/March 26 2012 Risha Slava 12 Av 5751/July 23 1991
Menachem Mendel 12 Cheshvan 5774/October 16 2013
Chaya Mushka "Mussie" 7 Cheshvan 5776/October 20 2015
-----------------------
Children of Avrohom Aba Halevi Raichik m. 11 Sivan 5774/June 9 2014 Chaya Mushka Piekarski 23 Tishrei 5754/October 8 1993
Leah 6 Iyar 5775/April 25 2015
Chaim 30 Tishrei 5777/November 1 2016
Sima Nechama 20 Nissan 5778/April 5 2018
-------------------
Yehoshua Shneur Zalman m. Chana Gourarie 25 Adar 5777/March 23 2017
Chaim 6 Nissan 5778/21 March 2018
Elimelech 22Av 5779/August 23 2019
---------------------------

**Grandchildren of Moshe Mordechai and Bluma Serebryanski**
Yoel m. 5 Elul 5778 / August 23 2018 Chaya Mushka Plotkin 15 Nissan 5758 / April 11 1998
Chaim 25 Sivan 5779 / June 28 2019
-----------------

**Grandchildren of Yoske and Doonie Mishulovin**
Basya m. 19 Adar 5778 / March 6 2018 Menachem Mendel Cohen 9 Shvat 5756 / January 30 1996
Brocha 16 Shvat 5779 / January 20 2019
-------------------------

**Grandchildren of Mendy and Miriam Simon**
Shneur Zalman m. 12 Elul 5778 / August 23 2018 Rina Ben Chayun 30 Nissan 5758 / April 26 1998
---------------

**Grandchildren of Debbie and Robbie Nossbaum**
Children of Lia Nossbaum m. 21 Shvat 5758 / February 17 1998 Sholom Meir Pesach "Shmop" Weisbord 10 Tishrei 5734/ October 6 1973
Ariela Bracha 6 Adar 5759 / February 22 1999
Reuven Yonah 29 Iyar 5761 / May 22 2001
Dalia 28 Kislev 5769 / December 19 2006
Koby 11 Tishrei 5772 / October 9 2011
------

Children of Eli Nossbaum m. 4 Nissan 5763 / April 6 2003 Tammy Holzer 27 Av 5743 / August 6 1983
Daniel Shimshon 11 Shvat 5767 / January 30 2007
Akiva Pinchas 7 Sivan 5769 / May 30 2009
Joshua 2 Elul 5773 / August 8 2013
Avigail Sara 10 Cheshvan 5778 / October 30 2017
--------------

Children of Sari Nossbaum m. 15 Tammuz 5769 / July 7 2009 Yair Givati 27 Av 5739 / August 20 1979
Yakira Rivkah 8 Elul 5772 / August 26 2012
Hyla Maya 20 Kislev 5775 / December 12 2014

Natanel Tishrei 5778

-------

Children of Tali Nossbaum m. 16 Av 5767/July 31 2007
Zalman Ainsworth 3 Teves 5743/December 19 1982
Mati 17 Elul 5769/Sept 6 2009
Abi 28 Adar 5772/March 22 2012
Emunah Bracha "Emmy" 6 Kislev 5775/November 28 2014
Boy 2 Elul 5778/August 13 2018

--------------------

**Grandchildren of Shlomie and Shyrla Werdiger**
Children of Dov Werdiger m. 14 Elul 5764/August 31 2004
Devorah Leah "Devi" Shlomo 10 Av 5742/July 30 1982
Freeda 17 Sivan 5765/24 June 24 2005
Yehoshua Shneur Zalman 19 Kislev 5767/10th December 2006
Rivka Naava 27 Sivan 5769/19 June 19 2009
Naomi 22 Teves 5772/January 17 2012
Nosson/Nathan 9 Adar 2 5776/March 19 2016
Yeshaya Chaim Tishrei 5779/Sukkos 2018

---------

Children of Maaryasha Bahdanna m. 1 Nissan 5767/20 March 2007 Shaya Rubinstein 3 Tammuz 5743/June 14 1983
Zohar Yosef Ohr Tzion 4 Teves 5770/December 21 2009
Selah Yehudah Lavi 11 Tammuz 5773/June 19 2013
Natan Mordechai Ziv 6 Adar 2 5776/March 16 2016

-------------

Children of Itta Rochel m. 26 Av 5765/August 31 2005
Mattisyahu Roth 25 Sivan 5738/June 30 1978
Yalta 5 Adar 1 5768/February 11 2008
Freda Belle 29 Iyar 5770/May 13 2010
Rashi 9 Adar 2 5774/March 11 2014
Zayit Nishaela Elul "Olive" 1 Elul 5776/September 5 2016

--------------

Children of Esther Chana m. 19 Sivan 5774/June 17 2014 Marcus Silverman January 19 1984
Nathan Akiva 5 Sivan 5776/June 11 2016

---------------

Children of Freeda m. 11 Av 5770/July 22 2010 Brendon Rothschild 16 Tishrei 5746/October 21 1985
Yehuda Raphael 3 Cheshvan 5773/October 19 2012

--------------

Children of Boruch Yehuda Aryeh "Boz" Werdiger m. 3 Elul 5772/August 21 2012 Chaya Denebeim 9 Tammuz 5750/July 2 1990
Malya Chana Werdiger 27 Kislev 5774/November 30 2013

-------------------

Children of Yehoshua Shneur Zalman Werdiger m. 1 Nissan 5773/March 12 2013 Mushky Kershenbaum
Fania Luria Werdiger 5 Av 5776/August 9 2016
Freda Ruby

--------------

**Grandchildren of David and Adira Werdiger**
Joshua m. Caylee Rachael Hyman 17 Adar 5775/March 8 2015
Aharon Moshe Yitzchok "Ari" m. Bat Sheva Vogel 14 Tammuz 5778/June 27 2018

--------------

**Grandchildren of Chaya Malka and Yitzchok Feiglin**
Children of Haddassa Feiglin m. 17 Kislev 5759/December 6 1998 Shimon Kessler 3 Adar 2 5736/March 5 1976
Tzvi Arye "Ari" 16 Kislev 5760/November 25 1999
Ayala – 16 Iyar 5761/May 9 2001
Penina Leah – 21 Iyar 5765/May 30 2005
Rivka Brocha "Rikki" – 8 Teves 5768/Dec 17 2007
Eliora – 5 Adar 5772/February 28 2012

---------------

Children of Yehudit Feiglin m. 22 Sivan 5762/2 June 2002 Binyomin "Bennie" Kazatsky 7 Iyar 5739/4 May 1979
Tova Shulamis 22 Cheshvan 5767/13 November 2006

Ellie 28 Sivan 5768 / I July 2008
Talya 9 Nissan 5771 / April 13 2011
Aviva 10 Shvat 5775 / January 30 2015
----------------

Children of Moshe Hendel Feiglin m. 20 Sivan 5767 / June 6 2007 Adena Firstman 20 Sivan 5743 / June 1 1983
Teruah Siman Geulah 20 Elul 5768 / September 20 2008
Nahara 11 Teves 5772 / January 6 2012
Kamiya 3 Elul 5773 / August 9 2013
Natan Tzur Yisroel 18 Elul 5776 / September 21 2016
--------------

Children of Avital Feiglin m. 19 Adar 2 5768 / March 26 2008 Gideon Harkhan 14 Av 5742 / August 3 1982
Neriya Yosef Hoshaya 19 Tishrei 5770 / October 7 2009
Hillel Aharon 27 Elul 5774 / September 22 2014
Shalva 27 Elul 5774 / September 22 2014
Elnatan 4 Tishrei 5779 / September 13 2018
-----------------------------------

Children of Bracha Feiglin m. 12 Sivan 5771 / June 14 2011 Avraham Yitzchok "Avreme" Cohney 10 Cheshvan 5747 / November 2 1987
Levana Tzipora 12 Elul 5772 / August 30 2012
Eden Emunah 4 Teves 5777 / January 2 2017
--------------------------

**Grandchildren of Miriam and Yirmi Goldschmiedt**

Children of Yossi Goldschmiedt m. 18 Iyar 5763 / May 20 2003 Shaina Gittel "Gitty" Schmidt 6 Shvat 5744 / January 10 1983
Elazar "Eli" 16 Shvat 5764 / February 7 2004
Esti 17 Shvat 5766 / February 14 2006
Efraim 5 Kislev 5768 / November 15 2007
Binyomin 19 Tammuz 5770 / July 1 2010
Bracha 11 Tammuz 5772 / July 1 / 2012
Shloime Zalman 14 Cheshvan 5775 / November 6 2014
----------

Children of Dvora Goldschmiedt m. 4 Tammuz 5764/June 23 2004 Zvi "Zviki" Ebert 27 Tammuz 5741/July 29 1981
Ahuva 17 Tammuz 5765/July 24 2005
Faigy 14 Tishrei 5767/October 6 2006
Binyomin 9 Adar 5769/March 4 2009
Menachem 11 Adar 5772/March 5 2012
Rachi 27 Shvat 5775/February 16 20015
---------

Children of Yehuda Goldschmiedt m. 1 Cheshvan 5767/ October 3 2005 Toby Gottleib 15 Tammuz 5748/July 1 1988
Yosef Binyomin "Yamin" 20 Tishrei 5767/October 12 2006
Chaim 11 Tishrei 5769/October 10 2008
Yehoshua Shneur Zalman "Shuki' 20 Elul 5770/August 30 2010
Shevi 14 Teves 5773/December 27 2012
Rochel Leah 5 Iyar 5775/April 24 2015
-------------

Children of Ori Goldschmiedt m. 20 Shvat Sari Aschkenazy 3 Adar 5747/March 4 1987
Reuven "Ruvi" 2 Elul 5768 /September 2 2008
Chani 2 Menachem Av 5770/July 13 2010
Yehuda "Yudi" 27 Teves 5773/January 9 2013
Nosson 14 Adar 5777/March 11 2017
----------

Children of Benyomin Goldschmiedt m. 2 Teves 5772/ December 28 2011 Sari Weinberg 29 Cheshvan 5751/ November 17 1990
Chaya Leah 12 Iyar 5773/April 22 2013
Brachi 2 Menachem Av 5775/July 18 2015
----------

Children of Brocha Goldschmiedt m. 4 Cheshvan 5774/ October 8 2013 Simcha Shreiber 20 Teves 5754/January 3 1994
Binyomin 22 Elul 5774/September 17 2014
Esther "Esti" 11 Kislev 5776/November 23 2015
Nossen 10 Sivan 5777/June 4 2017

# Why Genealogical Research Matters in General

by David Levy

Knowing your past helps you understand your present.

In antiquity and current times genealogy knowledge matters. In the Beit Hamikdash there were 24 rotations of Kohanim and Leveim. The Mishnah notes that musical instruments were played as the priests were rounded up from small villages and brought "up" to Jerusalem. This bringing up is a halakhic principle in that even the loaves of Challah that were on marble tables at the end of the mamadot rotation was transferred to a gold table. Thus, one always rises in holiness. Joseph mentions a Royal Archives on Har Habayit that Herod burnt down to obscure the fact that his mother was a Idumian princess and his father a ger. The Talmud in Ketubot mentions that to marry a bat Kohen one must have pristine yichus back 5 generations, some opinions hold 10 generations. It was so tragic when Herod had his wife Miriam's, [who he embalmed in honey], brother, Jason HaKohen, drowned in a swimming pool in Jericho and covered it up to look like a swimming accident. You see Miriam's brother was a direct and perhaps the only clearly traceable genealogical link to the Tzadakite priesthood to the Beit Rishon. When Mashiach arrives, we are told that the tribes will be distinct as when they marched through the 12 walls of clear water at Shirat HaYam Kriat Yamsuf. In the third Temple genealogy will decide who serves and Mashiach will know where each person belongs. In antiquity proof of such yichus was taken very seriously and seen as an important aspect required for priestly service. While some opinions hold that a mumzer who is a Talmud Chakham trumps a kohen who is an am ha-aretz. In general, showing that the "crown" of Torah learning is greater than the kehunah (priestly genealogy) and malchut (royalty) as per its various pirushim in Pirke Avot regarding the 3 crowns and their ranking. Yet in Maseket Berachot even Rabbinic leadership most often gave great respect and privilege to the ability to testify to a pure blood line of Jewish motherhood going back as far as possible. Thus, Rabbi Eleazar is chosen to be Rosh Yeshivah of the Sanhedrin in MS. Berachot because: "Hu Chakham, Hu Ashir, and Hu Asar Li-Ezra" (he is wise, he is wealthy, and he could count his genealogy back to Ezra Hasofer). That is why Rabbi Elazar was chosen to be head of the court when Rabban Gamliel was deposed for insulting Rabbi Yehoshua (a learned rabbi who earned his livelihood as a coal smith) over the question whether the evening shema is mandatory or optional in a public minyan. Tannaim like Rabbi Tarfon openly made known his priestly genealogy and great admiration was held for this sages yichus. Even a more assimilated secular writer, such as Josephus' prided himself on being a Kohen, and even the Roman nobles acknowledged his upright genealogical merit.

The genealogical research will describe the methods, strategies, and reliance at times on pure luck, Hashgahah Pratit, serendipity to uncover my family history of various members of the Levy-Gluskin family and place this account in its historical context. For example, there are more chances of being hit by a meteorite than being neighbors with Rabbi Dovid Katz of Baltimore whose father received semichah from Rabbi Eliezer Rabinowitch of Minsk- the father in law of my grandmother's brother

Rav Menachem Gluskin (ztsl). What luck to meet Haym Sheninn former rare books librarian at Graetz who did his dissertation under my great aunt Dr. Gita Gluskina! What chance to bump into a relative of the Gluskin Levy yichus while davening at the Kotel on a recent trip to Yerushalayim! The testimony is peppered with primary sources including interviews and many secondary sources in Hebrew. It notes some individuals who made major impacts in their Jewish community, Judaism, cultural history at large, and Eretz Yisrael. Rabbi Moshe Zev Gluskin (ztsl) was a confidant of Reb Chaim of Volozhin and gave a Hesped for the GRA whom he visited numerous times. Rabbi Mendel Gluskin (zts) was the last chief Rabbi (Av Bet Din) in Minsk. Rav Menacham Mendel was the son in law of Rabbi Eliezer Rabinowitch who in turn was the son in law of the Minsker Gadol, Rabbi Eliyahu Pearlman (Ztsl). Both Rav Menchem Mendel and Rabbi Eliezer Rabinowitch were imprisoned by the Communists for the actions on behalf of Yiddishkeit in the USSR under the surveillance of the KGB. The Gluskin family via Rabbi Aaron Gluskin of Paritich (Rabbi after the Chabad Luminary Rabbi Hillel of Paritich, son of Rabbi Yehoshua of Loyev who married the daughter of Rabbi Dan of Slonim who stems from Rashi and on his father's side from the Maharal of Prague among Rabbinic scholars and Tzadikim. The latter history of his long Rabbinic dynasty shows that there are many insights into life of Jews under persecution in the USSR and Rabbinic life in general that comes to light in the journey of uncovering this illustrious rabbinic past in Eastern Europe. This illustrious Rabbinic history also is peppered with bringing to center stage from the margins the Rebbetzins, scholars, and devoted wives, mothers, and daughters. There we see the personal side of the family as when in an interview Dr. Gita Gluskin remarked to me "all the women had crushes on Saul Lieberman who they felt was very good looking

(Lieberman was the brother in law of Rav Menachem Mendel Gluskin (ztsl), as Lieberman's 1st wife was Rochelle Rabinowitch and Rav Menachem's wife was Fraidl Rabinowitch. We learn from such anecdotes little hints of the personal lives of these family members. Thus, the overall book is not a Hagiographic work, but rather recoups the role of womens' history and the exemplary roles of individual women in my family and bring them center stage from the margins of rabbinic history. This is a journey for sacred MEMORY, as the Besht, notes, "Bizikranot yesh ha-geulah". We cannot do justice to the present unless we remember and learn from the noble deeds of our ancestors. Further we cannot know where we are going unless we know where we have walked in generations before us. This teaches us to trust the future, remember the past, and live the present informed and guided by the light of the holy soul sparks that shine as glistening "names" in Gan Eden. This book is not so much one in search of Yichus rather it is a journey to uncover the misrat nefesh of our ancestors who sacrificed to be proud Jews in trying times, for we are mere dwarfs in ruchnius, intellectual virtue, and moral and spiritual middot compared to our forefathers in Eastern Europe. We can only know where we are going if we walk by the light of their inspiring examples It is an attempt to turn to the past to guide the future, to make us better persons, seeking wisdom from the elders, as parasha Hazinu enjoins: זְכֹר יְמוֹת עוֹלָם, בִּינוּ שְׁנוֹת דֹּר-וָדֹר; שְׁאַל אָבִיךָ וְיַגֵּדְךָ, זְקֵנֶיךָ וְיֹאמְרוּ לָךְ

## Why Genealogical Research Matters for the Gluskin family and cousins by DBL

Interest in ancestors of the Gluskin family is a personal quest not merely a genealogical project, but for historical clarity about the life of our previous family members in previous generations, in Eastern Europe, and their scholarly activities as part of a journey for MEMORY, as the Besht, notes, "Bizikranot yesh ha-geulah". We cannot do justice to the present unless we remember and learn from the noble deeds of our ancestors. Further we cannot know where we are going unless we know where we have walked in generations before us. This teaches us to trust the future, remember the past, and live the present informed and guided by the light of the holy soul sparks that shine as glistening "names" in Gan Eden. My book is not so much one in search of Yichus. It is a journey to uncover the misrat nefesh of our ancestors, for we are mere dwarfs in ruchnius, intellectual virtue, and moral and spiritual middot compared to our forefathers in Eastern Europe. We can only know where we are going if we walk by the light of their inspiring examples. Yet I am not writing Hagiography.

Personally, the academic example of research librarian Dr. Aryeh Vilsker who suffered greatly from persecution of Jews in Russia by the Communists, is a role model I can only hope to emulate a tincture of, as Dr. Vilsker was a great research librarian beyond any measure of Judaica research librarians today and recent times. see AJL Charlottesville Proceedings at http://databases.jewishlibraries.org/node/51186 Dr. Vilsker orbits with great Jewish librarians such as Umberto Cassutto, Gershom Scholem, Menachem Schmelzer, and Malachi Beit Ari. Yet the models of Rabbis in our ancestry the likes of Rav Menachem Mendel Gluskin who also suffered under the Communists, great Av bet danyanim such as Rabbi Aaron Gluskin of Paritch, Rabbi Yehoshua Gluskin of Loyev, and Rabbi Moshe Zev Gluskin provide spiritual and moral/ethical examples as well as magnanimous greatness in the realm of intellect from which we have aions to learn from.

As per research of Dr. Rabbi Moshe Shualy (dissertation Dropsie College) Kohanide and Levitical families kept great care in preserving geneological documentation of ancestry in order to serve in the beit HaMikdash as part of the process of the Mamadot, or the going up to Jerusalem from the outskirts and villages described in the Mishnah as a ceremony whereby Kohanim and Leveim were rounded up with the accompaniment of music and procession to go up to the Jerusalem Temple to serve in 24 rotations during the year. Each rotation (mamadot) involved the elevation of 12 hallot from a marble table to a gold table to illustrate the process of elevating in kedushah. The Beit HaMikdash archive of yichusin was finally destroyed by fire in 70 C.E. by the Romans (Jos.Wars 6:354). The Sanhedrin examined the purity of priestly descent, on the basis of genealogical tables (Megillat or Sefer Yuhasin) which are known to have been preserved in the Beit HaMikdash. In Yevamot 5:4 we read, רבי שמעון בן עזאי אומר מצאתי מגילת יוחסין בירושלים

Further reference to genealogical documents is found in Tosefta Haggigah 2:9, 235; Yevamot 4:13, 49a-b. These documents of Yichus in the Beit HaMikdash at this time were guarded with great care. Josephus writes, "A member of the priestly order must, to have a family, marry a woman of his own race... he must investigate her pedigree, obtaining the genealogy from the archives (the genealogy of his own family taken from the public registers)" (Josephus, Apion 1:31)

Meseket Kiddushin Mishnah 4:4 attests to this emphasis on genealogical purity as noted when we read, הנושא אשה כהנת צריך לבדוק אחריה ארבע אמהות שהן שמנה אמה ואם אמה ואם אבי אמה ואמה ואם אביה ואמה ואם אבי אביה ואמה לויה וישראלית מוסיפין עליהן עוד אחת (One who weds a woman who is a priestess, must investigate after her for four mothers, which are eight; her mother, and the mother of her mother, and the mother of her mother's father and her mother, and the mother of her father and her mother, and the mother of her father's father and her mother. A Levite woman and Israelite woman- they add to them one more.) While Josephus mentions Tiberia (the last place for the relocation of the Sanhedrin from the Lishkat ha-Gazit of the Beit HaMikdash, to Yavne, Shefaram, Bet She'arim, and Sepphoris), the capital of Galilee being the seat of the royal bank and archives (Life, 38), rabbinic texts mention Sepphoris ( Kiddushin 4:5) and Gadera (Esther Rabba 1:3) as other locations for Jewish archives. For more on genealogical archives in antiquity see http://databases.jewishlibraries.org/sites/default/files/proceedings/proceedings2001/levydavidshort1.pdf

Dr. Benjamin Sax whose Yahrzeit is 5 Av (yahrzeit of HaAri HaKodesh of Safed) was killed in a tragic car crash when my mother (zl) was very young and my grandmother Miriam (was driving the car) and subsequently miraculously survived only after a hip, knee, shoulder, teeth, replacements. As the bionic women my grandmother always was an optimist and positive seeing the glass half full, and my mother (zl) took great care of my grandmother even like Rabbi Tarfon putting his hands on the cold floor so his mother's feet not become cold in the winter, and putting on her slippers and making sure all her needs were met etc.

## Sources on Jewish Genealogy

In the biblical period historical ethnographic genealogies (Gen 5:11; 6:92; 10:13), tribal genealogies (census lists in Numbers), and individual genealogies were kept. Examples of individual genealogies are (1) the house of David (I Chron. 2:10-154; 3:1-245), (2) the House of the

Zadokite priesthood (I Chron 5:28-416; 5:14) and individuals (II Kgs 22:37; Jer 36:148), The house of Saul is given in I Chron 8:3. Sometimes artisans, hokhamim, poets whose professions were hereditary were linked with some ancient ancestor (I Chron 2:55; 4:21, 23). Such later typcs of lists were used for national census, military service, or tax purposes. In Ezra 2:62 a list of priestly families returning to Zion sought proof of their pedigree but could not find it. Nehemiah (7:5) mentions "the book of genealogy of those who came up first."9 The existence of genealogies is etymologically correlated to certain idiomatic expressions linguistically (Ex 32:32; Ezek 13:9; Ps 139:16). The list of Aarons' geneology may go back to a text in which there existed generation skipping data (I Chron 5-6).10 In Megillos Esther written in the Persian period the lineage of Modekhai is given (Esth 2:511; I Sam 9:112). In I Chron 2:55 the names of families such as the Tirathites is given.13 Caleb, the husband of Miriam is also given in I Chron 2:42-49.14 Sometimes the given name of a tribe or family occurs in different contexts or compound lists. Aram is listed in Gen 10:23 as the father of Uz whereas in Gen 22:20-21 Uz is the son of Nahor and an uncleof Aram. In Gen 36:5, 14 Korah is a son of Esau, but in Gen 36:16 the clan of Korah is descended from Esau's son Eliphaz. In Chron 2:9 Ram is the son of Hezron and the brother of Jerahmeel, yet in the same chapter verse 27 Ram is the eldest son of Jerahmeel. A name can also be included in several genealogical lists Fr example Zerah, Korah, Kenaz are included in Edomite lists in Gen 36, are also found on the list o the families of the tribe of Judah in I Chron 2 and 4. Beriah appears asone of the sons listed as the sons of Reuben (Gen 46:9) and also as one of the sons of Perez son of Judah (Gen 46:12).

In Second Temple Period

Purity of descent is most emphasized in the Beit Sheni Tekufah with regards to Kohanim and those Israelite families who lay claims to eligibility of the daughters to marry Kohanim. Families who had no record of their descent but were not suspected of impure lineage were referred to as issah (good dough). The kohanim in order to preserve their pure status were restricted to marital ties with families whose purity of descent was not in doubt and were therefore required to know their genealogy in detail and that of families whose daughters married kohanim. Families claiming purity of blood kept ancestral lists. According to Josephus (Jos Apion 1:7) in the Beit HaMikdash Kohanide genealogies on all priestly families even in the diaspora was required for deposit in Jerusalem. According to Kiddushin Kohanim who performed avodah from the altar upward and from the dukhan upward and members of the Sanhedrin (1/2 of which were Kohanim) were usually not suspected of impure genealogy (Kid 4:4-5). We read:

משנה מסכת קידושין פרק ד

משנה ד

הנושא אשה כהנת צריך לבדוק אחריה ארבע אמהות שהן [*] שמנה אמה ואם אמה ואם אבי אמה ואמה ואם אביה ואמה ואם אבי אביה ואמה לויה וישראלית מוסיפין עליהן עוד אחת:

משנה ה

אין בודקין לא מן המזבח ולמעלה ולא מן הדוכן ולמעלה ולא [*] מן סנהדרין ולמעלה וכל שהוחזקו אבותיו משוטרי הרבים וגבאי צדקה משיאין לכהונה ואין צריך לבדוק אחריהן ר' יוסי אומר אף מי שהיה חתום עד בערכי הישנה של צפורי רבי חנינא בן אנטיגנוס אומר אף מי שהיה מוכתב באסטרטיא של מלך:

Likewise in Sanhedrin 4:2 we learn:

משנה מסכת סנהדרין פרק ד

משנה ב

דיני הטומאות והטהרות מתחילין מן הגדול דיני נפשות [*] מתחילין מן הצד הכל כשרין לדון דיני ממונות ואין הכל כשרין לדון דיני נפשות אלא כהנים לוים וישראלים המשיאין לכהונה

Further in Aruchin 2:4 performance of avodah lessened doubt, sufek, the gematria of satan:

משנה מסכת ערכין פרק ב

משנה ד

ועבדי הכהנים היו דברי רבי מאיר רבי יוסי אומר משפחות [*] בית הפגרים ובית צפריה ומאמאום היו משיאין לכהונה רבי חנניא בן אנטיגנוס אומר לוים היו

Certain sages were of noble birth such as Rabbi Yehudah HaNasi who lived in Beit Sharim in the winter and Tzipori in the summer, where the breeze provides relief from the summer heat since Tzipori as the name means is like a bird pirched on a hill. Yet the crown of torah trumped genealogy as Rabbi Akiva Resh Lakish, and Rabbi Meir learned later in life as baalei teshuvah. Al pi Kabbalah some of Hazal were said to descend in gilgulim from evil roots such as Sisera, Sennacherib, Haman, Nero, and a tikkun is made by their descendents becoming rabbinic scholars as it says the late descendents of Haman are in Bnai Brak learning torah.

The Hasmonians area special case who sought to defend themselves against the contention that only Davidic descendents could lay claim to kingshi. The Talmud recounds how they shed doubt on King davids blood line from Ruth which the Biblical text makes clear is pristine and fit for the mashiach to come from:

רות פרק ד

וִיהִי בֵיתְךָ כְּבֵית פֶּרֶץ אֲשֶׁר יָלְדָה תָמָר לִיהוּדָה מִן הַזֶּרַע אֲשֶׁר יִתֵּן יְקֹוָק לְךָ מִן הַנַּעֲרָה הַזֹּאת:

(יג) וַיִּקַּח בֹּעַז אֶת רוּת וַתְּהִי לוֹ לְאִשָּׁה וַיָּבֹא אֵלֶיהָ וַיִּתֵּן יְקֹוָק לָהּ הֵרָיוֹן וַתֵּלֶד בֵּן:

(יד) וַתֹּאמַרְנָה הַנָּשִׁים אֶל נָעֳמִי בָּרוּךְ יְקֹוָק אֲשֶׁר לֹא הִשְׁבִּית לָךְ גֹּאֵל הַיּוֹם וְיִקָּרֵא שְׁמוֹ בְּיִשְׂרָאֵל:
(טו) וְהָיָה לָךְ לְמֵשִׁיב נֶפֶשׁ וּלְכַלְכֵּל אֶת שֵׂיבָתֵךְ כִּי כַלָּתֵךְ אֲשֶׁר אֲהֵבַתֶךְ יְלָדַתּוּ אֲשֶׁר הִיא טוֹבָה לָךְ מִשִּׁבְעָה בָּנִים:
(טז) וַתִּקַּח נָעֳמִי אֶת הַיֶּלֶד וַתְּשִׁתֵהוּ בְחֵיקָהּ וַתְּהִי לוֹ לְאֹמֶנֶת:
(יז) וַתִּקְרֶאנָה לוֹ הַשְּׁכֵנוֹת שֵׁם לֵאמֹר יֻלַּד בֵּן לְנָעֳמִי וַתִּקְרֶאנָה שְׁמוֹ עוֹבֵד הוּא אֲבִי יִשַׁי אֲבִי דָוִד: פ
(יח) וְאֵלֶּה תּוֹלְדוֹת פָּרֶץ פֶּרֶץ הוֹלִיד אֶת חֶצְרוֹן:
(יט) וְחֶצְרוֹן הוֹלִיד אֶת רָם וְרָם הוֹלִיד אֶת עַמִּינָדָב:
(כ) וְעַמִּינָדָב הוֹלִיד אֶת נַחְשׁוֹן וְנַחְשׁוֹן הוֹלִיד אֶת שַׂלְמָה:
(כא) וְשַׂלְמוֹן הוֹלִיד אֶת בֹּעַז וּבֹעַז הוֹלִיד אֶת עוֹבֵד:
(כב) וְעֹבֵד הוֹלִיד אֶת יִשָׁי וְיִשַׁי הוֹלִיד אֶת דָּוִד:

The mashiach must come from Ruth as a righteous geyoret who is linked to Peretz the son of Judah and Tamar.

On the eve of the Hurban by the Romans Rabbi Yochanan ben Zakai who was smuggled out in a coffin from the sieged Jerusalem (See Avot De Rabbi Natan) and asked Vespasian for (1) a Yeshivah in Yavne, and (2) a physician to cure Rabbi Tzadok who was starving himself on fruit juice as mourning for the Beit HaMikdash, that no subsequent rabbinical court would deal with matters concerning genealogy (Eduy 8:3) as we read:

משנה מסכת עדויות פרק חמשנה ג
[*] העיד רבי יהושע ורבי יהודה בן בתירא על אלמנת עיסה שהיא כשרה לכהונה שהעיסה כשרה לטמא ולטהר לרחק ולקרב אמר רבן שמעון בן גמליאל קבלנו עדותכם אבל מה נעשה שגזר רבן יוחנן בן זכאי שלא להושיב בתי דינין על כך הכהנים שומעים לכם לרחק אבל לא לקרב:

Such a consideration led to a rejection previously in time of Sefer Yuhasin which was a Midrash on Chronicles (see Pes 62b).

During the period of the Amoraim in Pumpeditha, Suria, and Nehardaa we find the Talmud's recording of many families that sought to maintain genealogical purity engaging in the practice of an uncle marrying a niece to ensure the purity of the blood line (Yev 62b). During the Amoraim and Geonic periods many families in Babylonia are mentioned in the Talmud and Mishnah in placing importance on tracing back. Thus, in Tosefta Peah 4:11 we read:

תוספתא מסכת פאה (ליברמן) פרק דהלכה יא
היה משתמש בכלי זהב מוכרן ומשתמש בכלי כסף בכלי כסף מוכרן ומשתמש בכלי נחשת בכלי נחשת מוכרן ומשתמש בכלי זכוכית אמרו משפחת בית נבטלה היתה בירושלם והיתה מתיחסת עם בני ארנון היבוסי העלו להם חכמים שלש מאות שקלי זהב ולא רצו להוציאן חוץ מירושלם
הלכה יב

Likewise, in Ta'anit 4:5 such emphasis is made:

משנה מסכת תענית פרק דמשנה ה
זמן עצי כהנים והעם תשעה באחד בניסן בני ארח בן יהודה [*] בעשרים בתמוז בני דוד בן יהודה בחמשה באב בני פרעוש בן יהודה בשבעה בו בני יונדב בן רכב בעשרה בו בני סנאה בן בנימין בחמשה עשר בו בני זתוא בן יהודה ועמהם כהנים ולוים וכל מי שטעה בשבטו ובני גונבי עלי בני קוצעי קציעות בעשרים בו בני פחת מואב בן יהודה בעשרים באלול בני עדין בן יהודה באחד בטבת שבו בני פרעוש שניה באחד בטבת לא היה בו מעמד שהיה בו הלל וקרבן מוסף וקרבן עצים:
משנה ו

The list in Taanit 4:5 originates from the Persian period. This concern is again voiced in the gemarah in Yevamot 16b.

While a Jew is Jewish law is defined as someone whose mother is Jewish,

Jewish law legislates that a child is Jewish if the mother is Jewish, or one who had converted to Judaism according to specific halachic requirements. Jewish identity is thus not merely sociological and demographic (if Jews live in the land of Israel) nor ethnic (differences in customs, folkways, and liturgy and practice of Ashkenazi Jews vs. Sephardic Jews), but rather determined by a maternal hereditary religious blood covenant. The rabbis and the Talmud trace the determination of Jewish status through the mother from Deuteronomy 7:3-4. The paradigm of legitimate conversion to Judaism is Ruth who tells her mother-in-law Naomi, "Your people will be my people, where you go I will go, etc.," and it is from Ruth and Boaz that the messiah is traced back to Judah and Tamar. The convert in Jewish law engages in (1) ritual immersion for purification in a *mikveh,* (2) circumcision for males, (3) acceptance of the *mitzvot,* and (4) offering a sacrifice, when the Temple stood, and will be rebuilt. Tractate Demai requires a convert's substantive acceptance of the *mitzvoth – kabbalat ha-mitzvot.* The Chazon Ish understands the acceptance of the *mitzvot* in its theological rather than practical sense, a convert must accept the chosen uniqueness of the Jewish people as it relates to our role in the world. This acceptance must be acknowledged *al da'at bet din.* Rav Joseph B. Soloveitchik holds the halachic principle of *kibush* which would allow for a *beit din* and parents to convert a child without asking and rear the child in their own faith; thus the *ger katan* program. Rabbi Chaim Ozer Grodzinski is of the position that *kabbalat ha-mitzvot* need not be accompanied by full and complete observance but needs to be accompanied by observance of significant basics such as Shabbos observance, *kashrut,* and *taharat ha-mishpaha.* The details of this process are complex, with nuanced disputes among

*Rishonim* and later *Achronim*, and clarified in codes such as the *Tur, Mishneh Torah*, and *Shulchan Aruch*.

In 1950 the state of Israel passed the Law of Return, by which "every Jew has the right to come to the country as an *oleh*" which was amended in 1970 to include anyone with a Jewish grandparent and their spouses, unless they have *voluntarily* renounced Judaism.

The question of Jews who are forcibly converted to Christianity and wish to return to Judaism is addressed by the 13th century Rabbi Meir of Rothenburg [1215-1295]. While Rambam holds Christianity to be a form of heretical idolatry while Islam is monotheistic, Maimonides [1135-1204] advised the Jews of Yemen living in a Islamic culture to commit martyrdom only in order to avoid the three cardinal sins: idolatry, sexual improprieties, or murder. A further question arises about 16th and 17th Century Jewish Conversos/Maranos who were forced to convert to Christianity by the Inquisition. More recently Rabbi Yitzhak Herzog retrieved and brought to Israel children hidden in Catholic monasteries during the Holocaust. Rabbi Ephraim Oshry deals with the halachic status of these children and many more in his work *She'eilos Uteshuvos Mima'amakim*.

The question of intermarriage can be found in the time of Ezra (458 BCE) who upon his return to the land of Israel from Babylonia found that returning Jewish exiles had married non-Israelite women, and children had been born to them. Ezra (10:3) made the Jewish men divorce their non-Jewish wives "according to the commandment of our G-d and according to Torah." Ezra 9:2 and Nechemia 13:23 legislate that the offspring of non-Jewish wives are not Jewish and we are told that the marriage to a non-Jewish wife leads to the "diluting of the holy seed (*zera ha-kodesh*) among the people of the land" (Ezra 9:2). In the *Mishnaic* times while the house of Hillel would not marry with the house of Shamai, both were clearly Jewish. However, marriage with the Samaritans was prohibited by the *Tannaim*. Prohibition of marriage with Christians followed on theological difference and historically on Christian acceptance of gentiles into the Church. When the Karaites arose in the middle Ages, most authorities prohibited marriage to this sect which only accepted the Written Law and not the Oral Law.

Today, particularly with the increase of intermarriage, questions arise such as "how should children born to a mixed marriage be registered in categories of religion and nationality by the Israeli government?" The Lubavitcher Rebbe, Rabbi Menachem Mendel Schneersohn, along with other great rabbis, called for emending the law of return to require conversion according to an Orthodox traditional interpretation of Jewish law. However very recently, liberal groups, mis-citing the work of historian Shaye Cohen, have been urging definition of who is a Jew based on patrilineal descent. This is contrary to 19th century classical Reform Judaism which agreed in consensus with Orthodox leaders that the litmus test of the status of Jewish identity is if a child is born of a Jewish mother, as noted by Solomon Freehof. Also the large numbers of Russian Jews to Israel since the 1990s, many of whom do not have Jewish mothers, has led to its own controversies.

To further complicate matters, questions have arisen regarding Jewish communities that were separated from the major Jewish centers of the Middle Ages and early modern period, such as the Bene Israel Jews of India and the Ethiopian Beta Israel. While Rabbis Shlomo Goren and Ovadia Yosef ruled in 1973 that the Ethiopians were Jewish and deserved full rights in Israel, other rabbis such as

Rabbis Bakshi-Doron and Amar required symbolic conversion of all Ethiopians. Other questions arise over the conversion of adopted children.

A well-known Mishnah of every ten year old in Yeshivah learning Mishnah lists ten social groups who returned from Babylonian exile in 486 BCE in genealogical purity:

(1) Kohnanim

(2) Leveim

(3) Israelite

(4) Halalim (sons of marriages of disqualified kohanim

(5) Gerim (convets)

(6) Harurim (manumitted slaves)

(7) Mamzerim (bastards, children of a Jewish father and non-Jewish mother

(8) Nethinim (descendants of the Gibeonites who had brit milah at time of Yehoshua but not regarded as full Jews because their ancestor's conversion was incomplete

(9) Shetukim (silent ones, who do not know the identity of their father

(10)Asufim (foundlings, who know neither their mother or father

We read in Kidushin 4:1

משנה מסכת קידושין פרק ד

משנה א

עשרה יוחסין עלו מבבל כהני לויי ישראלי חללי גירי [*]
וחרורי ממזרי נתיני שתוקי ואסופי כהני לויי וישראלי
מותרים לבא זה בזה לויי ישראלי חללי גירי וחרורי
מותרים לבא זה בזה גירי וחרורי ממזרי ונתיני שתוקי
ואסופי כולם מותרין לבא זה בזה:

The Mishnah chapter 4 of Kiddushin is devoted to the relationships between these groups i.e. rules applying to intermarriage between one group and another. Yet the Mishnah states that a learned mamzer takes precedence over an uneducated Kohen Gadol as we read in Horayot 3:8:

משנה מסכת הוריות פרק ג

משנה ח

כהן קודם ללוי לוי לישראל ישראל לממזר וממזר לנתין ונתין [*]
לגר וגר לעבד משוחרר אימתי בזמן שכולן שוין אבל אם היה
ממזר תלמיד חכם וכהן גדול עם הארץ ממזר תלמיד חכם קודם
לכהן גדול עם הארץ:
נשלמה מסכת הוריות

The Talmud makes frequent mention to families of honorable genealogy who quarreled over yichus, stating "when men quarrel among themselves they quarrel over birth (Kiddushin 76a). The Amoraim proclaimed, "anyone with a family of stigma stigmatizes others and never praises anyone, "and Samuel adds, "he stigmatizes with his own stigma (Kiddushin 70b). Thus, it takes on to know one. "The Holy one is reluctant to uproot a name or family from its place in a genealogical tree (Genesis Rabbah 82:11; 11) Thus we read in Sukkah 5:8:

משנה מסכת סוכה פרק המשנה ח
חל להיות יום אחד להפסיק בינתיים משמר שזמנו קבוע [*]
היה נוטל עשר חלות והמתעכב נוטל שתים ובשאר ימות השנה
הנכנס נוטל שש והיוצא נוטל שש רבי יהודה אומר הנכנס נוטל
שבע והיוצא נוטל חמש הנכנסין חולקין בצפון והיוצאין בדרום
בילגה לעולם חולקת בדרום וטבעתה קבועה וחלונה סתומה:
סליק מסכת סוכה

The sages also protested against anyone who takes a wife not fit (Kid 70a) "because he disregards the importance of birth."

In the messianic era Hashem will purify the tribes to become distinct. As was clear in the parting of the Reed sea where each tribe walked through 12 walls of potable sweet water. The question arises in the gemarah what type of bracha does one say over the exotic fruits that sprung from the sea bed, as later commented on by the Nodeh biYehudah.

In the Geonic periods in Israel and Babylonian the Talmud takes great care to trace the Exilarchs back to the house of David as was made of the geonim such as Hai Gaon. In the Middle Ages Davidic lineage was claimed for some Gedolim such as Rashi and his grandsons Rabbi Jacob Meir (Rabbenu Tam) and Rabbi Shmuel ben Meir who descended from Rabbi Yonatan ha-sandlar (Sandlar a tanna who was a shoe maker, from the root of sandal), who in turn was regarded as being of Davidic descent.

Zekut avot continues into the modern period and particularly among Hasidic dynasties certain Tzadikim would marry their daughters to sons of other Hasidic dynasties. Thus Ger, Vishnetz, Burke, Chabad, Bobov, etc. would engage in marriage the equivalent lehavdil to the likes of the Kings of England, France, and other secular royal dynasties, in order to secure alliances amongst the Hasidic royal lines.

Some notes on Rabbinic Genealogy

A researcher will be lucky if they have rabbeim in the family if they are searching for genealogical documents.

This is because:

(1) Rabbinic culture cares about yichus

(2) Rabbinic biographical sketches can be found

(3) Rabbinic manuscripts sometimes include a family tree

(4) Sheolot ve-teshuvot may refer to a rabbinic family as the Nodeh BiYehudah describes the halakhic issue of his niece who was a perpetual niddah due to a blood condition that posed a problem for the marriage night and consummating marital relations

(5) Yizkor books note Rabbinic leadership and their families. Yizkor books are a treasure trove as they contain maps, photos, shtetl records, cemetery records, synagogue records, etc.

(6) Pinkasim of synagogue records include sometimes genealogical records

(7) Yahrzeits are often recorded for mystical reasons in Rabbinic documents. For example, Fraidl Rabinowitz shares the 13 of Kislev with her husband Rav Menachem Mendel Gluskin because "there souls were so bound up with each other."

(8) Roshe tevot can be used to trace rabbinic dynasties

(9) The books authored by rabbis are often named after family names in abbreviation such as Eked Sefarim.

(10)If a family maintains it is descended from Gedolim like the Besht, the GRA, or the Maharal of Prague their homework is done, once they trace back to these great scholars, because these rabbinic leaders themselves were able to produce and took pride in their genealogical roots. For instance, the Maharal can be traced back to Dovid HaMelech and thus the 7 Chabad rebbes go through the Maharal.

(11)For non-rabbinic families today archives such as YIVO (for Yiddish speaking Jewry from Eastern Europe), Leo Baeck (for Geman Jewry), Yad Vashem (for Shoah records), and Beit Tefusoth maintain Geneological research libraries and records. For Shoah survivors' databases that contain Holocaust testimony can be accessed at the Yale Fortunoff database, Yad Vashem database, and Shoah Visual History Foundation under the auspices of the University of Southern California. For a list of the similarities and differences of these 3 databases see paper by David B Levy on TC website

(12)For non-rabbinic families today archives such as YIVO (for Yiddish speaking Jewry from Eastern Europe), Leo Baeck (for Geman Jewry), Yad Vashem (for Shoah records), Holocaust Museum, and Beit Tefusoth maintan Geneological research libraries and records. There are a host of holocaust organiations that also maintain genealogical resources. Geneaological databases for the kindertransports exist. And refugees in general. International tracing service is another avenue. Research projects can be consulted. For Shoah survivors' databases that contain Holocaust testimony can be accessed at the Yale Fortunoff database, Yad Vashem database, and Shoah Visual History Foundation under the auspices of the University of Southern California. For a list of the similarities and differenes of these 3 databases see paper by David B Levy on TC website. Sepahrdic geneaology during the Holocaust is another impotant avenue of research. Sephardim some claim have taken a great pride in genealogy above and beyond ashkenaz.

(13) Public Records, including US records and records of organizations like the Joint, vital records, central Zionist archives, archives of local eastern European locations like Kaunas, Lithuania, and Zhitmir, bank records,birth records of Tzarist Russia, and central archives for the Jewish people in Poland, business directory records

(14)Historical Jewish press

(15)Library genealogical collections, i.e. LC, JTSA, and archives, and genealogical institutes finding aids and reference books, general starter guides, and knowledgeable librarian archivists

(16)Local archives of specific places such as Ukraine, eastern Europe, poland and minsk, southern Russia, Galicia, Spain, Hungary, central Europe Netherlands, Germany, Rhodes ,Province France,

Alsace France, Cheklosavakia, , southerin Germany, Poland, Italy, Salonika, New Zealand Ottoman Turkey, transcarpathia, Lithuania, Scotland, Romania, Byelrussia, Israel

**(17)**Genetics and genetic testing and DNA studies

(18)Tombstone inscriptions and epitaphs and cemetery records, burial books

(19)New Technologies such as database construction and databases, websites, interent, digitization, automated matching of family trees, search engines, CDROM. and trends

(20) Cartography[15] ( maps) and backround on town

(21)Photos

(22) Demographic studies and knowledge of Jewish geography

---

1 זֶה סֵפֶר, תּוֹלְדֹת אָדָם: בְּיוֹם, בְּרֹא אֱלֹהִים אָדָם, בִּדְמוּת אֱלֹהִים, עָשָׂה אֹתוֹ

2 אֵלֶּה, תּוֹלְדֹת נֹחַ--נֹחַ אִישׁ צַדִּיק תָּמִים הָיָה, בְּדֹרֹתָיו: אֶת-הָאֱלֹהִים, הִתְהַלֶּךְ-נֹחַ

3 וְאֵלֶּה תּוֹלְדֹת בְּנֵי-נֹחַ, שֵׁם חָם וָיָפֶת; וַיִּוָּלְדוּ לָהֶם בָּנִים, אַחַר הַמַּבּוּל

4 דברי הימים א פרק ב

וְרָם הוֹלִיד אֶת עַמִּינָדָב וְעַמִּינָדָב הוֹלִיד אֶת נַחְשׁוֹן נְשִׂיא בְּנֵי יְהוּדָה:

(יא) וְנַחְשׁוֹן הוֹלִיד אֶת שַׂלְמָא וְשַׂלְמָא הוֹלִיד אֶת בֹּעַז:

(יב) וּבֹעַז הוֹלִיד אֶת עוֹבֵד וְעוֹבֵד הוֹלִיד אֶת יִשָׁי:

(יג) וְאִישַׁי הוֹלִיד אֶת בְּכֹרוֹ אֶת אֱלִיאָב וַאֲבִינָדָב הַשֵּׁנִי וְשִׁמְעָא הַשְּׁלִישִׁי:

(יד) נְתַנְאֵל הָרְבִיעִי רַדַּי הַחֲמִישִׁי:

(טו) אֹצֶם הַשִּׁשִּׁי דָּוִיד הַשְּׁבִעִי

## דברי הימים א פרק ג 5

וְאֵלֶּה הָיוּ בְּנֵי דָוִיד אֲשֶׁר נוֹלַד לוֹ בְּחֶבְרוֹן הַבְּכוֹר אַמְנֹן
לַאֲחִינֹעַם הַיִּזְרְעֵאלִית שֵׁנִי דָּנִיֵּאל לַאֲבִיגַיִל הַכַּרְמְלִית:
(ב) הַשְּׁלִשִׁי לְאַבְשָׁלוֹם בֶּן מַעֲכָה בַּת תַּלְמַי מֶלֶךְ גְּשׁוּר
הָרְבִיעִי אֲדֹנִיָּה בֶן חַגִּית:
(ג) הַחֲמִישִׁי שְׁפַטְיָה לַאֲבִיטָל הַשִּׁשִּׁי יִתְרְעָם לְעֶגְלָה
אִשְׁתּוֹ:
(ד) שִׁשָּׁה נוֹלַד לוֹ בְחֶבְרוֹן וַיִּמְלָךְ שָׁם שֶׁבַע שָׁנִים
וְשִׁשָּׁה חֳדָשִׁים וּשְׁלֹשִׁים וְשָׁלוֹשׁ שָׁנָה מָלַךְ בִּירוּשָׁלִָם: ס
(ה) וְאֵלֶּה נוּלְּדוּ לוֹ בִּירוּשָׁלָיִם שִׁמְעָא וְשׁוֹבָב וְנָתָן
וּשְׁלֹמֹה אַרְבָּעָה לְבַת שׁוּעַ בַּת עַמִּיאֵל:
(ו) וְיִבְחָר וֶאֱלִישָׁמָע וֶאֱלִיפָלֶט:
(ז) וְנֹגַהּ וְנֶפֶג וְיָפִיעַ:
(ח) וֶאֱלִישָׁמָע וְאֶלְיָדָע וֶאֱלִיפֶלֶט תִּשְׁעָה:
(ט) כֹּל בְּנֵי דָוִיד מִלְּבַד בְּנֵי פִילַגְשִׁים וְתָמָר אֲחוֹתָם: פ
(י) וּבֶן שְׁלֹמֹה רְחַבְעָם אֲבִיָּה בְנוֹ אָסָא בְנוֹ יְהוֹשָׁפָט
בְּנוֹ:
(יא) יוֹרָם בְּנוֹ אֲחַזְיָהוּ בְנוֹ יוֹאָשׁ בְּנוֹ:
(יב) אֲמַצְיָהוּ בְנוֹ עֲזַרְיָה בְנוֹ יוֹתָם בְּנוֹ:
(יג) אָחָז בְּנוֹ חִזְקִיָּהוּ בְנוֹ מְנַשֶּׁה בְנוֹ:
(יד) אָמוֹן בְּנוֹ יֹאשִׁיָּהוּ בְנוֹ:
(טו) וּבְנֵי יֹאשִׁיָּהוּ הַבְּכוֹר יוֹחָנָן הַשֵּׁנִי יְהוֹיָקִים הַשְּׁלִשִׁי

---

דברי הימים א פרק ה 6

וּבְנֵי קְהָת עַמְרָם יִצְהָר וְחֶבְרוֹן וְעֻזִּיאֵל: ס

(כט) וּבְנֵי עַמְרָם אַהֲרֹן וּמֹשֶׁה וּמִרְיָם ס וּבְנֵי אַהֲרֹן נָדָב
וַאֲבִיהוּא אֶלְעָזָר וְאִיתָמָר: ס

(ל) אֶלְעָזָר הוֹלִיד אֶת פִּינְחָס פִּינְחָס הֹלִיד אֶת
אֲבִישׁוּעַ:

(לא) וַאֲבִישׁוּעַ הוֹלִיד אֶת בֻּקִּי וּבֻקִּי הוֹלִיד אֶת עֻזִּי:

(לב) וְעֻזִּי הוֹלִיד אֶת זְרַחְיָה וּזְרַחְיָה הוֹלִיד אֶת מְרָיוֹת:

(לג) מְרָיוֹת הוֹלִיד אֶת אֲמַרְיָה וַאֲמַרְיָה הוֹלִיד אֶת
אֲחִיטוּב:

(לד) וַאֲחִיטוּב הוֹלִיד אֶת צָדוֹק וְצָדוֹק הוֹלִיד אֶת
אֲחִימָעַץ:

(לה) וַאֲחִימַעַץ הוֹלִיד אֶת עֲזַרְיָה וַעֲזַרְיָה הוֹלִיד אֶת
יוֹחָנָן:

(לו) וְיוֹחָנָן הוֹלִיד אֶת עֲזַרְיָה הוּא אֲשֶׁר כִּהֵן בַּבַּיִת
אֲשֶׁר בָּנָה שְׁלֹמֹה בִּירוּשָׁלִָם:

(לז) וַיּוֹלֶד עֲזַרְיָה אֶת אֲמַרְיָה וַאֲמַרְיָה הוֹלִיד אֶת
אֲחִיטוּב:

(לח) וַאֲחִיטוּב הוֹלִיד אֶת צָדוֹק וְצָדוֹק הוֹלִיד אֶת
שַׁלּוּם:

(לט) וְשַׁלּוּם הוֹלִיד אֶת חִלְקִיָּה וְחִלְקִיָּה הוֹלִיד אֶת
עֲזַרְיָה:

7 מלכים ב פרק כב

וַיְהִי בִּשְׁמֹנֶה עֶשְׂרֵה שָׁנָה לַמֶּלֶךְ יֹאשִׁיָּהוּ שָׁלַח הַמֶּלֶךְ אֶת
שָׁפָן בֶּן אֲצַלְיָהוּ בֶן מְשֻׁלָּם הַסֹּפֵר בֵּית יְקֹוָק לֵאמֹר

8 ירמיהו פרק לו

וַיִּשְׁלְחוּ כָל הַשָּׂרִים אֶל בָּרוּךְ אֶת יְהוּדִי בֶּן נְתַנְיָהוּ בֶּן
שֶׁלֶמְיָהוּ בֶן כּוּשִׁי לֵאמֹר הַמְּגִלָּה אֲשֶׁר קָרָאתָ בָּהּ בְּאָזְנֵי
הָעָם קָחֶנָּה בְיָדְךָ וָלֵךְ וַיִּקַּח בָּרוּךְ בֶּן נֵרִיָּהוּ אֶת הַמְּגִלָּה
בְּיָדוֹ וַיָּבֹא אֲלֵיהֶם

9 וַיִּתֵּן אֱלֹהַי אֶל-לִבִּי, וָאֶקְבְּצָה אֶת-הַחֹרִים וְאֶת-הַסְּגָנִים
וְאֶת-הָעָם לְהִתְיַחֵשׂ; וָאֶמְצָא, סֵפֶר הַיַּחַשׂ הָעוֹלִים בָּרִאשׁוֹנָה,
וָאֶמְצָא, כָּתוּב בּוֹ

10 וְאֶחָיו, לְמִשְׁפְּחֹתָיו, בְּהִתְיַחֵשׂ, לְתֹלְדוֹתָם--הָרֹאשׁ יְעִיאֵל,
וּזְכַרְיָהוּ

11 אִישׁ יְהוּדִי, הָיָה בְּשׁוּשַׁן הַבִּירָה; וּשְׁמוֹ מָרְדֳּכַי, בֶּן יָאִיר
בֶּן-שִׁמְעִי בֶּן-קִישׁ--אִישׁ יְמִינִי

12 וַיְהִי-אִישׁ מבן ימין (מִבִּנְיָמִין), וּשְׁמוֹ קִישׁ בֶּן-אֲבִיאֵל
בֶּן-צְרוֹר בֶּן-בְּכוֹרַת בֶּן-אֲפִיחַ--בֶּן-אִישׁ יְמִינִי: גִּבּוֹר, חָיִל

13 וּמִשְׁפְּחוֹת סֹפְרִים ישבו (יֹשְׁבֵי) יַעְבֵּץ, תִּרְעָתִים שִׁמְעָתִים
שׂוּכָתִים; הֵמָּה הַקִּינִים הַבָּאִים, מֵחַמַּת אֲבִי בֵית-רֵכָב

דברי הימים א פרק ב 14

וּבְנֵי כָלֵב אֲחִי יְרַחְמְאֵל מֵישָׁע בְּכֹרוֹ הוּא אֲבִי זִיף וּבְנֵי
מָרֵשָׁה אֲבִי חֶבְרוֹן:

(מג) וּבְנֵי חֶבְרוֹן קֹרַח וְתַפֻּחַ וְרֶקֶם וָשָׁמַע:

(מד) וְשֶׁמַע הוֹלִיד אֶת רַחַם אֲבִי יָרְקֳעָם וְרֶקֶם הוֹלִיד
אֶת שַׁמָּי:

(מה) וּבֶן שַׁמַּי מָעוֹן וּמָעוֹן אֲבִי בֵית צוּר:

(מו) וְעֵיפָה פִּילֶגֶשׁ כָּלֵב יָלְדָה אֶת חָרָן וְאֶת מוֹצָא וְאֶת
גָּזֵז וְחָרָן הֹלִיד אֶת גָּזֵז: ס

(מז) וּבְנֵי יָהְדָּי רֶגֶם וְיוֹתָם וְגֵישָׁן וָפֶלֶט וְעֵיפָה וָשָׁעַף:

(מח) פִּלֶגֶשׁ כָּלֵב מַעֲכָה יָלַד שֶׁבֶר וְאֶת תִּרְחֲנָה

15 Maps are challenging to find because often place names have multiple transliterated spellings. Parichi appears as Paricze sometimes. Loyev appears as Lojew sometimes. Glusk appears as Hlusk sometimes. It's a bit of a challenge to balance the needs for detail, geographic context, and time period in map requests. And it's a cliché, when working with detailed map series to locate places in proximity with each other, that each locality will be found on the edges of different but adjoining sheets. So, true to form, here are citations to multiple maps from 3 different series in the NYPL Map Divison, that show the locations of **Hlusk (Glusk), Parichi, Loyev**, and (in 2 out of the 3 cases) Minsk:Topograficheskaia karta Minskoĭ guberniĭ, 1846, Scale 1:210,000. The place names on this map are in the Cyrillic alphabet. Minsk appears on Sheet VI, Glusk and Parichi on Sheet XI, and Loyev on Sheet XVI. Specialnia Karta Europeickoi Rossii, 1890-1914, Scale 1:420,000.Also in the Cyrillic alphabet. Minsk appears on Sheet 15 (1913), Glusk on Sheet 29 (1912), and Parichi and Loyev on Sheet 30 (1911).
This map series is not described in NYPL online catalog, but is listed under RUSSIA, EUROPEAN. SET in the *Dictionary Catalog of the Map Division*, vol. 8, page 761.
Generalkarte von Mitteleuropa in masse, 1:200,000, 1899-1918.
Minsk is too far north to appear on this set of maps, but Glusk appears on the sheet named Glusk (1900), Parichi appears as Paricze on the sheet named Bobrujsk (1914), and Loyev appears as Lojew on the sheet named Reczyca (1914).
This map series also is not described in NYPL's online catalog, but is listed under EUROPE, CENTRAL. SET in the *Dictionary Catalog of the Map Division*, vol. 3, page 815.
These maps have not been digitized for the NYPL Digital Collections, however the last set is available online at 2 other sites:
https://www.landkartenarchiv.de/oesterreich_gkm.php
http://lazarus.elte.hu/hun/digkonyv/topo/3felmeres.htm
One can also search for other maps that fit the researchers needs at oldmapsonline.org

**Levy family** Dates by David B Levy

Secular Dates:

Abraham Eisenberg October 24 186-January 26 1933
Linnie Eisenberg October 27 1866- oct 25 1940/23 Tishrei
Gustav Eisenberg April 28 1828-May 29 1917
Esther Eisenberg sept 20-1828-January 8 1909
Samuel Eisenberg nov 16-1826-October 23 1918
David Eisenberg March 24 1868- March 30 1937
Moses Bear June 29 1864-nov 11 1958
Dr Charles levy November 29 1893-February 24 1970/18 Adar
Ruth Bear Levy November 11 1898- October 8 1994/3 Cheshvan
Ruth Sax Levy born January 27 1937- march 18 2007/28 adar
Dr Robert I Levy March 18 1926
David Bennett levy born March 24 1967 (Ta'anit Esther)
Emily Bear Levy July 24 1991 married Gabriel Feingold

Hebrew Dates:

Rosa Cohen Levy 15 Av (1871-1961)
Yosef Yonah HaLevy 30 Shevat Rosh Hodesh Shevat (1870-1941) Rosh Hodesh
Rabbi Israel Samuel Cohen 24 Kislev
Hartz Bear (1815-1907) born Bavaria
Barbeta Jandorf Bear (1830-1898) born Wurtenberg, Gemany
Dr. Benjamin Sax 5 Av (1897-1949) killed in car crash , family from Poland
Miriam Helfgot Gluskin Sax (1898-2000) 13 Shevat New Year for Trees Tu bi shevat; David B Levy the grandson of Miriam gave Miriam on her birthday every year a card acknowledging the planting of trees in Eretz Yisrael with the JNF in her honor. Coincidentally Miriam passed away on the 15th of Shvat when the New Year for trees .

Rabbi Yakov Yitztak Helfgott zts (3 Tevet) ben Shneur Zalman
Keila Leiba Helfgott Gluskin zl 27 Tishri

Notez Bien: General Leopold Blumenberg a relation of the Bear family, the Levy/Eisenberg Family donated to the Jewish museum of Maryland the sword of General Leopold Blumenberg pro bonum. David delighted when he attended a conference at the Center for Jewish History in Manhattan in 2018 and saw the sword on loan for a display about Jews in the Civil War, as Blumenberg was the highest-ranking officer of the Union Army.

The Levy family also donated to the Jewish Museum of Maryland a cook book of homemade Jewish recipes that had been in the family for many generations where women of the family wrote down how to make certain Jewish foods including zimus, cholent, gefilta fish, kreplach, Knish, Latkes, etc.

(1) Eisenberg relationships explained

Gustav Eisenberg and Esther Eisenberg came from Hungary (Chibish Hungary) to America. Gustav Eisenberg and Esther settled in lonaconing Maryland; Gustav built the house in which the family lived and was a carpenter. The family worshiped at a synagogue in Cumberland

Gustav and Esther Eisenberg had children Linnie Eisenberg and Abraham Eisenberg [Abe was a big philanthropist in Baltimore) Below Donation of Abraham Eisenberg to Zionist Organization of America.

TELEPHONE, PLAZA 0725

ההסתדרות הציונית של ארצות הברית

# ZIONIST ORGANIZATION OF AMERICA



**BALTIMORE ZIONIST DISTRICT**

305 HEARST TOWER BUILDING
BALTIMORE, MD.

January 21, 1933.

Mrs. A. Eisenberg
Park Heights Ave. & Ford's Lane
Baltimore, Md.

My dear Mrs. Eisenberg,

The Zionists of Baltimore join the community in mourning the loss of your dear departed husband, Abraham Eisenberg, who for many years has maintained his membership in the Zionist Organization, which efforts he followed minutely from day to day.

We shall for a long while to come keenly feel the loss of his sweet personality and generosity which permeated his entire being during his life's sojourn. Accept our heartfelt condolence in this hour of your bereavement and may you be consoled by the recollection of themany significant and worthy deeds performed by your eminent departed husband.

Sincerely yours,

Simon J. Levin
Simon J. Levin
Executive Secretary.

SJL:ml.

Linnie Eisenberg married Moshe Bear
Moshe Bear was the son of Hartz Bear from Bavaria and Barbeta Jandorf from Wurtenberg Germany. Moshe Bear owned a small clothing store in Lonaconing Maryland. Moshe Bear was a member of the secret organization the Masons. Moshe and Linne made sure their daughter Ruth Bear received a good College education at Goucher College. Linnie was from a very cultured family and played the piano and her brother Abe the violin (see intro to book *Music and Medicine* by Robert I Levy)
Moshe Bear and Barbeta Jandorft were related to Leopold Blumberg the highest-ranking Jewish general in the Civil war, who was injured at the Battle of Antietam. General Leopold Blumenberg was from the province of Brandenburg, Prussia, Germany 1827 died in Baltimore MD 1876. He was unique among generals because he refused to shave his beard off although military thought soldiers should be clean shaven so enemies not grab one by the beard to be stabbed etc. He served with distinction in the Prussian Danish war of 1848 and promoted in Europe to Lieutenant, no small feat for a Jew. He was one of the few Jews to hold an army commission in Germany and anti-Semitism in Germany caused him to emigrate to Baltimore in 1954. With the outbreak of the Civil War, Lincoln called on Blumeberg to serve as a general given his vast experience in the military to serve for Union forces. Local Secessionists for the Confederates threatened to hang Blumenberg when he aligned with the Union anti-slavery faction. He organized the 5th Maryland Regiment as acting colonel at the time. He participated in the Peninsular Campaign as a member of the Mansfield Corps. At the battle of Antietam Blumenberg then a major was in command of the 5th Maryland Regiment, His horse was shot from under him and he was badly wounded. In 1863 after he had recovered partially from the wound he was appointed by Lincoln provost marshal in the

Maryland District for 2 years. He was then appointed brigadier general by President Andrew Johnson. In Blumemberg's personal life he championed Jewish philanthropy and served as president of the Hebrew orphan asylum of Baltimore as well as the president of the National Schuetzen Verein of America. Rabbi Dovid Katz has written an important article in Where, What and When Baltimore publication illustrating an important charitable act of Blumenberg for the Friedenwald family of Baltimore. Harry Friedenwald was a researcher and physician of Jewish in Medicine. His 4-volume set is a classic in the Field; see Friedenwald, Harry, The Jews and Medicine: Essays Intro by George Rosen, NY: KTAV Pub House, 1967

Friedenewald wrote many other important works on the history of Jews in Science. The Friedenwalds had a large family of sons. Most of the sons joined the Union, but one son joined the confederacy. Baltimore city was Union. But farms on the outskirts were often confederate. Because one son out of many sons joined the confederates the whole Friedenwald family was arrested on a Shabbos that fell out of Pesach. They were taken to Fort McHenry that was transformed into a prison with terrible conditions. The person who got the family out of this terrible prison at Fort McHenry for the crime of 1 son joining the confederacy was David Levy's ancestor Leopold Blumenberg who had connections with Abraham Lincoln as the highest-ranking Jewish military officer in the Union. Blumenberg even paid the large ransom required to free the Friedenwald family from the prison. Perhaps the reason why Blumenberg went out on a limb for this prominent Jewish family that was imprisoned (all of them) for McHenry for treason, was that he always admired most of all the Tannaim, Rabbi Ishmael who was very diligent (machmir) in performing the mitzvah of redeeming the captives, for Rabbi Ishmael himself had been a captive of the Romans after the churban and a wealthy Jew paid for his freedom too. Blumenberg was eclipsed however by the philanthropic acts of the Eisenberg family

Abraham and Linnie (Leah) Eisenberg were the children of Gustav and Esther Eisenberg from Hungary. Abraham started out as a peddler selling wares door to door but subsequently due to hard work and brains made a fortune in the department store business. However, he used his wealth to help the Jewish community. Abraham gave the money for the Dining Hall at Ner Israel Yeshivah (and the perpetuity of stocking it with food supplies) because Rabbi Ruderman was admired by him. The dining Hall bares the name of Helen Eisenberg, Abe's wife. Further Abraham gave money for the Hopkins University Ancient Near Eastern Studies department to have a perpetual book fund to buy Jewish books. A room in the Library is named "Eisenberg seminar room" because Eisenberg gave much funds to encouraging Jewish studies at Hopkins. At the time Eisenberg was friends with Rabbi Samuel Rosenblatt who was the Jewish studies professor at Hopkins. Eisenberg's gave charitably to many other Jewish causes including Baltimore Hebrew University and sponsored Zionist funding of the Yishuv.

Abe Eisenberg were very cultured and had musicals at their house on Sundays. Robert I Levy as a small child played the piano at these musicals as Robert is a talented pianist who attended Peabody music conservatory until 18 years when Robert was drafted into the navy in World War II. However, Robert would prepare and play a piece for the Sunday musicals at the Eisenberg house on Park Heights Avenue across from what is now the RAMBAM HS, formally Har Sinai Synagogue. Robert's grandmother Leah Eisenberg also was a talented pianist who played duets with her grandson and Robert Remembers her playing

"Hungarian Rhapsody" by Franz Lizt and many other pieces. Abraham played the violin and often a cellist attended so trios and duets were frequently played in a family setting. The Eisenberg house is now the cite of the Elmont Apartments next to Rabbi Loenbruns house.

Linnie Eisenberg (zl) and Moshe Bear (zl) had a child (daughter) named Ruth Bear (zl) who later in life painted after Charles passed on and was a student of the artist Herman Merill. Ruth's painting were categorized as in the genre of Impressionism and folk art. In fact her mother, Linnie Eisenberg Bear's family donated a number of impressionist paintings to the Baltimore Museum of Art (Eisenberg Collection) and the Eisenberg's donated a large precious Jewel to the Walter's Art Gallery in Baltimore.
Moshe Bear had a modest clothing store in Lonaconing Maryland and Moshe was a member of the secret organization known as the Massons, as was Mozart. Coincidentally Ruth S Levy was born on Mozart's birthday

Ruth Bear married Dr. Charles Levy (Urologist)
Photo of Dr. Charles Levy, Ruth Bear Levy, and David

Ruth Bear Levy zl and Dr. Charles Levy zl had a son named Dr. Robert I Levy bis hundert und zwanzig, lemeah ve-ezreim Shlita (for biography of the Bear Eisenberg family see intro to book Music and Medicine by Robert I Levy

Photo of Robert I Levy with Sefer Torah ca 1939

Dr. Robert I Levy married Ruth Sax (the granddaughter of Keila Leiba Gluskin Helfgott)

Dr Robert I Levy Shlita and Ruth Sax Levy (zl) had children David B Levy PhD. (a librarian and autodidact) and Elizabeth Malis (creative writing major at JHU under Edward Albee)
Below Thank you letter from Dr. Alan Kadish President of Touro University David's workplace

TOURO COLLEGE & UNIVERSITY SYSTEM
NEW YORK MEDICAL COLLEGE

*President*
*Touro College and University System*

DR. ALAN KADISH

*President*
*New York Medical College*
*a member of the Touro College and University System*

NEW YORK OFFICE
500 Seventh Avenue
New York, NY 10018
Tel: 646-565-6136
Fax: 212-627-3152
alan.kadish@touro.edu

VALHALLA OFFICE
40 Sunshine Cottage Road
Valhalla, NY 10595
Tel: 914-594-4600
Fax: 914-594-4145
alan_kadish@nymc.edu

August 9, 2016

Dr. David Levy, Head Librarian
Lander College for Women
227 West 60th Street
New York, NY 10023

Dear David,

I am writing to express my sincere gratitude for your ongoing and invaluable assistance in researching a wide variety of topics. Your availability and dedication have played a major role in my and Dr. Fishbane's ability to prepare and deliver lectures and essays in various locations and on a wide range of topics.

In areas ranging from Jewish medical ethics to the vast range of contemporary halachic issues confronting us today, your knowledge and your direction to appropriate and interesting sources continue to help make our presentations both timely and intellectually challenging.

I greatly appreciate your willingness to devote the time and effort to help in the development of material for discussion. Your thoughts and suggestions are always extremely informative and useful and your collaboration is an essential part of the process of identifying relevant themes and areas of interest.

Once again, my sincere thanks for your help and devotion to Touro.

Sincerely,

Dr. Alan Kadish
President

(2)

<u>Levy and Cohen relationships Explained</u>

Yosef Yona HaLevy (zl) married Rosa Cohen (zl) from a suburb of Kovna
Photo Yosef Yonah HaLevy and Rosa Cohen Levy

Yosef Yona HaLevy and Rosa Cohen had child Dr. Charles Levy (zl)

Yosef Yonah had a number of brothers including Ike (Isaiah), David, and Max. Yosef Yona in Baltimore owned what Ruth Bear Levy calls a "notions store" which sold a little bit of this and that. Later Yosef saved up to buy apartments which he named after his daughters.

Rosa Cohen came from a priestly family as her father was a Kohen named Rabbi Israel Cohen (ztsl) buried on end of row with picture of priestly hands etc Below Death Certificate of Rabbi Israel Cohen, Rabbi from Kovna settled in Baltimore

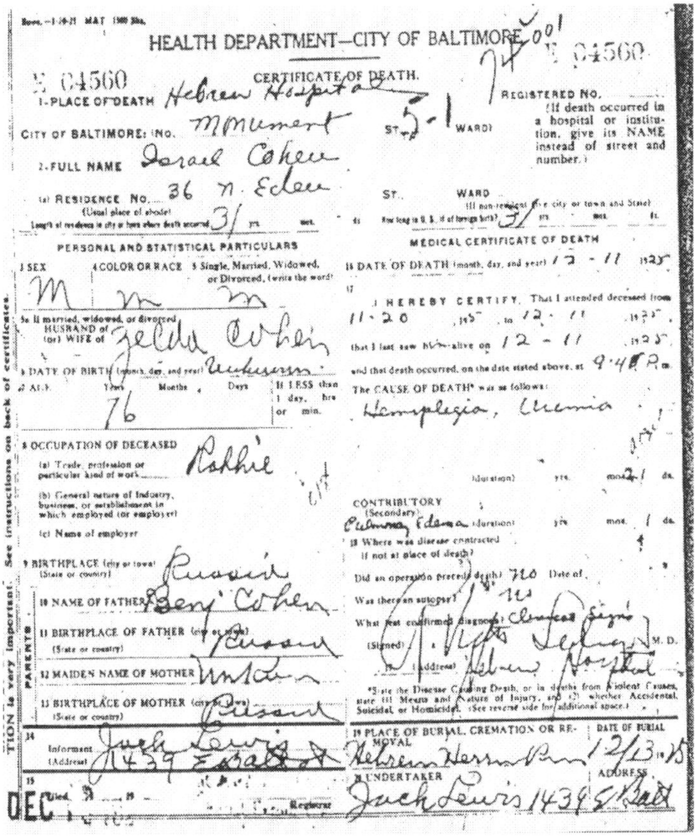

HEALTH DEPARTMENT—CITY OF BALTIMORE

CERTIFICATE OF DEATH.

04560

1-PLACE OF DEATH Hebrew Hospital

CITY OF BALTIMORE: No. Monument St. 5-1 WARD

REGISTERED No. (If death occurred in a hospital or institution, give its NAME instead of street and number.)

2-FULL NAME Israel Cohen

(a) RESIDENCE No. 36 N. Eden ST. WARD

PERSONAL AND STATISTICAL PARTICULARS

3 SEX M 4 COLOR OR RACE W 5 Single, Married, Widowed, or Divorced (write the word) M

MEDICAL CERTIFICATE OF DEATH

16 DATE OF DEATH (month, day, and year) 12 - 11 1925

5a If married, widowed, or divorced HUSBAND of (or) WIFE of Zelda Cohen

6 DATE OF BIRTH (month, day, and year) Unknown

7 AGE Years 76

I HEREBY CERTIFY, That I attended deceased from 11-20, 1925, to 12-11, 1925, that I last saw him alive on 12-11, 1925, and that death occurred, on the date stated above, at 9:40 P.m.

The CAUSE OF DEATH* was as follows: Hemiplegia, Uremia

8 OCCUPATION OF DECEASED (a) Trade, profession or particular kind of work Rabbi

CONTRIBUTORY (Secondary) Pulmonary Edema

9 BIRTHPLACE (city or town) (State or country) Russia

10 NAME OF FATHER Benj. Cohen

11 BIRTHPLACE OF FATHER (city or town) (State or country) Russia

12 MAIDEN NAME OF MOTHER Unknown

13 BIRTHPLACE OF MOTHER (city or town) (State or country) Russia

Did an operation precede death? No

Was there an autopsy? No

(Signed) M. D.

(Address) Hebrew Hospital

14 Informant Jack Lewis (Address) 1439 E Balt St

19 PLACE OF BURIAL, CREMATION OR REMOVAL Hebrew Herr... DATE OF BURIAL 12/13 1925

20 UNDERTAKER Jack Lewis 1439 E Balt

His Kever is in Hebrew Friendship cemetary in Baltimore. Documents exist in DBL's possession of Rosa Cohen in support of Eretz Yisrael. One thank you letter is from the chief rabbi of Israel to Rosa Cohen for a donation. Rosa Cohen was very pious. Rosa Cohen's *Last will and testament* gave her modest savings to worthy Jewish tzedakah organizations including Ner Israel Rabbinical College, Hospitals in Eretz Yisrael, Talmudical Academy of Baltimore, Hadasah, Yeshivah Kenessoth Israeol of Jersusalem, Histadruth Zionists organization etc. First page of will below:

LAST WILL AND TESTAMENT

OF

ROSA LEVY

* * *

I, ROSA LEVY, of the City of Baltimore, State of Maryland, do hereby make, publish and declare this as and for my Last Will and Testament, hereby revoking all other Wills and Codicils by me heretofore made.

I do hereby make the following disposition of all my property:

FIRST: I do hereby authorize my Executors, hereinafter named, to spend such sums for funeral expenses, the erection of a marker or monument at my grave, and the perpetual care of the lot in which I shall be buried (unless arrangements therefor shall have been made during my lifetime), as my said Executors may deem proper, and all such payments may be made by my Executors without regard to any limitation fixed by law and without the necessity of prior application to or subsequent ratification by any Orphans' Court or any other court. I direct that my Executors select a suitable person to recite the Kaddish Prayers, during the period of one year following my decease, and that they pay to said person the sum of Two Hundred Dollars ($200.00).

SECOND: I give, devise and bequeath unto the following charitable, religious and educational institutions, the respective amounts set out opposite their respective names:

| | |
|---|---|
| Jewish Welfare Fund of Baltimore City | $500.00 |
| Associated Jewish Charities of Baltimore City | 500.00 |
| Ner Israel Yeshiva, with the request that Kaddish Prayers be recited and a Memorial Light established in my memory | 300.00 |
| Levindale Hebrew Home and Infirmary | 300.00 |
| Talmud Torah, Etz Haim and Bicur-Cholim Hospital in Jerusalem, State of Israel | 300.00 |
| Talmudical Academy of Baltimore with the request that my name be placed upon a memorial plaque | 500.00 |
| Baltimore Chapter of Hadassah, for use in its work in Israel | 200.00 |
| Hebrew Yeshiva Knesseth Israel, P. O. Box 859, Jerusalem, State of Israel | 200.00 |
| Hadassah, the Women's Zionist Organization, Inc., a New York membership corporation, for use in the furtherance of its work for Youth Alyah | 300.00 |
| Histadruth, the Labor Zionist Organization | 200.00 |

Sara Shanker recalls that Rosa did not eat a morsel of breakfast until she davoned every morning for at least 2 hours. Rosa and Yosef Yona's first language was Yiddish, David B Levy has in his possession the tefillin of Dr.

Charles Levy that Yosef Yonah gave to Charles upon his bar Mitzvah. The day Charles passed on according to Charles wife Ruth Bear Levy, Charles had just returned from schacharit in Schul at Chizuk Amuno Congregation (which at that time was Orthodox, later became Conservative) but Charles insisted on laying tefillin at home again. According to Ruth Bear Levy it was just after removing the 2nd pair of Tefillin that Charles passed on. Ruth Bear in her merit relayed these tefillin to her only grandson David B Levy urging him to use them regularly. To Ruth Bear Levy's credit also she relayed to David an old sefer that had been brought over by Gustav Eisenberg in the 19th century from Hungary to Baltimore called Etz Chaim, which is a hodge podge of Rabbinic texts (midrashic, Halakhic, siddur) etc David cherishes this sefer published around 1750 in Lemberg. Amongst many rare sefarim, another given to David by Flora Atkin which belonged to her grandfather Hartogenesis whose rabbbinc family came from Amsterdam: (see https://www.jewishdowntown.org/sometimesyouhavetosayno ) Hartogensis took an active interest in Jewish affairs and was a member of the Baltimore Hebrew Congregation then worshipping in the Lloyd Street Synagogue. Strictly orthodox, he joined with other members who left Baltimore Hebrew in 1871 when that congregation shifted to Reform Judaism, and he served as the Recording Secretary of the new Chizuk Amuno Congregation for nineteen years. He helped establish a learning center for the shul and pledged money to build their permanent home on Lloyd Street, which is now the home of B'nai Israel. H. S. Hartogensis often served as a chazzan for the new shul. A brief biography of him in the 1910 book, The History of the Jews of Baltimore, states "He was highly esteemed as assistant chazan, officiating frequently, and always on holidays and fast days. Hartogenesis name is in this Mishnah Flora gave David which dates to the 17th century soon after the invention of the publishing press. It is one volume of Seder Kodshim of a mishnayot printed in Amsterdam. David notes that the Chofetz Chaim's Yeshivah in Radin was especially diligent to learn seder Kodshim in the mishnayot because in case the *beit ha Mikdash* would be rebuilt one has to know how to do the korbanot. The merit of learning korbanot is as if one offered them. The Chofetz Chaim kept a pair of Shabbos clothes at his doorway to go out to greet the mashaich!

Yosef Yonah HaLevy and Rosa Cohen HaLevy had a # of daughters. One was Eleanor. Elenor's granddaughter married an opthamologist from Haifa named Dr. Katz. The second daughter was named Anna and her child was Flora who married Moshe Atkin (Moshe worked for the Israeli Government as a business coordinator, i.e. to send food for example to Israel in times of famine, see Letter from Rabbi Levi Yitchak Herzog to Maury Atkin thanking Moshe for sending food including Cholov Yisrael Cheese to Israel, in Maury Aitkins autobiography). Flora Levy Aitkin's grandfather was Rabbi Hartegenosis from Amsterdam. Rabbi Hartogenesis in Baltimore came from many generations of rabbis in Amsterdam. Rabbi Hartogenesis in Baltimore wrote teshuvot in Hebrew that can be accessed

Photo of Rosa Cohen Donation to Kolel Shomre Harchomos of Jersusalem

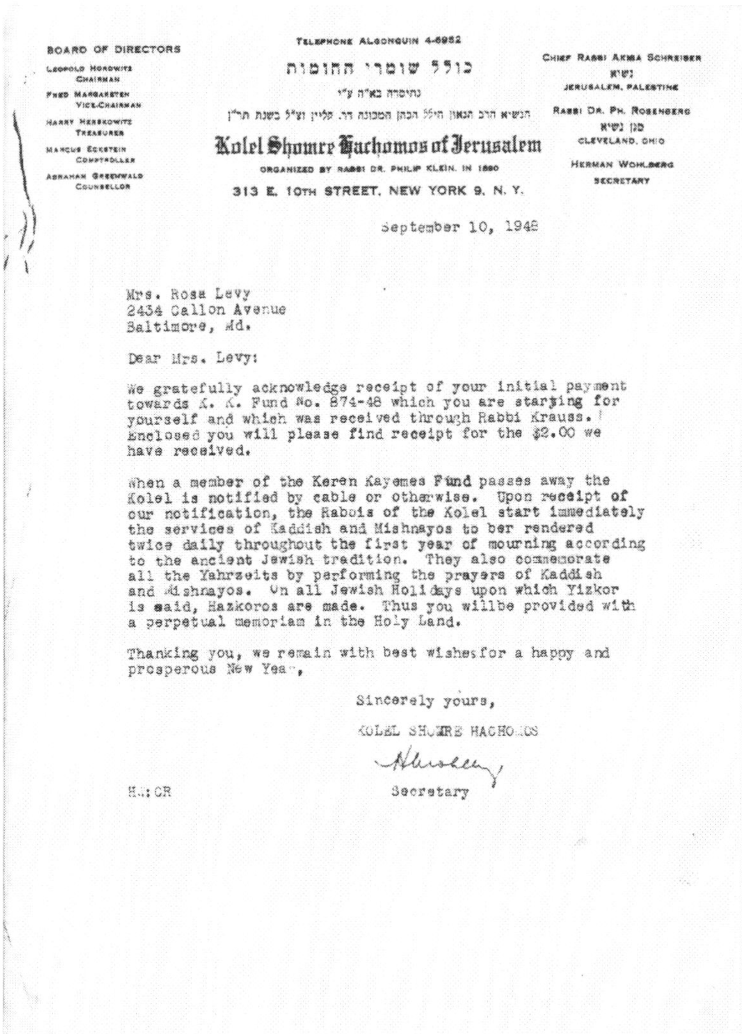

BOARD OF DIRECTORS
LEOPOLD HOROWITZ, CHAIRMAN
FRED MARGARETEN, VICE-CHAIRMAN
HARRY HERSKOWITZ, TREASURER
MARCUS ECKSTEIN, COMPTROLLER
ABRAHAM GREENWALD, COUNSELLOR

TELEPHONE ALGONQUIN 4-6952

כולל שומרי החומות
נתיסדה באה״ק ע״י
הנשיא הרב הגאון הילל הכהן המכונה דר. קליין זצ״ל בשנת תר״ן

**Kolel Shomre Hachomos of Jerusalem**

ORGANIZED BY RABBI DR. PHILIP KLEIN, IN 1890

313 E. 10TH STREET, NEW YORK 9, N. Y.

CHIEF RABBI AKIBA SCHREIBER
נשיא
JERUSALEM, PALESTINE

RABBI DR. PH. ROSENBERG
סגן נשיא
CLEVELAND, OHIO

HERMAN WOHLBERG
SECRETARY

September 10, 1948

Mrs. Rosa Levy
2434 Callon Avenue
Baltimore, Md.

Dear Mrs. Levy:

We gratefully acknowledge receipt of your initial payment towards K. K. Fund No. 874-48 which you are starting for yourself and which was received through Rabbi Krauss. Enclosed you will please find receipt for the $2.00 we have received.

When a member of the Keren Kayemes Fund passes away the Kolel is notified by cable or otherwise. Upon receipt of our notification, the Rabois of the Kolel start immediately the services of Kaddish and Mishnayos to ber rendered twice daily throughout the first year of mourning according to the ancient Jewish tradition. They also commemorate all the Yahrzeits by performing the prayers of Kaddish and Mishnayos. On all Jewish Holidays upon which Yizkor is said, Hazkoros are made. Thus you willbe provided with a perpetual memoriam in the Holy Land.

Thanking you, we remain with best wishes for a happy and prosperous New Year,

Sincerely yours,

KOLEL SHOMRE HACHOMOS

Secretary

HW:CR

(3)

My maternal grandmother Miriam (zl) told me she was born in what sounded like Loev went to Gomel (pogrom in Gomel) and then went to Yekatasrinislav. My grandmother Miriam earned a dental degree in Yekatsrinslav. However, when the Helfgott family eventually made migration to Baltimore (Dr. Nathan Helfgott served to support afadativ for family to settle in Baltimore, stories have it that Dr. Nathan was much admired by women for his good looks) Baltimore dental organization not accept dental degree of my grandmother from Yekatasrinsilav. Therefore, my grandmother Miriam earned a degree as a "nurse". She began serving as a nurse in the maternity ward at Sinai Hospital. That is where she met my mother's father Dr. Benjamin Sax a Radiologist. Rules at Sinai Hospital were that nurses could not marry physicians. Therefore, Miriam and Dr. Benjamin Sax went to Philadelphia to get married where two big Chabad Rabbis signed the Ketubah in Philadelphia. The Saxes then returned to Baltimore. However, in 1949 terrible car accident when my grandmother Miriam driving on NJ turnpike. Car hit from behind by a truck. Hit and run accident. Dr. Benjamin Sax was killed and Miriam serious hurt. Miriam had a hip, knee, shoulder, teethe replaced and terrible arthritis since accident. Doctors said Miriam would never walk again. Yet Miriam the miracle Bionic women with strength, courage, determination, and persistence eventually managed to walk again (with a cane). She eventually found a Job as a school nurse at Roland Park Public school that was closed on the weekends, did not require large amounts of standing, and allowed her not to work on Shabbos. Miriam's cousins thru her father Rabbi Helfgott were the Schotenstein's who later sponsored the Schotenstein Talmud translation. The Schotenstein owned a large farm between UMCP and Baltimore. Rabbi Helfgott's cousin was related to the Schotensteins. Many rabbis came to Rabbi Helfgott for advice according to Albert Sax. Rabbi Helfgott was a successful lumber merchant, like Bialik's father in Russia. Rabbi Helfgott lived in the house of Miriam. Rabbi Helfgott died in the house. Rabbi Helfgott taught was kind and taught Albert how to layn tefillin.

Albert although raised in yeshiva went of the derekh and is frei psychiastrist. After the accident in 1949 Albert threw the dobermin pintcher dog out of the window. Coping with the loss of the father was difficult for all of the children. Albert remembers that Keila Leiba droped the hot soup on Albert (age 3) and that Keila Leiba was distraut over Albert being burned. coCoAlbert Sax's Rabbi in cheder in Baltimore was Rabbi Shoham. The bar mitzvah party was very low key in the basement of the house on Eutaw street. Albert had a crush on a daughter of Dr. Ostrow. Dr Nathan Helfgott (general practitioner) brought the Rabbi Helfgott family over. Nathan's wife was Rose. Nathan's son was Aaron. Nathan's grandchild was the mayor of Annapolis. Coincidentally David Levy's fellow classmate in the doctorate program at BHU was Rabbi Moshe Pinchas Weisblum, who was a rabbi in Annapolis. David was asked to write the introduction for Rabbi Weisblum's book: **The Hermeneutics of Medieval Jewish Thought: Understanding the Linguistic Codes of Rashi and Nahmanides.**

In Moscow Miriam became a dentist and Yivesay and Griesha became doctors. Yivesay was a chief surgeon in the Red Army. Yivesay was not a communist but his wife was a communist. Griesha was sent to Siberia in the Jewish Doctor's plot. Miriam visited in the 1970s (during Breshhnav's reign) her family and had to meet on park benches because the apartments were bugged by the KGB. Miriam's sister Rochel's husband was a dentist who wrote a number of dental textbooks. Miriam's parents were often asked for money to support the gambling addiction of Iser. Iser's first wife's maiden name was Seravski. Their child was Lee who married a psychiatrist in NYC named Dr. Naiman. One of Lee's children Eric Naiman is a professor of Russian Literature at UCLA. Another child is a social worker in NYC. A third child of Lee Naiman is in finance.

Miriam was the oldest surving graduate off Sinai nurses as Miriam lived to the age of 105 years. She was an eternal optimist who overcame the adversity and the challenges of medical issues from the car crash by always seeing the glass half full. Miriam's longevity may be attributed not only to good genes but also to the great care that her daughter Ruth and son-in-law Robert gave to her, visiting her at North Oaks everyday and making sure all her needs were met. Ruth truly affirmed the mitzvah of כַּבֵּד אֶת-אָבִיךָ, וְאֶת-אִמֶּךָ and from Ruth's father imparted the importance of intellectual virtue and devotion to the life of the mind in pursuit of hokmah, binah, ve daas, as Dr. Benjamin Sax (David's middle name Benjamin) had a magnificent library. Benjamin Sax (born 1897) a radiologist's by profession, family was from Poland and Russia. They started off as peddler but his mother Sara Levy's family in New York was in the antiques business with the Ginzberg family. Benjamin's father was printer, publishing Yiddish works as well as printing for the Levy-Ginzberg antique business. He married Sara Levi. Her brother was named Ike Levy and his wife's maiden name of Ginzberg. The antique store furnished many works to the Metropolitna Museum of Art NYC, and the Imma Hog Museum in Texas. Benjamin was told that Ben Ginzberg (his wife Cora Ginzberg was an expert in fabrics) would take over the running of the antique business so Benjamin Sax went to University of Maryland Medical School to become a radiologist. Benjamin Sax prior to that was in the Navy at the end of WWI. Ben Sax finished College at City University of NY. His sister was named Rebecca a teacher in the public school system. Rebbeca also liked to paint and was an artist. Rebecca's brother Saul also taught in the NYC public schools. A turning point in the the Sax family's life was the car crash in 1949 where their father Benjamin was killed and the precious antiques from the family Levy-Ginzberg antique business were sold for pittance and the family moved into a small apartment. What my mother Ruth was allowed to keep were some of the books from her father's extensive library.

<u>**Gluskin families we hope we can learn more about**</u>

Some **Gluskin families** and names that we do not know of any connection. We mention a few here in order to show that there is still much more research to do. We have begun the work with this book.

-----------

Sonia daughter of Alena Hluskina, she has a brother, father and his brother, grandfather Mikhail Hluskin, his father Abraham and his father Shaul from Hlusk.

-------------

Yulia Gluskin daughter of Igor, grandparents from Tashkent moved there after WW2 Roman and Lidiya Gluskin.

-------------

Tatyana Gluskina born in Voronzeh, father, grandfather Lev born in Bobroysk brother Moshe/Michael, their father Yuda Gluskin married Nechama b. 1898

**Births**

Reiza Gluskin - father Meir, grandfather Aharon. Mother Shaina (father from Metislev) DOB 17/7/1838 7$^{th}$ of Av Minsk

Yuda Leib – Iyud leib Glushkin father Morduhk/ Mordechai, grandfather Isak/Yitzchak dob 1/7/1887 21 Tammuz Usvyaty (Velizk – Vitebsk), retired Soldier, mohel Beshkin. Mother Itka, Moushal, grandfather Moshe.

Izroil Gluskin father Itska, grandfather Izroil, mother Gitlia, grandfather Naftolya dob 2/2/1878 Mogilev.

**Deaths**

Shifra married to David Gluskin, Mogilev. Illness d. 7/10/1872 17 Tishrei age 45

Esther Chana (Khana) Gluskin father Esel, grandfather losef Itska – Itschak Mogilev residence Bobroysk d. 21/10/1889 8 Cheshvon age ¼ scartatina.
Shepsel Gluskin d. 31/1/1895 age 85 heart failure Bobruisk

**Duma Voters**

Nekhemia Gluskin 1906 Rechitsa (Minsk area)

**Marriage**

Tzira Gluskin father Shlema mother Gamshey from Parichi married 18/10/1916 in Gomel (Mogilev area) at age 25 to Leyba Tamarkin – 38 father psach from Mogilev
Feyga Pesya Glusskin – 23 father Evesy, m. in Gomel 13/7/1901 to Nokhim Velikovitch – 23 son of Aron from Gomel.
Sosia Gluskin – 29 father Tzemakh m. in Mogilev 7/11/1891 18 Kheshvan to Leiba Feigin (widower) son of Leizer wedding by Rabbi Katz-Kagan witness Boruch ber Shifrin (Zalman Shifrin).
Genya Simkha Glusskin – 22 father benyamin from Paritchi m. in Gomel 13/11/1892 Shlema Garelik – 28 son of Yosel from Rogachev (second marriage, farmer).
Ilia Gluskin – 25 father Abram from Paritchi m. in Bobruisk 2/9/1882 Tema Zakhaim- 20 son of David from Bobrouisk witnesses Mordechai Rizinkin and Sinai Kabakov.
Mikhel Gluskin – 29 father Abram from Paritchi m. in Gomel 27/3/1892 Dvera daughter of Vulf.
Gertzel Gluskin – 34 father Leyb m. in Gomel 13/8/1900 Khana Zakoshansky bas Mordukh from Mstislavl.
Esel Gluskin – 23 ben Gilel from Rechitza m. in Gomel 22/10/1913 Khana Brandin bas abram from Vetka
Sora Gluskin – 50 bas Leyb from Parítichi (widow) m. in Gomel Gershon Pain 62 ben yankel from Gomel (Second marriage, widower).

**Vitebsk**

Grigory Glushkin b. 1908 d. 1989 – 81
Leyb Glushkin b. 1853 d. 1914 – 61

**Vilna**

i.i. Gluskin b. 1896 d. feb 24 1958 buried Saltonishkiu cemetery Vilnius Lithuania
A Gluskina b. 1896 d 27 sept 1957
Berta Moiseevna Gluskin b. 1915 d. 1988
Elka Girshevna Gluskin b. 1885 d. oct 5 1969
-------
My great-great-grandfather was named David Gluskin and I believed he lived in the town of <u>Zelva</u> in the Grodno region (around 200 miles from Hlusk). He was married twice, to Esther (surname unknown) and Ida-Shifra Bublatsky. His children with Esther were Chanka, Sholom, and Anna. Some or all of that branch of the family perished in the Holocaust, some may have gone to France but my research has not turned up anything. His children with Ida Shifra were Kalman (1874-1911), Label (1874-1925), and Libby (my great-grandmother, 1880-1954). As far as I know, only Libby and perhaps Label immigrated to the U.S.

I know that Libby grew up in a very religious household and there is a branch of her descendants (my second cousins) who remain orthodox and live in Brooklyn and the Five Towns area. They are strict modern orthodox but not Hassidic.

Part of the Bublatsky line changed their name to Ratner and live in Sydney and Melbourne. Dan - Daniel Rice" danrice@gmail.com
--------------------------
Aharon Gluksins wife's maiden name was Wolfson but We do not know which ones. Aharon was in the lumber business before e became a Rov.

My Arkins, Kreitsers, Wolfsons, and Lifshitzes originated in Hlusk, migrated to the dorf Koslovichi, then

Babruisk. In 1908, they arrived in America. My Wolfsons were Mayer Wolfson, a melamed, and Yochevet Lifshitz Wolfson, whose family was in the lumber and grain business. Their children were Esther Wolfson Frakt, Masha Wolfson Arkin, Hymie, and William. Jeff, Jeffrey Arkin jebra47@gmail.com

Olga wife of … Gluskin son of Yaakov Gluskin son of Isser Gluskin from Slutsk.

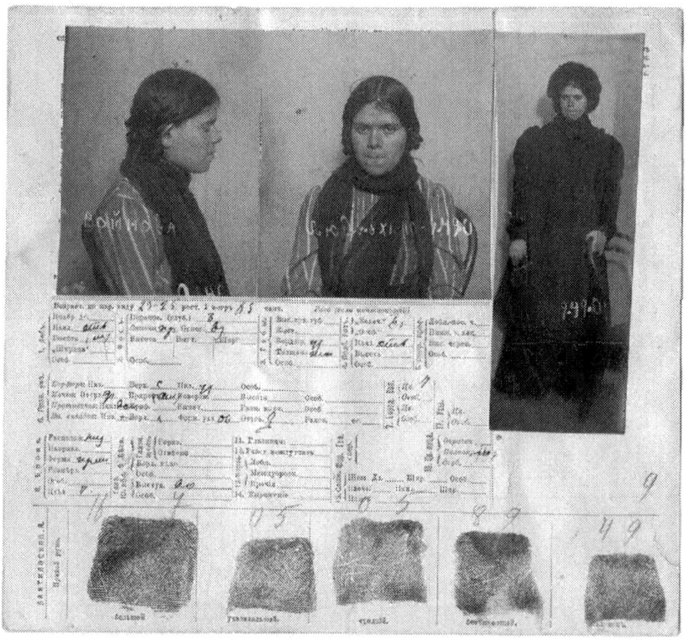

Simcha Leah Aronova Gluskina. On the police card she first named herself as Ludmila Voynova. Then the police found that she is a citizen of Paritchi and lived in Ekatrinislav and was born in Nezhin. Her father had been living in Paritchi for a lengthy period.

An unknown Aron Gluskin from Paritchi had a daughter Chana. She studied in the gymnasia in Rostov-on-Don and in Derbent where her uncle lived. In 1914 she wanted to study medicine in the Moscow University. Her father Aron wrote a letter agreeing for her to take on such an education. (There was a demand from the university at that time that the father must write a letter supporting his daughter's education in order for her to be accepted.) She was refused admission, but she worked in Moscow. In the letter Aron wrote that he is a citizen of Paritch living in Ekatrinburg. That is all we know.

This Aron was also the father of Rosa, both were born in Ekatrinislav; Chana in 1895 and Rosa in 1899. They both wrote about gymnasia in Derbent where their uncle lived. Rosa wrote that her father was a shop manager for the sale of Kerosene in Ekatrinislav. Rosa's mother died in 1913.

There is a policy questionnaire of Sorah Leah Aronova Gluskina in 1910. She is a citizen of Paritchi born in Nezhin. She had a brother Leon Aronov Gluskin who was written down as a metal worker in S. Petersburg. She is mentioned as being from the Saratov medical school.

Rosa became a communist party nomenklatura. She changed her name from Aronova to Arkadievna which is a standard Soviet variant for Aron. Rosa 1899-1968 and is buried in Novodeviche cemetery in Moscow. She is mentioned as a chemical engineer but was more of a party specialist not in chemistry.

МАРТИРОЛОГ РАССТРЕЛЯННЫХ
в Москве и Московской области

The computer database "Victims of political repression, shot and buried in Moscow and the Moscow region from 1918 to 1953" was compiled by the Sakharov Center on materials provided by the group on the perpetuation of the memory of victims of political repression under the guidance of Mindlin MB, State Archive of the Russian Federation, The central archive of the FSB of Russia, the FSB Directorate in Moscow and the Moscow region. e-mail:secretary@sakharov-center.ru

https://www.sakharov-center.ru/asfcd/martirolog/?id=5988&t=page
Year of birth 1895 Gluskina
Anna Arkadevna
Nationality Jewish Yerozhenka
Ekaterinoslav
Place of residence Simferopol, Vostochnaya St., 24, kv.2
Anna Arkadevna Gluskina
Higher education
Party membership was excluded from the CPSU (b) in 1929.
Place of work "Krymshveimprom" association
Occupation, position economist
Arrested August 9, 1936
Condemned by the Military Collegium of the Supreme Court of the USSR
On charges of participation in a counterrevolutionary terrorist
in execution on August 7, 1937
Rehabilitated on July 26, 1990, by decision of the Plenum of the Supreme Court of the USSR
Place of burial Don Cemetery, Tomb 1
Location of the file Central Archive of the FSB of Russia
Case number

Год рождения 1895 Глускина
Анна Аркадьевна
Национальность еврейка
Уроженка г. Екатеринослава
Место проживания г.Симферополь, ул.Восточная, д.24, кв.2 Анна Аркадьевна Глускина
Образование высшее
Партийность исключена из ВКП(б) в 1929 г.
Место работы объединение "Крымшвейпром"
Род занятий, должность экономист
Арестована 9 августа 1936 года
Осуждена Военной коллегией Верховного суда СССР
По обвинению в участии в контрреволюционной террористической организации
Приговорена к расстрелу 7 августа 1937 года
Приговор приведен
в исполнение 7 августа 1937 года
Реабилитирована 26 июля 1990 года, постановлением Пленума Верховного суда СССР
Место захоронения Донское кладбище, могила 1
Место хранения дела Центральный архив ФСБ России
Номер дела

***Post-Script:***

This genealogical research describes some of the methods, strategies, and reliance at times on pure luck, Hashgahah Pratit, serendipity to uncover the past family history of various members of the Gluskin family and place this account in its historical context. As well as the uncovering of an elite rabbinic history this study is unique in revealing maternal histories. The testimony is peppered with primary sources including interviews and many secondary sources in Hebrew (**see Hebrew Bibliography**). It notes some individuals who made major impacts in their Jewish community, Judaism, cultural history at large, and Eretz Yisrael.

Rabbi Moshe Zev Gluskin (ztsl) was a confidant of Reb Chaim of Volozhin.

Moshe Zev also gave a Hesped for the GRA whom he visited numerous times.

Rabbi Mendel Gluskin (zts) was a chief Rabbi (Av Bet Din) in Minsk and later Leningrad. Rav Menacham Mendel was the son in law of Rabbi Eliezer Rabinowitch who in turn was the son in law of the Minsker Gadol, Rabbi Eliyahu Pearlman (Ztsl). Both Rav Menchem Mendel and Rabbi Eliezer Rabinowitch were imprisoned by the Communists for the actions on behalf of Yiddishkeit in the USSR under the surveillance of the KGB. Many letters are preserved in the *Iggerot Kodesh* of the previous Lubavitch Rebbe to this effect.

The Gluskin family via Rabbi Aaron Gluskin of Paritich served as av bet din after the Chabad Luminary Rabbi Hillel of Paritich. Rabbi Aaron was the son of Rabbi Yehoshua of Lvov [who married the daugther of Rabbi Dan of Slonim- **see genealogical chart attached above**)] who stems from Rashi and the Maharal of Prague. The latter history of his long Rabbinic dynasty shows that there are many insights into life of Jews under persecution in the USSR and rabbinic life in general that comes to light in the journey of uncovering this rabbinic past in Eastern Europe.

This Rabbinic history also is substantiated with bringing to center stage from the margins the Rebbetzins, female scholars, and devoted wives, mothers, and daughters There we see the personal side of the family as when Dr Gita Gluskin notes she plucked flowers from her own small garden and gave them to the Chofetz Chaim who was visiting her father from Radin

Dr Gita Gluskin told David Levy in Givatayim in an interview in Givatayim that the Brisker Rav was at her Hatana with Dr. Leib Vilsker.

Dr. Gita Gluskin who remarked to me in Givatayim (1998) that "all the women had crushes of Saul Lieberman who they felt was very good looking ( Dr. Lieberman was one of the brothers in law of Rav Menachem Mendel Gluskin (ztsl), as Lieberman's 1st wife was Rochelle Rabinowitch Lieberman and Rav Menachem's wife was Fraidl Rabinowitch Gluskin were sisters.

We learn from such anecdotes little hints of the personal lives of these family members as when Dr Gita in an interview (1998) tells me that "it is no accident that the yahrzeit of Rav Menachem (my father) and Fraidl Rabinowitch Gluskin (my mother 5 years earlier) is both the 13 Kislev- "*Because there souls were so mystically bound up with one another... al pi Kabbalah.*"

Thus the overall book is not a Hagiographic work, but rather recoups the role of womens' history and the exemplary roles of individual women in my family and bring them center stage from the margins. Dr. Leah Gluskin for instance was a great scholar of the classics and 2nd temple Judiasm, but RAMBI does not note her many publications but rather her homage to her husband Dr. Joseph David Amusin, her husband who was a prolific scholar who encountered much antisemitism under the Communists. Dr Amusin published books in more languages than the fingers on the hand yet RAMBI only traces of few of his articles. To be a Hebraicist in the USSR was a difficult path. Persecution and misirat nefesh was not unique to Dr. Joseph David Amusin. For instance Esther Gluskin was arrested by the KGB and sent to Siberia for her involvement in a Zionist organization *HaShomer HaTzair* not to mention that Rav Menachem was imprisoned 2x by the Communists along with his father in law Rabbi Eliezer Rabinowitch. Sonia Gluskin was also a noble soul who also achieved a doctorate like Gita and Leah, but Sonia focused in the area of Russian linguistics and philology and literature, but encounterd much antisemitims professionally as did her brother in laws Dr. Joseph David Amusin (married to Dr. Leah Gluskin) and Dr. Aryeh Vilsker (married to dr. Gita Gluskina). These 4 remarkable sisters speak to the Jewish spirit to overcome adversity as was a trait of Rav Menachem Mendel's niece Miriiam Helfgott Gluskin Sax who in 1949 was in a car crash having a hip, knee, shoulder, and teeth replaced with terrible complications, yet always remaining upbeat, optimistic, and always seeing the class full rather than half empty. Miriam despite her adversity lived to the ripe age of 105. Her last words were "abba Abba" when Dr. Robert I Levy made a bikur holim visit at her badside, whereby Miriam may have confused her son-in law with her own father Rabbi Yakov Yitchak Helfgott (Ztsl). It is a testament of great fililial piety fulfilling the mitzvah of כַּבֵּד אֶת-אָבִיךָ, וְאֶת-אִמֶּךָ that Ruth S. Levy (Dr. Robert Levy's wife) took extradinary care of her mother Miiram, like Rabbi Tafron showed his own mother, putting on her slippers so that her feet not experience a cold floor in winter.

This is a journey not only for secular history, but *for sacred MEMORY, as the Besht, notes, "Bizikranot yesh ha-geulah"*. We cannot do justice to the present unless we remember and learn from the noble deeds of our ancestors to guide us in the future. Further we cannot know where we are going unless we know "where we have walked" in generations before us. This teaches us to "trust the future, remember the past, and live the present," informed and guided by the light of the holy souls sparks that shine as glistening "names" in Gan Eden. The book is not so much one in search of Yichus. It is a journey to reveal the nobility of the Jewish souls who preceded us, and the *misrat nefesh* of our ancestors who sacrificed to be proud Jews in trying times, accomplishing greatness in Torah learning, for we are mere dwarfs in *ruchnius,* intellectual virtue, and moral and spiritual middot compared to our forefathers and matriarchs in Eastern Europe. We can only know where we are going if we walk by the light of their inspiring examples. It is an attempt to turn to the past to guide the future, to make us better persons, seeking wisdom from the elders, as parasha Hazinu enjoins:

זְכֹר יְמוֹת עוֹלָם, בִּינוּ שְׁנוֹת דֹּר-וָדֹר; שְׁאַל אָבִיךָ וְיַגֵּדְךָ, זְקֵנֶיךָ
וְיֹאמְרוּ לָךְ

**Photos and Images Sources**
**Provenance:**

Categories:

(1) Photos Emanuel Gluskin prvate collection= photos of Gluskin family posted on Facebook page by Dr. Emanuel Gluskin
(2) Photos Rabbi Yosef Serebranski private collection= photos of Serebranski family and photo of Zev Gluskin library
(3) Photos Rabbi Yitzchok Gorowitz private collection= photos of
(4) Photos private collection of David B Levy and Levy family
(a) Photo of David benching daughter Ruth Levy in Levi Yitchak Library in Cedarhurst
(b) Photo of David in Lander College Library
(c) Photo of David at Kotel
(d) photo of Rabbi Yakov Yitchak Helfgott ztsl (great grandfather of David)
(e) photo of Miriam and Rabbi Yakov Yitchak Helfgott (Miriam's father)
(f) photo Anna Helfgott owned by Esther Helfgott
(g) Keila Leiba Helfgott zl matzevah (great grandmother of David) shot by David Rosedale Cemetery
(h) PHOTO of Saltkov Shedrin library retrieved by David from Wikipedia commons
(i) PHOTO of Israeli Newspaper HaDoar; Hebrew newspaper given by Dr Emanuel Gluskin to David Levy handouts at http:// databases.jewishlibraries.org/ node/51186
(j) Hebrew newspaper given by Dr. Emanuel Gluskin to David handouts at http:// databases.jewishlibraries.org/ node/51186

(k) Hebrew newspaper given by Dr. Emanuel Gluskin to David handouts at http://databases.jewishlibraries.org/node/51186
(l) Photo of Miriam Helfgott (grandmother of David)
(m) trees for Israel receipt gift given to Miriam at 100 year birthday party, owned by David
(n) Photo David planting trees in EY
(o) Photo of Ketubah of Miriam Sax (grandmother of David)
(p) photo Ruth on bima at Chizuk Amuno for bat mitzvah (not confirmation?) (mother of David)
(q) photo Ruth Sax owned by David Levy
(r) photo of Yossi Gluskin, David B Levy, and Dr. Emanuel Gluskin (Yerushalyim 2005), date photo
(s) photo David learning Mishnah from his Grandmothers, Miriam and Ruth Bear PHOTO
(t) ZOA letter to Abraham Eisenberg (brother of grandmother (Leah) of Dr. Robert I Levy
(u) Dr. Charles Levy, Ruth Bear Levy, David B Levy photo (mother of Dr. Robert I Levy)
(v) photo Robert I Levy holding sefer Torah (David's father bis hundert und zwanzig, le meah ve-ezreim)
(w) Dr Kadish Letter President of Touro College, regarding david's help with research
(x) photo of Rosa Cohen Levy and Yosef Yonah Levy (grandparents of Dr. Robert I Levy)
(y) Rabbi Samuel Cohen record death certificate (father of Rosa Cohen Levy)
(z) Last will and testament of Rosa Cohen donations to TA of Baltimore, Ner Israel of Baltimore, orphans in Jerusalem, Hadassah, etc (mother of Dr. Charles Levy)
(aa) photo donation to Kollel in Yerushalayim by Rosa Cohen Levy (mother of Dr. Charles Levy)

The pictures in Russia are part of the articles that are translated and have a url for the article.

Original Article on Dr. Aryeh Vilsker, 2016 AJL Proceedings, Charleston, SC., copyright AJL 2016, web address of Vilsker paper= http://databases.jewishlibraries.org/node/51186

The picture of Sefer Hamaros Hatzovos is taken from Otzar Hachochmoh but it is also on Hebrewbooks.org. and in the Central Lubavitch Library in Brooklyn.

The picture of the Gluskin Library was bought by Yosef Serebryanski when copies of it were sold online on ebay
The colored Belarus map in English in two places in the book is part of a map published by the *Union of Religious Jewish Congregation of the Republic of Belarus*, by giving them a donation they will send you map.

Picture on Dnieper river in Loyev – Wikipedia commons
Cemetery in Loyev –the source is mentioned in the article on the page Кладбище в Лоеве. Где старые памятники? | Aviv

Printed under the picture - This semicha was given to Yisroel son of Yaakov Tuvia Rapaport on Wednesday Elul 3 5687/August 31 1927, printed in **Ner Yisroel** p.19 Tel-Aviv 5758 a sefer Zikaron by Aharon Surski.

This semicha was given to Yaakov Tuvia Rapaport Elul 5 5690/August 29 1930. *Published in Ner Yisroel, Sefer Zikaron Tel Aviv 5758 p. 72 by Aharon Surski.*

The matzevah stones of the Perelman and Gluskin family after they were moved from Minsk https://www.geni.com/people/Freidel-Gluskin/2211200

The plate of the shul in S. Petersburg was given to Rabbi Chaim Serebryanski as a gift from a dinner that was made in honor of the shul. It is owned by Yosef Serebryanski.
The stone of Esther Gluskin. Rabbi Yosef Serebryanski heard from Rabbi Yitzchok Gorowitz that Esther was buried in the old Chabad section in Staten Island cemetery. Never having been there, Yosef found out where it is and called the cemetery and went to the office where they gave him a map of the cemetery and where people are buried, and after the detective work found the kever.

Shimon of Zelichov – the picture is printed in a few places, this was found through Otzar Hachochma.

Picture of Itche the masmid, Yizchok Gorowitz was found and published by Rabbi Mordechai Glazman of Latvia.

p. 91 photo of Rav Menachem Gluskin from Gedolei Mi Minsk (Feldheim pub)

p.98 photo of Fradel Rabinowitz and Rabbi Eliezer Rabinowitz, (Gedolei mi minsk, (Feldheim pub)

p.103 photo Rabinowitz family from sefer Godolei mi minsk (Feldhiem pub)

Emmanuel Gluskin archives - Picture of Gita May 1945, picture of Leah Emik and Sonya 1960, Lisa Ilinichna Volpert (March 30 1926 – October 1 2017) married Pavel Semenovich Reyfman, Sonya and Emmanuel 1989, Sonia and Emik in Israel, Emmanuel, Sonia and Gita in Hospital, Sonia tombstone, pictures of Alexander Mintz, picture of Alexander and Esther,

Pictures of Sonya with her school principal and other teachers and students - reifman.ru/memoirs/o_pskove/
Yosef Serebryanski private collection– pictures of Chaim Serebryanski with his siblings, picture Nechama Serebryanski with Sterberg sisters, picture of Chaim Serebryanski, picture of handwritten letter to the Rebbe from the archives of  Central Chabad Library, tombstone Eliyahu Serebryanski, Reb Zalman Serebryanski, Brocha Serebryanski from Central Chabad archives, Serebryanski family picture,

Picture of Zev Gluskin - Zichronos/memories Slutsk yizkor book

Yitzchok Gorowitz private collection – photos of Sarah Simcha, Ita Freida, Eliezer Gorowitz, Sarah Gorowitz and Zelda Rochel Edelstein tombstones on Mount Olives, Zelda Rochel's wedding, Shmuel and Esther Gorowitz.

**Concluding Dedication to my beloved Daugther Ruth from Dovid HaLevy[1]**

**היקירה רות שלי בת את לברך בשביל הזה הספר**
**הָרָקִיעַ כְּזוֹהַר וטְהוֹרִים קְדוֹשִׁים בתורה גדולי אזכרה**
**אלה**
**ואמהות אבות בזכות**
**גאולה יש בזיכרון**
**וּלְמִי, כָּל-חֶמְדַּת יִשְׂרָאֵל--הֲלוֹא לְךָ, וּלְכֹל בֵּית אָבִיךָ**

**(I Sam. 9:20)**

**וַתֹּאמַרְנָה הַנָּשִׁים, אֶל-נָעֳמִי, בָּרוּךְ יְהוָה, אֲשֶׁר לֹא הִשְׁבִּית לָךְ**
**גֹּאֵל הַיּוֹם; וְיִקָּרֵא שְׁמוֹ, בְּיִשְׂרָאֵל**

**(Ruth 4:14)**

**וְזֹאת הַתְּעוּדָה, בְּיִשְׂרָאֵל**

**(Ruth 4:7)**

**"And for whom is all Israel yearning if not for you and your entire ancestral house?" (see I Sam. 9:20) so that there "will not be withheld from you a redeemer" (see Ruth 4:14) on behalf of the Torah, as ".... Was formerly done in Israel...." (Ruth 4:7).**

**I pray regularly for you my daughter Ruthie- the preservation of your tranquility, the abundance of your bounty, and for the lengthening of your days. May you be blessed with the blessing of the fields that the L-rd has blessed** כְּרֵיחַ שָׂדֶה, אֲשֶׁר בֵּרְכוֹ יְהוָה **(Gen. 27:27). You are more precious than rubies** וְרָחֹק מִפְּנִינִים מִכְרָהּ **(Proverbs 31:2), more precious than the finest gold** הַנֶּחֱמָדִים--מִזָּהָב, וּמִפַּז רָב **(Ps. 19:10)**

**Blessed be the L-rd "who has not withheld a redeemer from you" and "He will renew your life and sustain your old age." Surely you shall be called bat shevet levi to whom was designated the Thumim and Urim וּלְלֵוִי אָמַר, תֻּמֶּיךָ וְאוּרֶיךָ לְאִישׁ חֲסִידֶךָ (Is 61:6) --וְאַתֶּם, כֹּהֲנֵי יְהוָה תִּקָּרֵאוּ מְשָׁרְתֵי אֱלֹהֵינוּ, יֵאָמֵר לָכֶם; חֵיל גּוֹיִם תֹּאכֵלוּ, וּבִכְבוֹדָם תִּתְיַמָּרוּ and you will emerge first among all the valiant within the L-rd's camp for you are the "L-rd's portion" (Deut 32:9) and "his allotment" כִּי חֵלֶק יְהוָה, עַמּוֹ (Deut 32:9) who "yearned after" וַיִּנָּהוּ כָּל-בֵּית יִשְׂרָאֵל, אַחֲרֵי יְהוָה (I Sam 7:2) Him as in former years, who are encamped about his banner (His sanctuary), who minister before Him always in his beit hamikdash limatah and esoteric spiritual holy Temple, beit mikdash memalah**

**"Bless O L-rd his substance"בָּרֵךְ יְהוָה חֵילוֹ, וּפֹעַל יָדָיו תִּרְצֶה; מְחַץ מָתְנַיִם קָמָיו וּמְשַׂנְאָיו, מִן-יְקוּמוּן (Deut 33:11). The Torah scroll was handed down to you, and "from the time the regular offerings were abolished" (Dan 12:11), it was not abolished from you, All who search for the L-rd "is obedient to your bidding" וּמִי בְכָל-עֲבָדֶיךָ כְּדָוִד נֶאֱמָן, וַחֲתַן הַמֶּלֶךְ וְסָר אֶל-מִשְׁמַעְתֶּךָ וְנִכְבָּד בְּבֵיתֶךָ (I Sam 22:14). It was long ago decreed that it is yours to interpret and teach the statutes and the laws, for "you are the guardian" (Deut 33:9) of "the words of the L-rd, "which are pure words :אִמְרוֹת יְהוָה, אֲמָרוֹת טְהֹרוֹת: כֶּסֶף צָרוּף, בַּעֲלִיל לָאָרֶץ; מְזֻקָּק, שִׁבְעָתָיִם (Ps. 12:7)- "guardians of the brit (Deut 33:9) as in former years. "Renew our days as of old. הֲשִׁיבֵנוּ יְהוָה אֵלֶיךָ ונשוב (וְנָשׁוּבָה), חַדֵּשׁ יָמֵינוּ כְּקֶדֶם**

מְנֻחָתוֹ וְהָיְתָה דְּרֹשׁוּ גּוֹיִם אֵלָיו עַמִּים לְנֵס עֹמֵד אֲשֶׁר יִשַׁי שֹׁרֶשׁ
הַהוּא בַּיּוֹם וְהָיָה

כָּבוֹד

---

1 Revised by DBL from Maimonides' "Epistle to the Scholars of Lunel" which can be found translated into English in (1) Leon D. Stitskin, Letters of Maimonides, New York (N.Y.) Yeshiva University Press 5737=1977, (2) Isidore Twersky, Introduction to the Code of Maimonides, New Haven : Yale University Press, 2010,(3) Sheer, Charles, H., Maimonides Grand Epistle to the Scholars of Lunel: Ideology and Rhetoric, Boston: Academic Studies Press, 2019. Hebrew in edition by Y. Blau

Made in the USA
Middletown, DE
13 January 2020

83125868R00288